MAKING SENSE OF MATHEMATICS TEACHER EDUCATION

Making Sense of Mathematics Teacher Education

Edited by

Fou-Lai Lin

*National Taiwan Normal University,
Taipei, Taiwan*

and

Thomas J. Cooney

*University of Georgia,
Athens, GA, U.S.A.*

KLUWER ACADEMIC PUBLISHERS

DORDRECHT / BOSTON / LONDON

A C.I.P. Catalogue record for this book is available from the Library of Congress.

ISBN 0-7923-6985-8 (HB)
ISBN 0-7923-6986-6 (PB)

Published by Kluwer Academic Publishers,
P.O. Box 17, 3300 AA Dordrecht, The Netherlands.

Sold and distributed in North, Central and South America
by Kluwer Academic Publishers,
101 Philip Drive, Norwell, MA 02061, U.S.A.

In all other countries, sold and distributed
by Kluwer Academic Publishers,
P.O. Box 322, 3300 AH Dordrecht, The Netherlands.

Printed on acid-free paper

Printed in the Netherlands.

TABLE OF CONTENTS

PREFACE

This is a research-based book on mathematics teacher education. It is about the learning of prospective and inservice mathematics teachers, mathematics educators, and researchers. The text is intended for a broad audience including teacher educators, mathematics educators, graduate students in mathematics education, and mathematics teachers at all levels of schooling.

In offering an examination of teacher education programs from different societies and cultures, this book provides an international perspective on mathematics teacher education. Practical situations associated with related theories are studied critically throughout the chapters. The possibilities and constraints of making an analogy between mathematics learning theories and mathematics teachers' learning theories are argued and examined. New perspectives on mathematics teacher education are presented along with relevant examples thus enhancing the book's readability for international readers.

BACKGROUND OF THE BOOK

The book was inspired by the obvious need to address issues in mathematics teacher education. In particular, the following mission statement for the newly established Journal of Mathematics Teacher Education (JMTE) reflects the mission of this book as well.

> The Journal of Mathematics Teacher Education is devoted to topics and issues involving the education of teachers of mathematics at all stages of their professional development. JMTE will serve as a forum for research on teachers' learning, for considering institutional, societal, and cultural influences that impact the education of mathematics teachers, and for creating models for teachers of mathematics. (Editorial, JMTE, 1(1), p. 2, 1998))

Conferences, particularly those with international perspectives, constitute one way of contributing to this mission. The conference which led to the writing of this book was conceived with this idea in mind, as F. L. Lin and other mathematics educators considered the feasibility of organizing an international mathematics teacher education conference when they met at the International Group for the Psychology of Mathematics Education annual meeting held in July, 1998, in Stellenbosch, South Africa. These initial conversations led to a broader discussion involving authors of the chapters herein and ultimately to the organization of the International Conference on Mathematics Teacher Education which was held in Taipei, Taiwan, in May, 1999. The intention of editing the conference proceedings and revising the papers so as to form this book was decided by the fourteen plenary speakers, who represented eight countries, and the conference organizer, F. L. Lin.

F.-L. Lin & T. J. Cooney (Eds.) Making Sense of Mathematics Teacher Education, 1—8.
© 2001 *Kluwer Academic Publishers. Printed in the Netherlands.*

In addition to their plenary addresses, speakers were invited to make a contribution to one of the following four themes which were the subject of plenary panel sessions.

- Theoretical Perspectives
- Mathematical Experience
- Inservice Teacher Education
- Relevance of Research

These four themes constituted a starting point for structuring this book. A subgroup of plenary speakers modified these themes into the book's present organization.

ORGANIZATION OF THE BOOK

The book consists of fourteen chapters organized into five sections. The first section presents alternative research perspectives on mathematics teacher education. Sections two through four address various issues involving teacher learning. Section five addresses issues related to the complexity of teacher education and how teacher educators themselves can grow in addition to supporting the growth of mathematics teachers.

Section One: Perspectives on Teacher Education

Different research perspectives on mathematics teacher education, including extant and needed perspectives, are considered and analyzed. Chapter 1 focuses on the perspective of teacher change. This chapter is about conceiving teacher development as a personal journey from a static world to one in which exploration and reflection are the norms. The notion of teacher change, particularly as related to change in beliefs about mathematics and mathematics teaching, is used to describe this journey. Cooney offers a theoretical analysis on how beliefs are constructed and how beliefs might be changed. He notes that prospective teachers often enter teacher education programs in search of teaching methods that help ensure certainty and predictability in the classroom. These expectations are in contrast to reform-oriented teacher education programs that encourage reflection, highlight attention to context, and characterize mathematics and its teaching as problematic. Based on his theoretical analysis and observations in teacher education programs, Cooney emphasizes that mathematical activities that integrate content and pedagogy in a reflective way can serve as powerful entry points for preservice teachers' reconceptualization of the enterprise of teaching mathematics. Examples of mathematical activities that integrate content and pedagogy are described.

In Chapter 2, Lerman reviews various research perspectives from the point of view of both implicit and explicit theories of teacher learning, such as changes in beliefs, reflective practice, pedagogical content knowledge, constructivism, and teachers' growing awareness of the complexity of classroom discourse. He argues that, although we have well-developed theories of children's learning, these theories are not appropriate for describing teachers' learning. Among the concerns he discusses are: (a) whether constructivism, with its notion of reflective abstraction and the construction of cognitive structures, can be applied to teachers' learning and (b) whether the study of beliefs is too static to describe the connections between theory and practice. Lerman suggests that theories that address the complexity of motives, goals, knowledge/power, and the forming of identity in social contexts need to be included in the study of teacher education. This suggestion is based on his review of different research perspectives that are related to the contexts in which teachers teach. Lerman provides a description of these perspectives.

Section Two: Making Sense of Mathematics

One of the primary goals of teaching mathematics is to enable students to make sense of mathematics. What kind of mathematical experiences can help teachers achieve this goal in their classrooms? How should teachers' mathematical experiences be conceptualized in terms of theoretical/philosophical perspectives? These are the primary issues addressed in section two.

Ponte reasons that investigations should be carried out both in learning mathematics and in learning how to teach mathematics. On the one hand, he analyzes mathematics investigations both in the curriculum and in the classroom. On the other hand, he considers investigations in teacher education and professional development as a vehicle for developing teachers' knowledge. In addition to the preservice and inservice teachers' narratives about their learning in mathematical investigations, Ponte claims that the investigation paradigm is a good framework for discussing pupils' work in the classroom as well as teachers' activities and professional development. This chapter describes six different teachers' roles in investigation classes: defy pupils, support pupils, evaluate pupils' progress, reason mathematically, supply and recall information, and promote pupils' reflection. This system of teachers' roles is a good framework for both research and practice in teacher education.

Tirosh, Stavy, and Tsamir emphasize their belief that enhancing teachers' acquaintance with students' ways of thinking is an important aim in teacher professional development. They argue that the intuitive rules theory could be used as an organized, general framework to assist teachers in their attempts to understand and predict children's responses to a wide variety of mathematical and scientific tasks. "More A- More B," "Same A- Same B," "Everything comes to an end," and "Everything can be divided" are the four intuitive rules that the authors describe and illustrate. Two specific sequences of teaching approaches, viz., teaching by analogy and conflict teaching, are applied based on knowledge about the effects of the intuitive rules on students' responses to apparently different but essentially similar tasks. The intuitive rules theory, given its predictive power, provides a tool for teachers to identify tasks to be used in the classroom. Some of the teachers who had participated in an inservice teacher seminar program that focused on the intuitive rules saw considerable value in this theory for their own teaching.

Laborde presents the results of a study involving a team of teachers with varied teaching backgrounds and experiences with Cabri Geometry as they designed teaching sequences for their students. Laborde observed evolutionary stages of the role given to technology by the teachers as they attempted to integrate technology into their teaching. She identified six stages which progressed from a scarce use of technology for activities to the stage in which technology was fully incorporated into the teaching activities. Laborde analyzed how the nature and the content of the teacher-designed tasks evolved over a three-year period. She concluded that in the first two stages technology is used as an amplifier but is not fundamental to the lesson. It is only in the following stages that teachers' mathematical knowledge is reorganized by linking it intrinsically to technology and that the meaning of mathematical knowledge is constructed through technology. Laborde describes her project as a "teaching learning" situation for teacher development.

Section Three: Making Sense of Teaching

Not only preservice teachers but also inservice teachers, teacher educators, and researchers are concerned with the mission of making sense of teaching. Among the issues related to this mission, the followings objectives are considered central.
- To elaborate the complexity of teaching,
- To represent and bring real teaching situations into teacher education programs,
- To motive student teachers to the need and advantage of conceptualizing and theorizing teaching,
- To design strategies and develop tools for teachers to make sense of a particular aspect of teaching,
- To design teacher education programs in which research findings and processes facilitate teachers' professional development, and
- To develop theories that help conceptualize the complexity of teaching.

What seems clear is that preservice teachers, inservice teachers, teacher educators, and researchers all have an important stake in dealing with these objectives. Means of addressing issues stemming from these objectives are addressed in this section.

In Chapter 6, Goffree and Oonk introduce their MILE project. This project provides a rich source of practical knowledge captured through authentic case studies of classrooms. The case studies are presented in a digital context so that they are easily accessible to student teachers. The cases also provide a context for theoretical reflection in which student teachers can learn from real teaching episodes. Indeed, based on seven theoretical perspectives, Goffree and Oonk provide their views on the designing of their digital learning environment and its use by student teachers. These seven perspectives include developmental research, practical knowledge, reflective practice, narrative, socio-constructivist, investigation, and adult learning. The authors analyze the learning process of two student teachers who were learning to teach by investigation in the context of MILE for two years. It was observed that the process of knowledge construction consisted of four different levels, namely assimilation of practical knowledge, adaptation and accommodation of practical knowledge, integrating theory into practice, and theorizing more generally. With digital representation of real teaching available in their teacher education program, Goffree and Oonk argue that acquiring practical knowledge becomes a natural way of knowing and can reach the level of reflective knowledge. The acquisition of this knowledge, which is an active and constructive process, occurs by means of in-depth and focused investigations of teaching practice. This investigation process can serve as a vehicle for teacher learning.

Sullivan and Mousley focus on one particular aspect of teaching, namely, seeing mathematics teachers as active decision makers. They used three-dimensional considerations related to the choice of particular classroom tasks to illustrate the complexity of teaching. The three dimensions are perspectives on learning and teaching; social and attitudinal aspects; and the mathematics content. They argue that given teaching is complex and multidimensional, then teachers need to be active decision makers who determine their own priorities rather than merely implement standard directions, plans, and routines. They developed an interactive multimedia CD "Learning about Teaching" that captures the complexity of mathematics teaching. They conclude that detailed analysis and consideration of the complexity of teaching situations drawn from classroom practice can both raise awareness of this complexity and suggest alternative ways of resolving issues arising from this complexity.

Ruthven considers the relevance of research to teacher education and classroom teaching through the example of a postgraduate pre-service education program at Cambridge, UK. He adopted the idea of "practical theorizing" within teacher education from R. J. Alexander. The notion of practical theorizing emphasizes that learning to teach must be a continual process of hypothesis testing framed by detailed analysis of the values and practical constraints fundamental to teaching. Ruthven provides a strategy to support practical theorizing through professional exercises. The collection of professional exercises entitled "Investigational Work in School Mathematics" was developed by Ruthven to illustrate this approach. In addition to the qualitative evaluation that focuses on the extent to which the professional exercises promote the development of thoughtful practice, Ruthven argues that in the practical theorizing approach, research is granted no privileged status; it must prove its value by providing insight about teaching and support for improvement.

Sfard focuses on a reformed classroom in which mathematics learning takes place in a peer-interactive setting. In this approach, the teacher abandons her traditional role as the center of the class and assumes the role of an unobtrusive helper and navigator. Sfard argues that one of the major reasons for the present ineffectiveness of teacher preparation is our insufficient understanding of the dynamics of learning in the reformed classroom, and our uncertainty with regard to the role of the teacher who uses this reform-based approach. Sfard introduces and illustrates a tool for analyzing classroom interactions and the possible reasons for the ineffectiveness of these interactions in traditional settings. The analysis of a sample of a few episodes of classroom interactions can have an eye-opening effect on teachers. Teachers can use this tool for self-improvement. They also can learn from such analysis about the mechanisms, advantages, and disadvantages of the students' interaction. Sfard suggests that if discourse is to be effective and conducive for learning, the art of communicating has to be taught. She concludes that the role of the teacher in making classroom discourse productive is much more complicated than was previously assumed.

Section Four: Making Sense of the Context of Teaching

This section emphasizes the complexity of teacher development and the relevance of the context of teaching, including the classroom, the institution, the professional teaching community, texts, and values, to that development.

In Chapter 10, Cobb and McClain focus on an analytical approach that supports teachers' learning within the social context of both the professional teaching community and their classroom. The authors reflect on a school-based, teacher development research program that has been ongoing for more than 13 years. The program started with the renegotiation of classroom social norms as a means of initiating a long-term learning process for teachers. After they had worked with the teachers for a period of time, the authors began to switch their focus from that of the teachers' learning to the professional teaching community as they realized that teachers' development is encased in the professional community in which they practice. In order to encourage teachers to become actively involved in the process of improving and adapting the instructional sequences, they asked teachers to take responsibility for documenting 1) their instructional designs, 2) observations of instruction, and 3) students' learning. The researchers organized the teachers' documentation and distributed syntheses based on the documentation to all participants who constituted the professional teaching community. This kind of collaboration among teachers and researchers resulted in instructional sequences that can be used as resources for the development of professional teaching communities.

Both Chapters 11 and 12 address the issue of which values in mathematics education are consistent with the theme of making sense of the context of teaching. The former chapter presents theoretical perspectives and the later chapter offers an empirical perspective.

Bishop describes the need to address values in mathematics teacher education. He argues that values in mathematics education, often implicit in teachers' teaching, have strong influences on students' learning. Bishop analyzed texts in Australia and found that values are present in both the intended curriculum and the implemented curriculum. In addition, students' own values, often rooted in classroom interactions, influence the attained curriculum. Textbooks are also carriers and shapers of values. Bishop cites research that demonstrates textbooks strongly encourage some dichotomized values of mathematics learning: formalist view vs. activist view, instrumental understanding vs. relational understanding, process vs. tool aspects. Bishop presents three types of activities for student teachers that address the question of values in mathematics education. These activities are designed to sensitize students to the very notion of values in mathematics education and to allow them to clarify their own values.

Chin, Leu, and Lin address the role of pedagogical values in mathematics teachers' thinking and classroom practices as these values relate to improving the quality of teacher education programs and mathematics teaching. The authors use two case studies to elaborate two issues related to chapter eleven: How can teachers' values be interpreted and represented? and Can the teaching of mathematics be improved through value clarification? Chin, Leu, and Lin describe teachers' pedagogical values from two points of view: pedagogical identities and products of valuing. Furthermore, they distinguish different degrees of value clarification. In terms of their observations of the two experienced teachers, they conclude that the more mathematics teachers understand about their own pedagogical values, the more flexible they will be in thinking about the role of values in their own classroom practice. The authors take the position that the more we understand about value clarification, the better able we will be in developing relevant teacher education activities on pedagogical values.

Section Five: Making Sense of the Complexity of Teacher Education

This section considers the complexity of teacher education based on the interconnections among the growth of individual teachers, groups of teachers, the schools, and educational systems. The two chapters in this section emphasize the importance of this interconnectedness among the participants in teacher education as issues stemming from this complexity are addressed.

Krainer tells a story that illustrates the complexity of teacher education as he studied and reflected on the case of Gisela, a mathematics teacher and vice-principal at an Austrian secondary school. He not only describes her individual development, but also sketches how this development is interconnected with the development of her school and even with the Austrian educational system. He found that the systematic enhancement of the quality of teaching is not only a function of the professional development of selected individual teachers, but also a function of the conditions and expectations of entire schools and regions in which teachers teach. Relevant stakeholders, such as department heads, principals, superintendents, teacher educators, parents, and students, must all be a part of a system of development. Krainer concludes that in order to deal with the full complexity of teacher education, we need to interconnect classroom development, school development, and the development of the entire educational system.

Jaworski examines the complexity of teacher education from a perspective that particularly focuses on the co-learning partnerships of teachers, teacher educators, and researchers within teacher education programs. She calls our attention to the value of teachers, as well as teacher educators, who are engaged in research on developing mathematics teaching. Reference is made to a particular program in Pakistan in which mathematics teachers and teacher educators have worked together for the development of both teachers and teacher educators, sometimes jointly and sometimes in parallel. In order to study the teacher as learner as well as the teacher educator as learner, Jaworski identifies three levels of cooperation between teachers and teacher educators:

Level 1. Creating classroom mathematical activities for students,

Level 2. Reflecting on ways in which teachers can think about developing their approaches to teaching, and

Level 3. Reflecting on the roles and activities of teacher educators in contributing to developments in (1) and (2).

Teachers work mainly at Level 1, with some thinking at Level 2. Teacher educators, as learners, are primarily engaged in Level 3 activities. Jaworski points out the significance that lies in the complementary roles of both teachers and teacher educators, so that both can be learners and contribute to the development of teaching.

CONCLUSION

We believe that this book provides significant insights into the processes of teacher education, insights that can benefit all participants of teacher education programs. Teacher education is not only an activity but a research site for those who make the task of educating teachers their life's work. It is our hope that the chapters contribute to the readers' understanding of teacher education as much as their development has contributed to our understanding.

The Editors wish to thank Dr. Heide G. Wiegel for her extensive effort in putting the individual chapters into the final form in which they appear in this book. Her help was invaluable and greatly appreciated by the contributing authors.

Fou-Lai Lin
Thomas J. Cooney
Editors

THOMAS J. COONEY

CONSIDERING THE PARADOXES, PERILS, AND PURPOSES OF CONCEPTUALIZING TEACHER DEVELOPMENT

ABSTRACT. Mathematics teacher education is a composite of many influences and purposes not the least of which is the propensity of many teachers to provide students with a caring environment in which to learn mathematics in an efficient manner. But reform teaching, rooted in Dewey's notion of education in a democratic society, is predicated on processes that evoke reasoning and problem-solving not just efficiency of providing information. The education of teachers to teach from such a process-oriented perspective is fraught with difficulty and thus presents a certain moral dimension which is considered in this chapter. Research indicates that change away from predictability and toward the problematic is often a difficult journey for teachers. A theoretical perspective for conceptualizing teachers' professional development is offered along with an analysis of the paradoxes and perils associated with implementing reform-oriented teacher education programs.

The business of teacher education has many purposes. On the one hand, teacher educators are expected to educate teachers who can survive, if not thrive, in today's classrooms with all the complexity and turbulence that entails. As such, the task is essentially one of promoting the status quo, keeping society and education on an even keel. Witness the large amounts of time spent on acclimating preservice teachers to the conditions of the schools and of life in the classroom. Further, the school-based components of teacher education programs are the most popular among the participant preservice teachers. These also are the components of teacher education that have the most validity among those who create policies that impact teacher education. On the other hand, teacher educators are expected to educate teachers so that they can become reformers of the teaching of mathematics. Usually this reform has its roots in a more process-oriented instructional style in which considerable emphasis is placed on conceptual understanding and problem solving. This polarization of perspectives provides a sort of continuum on which most teacher education programs fall.

With respect to inservice teacher education, the scene is somewhat different in that familiarity of the classroom is assumed, a familiarity that can be a double-edged sword. Familiarity helps provide continuity with professional development programs but it can also narrow the vision of what might be. Myopia is not a friend of reform. Teacher educators and teachers live in different worlds. In some sense, the role of the teacher educator is to reveal and make evident the complexity of teaching and then propose alternatives for dealing with that complexity. Teachers, on the other

Familiarity = Comfort

F.-L. Lin & T. J. Cooney (Eds.) Making Sense of Mathematics Teacher Education, 9—31.
© 2001 *Kluwer Academic Publishers. Printed in the Netherlands.*

hand, live in a very practical world. They have neither the luxury, nor the resources, to experiment, to fantasize a different school environment. Indeed, in most schools, the teacher's job is to stay within certain boundaries, boundaries that are determined by school authorities who have the power to hire and fire. Reform becomes an issue to those outside the field of mathematics education when it is perceived that reform could alter the status quo. Today's students and tomorrow's workers need problem-solving skills and a flexibility of thinking that allow for changing conditions in an ever increasingly technologically oriented society. But just as often, the pendulum swings the other way in that the time-honored basics are seen as the cure that solves educational ills. Witness the back-to-basic movements in the United States during the 1970s and the 1980s and the strong emphasis on basic skills that is not far below the surface in most school programs today. It was out of this concern for basic skills and accountability that led education to the notion of competency based education in which objectives detailing pedagogical skills were as prevalent in teacher education as was skill development in school programs.

For preservice teachers, reform is more of an intellectual exercise in which they have the opportunity to grapple with interesting problems. The risk is very low, for they will learn the real art of teaching during student teaching. For the inservice teacher there is considerable peril. Teachers, like the rest of us, strive to make sense of their lives and to find a comfort level that allows them to function in a reasonably orderly fashion. But reform is not always consistent with order as problems and perturbations, both essential components of reform-oriented teaching, often promote uncertainties in the teaching process. The question then becomes one of how much uncertainty teachers or students, both operating under an assumed didactical contract, can reasonably tolerate. The clever teacher educator is the one who envisions a different world of teaching but does so in a manner that honors the existing world of the teacher. Similarly, the clever teacher is the one who envisions a different world and searches for ways to realize that world within the usual classroom constraints. In some sense, we might think of teacher education as the process by which we develop clever teachers so defined.

Perhaps it is the case that reform is not for everyone, albeit we seldom talk or act that way for fear of sounding like elitists. But reform can be conceived in another way, one that sees reform as a form of liberation rather than as a movement toward something perceived to be better. This paper is about conceiving teacher development as a personal journey from a static world to one in which exploration and reflection are the norm. I will begin by considering the notion of teacher change.

1. EXAMINING THE NOTION OF TEACHER CHANGE AND ITS MORAL IMPLICATIONS

The obvious question associated with the notion of teacher change is, "Change from what to what?" That is, what compass defines change? Often discussions about reform become polarized in the sense that traditional teaching is contrasted with reform-oriented teaching. But what is it that constitutes traditional teaching? Typically, traditional teaching is equated with telling, which—as some assume—leads to rote learning with a heavy reliance on memorization. Although this view has considerable currency in the literature, it is not commonplace among teachers. I have never met a teacher who believed that he/she was teaching for rote learning. Teachers talk of enabling their students to solve problems and develop reasoning skills. Nevertheless, the evidence clearly shows that lecture is the dominant means of teaching in most school settings. Davis (1997) found that teachers' views of their own teaching were not dramatically different from positions reflected in the NCTM *Standards*. Yet, observations of their teaching revealed a heavy reliance on telling and lecturing. This discrepancy results, no doubt, from a difference as to what constitutes meaningful learning. Teachers live in a practical and parochial world as they are necessarily commissioned to deal with specific students in specific classrooms in a specific cultural setting. For most teachers, order is important—both in the sense of order from a management perspective and from an intellectual perspective. It is no accident that teachers often use the words "step-by-step" to describe their teaching of mathematics, a connotation that necessarily evokes procedural knowledge. Such an orientation is the frame in which their professional lives exist.

If traditional teaching refers to what teachers traditionally do in some normative sense, then a case can be made that traditional teaching involves a kind of teaching in which the teacher informs students about mathematics through the primary scheme of telling and showing. Knowledge is presented in final form. What kind of learning results from this, meaningful or otherwise, is an empirical question, not a definitional one. Traditional teaching, so conceived, allows us to consider a different kind of teaching, one which involves less telling and showing and more creating mathematical communities in which process and communication transcend product. We can call this kind of teaching *reform teaching*, and we can conceive of teacher change as moving from the traditional mode to the reform mode. Again, it remains an empirical question as to what kind of learning results from this kind of change although educators frequently speculate that students become more conceptual and adept at solving problems. Although I acknowledge the legitimacy of the empirical nature of connecting learning outcomes to any kind of teaching, I suggest that there remains a philosophical perspective that suggests a reform-oriented classroom is more consistent with the kind of society most of us would embrace. I do so under the assumption that the teaching of mathematics, or any subject for that matter, is ultimately a moral undertaking.

Polya

1.1 The Moral Dimension of Reform Teaching

The history of teacher change has many roots and can often be traced to scholars who see education in its broadest sense. Dewey (1916), for example, examined the purpose of education in a democratic society. His use of the word *transmission* might seem limited when he writes, "Society exists through a process of transmission quite as much as biological life. This transmission occurs by means of communication of habits of doing, thinking, and feeling from the older to the younger" (p. 3). But we see a much deeper meaning of transmission when he continues, "Society not only continues to exist *by* transmission, *by* communication, but it may fairly be said to exist *in* communication (emphasis in original)" (p. 4). Dewey's emphasis on reflective activity is one of the hallmarks of his philosophy of education. We begin to sense the immense complexity of Dewey's ideas when he defines education as the "reconstruction or reorganization of experience which adds to the meaning of experience, and which increases ability to direct the course of subsequent experience" (p. 76). Later he adds,

> The other side of an educative experience is an added power of subsequent direction or control. To say that one knows what he is about or can intend certain consequences, is to say, of course, that he can better anticipate what is going to happen; that he can, therefore, get ready to prepare in advance so as to secure beneficial consequences and avert undesirable ones. (p. 77)

From Dewey's perspective (1916),

> Democracy cannot flourish where the influences in selecting subject matter of instruction are utilitarian ends narrowly conceived for the masses, and, for the higher education of the few, the traditions of a specialized cultivated class. The notion that the 'essentials' of elementary education are the three R's mechanically treated, is based upon ignorance of the essentials needed for realization of democratic ideals. (p. 192)

When education is seen as the backbone of democracy, education takes on a certain moral dimension. Moral education, according to Dewey, involves providing the means by which the educated can best control their own destiny and that of society. We often mistake, I believe, moral education as prescriptions of the sort "Johnnie be good," rather than the fusion of knowledge and conduct in which the former informs the latter.

From this perspective, Green's (1971) distinction between indoctrination and teaching seems quite relevant. Both seek to inform, but only the latter informs with evidence. We must keep in mind that the teaching of mathematics, or any subject for that matter, educates the learner in two ways. First, it provides the learner with access to what Schön (1983) called technical knowledge. Second, the learning process is also a learning outcome whether that outcome is learning by reasoning or learning by imitation. Although we might not feel comfortable thinking about the teaching of mathematics as indoctrination, the reality is that this is exactly the kind of teaching we often criticize and characterize as traditional teaching.

Ball and Wilson (1996) echoed Dewey when they conclude, with respect to teaching, that the intellectual and the moral are inseparable. In what sense are the intellectual and the moral inseparable? Because of its inherent abstractness and certainty, mathematics is often seen as the sine qua non of ammorality. But we can ask the question of what makes any subject moral, immoral, or amoral. Given the often perceived ammorality of mathematics, the leap is often taken that its teaching, then, is largely an ammoral activity. But if we examine the question of what it means to know, then we have a different slant that suggests the teaching of any content area is subject to the question of whether or not it is a moral activity. The issue centers on what kind of evidence supports one's knowing. The presence of evidence is what fuses the intellectual and the moral.

What is our rationale for teaching functions, congruence, or literary classics? The answer lies not in the information itself, although that is not inconsequential, but in the underlying reasoning processes that allow students to make connections and reasoned judgments. Those reasoning processes are what distinguish knowledge from information. A student may know the Quadratic Equation in the sense of being able to apply it in a given and predetermined setting. But it would seem strange to say that a student knows the Quadratic Equation if he/she has no idea how it is developed or in what contexts it can be used. Information is not to be confused with knowledge.

Rokeach (1960) used the term *closed mind* to describe situations in which what one knows or believes is based on other beliefs that are impermeable to change. Green (1971) called beliefs that are impermeable to conflicting evidence *nonevidentially held beliefs*. These two constructs are closely related and speak directly to the importance of students having experiences with processing different kinds of evidence. The encouragement of students to acquire information in the absence of evidence and reasoning is not what I would call a moral activity. The challenge, then, becomes one of educating teachers so that they can provide contexts for students to experience the processing of evidence. Professional development, then, can be conceived of the ability of the teacher to promote such experiences and to engage students in the kind of reasoning that reflects the essence of most reform movements in mathematics education.

There is a certain moral dilemma associated with acknowledging a student's reasoning process when, in fact, that process leads to a mathematically incorrect statement. Ball and Wilson (1996) addressed this point. Teachers usually are reluctant to honor such reasoning processes particularly if they hold a product-oriented view of teaching and learning. Therein lies the dilemma. If only those reasoning processes that lead to correct results are appreciated, then, in some sense, process and product become fused and inseparable. If teaching is viewed from a constructivist perspective in which teaching is based on students' mathematical understanding wherein that understanding and the so-called curriculum are one and the same, then there is no dilemma because there is no absolute to which understanding can be compared. Most teachers feel uncomfortable with this perspective, if for no other reason than that the curriculum becomes entirely problematic. Indeed, few classrooms are organized from a constructivist perspective. → scarcity Witness, for example, teachers' emphasis on objective tests and the paucity of alternative assessment items on those tests (Cooney, Badger, & Wilson, 1993; Senk, Beckmann, & Thompson, 1997).

A related issue is what students learn to value. Glasser (1990) observed that students' responses to the question, "Where in school do you feel important?" inevitably evokes responses that entail extracurricular activities such as sports, music, or drama; rarely mentioned are experiences with academic subjects. Glasser's observation paints a rather bleak picture that captures the failure of the classroom to create an intellectual community in which students are honored as much for their thinking as for their doing. Unfortunately, I suspect his conclusions are not specific to any particular school or subject. This, again, suggests that students fail to see their reasoning processes honored as an intellectual activity in and of itself.

1.2   The Notion of Good Teaching

What circumstances lead to a product-oriented view of teaching? Teachers often see themselves as wanting to provide an environment free of anxiety, one in which fear of the subject is neutralized or at least minimized. Cooney, Wilson, Chauvot, and Albright (1998) found that teachers' beliefs about teaching often center on the notion of caring and telling. One preservice teacher, Brenda, wrote in a journal entry, "A good mathematics teacher explains material as clearly as possible and encourages his students to ask questions." When preservice teachers are asked to select an analogy that best represents teaching (choices consist of newscaster, missionary, social worker, orchestra conductor, gardener, entertainer, physician, coach, and engineer), a popular choice is coach because a coach must establish fundamentals, show, cheer on, and explain. Another popular choice is gardener because gardeners nurture, provide support, and facilitate growth. When preservice teachers are asked what famous person they would like to be as a teacher of mathematics, a fairly common response is the identification of a comedian. The rationale they provide is based on the assumption that mathematics itself is a rather dry subject and hence it takes a special personality to make it interesting. These and other metaphorical descriptions reveal the various forms that telling and caring take. What these descriptions do not suggest is a kind of teaching in which students grapple with problematic situations or engage questions of context and what might be. If we think of mathematics as the science of creating order out of chaos or as pattern recognition as suggested by Steen (1988), then it follows that a reductionist view of mathematics is inappropriate.

I recall a conversation with one of my advisees that went something like this.

TC: How is this term going?

ST: My math professor is great this term.

TC: Wonderful. Why is he great?

ST: He is clear. He goes at a reasonable pace. He answers our questions.

This exchange conveys something about what this student considers good teaching to be, vis-à-vis, be clear and present material at the students' level. The anecdote is consistent with the way preservice teachers speak of coach, gardener, and other metaphorical selections. As laudable as being clear and teaching at the students' level may be, they hardly constitute the kind of process or reform-oriented teaching advocated in most teacher education programs.

When I observe a teacher who is doing a good job of teaching procedural mathematics with an emphasis on basic skills, what should my reaction be? Should I feel good if the class is conducted in an orderly way and students are learning the basics? Or should I be upset that students are only getting the basics (assuming this is true) and that they are not experiencing mathematics as an exploratory science? The issue goes deeper than just striking a balance between skill and meaning as Brownell (1956) urged long ago. Rather, it strikes at the heart of what education is all about and what we intend schooling to be. Although we urge student teachers to try new things and to find ways to bring problem solving to the forefront of their teaching, seldom do we easily succeed. I remember a conversation with a student teacher who had attempted to change her teaching. She reasoned that she did not have time to do problem solving since she was only teaching for 10 weeks. But she indicated that her cooperating teacher (who emphasized basic skills almost exclusively) would have time to do problem solving since she would be teaching for the entire year. This perspective of teaching places an emphasis on time. Good teaching then becomes defined in terms of the efficient use of time, a not uncommon occurrence. The perspective taken here, however, is that good teaching involves much more than being efficient, as it must also attend to the processes previously mentioned.

1.3 The Moral Dimension of Teacher Education

Perhaps more than any other educators, teacher educators have considerable latitude in terms of defining their curricula. By what principles do they make their curricular decisions? To what extent do they invite teachers, particularly preservice teachers, to consider what philosophers and experienced educators often see as problematic but what often goes unchallenged by teachers? Wilson and Padron (1994) argued for a culture-inclusive mathematics that is representative of more than the Western mathematics that typifies school mathematics programs at least in the United States. Gerdes (1998) and Presmeg (1998) have argued how culture-inclusive mathematics can play a central role in the education of teachers. Both Gerdes and Presmeg note that often teachers fail to see the mathematics that underlie their own backgrounds and experiences. Davis (1999) asks his preservice teachers to consider the question, "What is mathematics?" as a starting point to consider what it really means to teach the basics. He noted that it is not uncommon for teachers to provide dictionary definitions in response to this question, pushing their own mathematical experiences to the background.

The evidence suggests that teachers commonly divorce their own experiences from this perceived predetermined mathematics, which further isolates mathematics from the human condition. Taken to the extreme, this perspective relegates teacher education to an emphasis on acquiring pedagogical skills that enable teachers to effectively deliver the curriculum. Without question, these kinds of skills are important if teachers are to become good classroom managers and successful teachers; but neither should they represent the whole of teacher education. The question for teacher educators is to find some sort of balance between helping teachers develop pedagogical skills and enabling them to appreciate how mathematics is connected not only to their lives but to their students' as well. In short, they need to see school curricula as much more problematic than it is often considered to be. The defining of this balance promotes a moral overtone to teacher education that goes largely unrecognized in the profession. In part, this moral dimension of teacher education traces back to what we mean by good teaching.

The notion that good teaching consists of a telling process embedded in a humanistic, caring environment, assumes that the learning process should avoid frustration and not place students in a cognitively challenging environment. The irony is that the caring assumes that the student is unable to develop the ability to cope and is thereby dependent on the person who provides the care, a position inconsistent with Dewey's notion of education. Further, the planned avoidance of frustration places the responsibility for learning with the teacher and results in a reductionist view of the teaching/learning process. From a reductionist perspective, the logic of teacher education should be hortatory in nature wherein teachers are provided with the knowledge and skills necessary to become caring and telling teachers. That is, teacher education would be about delivery just as the teaching process would be about delivery. But this perspective is not consistent with the intent of a reform-oriented teacher education program that relishes a certain unpredictability of classroom events based on students' mathematical thinking.

If we take the position that we want teachers to be reflective practitioners who are adaptive and attend to students' understanding, we must provide them with opportunities to engage in reflective thinking. We should think of reflection as something other than simply recalling or looking back. Von Glaserfeld's (1991) notion of reflection requires the individual to step away from the events being reflected upon and to examine the situation from "afar" as if one could step out of oneself and re-represent events. Unless one engages in a sort of motivated blindness, there is a certain tension associated with examining one's own beliefs in the face of existing evidence. But this examination is critical to the process of becoming a reflective practitioner and of being adaptive. As desirable as this dynamic aspect may be, it provokes uncertainty which may conflict with the certainty that many teachers desire. Predictability is a circumstance that is a friend to most teachers, especially to beginning teachers; and so, there may exist a certain conflict between the expectations of teachers and those of *their* teachers. Concomitantly, it puts at risk teacher education programs whose goals differ from those that promote teaching methods which help insure predictability.

There are many issues lurking beyond the moral dimension of teacher education. Perhaps the greatest of them all is the challenge we face in enabling teachers to see knowledge acquisition as power so that they can enable their students to acquire that same kind of power. If teachers' ways of knowing are rooted in a cycle of received knowing, then it is predictable that their students' ways of knowing will be received as well. This presents a significant moral dilemma in that the received knower has less intellectual control over decisions that affect his/her life. To the extent that we think that the goal of teaching is to educate, then we have an obligation to provide teachers with a similar education.

2. RESEARCH ON TEACHER CHANGE

There is a growing body of literature that addresses the issue of teacher change. I will consider some of this literature, as I believe it provides a context for considering theoretical issues related to teacher change. Wilson and Goldenberg (1998) studied one experienced middle school teacher's efforts to reform his teaching of mathematics. During the first year of the two-year study, Mr. Burt's interactions with students were primarily of the form teacher-to-student with minimal student-to-student interactions. This changed somewhat during the second year as Mr. Burt allowed students to explain alternative solution methods, although his basic teaching style was still directive. When students used manipulatives, their use was limited to situations in which Mr. Burt was confident he knew the direction and outcome of the lesson. During the second year of the project he placed a greater emphasis on conceptual understanding and on the way students learned mathematics, being somewhat more process oriented. Students answered questions following presentations by their classmates. Mr. Burt recognized the positive results that accrued from organizing students into cooperative learning groups. Nevertheless, Wilson and Goldenberg drew the following conclusion.

> Although he let students explore and work cooperatively, he still insisted on telling many of the important points, emphasizing what he considered to be correct ways to think about things. In other words, although he intervened less frequently than usual, the nature of his intervention was still quite directive. (p. 285)

Mr. Burt felt that he was making significant changes, albeit the classroom observations indicated the changes were not fundamental, a position borne out by the students who indicated that "Mr. Burt talks too much" (p. 286). This circumstance led the researchers to conclude that "the case shows just how little progress even well-intentioned teachers like Mr. Burt may make toward implementation of the *Standards* (NCTM, 1989, 1991) unless they are also undergoing a significant pedagogical and epistemological shift" (p. 289).

Grant, Hiebert, and Wearne (1998) studied 12 primary grade teachers who attempted to reform their teaching. Predictably, some did realize reform and some did not. The authors found that teachers who had a more pluralistic view of mathematics were more likely to appreciate and realize reform than were their counterparts who saw mathematics from a limited perspective. Those who thought of mathematics as a collection of basic skills tended to focus on the more transparent aspects of reform, such as using physical materials and the like without accepting any of the deeper, more process-oriented teaching methods. With respect to the linkage between the teachers' beliefs and their instructional practice, Grant et al. reached the following conclusion:

> Teachers who hold a mixed set of beliefs, viewing mathematics as skills and understanding, are able to see some of the goals of reform-minded instruction. However, when these goals are translated into plans for action, they can easily deteriorate into a set of teaching strategies that are assimilated into the teachers "instructional habits" (Thompson, 1991, p. 14). For those teachers whose beliefs are at the process/student responsibility end, the spirit and the specifics of the instructional approach can be internalized through observations of reform-minded teaching. (p. 233-234)

Grant et al. (1998) conclude that the process of teacher change is very complex as it is rooted in what the teachers believe about mathematics and its teaching.

Schifter (1998) explored the relationship between a middle school teacher's understanding of mathematics and her instructional practice. Spurred by her participation in a seminar for teachers in which big ideas in mathematics were examined, Theresa Bujak's teaching, by her own account, began to change dramatically. Bujak's own mathematical explorations opened up new possibilities for her as a teacher of mathematics in that she began to organize her teaching around communal inquiry into mathematical ideas. Another teacher, Beth Keeney, also profited from her study of mathematics and realized that her confusion paralleled that of her students. Both teachers began to realize the problematic nature of students' mathematical thinking as they reflected on the problematic nature of their own mathematical learning. With respect to the influence of their professional development program on their teaching, Schifter (1998) reached the following conclusion:

> The cases of Theresa Bujak and Beth Keeney have been used to illustrate how teachers call upon learnings from a professional development program—learnings about mathematics and about children's mathematical thinking—as they engage their students in a study of fractions. Indeed, the two cases indicate quite specifically which aspects of their professional development experiences proved most transformative for their practice. (p. 83)

Jaworski (1998) embarked in a kind of action research with teachers as she engaged them in a kind of reflective practice. Her evolutionary approach with the teachers led to fundamental changes in some of the teachers' instructional practices as they engaged in their own defined research projects. This innovative approach was intially troublesome for the teachers as their conception of research was quite formalized. But by linking the research to the teachers' actual concerns, research and reform in the teaching of mathematics became intertwined. Jaworksi drew several conclusions based on her study. She saw the teachers' research as "consisting of cycles of reflective activity through which knowledge grew and was refined" (p. 26), knowledge being defined in terms of "teachers' own individual learning related to their substantive concerns" (p. 27). Jaworski's notion of the development of teaching is predicated on the cyclical and reflective process of teachers questioning and examining their own teaching. Central to this process are a concern for pupils' mathematical understanding and various issues related to the generality of mathematical processes.

Frykholm (1999) studied 63 secondary mathematics teachers over a three-year period as they progressed through a reform-oriented teacher education program. He found that many of the students equated reform with the NCTM *Standards*, held a rather rigid interpretation of the Standards, and uncritically accepted them as the "Bible of mathematics education." Perhaps this rigidity led to the teachers' feeling that implementation of the standards would be difficult if not impossible given their anticipated classroom constraints. Frykholm concluded that the preservice teachers saw the standards as a body of content that was to be learned as part of the teacher education curriculum. There appeared to be little recognition of the Standards as simply one of many representations of a philosophy of education. Frykholm pointed out that the student teachers recognized the duality of their thinking although this realization did little to impact instruction. The students expressed frustration over the mismatch between what they knew to be possible in mathematics classrooms and what they were actually doing.

Combined, these five studies reveal several issues related to the notion of teacher change. Clearly teachers' conceptions about mathematics and mathematics teaching strongly influence if not dictate their movement toward a reform-oriented teaching environment. Mr. Burt (Wilson & Goldenberg, 1998) wanted to reform his teaching yet was reluctant to move too far from the land of certainty that characterized his teaching. The Grant et al. (1998) study revealed that teachers with limited conceptions of mathematics were not likely to accommodate reform measures into their teaching in any real way. Frykholm (1999) demonstrated that beliefs do not necessarily translate into reform-oriented teaching even when teachers are aware of the contradiction between their beliefs and practice. That is, beliefs about the Standards may have been peripheral to more conservative but core beliefs. On the other hand, Bujak and Feeney (Schifter, 1998) seemed more amenable to change, perhaps because of their professional development program, but perhaps also because of their willingness to be reflective individuals as were the teachers in the Jaworski (1998) study. Thus a teacher's disposition to be reflective may be a significant predictor of his/her ability to not only question the practice of teaching but to actually reform that teaching. Schifter's (1998) seminar was explicit about changing beliefs as a prelude to changing teaching behavior. Jaworski (1998) accepted the premise that teachers should first buy into the notion of reflective thinking, couched in terms of research, in order for teaching to change. In general, the premise is that change in beliefs either precedes or occurs simultaneously with changes in teacher behavior.

Guskey (1986), however, posited an alternative perspective as indicated in the following model:

Staff Development ➔	Change in TEACHERS' CLASSROOM PRACTICES ➔	Change in STUDENT LEARNING ➔	Change in TEACHERS' BELIEFS AND ATTITUDES

He raised the question as to whether change in teaching behavior accompanied by a change in student performance is a prerequisite for change in teachers' beliefs. He put it in the following way:

> The three major outcomes of staff development are change in the classroom practices of teachers, change in their beliefs and attitudes, and change in the learning outcomes of students. Of particular importance to the change process and to efforts to facilitate change, however, is the order of occurrence of these outcomes. In what temporal sequence do these outcomes most frequently occur? (p. 6)

Guskey's claim seems to run counter to much of the research in mathematics teacher education. Sue (Cooney, 1994), for example, was very explicit about her change in beliefs about the teaching of mathematics as a prelude to her change in teaching. Nevertheless, it might be argued that the reason that change is not more evident in many cases is because teachers either do not see improved learning or they are reluctant to experiment with change to see if student learning is enhanced. When working with a group of teachers in which the intent was to alter their assessment practices in favor of using a greater variety of open-ended assignment items, I found that some teachers were surprised by what their students could do. One teacher was so enthralled with her students' thinking when they responded to various open-ended questions that she became quite convinced that the use of open-ended

H.S. math teachers become math teachers b/c they enjoy and are good with mathematics. This somewhat taints the perspective/beliefs concerning mathematics and the teaching of.

questions could improve her teaching of mathematics. Her case beautifully illustrates Guskey's model. Lurking in the background, however, is the question of what it means to improve learning as mathematical outcomes are not linearly ordered.

There is also the question of the evidential nature of teachers' beliefs. If a teacher's beliefs tend to be held nonevidentially, what would have to be the extent of change in student performance to warrant an epistemological shift in the teacher's teaching? Indeed, what would count as evidence? It is not difficult to envision a classroom in which a teacher introduces various problem-solving techniques only to witness the element of uncertainty in classroom discussions that might be perceived as undermining other, more important, outcomes. On the other hand, if evidence does influence one's beliefs to any great extent, then Guskey's model might make sense. The cases addressed by Grant et al., (1998) and Frykholm (1999), in which teachers did not change their teaching behaviors, might have had different outcomes if evidence of student performance had been gathered and emphasized.

The question of what precedes what, beliefs or practice, is not entirely an empirical question. One cannot dismiss that a teacher's beliefs about mathematics and teaching determine what counts for evidence. But there is another issue as well. And that has to do with the way those beliefs are structured, the subject of the next section.

3. A THEORETICAL PERSPECTIVE FOR TEACHER CHANGE

It is well established that there is some sort of a connection between beliefs and practice (Thompson, 1992), regardless of the temporal issue. What has received much less attention in the literature is how beliefs are structured, an understanding that might shed light on how beliefs are formed and how they might get changed. To begin this analysis, I will present a brief explication of belief.

3.1 · The Construct of Belief

The question of what it means to know or to believe something cries for both epistemological and empirical considerations. In some sense knowing and believing are intertwined. It would be strange to say, for example, that it is cold outside but I don't believe it. On the other hand, it would not be strange to say that I believe it is cold outside but I don't know that for sure. In this sense, knowing is a stronger condition than believing. That is, knowing assumes certain kinds of evidence that believing does not. It seems reasonable to call for explicit and incontrovertible evidence if one claims that he knows it is cold outside, evidence that is stronger than one indicating that he believes it is cold outside.

Scheffler (1965) provides the following definition for the condition of knowing.

> X knows Q
> if and only if
> (i)   X believes Q,
> (ii)   X has the right be be sure that Q, and

(iii)   Q

The critical issue is one of being sure and having a legitimate right to be sure. It would not make sense to say, " I know it is cold outside but I am not really sure about it." Neither would it make sense to think that somebody knows something because he/she is sure of it but without any legitimacy for his/her certainty. If, in fact, we saw people walking outside wearing bathing suits and saw them perspiring, it would be strange to say, "I know it is cold outside." If a student said she knew that a whole number ending with the digit 3 was prime, citing examples such as 13, 23, and 43, we would likely say that she believes that such numbers are prime but she doesn't know it. *positiveness when stating matters of opinion*

Pepper's (1942) notion of dogmatism applies to those individuals whose beliefs exceed the grounds that support those beliefs. To say it another way, a person may believe Q but it is not clear that the person has the right to be sure that Q is the case. A person could quite stubbornly maintain that it is cold outside based on the evidence that it was cold yesterday, the last time he was outside. Often, the dogmatist relies on evidence proclaimed by an authority, that is, one whose knowledge is considered irrefutable. Such an authority could be a person in power—a teacher, an administrator, a person in high office, or written proclamations such as the Bible. Evidence based on authority seldom passes careful scrutiny in the absence of other kinds of confirming evidence. Stereotypes such as "Some children can't learn mathematics" are often borne out of a dogmatic state. Evidence may exist to support a particular position, but counterexamples go unrecognized or unacknowledged.

Evidence is the foundation for both beliefs and knowledge. But evidence may consist of not observations but, rather, of other beliefs; or those other beliefs may dictate what counts for evidence. Evidence for nonevidentially held beliefs, often the product of a closed mind, is circular in nature and allows no new evidence to penetrate one's belief systems. Thus, when we encounter Scheffler's (1965) conception of belief, "Belief is, then, let us suppose, an abstract thing, in the nature of a habit or readiness, a disposition to act in certain ways under certain circumstances" (p. 76), we encounter several difficulties. First, we can not always be sure what kind of evidence has led to what the person believes to be the case. This is critically important information if teacher educators are to provide contexts in which teachers reflect on their beliefs. Second, the evidence we gather about what one believes should be multi-dimensional. Verbal proclamations alone do not constitute strong evidence of beliefs. Actions, consistent with the stated beliefs, must be evident as well.

For this reason it is important to think of beliefs as dispositions to act, which include both utterances and actions. Scheffler (1965) elaborates on his notion of belief.

> A belief is a cluster of dispositions to do various things under various associated circumstances. The things done include responses and actions of many sorts and are not restricted to verbal affirmations. None of these dispositions is strictly necessary, or sufficient, for the belief in question; what is required is that a sufficient number of these clustered dispositions be present. Thus verbal dispositions, in particular, occupy no privileged position vis-à-vis belief. (p. 85)

It follows that the determination of one's beliefs is a multifaceted thing and requires multiple contexts to form a viable interpretation of one's beliefs. Thus, to believe that a person thinks that problem solving is an important aspect of teaching mathematics, one must have evidence of several types, including supporting statements but also including actions that are consistent with the stated belief.

How is it that beliefs can change? To answer this question, let us consider Green's (1971) metaphorical analysis on how beliefs are structured.

> We may, therefore, identify three dimensions of belief systems. First, there is the quasi-logical relation between beliefs. They are primary or derivative. Secondly, there are relations between beliefs having to do with their spatial order or their psychological strength. They are central or peripheral. But there is a third dimension. Beliefs are held in clusters, as it were, more or less in isolation from other clusters and protected from any relationship with other sets of beliefs. Each of these characteristics of belief systems has to do not with the content of our beliefs, but with the way we hold them. (pp. 47-48)

If we think of core beliefs as those that are central to a person and related beliefs as those that are peripheral, it seems clear that peripheral beliefs would be more permeable. Similarly, it seems reasonable to assume that primary beliefs are much less amenable to change than are those derived from the primary beliefs. The point is that not all beliefs are held with the same intensity which speaks directly to the issue of change.

There are two key elements in any changes in one's beliefs: doubt and evidence. If one has no reason to doubt what one believes, then there is no reason to change one's beliefs. The second component is evidence. The problem with evidence is that one has to accept certain conditions as constituting evidence. If a person believes that it is cold outside and yet sees a person walking around outside in short sleeves, does the person count this as evidence that it might not be cold outside thereby inflicting doubt on the belief, or does the person cling to the belief that it is cold outside and conclude that the person is not properly dressed?

If the position is taken that change in beliefs precede change in practice, then it behooves teacher educators to consider what kinds of experiences can provide evidence for change. On the other hand, if one holds that change in beliefs must be preceded by a perceived change in student performance, then the question arises as to what kind of evidence accounts for increased performance—a sort of belief cluster in itself. Either way, the notion of doubt is of paramount importance. Even in Guskey's (1986) model, change in beliefs must be accompanied by doubts about the prevailing instructional program. In short, the element of doubt is an essential piece of the puzzle with respect to both change in teachers' beliefs and change in practice.

For this reason, I am attracted to the writings of those who address the notion of authority and how an individual is positioned with respect to authority as a source of knowledge. This seems quite relevant to the teaching of mathematics. Documents such as the Standards (NCTM, 1989, 1991) emphasize that the authority for one's knowing should rest in the logic of the subject and not in the proclamations of those teaching the subject.

3.2 Schemes for Ways of Knowing

Given that the element of doubt is central to change, it makes sense to consider various schemes that attend to an individual's willingness to doubt. Perhaps the foremost work in this area is that of Perry (1970) whose research is the standard bearer for the creation of intellectual developmental schemes. Perry identified nine stages of intellectual development which are primarily grounded in an individual's willingness to see situations contextually. In the first few stages of his nine-stage theory we have basic dualism in which there is no distinction between authority and absolute truth. From this perspective "authority is omniscient and the structure would appear to be a closed system" (p. 61). Out of this duality emerges multiplism, which allows for pluralism but only in a temporary sense as the individual remains a loyal adherent to Authority. Perry (1990) puts it this way:

> In any epistemological sense, therefore, Multiplicity remains a mere appearance; difference of opinion is allowed into the family, but only because it is quite temporary, good for the mind, resolvable, and therefore ultimately unreal (emphasis in original). (p. 78)

Pluralism becomes a legitimate domain at the expense of the authority's claims. The situation is then ripe for a revolutionary stage (about position 5) in which an individual begins to see the world from the point of view that knowledge is a "radical reperception of all knowledge as contextual and relativistic," (p. 109). It is not surprising that at this point Perry makes mention of Kuhn (1962) given that the individual is undergoing a restructuring of his/her knowledge, a restructuring that represents a significant paradigm shift. Whereas multiplism allows for a certain assimilation of evidence, relativism requires accommodation as the individual sees the world as contextually defined. Contextuality breeds doubt, a condition for change. Perry's subsequent stages of relativism and commitment follow the individual through a rational process by which beliefs are based on evidence, the more the evidence, the more the commitment.

Perry's (1970) work is controversial because his subjects consisted solely of men studying at Harvard. Consequently, others have embarked on similar work but with different populations. Belenky, Clinchy, Goldberger, and Tarule (1986) developed a scheme based on interviews with only women. Although they make no claim that their scheme is developmental, they do identify different positions that reflect Perry's basic positions. Using the metaphor of voice, Belenky et al., describe the following positions:
- silence—having no voice
- received knowledge—listening only to the voice of others
- subjective knowledge—listening to the voice of inner self and questing for self-identity
- procedural knowledge—applying the voice of reason in separate or connected ways
- constructed knowledge—integrating voices.

These researchers see a shift in the subjective knowledge position in which "an externally oriented perspective on knowledge and truth eventuates in a new conception of truth as personal, private, and subjectively known or intuited" (p. 54). This shift is similar to Perry's revolutionary change at about position 5.

Baxter Magolda (1992) studied 101 men and women as they progressed through their college years and found four distinct stages of thinking among the students: absolute knowing, transitional knowing, independent knowing, and contextual knowing. Her characterizations have a distinct Perry flavor in that one moves from accepting an authority as omniscient to seeing the world as a contextual place. According to the author, the absolute knower sees knowledge as quite certain. She expressed it in the following way, "Uncertainty only exists because students don't have access at the time to absolute knowledge" (p. 36). Authorities have all the answers. Transitional knowers accept that some knowledge is uncertain. "Although transitional knowers still believe that absolute knowledge exists in some areas, they have concluded that uncertainty exists in others. Discrepancies among authorities in these uncertain areas are viewed as a result of the answers being unknown." (p. 47). For Baxter Magolda, the shift similar to the one described by Perry (1970) and reflected in the work of Belenky et al. (1986) occurs in the independent knowing stage. Baxter Magolda provided the following analysis.

> Independent knowing represents a shift to assuming that knowledge is mostly uncertain. Viewing knowledge as uncertain changes substantially the learning process and the sense of where knowledge resides. Differences in the opinions of various authorities represent the range of views possible in an uncertain world. Moreover, these authorities are no longer the only source of knowledge; instead, students begin to see themselves as equals and hold their own opinions as valid. (p. 55)

This analysis is similar to Belenky's et al. (1986) description of subjective knowledge in that the individual sees others as having legitimate claims to knowing as does one's self. Finally, Baxter Magolda describes contextual knowing as the condition in which all knowledge is uncertain in that it is contextually defined. But some knowledge claims are recognized as having more legitimacy than others:

> When all perspectives are no longer equal, learning changes from thinking independently to thinking through problems and integrating and applying knowledge in context. Although the student still creates a point of view, it must be supported by evidence. The instructor is expected to foster learning environments that promote application of knowledge in a context, evaluative discussion of perspectives, and opportunities for the student and teacher to critique each other. (p. 69)

The issue of contextuality is readily apparent in this stage as it is in the latter positions of the Perry and the Belenky et al. (1986) schemes.

Baxter Magolda found that most of the absolute knowers in her study were first or second year college students. Most all of her college students had left this stage by the time they were seniors. Independent knowers readily increased from virtually none among the first two years of college to 57% of those who had graduated from college. She found only a handful of undergraduates at the contextual knowing stage; only 12% of the graduates were so classified. This leads to a question regarding the status of preservice teachers.

Usually we encounter preservice teachers in their methods courses or during student teaching, that is, in the latter part of their junior year and during their senior year of college. Both the Perry and the Baxter Magolda schemes suggest that these students should be at least at the transitional stage of development although evidence exists that many student teachers hold a dualistic or multiplistic view of mathematics and teaching (Thompson, 1992). Perhaps we should think of our preservice teachers less in terms of their number of years of college and more in terms of their stages of professional development This might explain why dualism or multiplism abounds among young teachers or perhaps even experienced teachers who have minimal experiences in professional development programs.

A critical part of the developmental process is the individual's propensity to be reflective. King and Kitchener (1994) developed a model of intellectual development that involves three levels of reflective thinking: pre-reflective, quasi-reflective, and reflective. At the first level, the individual is unlikely to perceive that situations exist for which there is no single correct answer. Knowledge is absolute much as in Perry's (1970) dualistic state. Quasi-reflective thinking involves the recognition that knowing does not require certainty and that every person is entitled to his or her own opinion, a position much like Perry's multiplism. More advanced quasi-reflective thinking involves recognizing that knowledge is contextual, a sort of relativistic stage. Finally, reflective thinking, according to King and Kitchener (1994) requires that knowledge is understood contextually and that evidence in support of that knowledge is continually open to reevaluation. The authors found that reflective thinking was more likely to occur in graduate students and that other students are better characterized by one of the two other reflective categories. This finding is similar to that of Baxter Magolda (1992) who found that only the more advanced students demonstrated extensive relativistic thinking.

In an effort to conceptualize a framework for considering teachers' beliefs specific to mathematics, Cooney, Shealy, and Arvold (1998) described four positions that characterized the teachers they studied: isolationist, naïve idealist, naïve connectionist, and reflective connectionist. Roughly speaking, these four positions reflect the extent to which teachers resist or accommodate new teaching methods into their teaching schemes and exhibit a reflective orientation toward mathematics and teaching. The isolationist is a rather dualistic person who resists new ideas and who assimilates only those ideas into his/her belief system that are consistent with those beliefs. That is, the beliefs act as a filter for the acceptance or rejection of new ideas regardless of the rationale or evidence in support of those ideas. In short, the isolationist is firm about what he/she believes and exhibits a closed mind when it comes to new ideas about teaching. The naïve idealist accepts uncritically what an authority suggests. Their reliance on authority may not be that much different than the isolationist, but they are more accommodating and hence accept whatever the authority recommends or states. The naïve connectionist is a reflective individual who sees connections between content and pedagogy, and who can identify certain tensions in the teaching of mathematics but who fails to see the significance of the connections and makes no attempt to resolve tensions that have been identified. The reflective connectionist is akin to Schön's (1983) reflective practitioner and accommodates pedagogical ideas as belief systems are restructured.

The aforementioned schemes address the basic epistemological issue of determining ways that individuals come to know. Recall Scheffler's (1965) ideas about beliefs and the importance of doubt in changing beliefs. For the isolationist, a change even in one's peripheral beliefs would be difficult, for on what basis would those beliefs change? One could argue that a teacher educator's proclamations might move the isolationist in light of the authority teacher educators usually hold. But if these proclamations run counter to the preservice teacher's own beliefs, beliefs accumulated through years of schooling as a student and further contradicted by traditional teachers in the field, the result is predictable. Indeed, this was exactly the case with Henry (Cooney, et al., 1998) who nearly dropped out of his teacher education program because he saw his beliefs being continually contradicted by his instructors. As luck would have it, his student teaching placement was with a very lecture-oriented teacher who reinforced Henry's view of teaching as effective teaching. Henry reached the conclusion that his teacher educators held inappropriate views of teaching. There was no doubt in Henry's mind. Nor was there in Harriet's mind, another preservice teacher who participated in a reform-oriented teacher education program. Her beliefs about teaching were rooted in her mother's perspective about teaching and as such were not permeable (Cooney & Wilson, 1995). She closed her mind to new ideas about teaching, save for the use of technology and a few ideas about the use of alternative assessment methods. But even here, these ideas were only minimally assimilated into her thinking and perhaps only in a way that allowed her to be the dominant dispenser of information. On the other hand, the preservice teacher Greg was a reflective individual whose beliefs were permeably. Although he initially rejected the use of technology in his teaching, he later became a firm advocate of using technology (Cooney, et al., 1998).

If we wish to engender in teachers the notion that the value of an activity or of any particular teaching strategy is context dependent, it seems clear that they must have experiences with evaluating those contexts. The epistemological issues raised in this section can provide a gyroscope both for theorizing the professional development of teachers and for providing a framework for developing activities that engage teachers in such evaluation. The key is to enable teachers to understand that activities or teaching methods in and of themselves are neither good nor bad. Rather, it is the context that makes them effective or not. As teacher educators, we need to develop a means for understanding how teachers can come to such understanding. Hofer and Pintrich (1997), after an exhaustive review of issues related to the conceptualization and use of various epistemological theories, put it this way: "In any case, the examination of the development of epistemological theories will help us to understand students' and teachers' beliefs about knowledge and their thinking about knowledge. This information will then help us better understand the teaching and learning processes in classrooms" (p. 133). These schemes can help map the conceptual terrain of teacher education. In the following section, I will describe a context that illustrates the perspective of which Hofer and Pintrich speak.

4. A MATHEMATICAL CONTEXT FOR TEACHER DEVELOPMENT

Based on my experience with educating preservice teachers, I have come to conclude that the best entry into their belief systems about mathematics and the teaching of mathematics is through the study of school mathematics. It is here that reflection can become commonplace with respect to both mathematics and pedagogy. Consequently, I submit that the integration of content and pedagogy is a strategic site for encouraging reflection and the consequences of that reflective thinking.

Preservice teachers often miss many of the important mathematical connections in school mathematics and frequently exhibit their own misconceptions. This seems to be true for high achieving students as well as for those who struggle with collegiate level mathematics. For example, I vividly remember one preservice secondary mathematics teacher who was an honor student with all As in her top level mathematics courses. Her teaching of a middle school lesson involved the identity element for rational numbers which she claimed was 0/0! There is a multitude of evidence that suggests elementary teachers lack mathematical sophistication (Brown, Cooney, & Jones, 1990). We have less evidence about what secondary teachers know about mathematics. What evidence does exist suggests that secondary teachers' understanding of school mathematics is neither sophisticated nor connected. Cooney, et al. (1998) studied preservice secondary teachers' understanding of mathematical functions and found that their view of function was generally shallow and often computational in nature. The preservice teachers seemed to believe that mathematics is useful, yet their examples tended to be computational in nature, a finding consistent with Owens' (1987) study of preservice secondary teachers.

Perhaps this should not be surprising, given that preservice teachers have rarely encountered secondary school mathematics during their collegiate career save those skills or concepts that are required to do calculus. Often lost in the shuffle is geometry, a particularly troublesome area for preservice teachers. This presents both a dilemma and an opportunity for those involved in mathematics teacher education. Do we find ways to "fill" the mathematical deficiencies or do we use this circumstance as an opportunity to encourage reflection about the nature of mathematics and what it means to study and do mathematics?

Cooney, Brown, Dossey, Schrage, and Wittmann (1999) developed materials that integrate content and pedagogy involving the topics of functions, the Pythagorean Theorem, modeling, combinatorics, and problem posing. The materials are designed to present different mathematical situations and engage teachers in problem solving in which they encounter such questions as "What happens if?" and the concomitant pedagogical issues that are embedded in the mathematical considerations. This effort to integrate pedagogy and content provides a context for teachers to reflect on their own understanding of mathematics and consider the implications of their beliefs about mathematics for their teaching of mathematics.

I have previously written about how mathematical situations have been posed to promote teacher development (Cooney, 1999). Another context is to take an apparently obvious situation and to ask teachers to consider what might be problematic about the situation. Consider, for example, the following systems of equations and their respective graphs. Preservice teachers are quick to respond that the first set represents a pair of parallel lines,

Set 1	Set 2	Set 3
$y = 2x + 3$	$y = 2x + 3$	$y = 2x + 3$
$y = 2x - 1$	$y = -0.5x - 2$	$y = -x + 6$

the second set represents a set of perpendicular lines, and the third set represents lines that intersect at the point (1,5). When pressed, they remain steadfast in their beliefs albeit they are a bit suspicious. They are then asked to consider whether their characterizations of the three pairs of equations are based on the assumption that they would be graphed in the Cartesian plane with orthogonal axes and what might happen if the axes intersected at a 60 degree angle. The question catches the teachers off guard because they never considered a situation in which the representational system was viewed as problematic.

In another context, I ask teachers to solve the following problem.

> Jack is in a race with 15 other boys. At the beginning of the race Jack is fifth from the last. At the end of the race he is third. How many boys did he pass? (Cooney, et al., 1999, p. 11)

What is interesting about this rather simple problem is that it cries for definition. If Jack passes Mark, then falls behind Mark, and then passes Mark again, is that one pass or two? Does the order of finish make any difference? Suppose two boys that were behind Jack finish ahead of Jack at the end of the race. Does this yield the same answer as the case in which the boys who were originally first and second finish first and second? Further, the problem allows for a sort of symbolic representation so that problem extensions that might involve 200 girls in a race could be easily solved.

These and other problems provide a rich context for preservice teachers to engage in pedagogical problem solving as well as mathematical problem solving. The problems can be used to generate "What happens if" questions and to engage in reflective thinking, both significant aspects of professional development. Many problems can promote this kind of professional development. What is critical is that the contexts in which the problems are presented are considered so that teachers have the opportunity to re-consider their beliefs about mathematics and its teaching and to begin developing their own personal philosophy of teaching mathematics. The mathematics is critical because it is the very essence of what teaching is all about. The movement into more pedagogical considerations flows more naturally once the mathematical tasks have been examined.

5. PARADOXES, PERILS, AND PURPOSES

Preservice teachers come to us with rather fixed views of mathematics. In many cases they want to emulate their teachers, who often exemplified traditional teaching methods. They want to "stand and deliver" as their teachers have done. They want certainty. They want prescriptions for generating that certainty. They care about kids. They want to be fair. They do not want their grading of students to be capricious, and consequently they favor methods that have the façade of being objective. And what do we do? We encourage doubt, reflection, consideration of context, and try to develop in them an experimental notion of teaching wherein instruction is based on what students know and understand. What a study in contradiction! There is peril in this polarity as I am sure all of us recognize. Push too far on the doubt and reflective end and we either destroy the confidence of the young teacher or alienate the teacher to the extent that our credibility as teacher educators is challenged.

A good dose of common sense can help avoid this peril as can the development of constructs that map the terrain we are traversing. The theoretical perspectives previously discussed present one attempt to do this. These perspectives can not only serve as a basis for generating activities that engage teachers in the exercise of reflective thinking, it can also provide us with an understanding of where teachers are located in their own struggle to develop a philosophy of teaching. Consider the case of Henry (Cooney, et al., 1998). Once an isolationalist always an isolationalist? No, of course not, as that would be isolationalist thinking in itself. But we might react differently to Henry if we had realized that his world views differed from ours and that those views led him to react negatively to much of his teacher education activities.

The argument for developing models of children's understanding of mathematics is that teachers can then use those schemes as a basis for educating children. Consider, for example, Cognitively Guided Instruction (Carpenter, Fennema, & Franke, 1996). Similarly, we could use models for conceptualizing how teachers make sense of their worlds so that the effect of our instruction is purposeful and not random. Just as we would like teachers' teaching to be scientific in the sense that it is based on what students know, so should our teaching of teachers be based on viable interpretations of their worlds. This is the science of teacher education that can provide us with the kinds of insights we need for our work with teachers.

Earlier in this article I tried to make the case that the education of teachers is not simply a matter of developing a better product but in fact engenders considerable moral authority. Responses to questions such as, "What constitutes good teaching?" and "What and whose mathematics should we be teaching?" provide moral lighthouses that can guide our journey in conceptualizing and conducting teacher education programs. Do we have the moral right, or the moral courage, to produce reflective practitioners? Arvold's (1998) Monica represents a teacher who was mathematically competent as determined by any reasonable standard. But her view of mathematics and her teaching of mathematics were limited and primarily dualistic. Hers was a classroom laced with certainty. She was a product of our reform-oriented teacher education program and, according to her grades, she learned the lessons well. By what moral compass do we judge her teaching? Were we blinded by her intelligence so that we failed to see this coming when she was our student? What could we have done differently? Should we have done anything differently? Is it her choice alone to teach mathematics in a highly directive, prescriptive, and dualistic manner? What say ye, John Dewey, that could alleviate our concerns?

The paradox in all of this is that despite our best efforts we run the risk of communicating specific teaching methods rather than a more reflective, adaptive approach. Recall Frykholm's (1999) finding that preservice teachers tended to see the *Standards* as content and not as a philosophy of teaching. An anecdote that was particularly striking to me occurred a few years ago when I engaged my preservice teachers in a variety of situations in which they had to create mathematical models of situations that were reasonably within the grasp of secondary students. The preservice teachers seemed to enjoy the mathematics and the accompanying pedagogical questions, including weighing the potential gains against the risks of doing investigative, data driven activities with secondary students. At some point near the end of the discussion, a bright young woman proclaimed, "I finally know the right way to teach." It was a bittersweet moment. Complimentary as it was, it exemplified the difficulty of helping teachers grapple with issues associated with any specific teaching method as opposed to advocating one. It was one more reminder of how fragile preservice teachers' knowledge really is and what extensive care must be taken to develop that knowledge. This realization alone should give those of us involved with teachers considerable pause as we reflect upon our own practice of educating teachers.

REFERENCES

Arvold, B. (1998). *Becoming a secondary mathematics teacher: A case study.* Unpublished doctoral dissertation, University of Georgia, Athens.

Ball, D. & Wilson, S. (1996). Integrity in teaching: Recognizing the fusion of the moral and intellectual. *American Educational Research Journal. 33* (1), 155-192.

Baxter Magolda, M. (1992). *Knowing and reasoning in college.* San Francisco: Jossey-Bass Inc.

Belenky, M., Clinchy, B., Goldberger, N., & Tarule, J. (1986). *Women's ways of knowing: The development of self, voice, and mind.* New York: Basic Books.

Brown, S., Cooney, T., & Jones, D. (1990). Mathematics teacher education. In Houston (Ed.), *Handbook of research on teacher education* (pp. 639-656). New York: Macmillan Publishing Co.

Brownell, W. (1956). Meaning and Skill—Maintaining the Balance. *Arithmetic Teacher. 15,* 129-136.

Carpenter, T., Fennema, E., & Franke, M. (1996). Cognitively guided instruction: A knowledge base for reform in primary mathematics instruction. *Elementary School Journal, 97,* 3-20.

Cooney, T. (1994). In-service programs in mathematics education. In S. Fitzsimmons & Kerpelman (Eds.), *Teacher enhancement for elementary and secondary science and mathematics: Status, issues, and problems* (pp. 8.1-8.33). Cambridge, MA: Center for Science and Technology Policy Studies.

Cooney, T. (1999). Conceptualizing teachers' ways of knowing. *Educational Studies in Mathematics. 38,* 163-187.

Cooney, T., Badger, E., & Wilson, M. (1993). Assessment, understanding mathematics, and distinguishing visions from mirages. In N. Webb & A. Coxford (Eds). *Assessment in the mathematics classroom.* Reston, VA: National Council of Teachers of Mathematics. pp. 239-247.

Cooney, T., Brown, S., Dossey, J., Schrage, G., & Wittmann, E. (1999). *Mathematics, pedagogy, and secondary teacher education: Reweaving the frayed braid.* Portsmouth, NH: Heinemann.

Cooney, T., Shealy, B., & Arvold, B. (1998) Conceptualizing belief structures of preservice secondary mathematics teachers. *Journal for Research in Mathematics Education, 29,* 306-333.

Cooney, T., Wilson, P., Albright, M., & Chauvot, J. (1998). Conceptualizing the professional development of secondary preservice mathematics teachers. Paper presented at the American Educational Research Association annual meeting. San Diego, CA.

Cooney, T. & Wilson, P. (1995). On the notion of secondary preservice teachers' ways of knowing mathematics. In D. Owens, M. Reed, & G. Millsaps (Eds.), *Proceedings of the Seventeenth Annual Meeting of the North American Chapter of the International Group for the Psychology of Mathematics Education* (pp. 2.91-2.96). Columbus, Ohio: ERIC. Davis, B. (1999). Basic irony: Examining the foundations of school mathematics with preservice teachers. *Journal of Mathematics Teacher Education, 2,* 25-48.

Davis, E. (1997). *The teaching of mathematics in Georgia's schools.* Unpublished manuscript, University of Georgia, College of Education, Athens.

Dewey, J. (1916). *Democracy and education.* New York: The Free Press.

Frykholm, J. (1999). The impact of reform: Challenges for mathematics teacher preparation. *Journal of Mathematics Teacher Education, 2,* 79-105.

Gerdes, P. (1998). On culture and mathematics teacher education. *Journal of Mathematics Teacher Education, 1,* 33-53.

Glasser, W. (1990). *The quality school.* New York: Harper and Row.

Grant, T., Hiebert, J., & Wearne, D. (1998). Observing and teaching reform-minded lessons: What do teachers see? *Journal of Mathematics Teacher Education. 1,* 217-236.

Green, T. (1971). *The activities of teaching.* New York: McGraw-Hill.

Guskey, T. (1986). Staff development and the process of teacher change. *Educational Researcher, 15*(5), 5-12.

Hofer, B. & Pintrich, P. (1997). The development of epistemological theories: Beliefs about knowledge and their relation to learning. *Review of Educational Research. 67,* 88-140.

Jaworski, B. (1998). Mathematics teacher research: Process, practice, and the development of teaching. *Journal of Mathematics Teacher Education, 1,* 3-31.

King, P. & Kitchener, K. (1994). Developing reflective judgment. San Francisco: Jossey-Bass, Inc.

Kuhn, T. (1962). *The structure of scientific revolutions.* Chicago. University of Chicago Press.

National Council of Teachers of Mathematics. (1989). *Curriculum and evaluation standards for school mathematics.* Reston, VA: Author.

National Council of Teachers of Mathematics. (1991). *Professional standards for teaching mathematics.* Reston, VA: Author.

Owens, J. (1987). *A study of four preservice teachers' constructs of mathematics and mathematics teaching.* Unpublished doctoral dissertation, University of Georgia, Athens.

Pepper, S. (1942). *World hypothesis.* Berkeley: University of California Press.

Perry, W. (1970). *Forms of intellectual and ethical development in the college years.* New York: Holt, Rinehart, & Winston.

Presmeg, N. (1998). Ethnomathematics in teacher education. *Journal of Mathematics Teacher Education, 1,* 317-339.

Rokeach, M. (1960). *The open and closed mind.* New York: Basic Books Inc.

Scheffler, I. (1965). *Conditions of knowledge.* Chicago: Scott Foresman and Company.

Schifter, D. (1998). Learning mathematics for teaching: From a teachers' seminar to the classroom. *Journal of Mathematics Teacher Education. 1,* 55-87.

Schön, D. (1983). *The reflective practioner: How professionals think in action.* New York: Basic Books Inc.

Senk, S., Beckmann, C., & Thompson, D. (1997). Assessment and grading in high school mathematics classrooms. *Journal for Research in Mathematics Education, 28,* 187-215.

Steen, L. (1988). The science of patterns. *Science, 240,* 611-616.

Thompson, A. (1991). The development of teachers' conceptions of mathematics teaching. In R. Underhill (Ed.) *Proceedings of the Thirteenth Annual Meeting of the North American Chapter of the International Group for the Psychology of Mathematics Education* (Vol. 2, 8-15). Columbus, OH: ERIC Clearinghouse for Science, Mathematics, and Environmental Education.

Thompson, A. (1992). Teachers' beliefs and conceptions: A synthesis of the research. In D. Grouws (Ed.), *Handbook of research on mathematics teaching and learning* (pp. 127-146). New York: Macmillan.

Von Glasersfeld, E. (1991). Abstraction, re-presentation, and reflection: An interpretation of experience and Piaget's approach. In L. Steffe (Ed.), *Epistemological foundations of mathematical experience.* New York: Springer-Verlag.

Wilson, M. & Goldenberg, M. (1998). Some conceptions are difficult to change: One middle school mathematics teacher's struggle. *Journal of Mathematics Teacher Education, 1,* 269-293.

Wilson P. & Padron, J. (1994). Moving towards a culture-inclusive mathematics education. In M. Atwater, K. Radzik-Marsh, & M. Strutchens (Eds.), *Multicultural education: Inclusion of all* (pp. 39-63). Athens, GA: The University of Georgia.

Department of Mathematics Education
The University of Georgia
Athens, GA 30602

STEPHEN LERMAN

A REVIEW OF RESEARCH PERSPECTIVES ON MATHEMATICS TEACHER EDUCATION

ABSTRACT. Research on mathematics teachers and mathematics teacher education has grown substantially over the last 10 to 20 years with the recognition of the enormous influence of the teacher on children's learning of mathematics. This chapter argues that theoretical frameworks for such studies are not always coherent, nor are they well examined in the literature, remaining largely implicit. The chapter attempts an overview of research and an investigation of the implicit assumptions about the process of teacher learning. I propose that social theories of teacher learning that draw on notions of developing identities are more relevant and fruitful for these domains of educational research.

There is considerable recent interest and development in research on teacher education, as evidenced by the appearance of the new *Journal for Mathematics Teacher Education*, by the publication of the book *Mathematics Teachers in Transition* (Fennema & Nelson, 1997), and of course this present volume. There have been teacher education working groups at meetings of the International Group for the Psychology of Mathematics Education (PME) for about a decade, with published productions from some of them. Those of us who have been working in the area for some years are very gratified to see this. We have been aware for many years that the teacher is a key element in students' learning of mathematics. The complexity of the field today, in terms of theoretical perspectives and empirical approaches, is evidence of how much there is to say and how much there is still to learn.

The terms *teacher education, teacher development,* and *teacher change* all appear in the literature at different times and in different contexts. Teacher education seems to be more generally used when the issue is concerned with pre-service students. Teacher development and teacher change are more frequently used in relation to in-service programmes and teachers' changing roles through curriculum innovation, or in research projects. These terms seem appropriate when there is a specific educational change to be effected (Fullan & Hargreaves, 1992), instigated by individual schools, school districts, subject groups (for example the reform in the US) or national governments (the UK situation). In these situations teachers are expected to change their practices towards particular goals, which are usually made quite explicit by the implementers. There are occasions when one finds in the literature an implicit set of goals of the researchers, whereby a particular style of teaching may be uncontroversially presented as the preferred direction, and the research is examining or measuring the change or development towards those goals.

F.-L. Lin & T. J. Cooney (Eds.) Making Sense of Mathematics Teacher Education, 33—52.
© 2001 *Kluwer Academic Publishers. Printed in the Netherlands.*

I don't believe that the field of study benefits by research that masks the values of the researchers. On the other hand development or change can be used by teachers to describe a process they are going through when they work on their own teaching in order to learn more about teaching mathematics and to improve their practice (for example. Jaworski, 1998). The goals for the teachers are their own, although the community within which they are engaged in the research process is clearly a key element that must be taken into account (Jaworski, 1998, p. 26).

Researchers have adopted a range of approaches to teacher education, development, and change. Grant, Hiebert, and Wearne (1998), for example, mention three successful approaches, in terms of "how to bring teachers into the reform process" (p. 218): discussion with teachers about their beliefs and practices (for example, Simon, & Schifter, 1991); cognitively guided instruction (for example, Fennema, Franke, Carpenter, & Carey, 1993); and working intensively with teachers (for example, Heaton & Lambert, 1993). They then propose their own method, that of teachers observing others teaching their own classes in a reform-orientated way. There are, of course, other research perspectives, and it is my intention to examine them in this chapter. I do not claim to have been exhaustive in this study, but I hope to have discussed the major trends in research in this field.

Although the domains of pre-service, in-service, curriculum innovation, and research projects are different, one to the other, in terms of teacher education/development/change, I want to suggest that there is a common underlying notion, that of teachers learning about teaching mathematics. It seems that we fight shy of using *learning* in relation to adults, perhaps because whoever is organising the project or the course will be put into the position of teacher, or perhaps because it suggests an absence of knowledge in the learners. Development or change may therefore appear more acceptable, even more democratic. However, I will not be suggesting that teaching is a body of knowledge, nor, for that matter, is education, pedagogy, or didactics. I do not think teaching is analogous to mathematics, in which there is a section of the library labelled Mathematics where accepted texts and journals are to be found, although of course we struggle over whether mathematics is a body of universal truths or is historically and culturally contingent, and what the implications of such positions might be (Lerman, 1983). Teaching (especially "good" teaching) and its associated terms are always disputed, except perhaps by governments. In this paper I will suggest that in pre-service, in-service, curriculum innovation, and research projects teachers are potentially learning different ways to be, as a teacher, and I think it is helpful to call this process learning. Of course we have well known ways of theorising children's learning, but we are not so well served when thinking about adults' learning, especially learning about their work. In this paper I intend to interrogate the approaches we use in research on teacher education, development, and change for the underlying assumptions about the learning process for teaching mathematics. In the past, I have engaged in studies of teachers' beliefs (Lerman, 1986, 1990), and have drawn on reflective practice as a theory of learning (Lerman, 1994). In this chapter, I will be offering a critique of my own work, as well as that of others, in a search for theories of learning appropriate to mathematics teachers (Lerman, 1997).

1. RESEARCH PERSPECTIVES: TEACHERS AND THEIR BELIEFS

1.1 Teachers' Beliefs

Much work has gone into the analysis of teachers' beliefs about mathematics and about mathematics education, and into the analysis of the possible connections between the two, and it remains of great interest today. It is perhaps the predominant orientation in research on teachers and teacher education. It has been argued (for example, Thompson, 1984) that teachers' beliefs are critical factors determining how they teach. So-called mismatches between theories and practices have been discussed in the literature (Cooney 1985; Thompson 1982, 1984, 1992; Lerman 1986, 1990), although it is sometimes referred to as espoused and enacted theories of mathematics teaching (Ernest 1989). In her review of the research in this field, Thompson (1992, p. 138) suggested that the relationship between teachers' conceptions of mathematics and their practice is complex and argued for viewing the relationship as a dialectic one, citing the work of Cobb, Wood, & Yackel (1990).

At the heart of this body of literature is the argument that teachers' beliefs and conceptions need to change for their teaching to change. Beliefs are taken to be an internal mental landscape which can be charted by suitable research instruments, but each person's landscape is assumed to be stable across the range of teaching sites and across the researcher's data collection sites. Beliefs are assumed to be amenable to change over time as a result of some processes, although the process of change is often not specified. Indeed it is argued that teachers' beliefs must change for their teaching to change. One must question, at this stage, what right anyone has to try to change someone's beliefs or their teaching. Teachers are quite likely to be perfectly happy with the way they teach. In the name of reflexivity, I feel sure that teacher educators and researchers should be explicit about their own beliefs about teaching mathematics and what constitutes better teaching for them.

The analysis and classification of teachers' beliefs forms one major focus of research; and monitoring changes in teachers' beliefs over time, and through periods of curriculum change, advanced study, or research programmes, form another focus. This chapter will begin with an examination of these two aspects of the research into mathematics teacher education.

Beliefs research. Research (Lerman, 1986; da Ponte, 1994; Pehkonen & Törner, 1996) which examines teachers' beliefs and theories in one context and attempts to examine practice, or beliefs about practice, in another context is based on a notion that the core of a subject's identity, at least in relation to teaching mathematics, is unified and decontextualised. It is as if the teacher brings his or her theories (relatively stable mental objects) to bear on practice (empirical setting). Given this separation, attitudes and beliefs about the teaching of mathematics can be examined by an instrument in one setting, interviews in a laboratory or questionnaire completion on one's own, for example, and their impact examined in another setting, the classroom. There is then the argument that whatever mismatches there appear to be result from the influence of one particular factor, in a school environment perhaps, that distorts or over-rides beliefs. In the literature of research in this area one finds the following examples:

> By virtue of working within a larger organization—in this case the school—constraints are placed on an individual teacher's decision-making power. This tends to result in an apparent within-school conformity of thought and idea. (Post, Ward, & Willson, 1977, p. 339)

> For some teachers, these conceptions (*about teaching in general and about students, and the social and emotional makeup of the class*) [italics added] are likely to take precedence over other views and beliefs specific to the teaching of mathematics. (Thompson, 1984, pp. 124-125)

> A strong candidate for explanation of this uniformity may be that the ethos of the school and the particular mathematics department may be the most significant factors in determining the way that teachers teach. (Lerman, 1986, p. 128)

These writers recognise that the shift from one setting to another allows the appearance of factors that significantly change teachers' actions from those they would profess to apply or would wish to apply, but there is no clear sense of any mechanism or relationship between settings and actions and/or beliefs. In my research (Lerman, 1986, 1990), I developed a questionnaire to examine teachers' beliefs and attitudes to mathematics and mathematics teaching, and invited all the mathematics teachers from one school to complete the questionnaire in their own time. Shortly afterwards I conducted structured interviews in the school staff room, and then observed each teacher's classroom on a number of occasions. I found a wide variety of beliefs and attitudes in the questionnaire and interview responses, but a uniformity in teaching styles (as determined by an interview schedule), and I gave the explanation above for this phenomenon.

I now feel that these explanations are not adequate. I want to suggest that whilst there is a family resemblance between concepts, beliefs, and actions in one context and those in another, they are qualitatively different by virtue of those contexts. I want to argue that contexts in which research on teachers' beliefs and practices are carried out should be seen as a whole, in the sense that the cognitive and emotional responses of the subject(s), through and with the methods, tools, and social structuring as related to the researcher(s'), language, and so forth, form the findings; they are not separable. So, too, the classroom must be seen as a specific context. It is not that the opinions and beliefs of a teacher in, say, an interview context are unrelated to that teacher's practice. I have characterised it as a family relationship in that there are strong links and resemblances, but the classroom is its own setting.

For example, Gattuso (1994) describes the effect of mood, personal relationships to students, and other factors on teaching styles. She came to the classroom with a set of beliefs about how one should teach and, indeed, of how she herself taught, but a monitoring of her teaching demonstrated the differences between her beliefs and her actions. Again, it is not to be seen as some factors interfering with a set of beliefs; those beliefs are related to the context within which they are elicited, and cannot be otherwise. I am suggesting that it makes no sense to claim that, for example, the way in which at the time Gattuso was reacting to a student with whom she felt unsympathetic in a formal manner, simply giving rather curt answers to his questions, can be described as a mismatch between espoused and enacted beliefs.

To take another example, in the second stage of the research I carried out some years ago (Lerman, 1986, 1990), in order to find another way of eliciting teachers' beliefs about mathematics teaching I showed a video extract of a mathematics lesson separately to four students on a pre-service mathematics teacher education course. The students were chosen because their responses to the questionnaire placed two of them at each of the extremes of the spectrum, as identified by the questionnaire. The lesson content was an introduction to solving simultaneous linear equations, and the friendly, informal atmosphere of the classroom tended to mask a quite didactic teaching style. In detailed interviews following the video, the two students whose views in the questionnaire placed them at the open end of the spectrum expressed the opinion that the teacher was too prescriptive in her teaching style. They wanted to see a more investigative approach, as discussed in greater depth by da Ponte in this volume. The two student teachers from the other end of the spectrum thought her not sufficiently directive and felt that the teacher had left the students floundering. They wanted to see more *transmission*. Thus, in contrast to the first stage of the study in which I had found a uniformity of teaching styles amongst a group of teachers, this methodology revealed strong differences. I suggest that the video elicited comments that may be closer to how those student teachers might have reacted if I had been able to interview them during their teaching practice whilst they were in the act of teaching, than would be seen in an interview without a video, or the completion of a questionnaire as in the first stage of my study. In the sense of a family resemblance of people's utterances in different situations, this method perhaps sits between the classroom and the more detached data-gathering methods. Nevertheless, all these situations/contexts are distinct, and research findings need to recognise this. Teachers' beliefs are contextualised: to the data-gathering situation; to the interviewer/interviewee relationship; to the location of classroom, laboratory or other setting; to the particular group of students, and so forth. Teacher's beliefs are related to practice and beliefs about practice, but they are not simply able to be mapped one to the other.

Changes in beliefs. Many studies on change in teachers' beliefs take place in a programme of intervention. I will begin, however, by examining a recent paper by Wilson & Goldenberg (1998) in which they studied change in beliefs without an explicit programme of intervention. They first presented a model for mapping teachers' belief, based on Perry (1970), and then used that framework to examine one teacher over a two-year period. Their version of the Perry model used 4 categories of beliefs of increasing sophistication: dualism, pluralism, extreme relativism, and experimentalism. They claimed that these are not to be seen as stages in teacher development, although they searched for progress through them towards experimentalism, which they see as the desirable perspective for reform teaching. There was no explicit agenda on the part of the researchers to bring about change, although the teacher was observed, by their research methods, to have moved through the categories to some extent. What is remarkable in that study is the absence of any discussion about what might lead to changes in beliefs or, indeed, a lack of changes. There is a brief mention of the support, mainly teaching materials, provided by university personnel "which may account for some of (the teacher's) instructional decisions" (p. 284), but in terms of processes of change, or what I would wish to call learning, there is no mention of theory. This is typical of much research on teachers' beliefs. Many readers would conjecture that a teacher being observed and interviewed over a two-year period by university researchers would construct a picture of the researchers' agenda and point of view, which might lead to changes in their practices and beliefs. In fact it would be remarkable were there to be no influence, although the authors claimed "We remind readers that we did very little to intervene in Mr Burt's practice or to sway his beliefs, and that we eschewed opportunities to more actively cause change along the lines of our model." (p. 290).

As an example of research that monitors changes in beliefs during a programme of intervention, I will discuss the paper by Grant, Hiebert, and Wearne (1998). The paper describes a project in which nine teachers watched reform oriented lessons taught by three project teachers over a number of weeks. According to the researchers, four teachers missed "the point of the instruction. They tended to focus on individual features, predominantly the use of manipulatives, as the crux of the alternative instruction" (p. 225). Three other teachers "recognised some of the features of the instruction ... However ... they did not connect these features with larger goals but treated them in narrow, overly-constrained ways" (p. 226). The final two teachers "tended to recognize and internalize the instruction" (p. 227). The research also examined the beliefs of the three project teachers, and found that they "were all quite articulate in discussing the intent of the instruction and its salient features in a way consistent with our views" (p. 230). In the face of this evidence, Grant, Hiebert, and Wearne attributed the key to the teachers' beliefs filtering "what they see and what they internalize" (p. 233). Again, the question that is not addressed is how beliefs might change, what the mechanics of this process might be. One might conjecture, for example, that the culture of the community of the project team as a whole, engaged in teaching expert lessons to measure the changes in beliefs of the observing teachers, might play a significant role in the project teachers' developing perceptions of the nature of teaching and learning mathematics. The researchers refer to Guskey's (1986) suggestion that teachers' beliefs may change when there is an intrinsic reward, such as seeing their students' improved success; but although that did occur here, in the form of students' improved end of year scores, it did not seem to bring about the changes hoped for by the research project in a larger number of the observing teachers.

Grant, Hiebert, and Wearne (1998) refer to Schifter's work as a successful example of changing beliefs. In a recent paper, Schifter (1998) explores two "avenues for promoting teachers' mathematical investigations. The first avenue is *exploration of disciplinary content* ... The second avenue is *examination of student thinking*" (p. 57). A total of 36 elementary school teachers and 6 staff members from three institutions are engaged in a four-year teacher-enhancement project. During sessions in college, teachers engage in mathematical investigations at their own level, and experience models of different mathematical learning experiences, including problems being set without prior instruction, group problem solving, and so forth. Through reflection on the nature of their own learning experiences in mathematics some, at least, of the teachers recognise possibilities for transforming their own classrooms. At the same time, the journals that they keep include records of their students' mathematical activities and analysis of their thinking. Schifter also refers to assigned readings as an element that contributes to teachers' changing practices. Schifter demands yet more, though, the development by teachers of "a new ear, one that is attuned to the mathematical ideas of one's own students" (p. 79). Narratives of incidents in their classes, as well as narratives from the staff members of the project team, offer opportunities for the teachers to discuss their students' learning with other teachers in the project. The final element is that of staff visits to their classrooms, in which the staff help teachers to work on aspects of their lessons which the teachers identified at the beginning of the year.

The reports of teachers' development are impressive, as they are in other of Schifter's writings (for example, Schifter, 1995). The range of experiences in which teachers engage, during the project, clearly has a significant effect on their perceptions of their own teaching. From the accounts in these papers it seems clear that many of the teachers have learnt a great deal about mathematics and about listening to and analysing their students' mathematical activity, and their practice has been transformed. The question remains, though, a question which might enable us to distinguish between the experiences of the teachers in the Grant, Hiebert, and Wearne (1998) study and the present one: Is the difference due to the range of experiences undertaken by these teachers, or the activity of the teachers in the Schifter study as opposed to the mere observation in the Grant, Hiebert, and Wearne study, or to other factors? What is the effect of the writing, of the work on their mathematics, of the length of the project, or of the group discussion between the teachers? In short, what leads to teachers' learning (or not)? What theory do the project team have which they and other researchers are able to draw on in order to construct suitable activities, both for teachers' learning and for research? This is not discussed in the Schifter paper, except for "a disposition to inquiry" (p. 84) and the ubiquitous, but uncritically stated, process of reflection (see, for example, p. 83). *found everywhere*

1.2 Reflective Practice

I will turn now to examine this notion that appears, often without elaboration, in many papers about teacher education/development/change. So many articles refer to teachers and student teachers reflecting on their experiences, as if the evocation of it is sufficient in itself for learning (for example, Lerman, 1994).

One of the most significant moves in thinking about teaching in the last few decades has been that of reflective practice and its association with critical theory and action research. Reflective practice offers a view of how teachers act in the classroom as informed, concerned professionals and of how they continue to learn about teaching and about learning, about themselves as teachers, and about their pupils as learners. It encourages and feeds the notion of the autonomous, emancipated teacher who is not dominated by government rhetoric in choosing the way she or he wishes to conduct the classroom interactions, nor by the self-interests of some university-based researchers in defining what constitutes valid research in the classroom. At the same time, the association of reflective practice with critical theory invites an engagement with the institutions of schooling in actions to change those structures; emancipate thinking and acting; and lead to the emergence of autonomous teachers. It injects a relativism into what we can know about teaching: In this classroom, with these students, this learning material, certain things happened which might be explained thus and were acted upon thus. It seeks to avoid the traps of extreme relativism, however, by emphasising principled thinking, reason, and critical judgement. The critical, reflective practitioner:

> thinks and acts in accordance with, and values, consistency, fairness, and impartiality of judgement and action. Principled, critical judgement, in its rejection of arbitrariness, inconsistency, and partiality, thus presupposes a recognition of the binding forces of standards, taken to be universal and objective, in accordance with which judgements are made. (Siegel, 1988, in Parker, 1997, p. 44)

It is precisely here that a critique must enter, the critique of the postmodern. Briefly, it can be said that postmodernism focuses on the problem of representation. Language(s), which people learn from the culture(s) in which they grow up, carries the meanings we can make from what we see, and the possibilities of how we think. Meanings are not, therefore, transparent, they are opaque. Words signify things, and it cannot be taken for granted what they signify, whereas in earlier times the link between a concept, the signifier, and what that concept refers to, the signified, might have been thought to be both fixed and apparent. As a consequence, postmodern research in education examines how language constructs the objects of its study and how it carries relations of power, often hidden. With regard to the construction of the objects of its research, Walkerdine (1984) shows how developmental psychology constructs what is a normal child, and how the child is produced within school practices, marginalising those children who do not conform to the notion of the normal child. With regard to how language hides the relations of power, one can re-examine certain words usually taken as unquestioned, and deconstruct them. For instance, the term enlightenment suggests that there is a place with light that can shed its light onto a dark area. There is an assumption that one place is enlightened, having knowledge, wisdom and the right way, that only people in the enlightened place can see the darkness and can bring light to it. In this way, the enlightenment project can be seen to carry implicit values.

In relation to reflective practice and its power to bring freedom from bias, there has to be a presupposition of autonomy in order to argue for autonomy. Unless one is free and emancipated, how can one recognise when the dominated teacher steps out from his or her chains, whether that teacher is oneself or someone else? From which Archimedian position can one identify that autonomy? Positivists appeal to the transcendental to resolve this, that the truth of the transcendental argument presupposes even being able to ask the question. Habermas uses the ideal speech situation in this way: "all speech, even intentional deception, is oriented towards the idea of truth... . Insofar as we master the means for the construction of an ideal speech situation, we can conceive the ideas of truth, freedom and justice" (Habermas, 1970, in Parker, 1997, p. 58). Similarly, rationality is claimed to be a transcendental notion. To argue about rationality is to presuppose rationality. The problem is that reasoning is a process, a language game, whilst what counts as justification for reasons, or validity of reasoning, is specific to a social context or is overlapping across a range of social situations and is entirely part of the grammar of the particular language game. Rationality, then, is deconstructed, it needs to be placed under a sign of erasure, what Derrida calls *sous rature*, and written ~~rationality~~, which highlights the absence of a foundation whilst it claims to provide a foundation; so too with ~~autonomy~~ and ~~enlightenment~~.

Second, from where is the criticism, rejecting arbitrariness, and so forth, to come? Views are positions, perspectives from where one is situated. A critical view is another view. Now the claim of critical theory is that one can become aware of how one's intentions may have become distorted by self-interest or by false ideology, and one can reject and remove these distortions:

> a critical social science will seek to offer individuals an awareness of how their aims and purposes may have become distorted or repressed and to specify how these can become eradicated so that the rational pursuit of their real goals can be undertaken (Carr & Kemmis, 1986, p. 136)

There is no doubting that each of us has aims, purposes, and goals but, first, they are always context-specific and, second, what might it mean to describe them as distorted or repressed? Indeed the goals of critical theory have been seen by some as far from emancipatory (Ellsworth, 1989). What concerns me here is the inadequacy of the notion of reflective practice as a theory of how adults, and in this situation pre- and in-service teachers, learn about teaching. In its appeal to the transcendental it implicitly assumes a direction of development, and it ignores relations of power. "Reflection" *per se*, does not give us enough to serve as a process of learning. This is not to say that we don't reflect, only that for reflection to say something about how people learn involves others in one way or another. Reflective practice takes place in communities of practice, as groups of teachers in a school, teachers attending in-service courses, or other situations, and learning can be seen as increasing participation in that practice.

1.3 Subject Matter Knowledge and Pedagogic Content Knowledge

In Schifter's (1998) study discussed above, she was interested both in teachers' own mathematics and in their reflections on their students' mathematical thinking. Study has also been made of the connections between them, that is, between teachers' knowledge of mathematics and their knowledge of pedagogy (Shulman, 1986, 1987; Even, Tirosh & Markovits, 1996). For the most part, the Shulman (1987) model, a taxonomy of seven types of teacher knowledge, is a descriptive one, and Mason (1998) has pointed out that it is "daunting in the extreme, and the many inter-connections between types mean that the taxonomy is rather unstable in practice. The trouble with such a list is that it comes across as factual knowledge, knowing-that, and as rigid and discrete." (p. 244). Implicit in the model, though, is the notion that they are inter-connected, and thus learning in one domain is necessary for, and can result in, learning in another domain. Even (1990) and Even, Tirosh, and Markovits (1996) make this the focus of their work with pre-service and in-service teachers. In one part of their work, they introduce content to teachers through offering them scenarios where a class of students propose alternative solutions to some mathematics, and invite the teachers to engage in the mathematics through examining how students might have arrived at those different answers and through considering how they might respond, as teachers. For instance, they present a situation in which students, when asked to add two fractions with different denominators, offer both a standard answer found by common denominators, and another answer by adding the two numerators together and the two denominators. In this way subject matter knowledge and pedagogic content knowledge are brought together in mutual interaction.

Even, Tirosh, and Markovits (1996) measure change by teachers' self-reports, and reports of supervisors, principals, and fellow teachers. "Our findings indicate that when asked to respond to specific suggestions made by students, teachers are pushed to articulate their own understanding. Thus, in turn, they provide teacher educators with an opportunity to study adult learners' cognitive processes and conceptions" (p. 128). Learning is through cognitive conflict, brought about by the situations the teachers encounter. Thus Piaget's model of learning through adaptation is extended into adult learning. Is this a suitable model? Where Piaget's ideas are applied to children developing mental structures for addition or multiplication, for example, there is a clear sense of what is to be expected, from the extensive body of research available (Sowder, Armstrong, Lamon, Simon, Sowder, & Thompson, 1998). What structures are understood here, though? What hierarchies does reflective abstraction lead to in relation to pedagogical content knowledge? Before pursuing this further, I will look at research that draws explicitly on constructivist theories in relation to teachers.

1.4 Constructivism

Constructivism offers a clear theory of learning when applied to children, but it has also been used to explain teaching which is compatible with constructivist theories of knowing (Steffe, 1991), and to explain teachers' learning (for example, Simon, 1995; Steffe & D'Ambrosio, 1995). Piaget's constructivism, taken up and developed by the radical constructivists, focuses on the process of equilibration, whereby conceptions remain stable unless they meet a perturbation, a situation that leads to disequilibrium. Learning is then seen as cognitive reorganisation by the individual. The two alternative aspects of the process are assimilation and accommodation. Steffe and D'Ambrosio (1995) distinguish between situations, and problems or tasks, as used by Simon (1995), arguing that in their use of the former they are attempting "to bring forth, sustain and encourage, and modify the mathematics of students" (p.157). They advocate "situations that involve assimilating generalisation," which they suggest is the constructivist way of speaking of transfer of knowledge (Steffe & Wiegel, 1994). The emphasis is on the neutralisation of perturbations. The latter, problems and tasks posed by the teacher educator at key points where she or he considers it necessary, aim rather at accommodation through setting up cognitive conflicts for student teachers: "I tried in different ways to promote disequilibrium so the students would reconsider the issue" (Simon, 1995, p.129). Simon's work faces the same problem as that of Even, Tirosh, and

Markovits (1996), namely, What is the direction of development? For Piaget, and others, the given mathematical structures provide the direction for the teacher to attempt to facilitate learning in the students, and for the researcher to study. In a similar way, if constructivist researchers such as Simon have a model of correct teaching, albeit an implicit model, then cognitive conflicts could be thought to lead to appropriate learning, as development. The direction of development towards better teaching is either towards the views of the teacher educator or towards the cognitive structure of better teaching. The former might make sense from the point of view of a community of practice for teaching mathematics but not, I suggest, the latter. Steffe and D'Ambrosio, however, are more careful. They talk of teaching that is compatible with constructivist theories of knowing as the construction of second-order models of students' mathematics, which are themselves first-order models arising from their mathematical activities (Steffe & Thompson, 2000). Teachers then learn about the adequacy or appropriateness of their own models by offering their students further activities and observing their actions. Improving teaching is a matter of improving the quality of one's second-order models, judged by their adequacy and viability.

I have offered a critique of constructivism, whether applied to children or to teachers, elsewhere (Lerman, 1996, 2000a), on the basis of its marginalisation of the socio-cultural (although see Steffe & Thompson, 2000). I will pick up on this issue below.

1.5 Teachers' Learning as Teachers' Growing Awareness

I have briefly mentioned Jaworski's work above (for example, 1998). Her research is focused on teachers identifying "hard questions" (p. 3) for themselves, questions which enable them "to delve deeply into their own purposes and become more overtly aware of personal theories motivating their practice" (p. 4). Jaworski sets the theoretical perspective within reflective practice. "The essence of reflective practice in teaching might be seen as the making explicit of teaching approaches and processes so that they can become the object of critical scrutiny. Through such critical scrutiny, by teachers, teaching develops" (p. 7). This is a strongly individualistic, internalist theory of learning. What is to be learnt is already within one's head, one's own purposes, and personal theories, but before undertaking the research one is not yet aware of what they are. The project which Jaworski and her colleague have set up is "a key factor in what was observed" (p. 26) in that a particular style of questioning one's own practice was developed and encouraged. I would conjecture that the project is an even more crucial element than Jaworski suggests, in that environments such as the project are actually *creative*, not reflective, of inner reality.

Mason (1998), for example, has a similarly internalist theory. He describes teacher education as a three-fold task:
- working with teachers to help them educate their awareness of their own, and hence of their children's awareness-in-action;

- working with teachers to educate their awareness-in-discipline so they are sensitised mathematically to work with their students in a mathematically informed and appropriate fashion; and
- working with colleagues to educate their own awareness-in-counsel. (p. 264)

Awareness is all that is educable, according to Mason, an idea that comes from Gattegno (1987). The levels of awareness are mental powers. For instance, Mason exemplifies awareness-in-action as powers of construal including: "the power to select, distinguish, demarcate, discern, detect difference; the power to see (construct) similarity, commonality, genericity" and so forth (p. 257). It appears from my reading of Mason's work that these powers are assumed to be innate, as potential, to be drawn out by a teacher or, indeed, by reading, or not drawn out if suitable circumstances do not arise.

Alternatively, one can look at Mason's writing (as at Jaworski's and others') as *productive* of ways of thinking mathematically and as a teacher. What arises for me from the review and critique of research perspectives so far is the alternative explanation that can be proposed in all this work: that it is not the internal map of beliefs and awarenesses which in an unobservable (mysterious) manner changes, but rather the new language, psychological tools, through dialogue and communities provided by the writers, researchers and exemplary teachers which bring teachers' learning as emerging identities. If this is so, then we have an observable theory of learning, to do with dialogue and community, interests and goals of teachers involved in courses, research projects, and curriculum changes.

2. RESEARCH PERSPECTIVES: TEACHERS IN THEIR CONTEXTS

There are three other research perspectives that I will discuss here, but they differ from those above in that they treat learning, including learning about teaching, as socio-cultural activities. I have suggested above that research situations, as well as communities of teachers working together in one situation or another, are productive of beliefs, practices, purposes, and goals, not reflective of them. Research on teaching, which feeds into teacher education, and research on teacher education, needs to look at individual teachers through their social settings (Lerman, 1998), and this perspective characterises the research examined in this section.

The work of Vygotsky and followers (1978, 1986) provides the stimulus for the first two perspectives, Lave's work and activity theory, as well as for some overlapping ideas with the third, postmodernism. Vygotsky's theory comprises at least three important factors: First it offers a coherent single framework for learning throughout life that applies to young children and equally to mature adults; second it attempts to integrate affect and cognition in focusing on meaning as its unit of analysis; and thirdly it offers a method for rooting knowledge and action in socio-historical-cultural settings. The classroom and seminar room are complex sites of political and social influences, socio-cultural interactions, and multiple positionings involving class, gender, ethnicity, teacher-student relations, and other discursive practices in which power and knowledge are situated. I believe that individualistic accounts cannot do justice to these forces.

2.1 Community of Practice Models

Studies of how people learn in out-of-school situations, particularly work environments (Lave, 1988; Lave & Wenger, 1991), have offered valuable perspectives of the nature of the alignment of goals and desires by the learner and the teacher, the latter as mentor or master (I use this gendered term in the absence of a more suitable one). The learner, as apprentice, learns the skills at the same time as becoming a part of the social practice. The mathematical methods used in specific social and workplace situations, or to be more precise, those methods used in social practices that are seen as mathematical by the observer, are specific to those situations for the participants. They are generally not seen as the transferring of decontextualised mathematical knowledge acquired in school. The 'master' in the workplace is not intentionally teaching, but apprenticing people into the practice, usually for increased efficiency or profitability. Learning, from this perspective then, is seen as increasing participation in the community of practice.

In order to bring those notions into her discussion of schooling Lave (1996) draws on both Olsen's study of the way that schooling shapes the identities of newcomers to the United States in terms of the "racialization of social relations and identities" (p. 159) and work in mathematics classrooms (Lave, 1997) where students create their own communities of practice and develop ways of working that are not those necessarily preferred by the teacher. Describing learning in terms of students becoming, in our case, motivated participants in school mathematics and of student teachers as apprentices, it seems to me, is where Lave's approach is particularly fruitful for us as teachers of mathematics and as researchers in mathematics teacher education. Lave's focus on the shaping of identity in social practice emphasises the centrality of the social relationships constituted and negotiated during classroom learning.

There are as yet few programmes of teacher education or research on teacher education that draw on Lave's ideas to structure their programmes (although see Boaler, 1997). Brown, Stein, and Forman's (1996) QUASAR project is based on Tharp and Gallimore's theory of assistance (1988), which is itself a development of Vygotsky's zone of proximal development. They reinterpret their work in terms of community of practice theories in a later publication (Stein & Brown, 1997).

In analysing the process of student teachers' learning about teaching, the effects of inservice courses, perhaps in times of curriculum change, or teachers involved in research projects we can fruitfully talk of teachers' changing participation in communities of practice. Identities emerge and develop as the practices develop and their involvement in those practices increases. The analysis of the researcher requires considering the person-in-practice, an essentially social unit of analysis for research, as distinct from beliefs or awarenesses, or second-order models, which are essentially individualistic units of analysis. In the review and critique of theories underpinning research on teacher education I have argued that teachers' actions and utterances, that is to say their classroom practices and the responses they give to interviews, questionnaires, or other research methods, are contextualised and cannot be interpreted outside of a consideration of the social situation. They also are productive of emerging identities in practices. Lave's model offers a way of interpreting teachers' learning in a social formulation which is observable. There are aspects of her theories that need work by researchers, such as that student teachers are learning about teaching from a teacher educator in a university setting, not a school setting. The teacher educator is not the master of the teaching practice, and some elaboration is required in terms of models of mastery being offered rather than the practices of the master (Lerman, 2000b).

Activity theory. A rich inheritance from the Vygotskian school in terms of educational research has been activity theory (Leont'ev, 1978). Vygotsky pointed out the centrality of the notion of the acting person and emphasised meaning as mediating the world for every individual. Through tools, and cultural tools in particular, society and culture are mediated for the child although thought and language are to be seen as a dialectic. Language offers the child inherited historical-cultural meanings, but each participant in the conversation or other activity uses those tools to intersubjectively re-shape meanings in communication and action. According to Leont'ev's view, the *activity* orients the participants and provides the initial meaning and motivation. Meanings have a social ontogeny, whereas sense is the individual's perspective and the *actions* of individuals within the activity are always motivated by sense, which incorporates cognition, culture, and affect. Finally, there are *operations*, the specific moves, often automatic, that individuals make in response to specific phenomena. To take a well-known example of Leont'ev's, in a group *activity* of hunting, one person, the beater, will have the role of circling around the prey to beat the undergrowth and usher the prey towards the hunters. The *actions* of that person only make sense within the context of the activity. If there is a boulder in the way the beater will go around it; this is an *operation*. The notion of activity incorporates the cultural artefacts, the social setting, and the motives and goals of the participants into a whole, thus embodying in a research perspective the unity of human actions that Vygotsky sought as a unit of psychology.

In an attempt to engage student teachers, in the final year of their course, with their still unchallenged assumptions about the role of the teacher, Crawford & Deer (1993) devised an activity in which the students had to work in groups to develop a programme of mathematics which was centred on the children's environment, rather than a prescribed syllabus. The students found this very hard and experienced "initial ecstasy, shock of recognition, crisis, realism and commitment" (p. 116). The outcome was at least a recognition by the students of having a wider range of skills upon which to draw and in many cases new-found confidence in their ability to create "a very different learning environment ... from the one that they had experienced themselves" (p. 118). Elsewhere Crawford writes:

> The course was designed to create a "zone of proximal development" for student teachers as a way of expanding their knowledge of the dialectic process of teaching and learning through conscious experience of the process. They were engaged in a learning activity. (Crawford, 1994, p. 6)

Bartolini Bussi (1996) draws on activity theory as part of her theoretical toolkit in a study of the teaching and learning of perspective drawing. She structured the tasks in terms of teaching-learning activities, using Leont'ev's analysis, and examined students' motives and needs in their learning. In a recent study (Lerman, 1997) I set teaching-learning activities to students on a pre-service primary teacher education course. Modelled on Crawford and Deer's research, the student teachers were put into a situation of discomfort, being asked to present a seminar on a mathematical topic and on a teaching-learning topic with which they were unfamiliar. It reorientated the students' goals and motives and resulted in interesting reactions from the students illustrating their learning: "I really learnt a lot from this about how you should fully understand something before teaching it."

Postmodern theory. Teachers and student teachers come to pre-service and in-service courses, curriculum innovation and research projects as persons of multiple, overlapping subjectivities, with different goals, interests, and needs. Different elements of those subjectivities are called up by different aspects of projects and courses of teacher education/change/development, and are expressed through identities of powerfulness or powerlessness. At the same time, new subjectivities are constituted in the social relationships and forms of communication which make up these activities. Rather than the intention of teaching as the handing over, or the individual construction, of ultimately decontextualised mathematics, teaching can be conceived of as enabling students to become mathematical actors in the classroom and beyond. The goals and needs of pupils, and the ways of behaving and speaking as school mathematicians, become the focuses of the teacher's intentions. This does not translate into either side of a traditional-drill-and-practice/progressive-group-learning dichotomy, however. Both may well be appropriate at different times. That dichotomy, like so many others, is irrelevant and uninteresting; clearly so when seen from a postmodern perspective. The same applies to student teachers in teacher education.

Ellsworth (1989) argues that a classroom based on a practice:

> grounded in the unknowable is profoundly contextual (historical) and interdependent (social)... What remains for me is the challenge of constructing classroom practices that engage with the discursive and material spaces that (the removal of the privileged self-image of the critical pedagogue) opens up (p. 323).

Klein (1997a) describes a shift in her teaching in which she saw her "practice as being coercive in that students always had to arrive at the authoritative 'truth' as portrayed throughout my subject and discriminatory in that students not adhering to my construction of the 'autonomous' student were classified as unmotivated" (p. 291). In this case Klein's strongly held theory was constructivism, whose tenets she was attempting to encourage student teachers to learn and adopt. She found that a poststructuralist focus enabled her to critique her practice and offered her a language for reconceptualising the function of the support that teachers give to move away from coercion to a position of enabling students' voices.

In a critique of reflective practice and critical theory, Parker (1997) suggests that it can be rehabilitated within a postmodern perspective. It is not that postmodernism means a rejection of reflective practice or the possibility of change in one's classroom, school, university, or region. It means a re-inscription of these activities into a language of the recognition of difference; of a rejection of the expectation of closure but not of a loss of meaning and values; of deconstruction of reason, rationality, and emancipation.

3. CONCLUSION

In this paper I have reviewed many of the research perspectives in mathematics teacher education from the point of view of the implicit or explicit theories of learning of the researchers. I have argued that, whilst we have well-developed theories of children's learning, they may not be adequate or appropriate to teachers' learning. Amongst the concerns I have discussed are whether constructivism, with its notion of reflective abstraction and the construction of cognitive structures, can be applied to teachers' learning, and whether the study of beliefs is too static and mentalist to be able to describe the connections between theory and practices. I suggest that theories that address the complexity in social practices are more appropriate for the study of teacher education.

Many teacher educators will be familiar with the problem that "Inservice teachers' resistance to change and preservice and beginning teachers' reversion to teaching styles similar to those their own teachers used are legendary" (Brown, Cooney, & Jones, 1990, p. 649; see also Crawford & Deer, 1993; Lerman, 1997; Klein, 1997b). It appears that courses do not provoke students to confront their naive notions of teaching mathematics. The reversion may be related to the different context of the teacher education course from the site of practice, the school. Ensor's (1999) study of the process of recontextualisation from one site to the other sheds some important light on the issue. It may also be expressed in Lave's terms, that student teachers have a sense of who and how they will be as teachers before coming to the course, or in Vygotsky's terms, as spontaneous concepts of teaching. The ideas that we offer, and even the essays that the students write to which we give credit, do not impinge on that initial sense of being a teacher. At the same time, the messages that teacher educators may be attempting to convey, explicitly and implicitly, about what they consider is good teaching, or what they consider student teachers should know will, in some measure, be oppressive to the extent that they deny agency to student teachers. In an analogous way to a postmodern pedagogy for schools, a postmodern pedagogy in teacher education would: encourage the expression of difference; teach methods of critique of orthodoxies concerning mathematics and mathematics education; and encourage theorising about teaching and learning mathematics. It would find ways of confronting student teachers with their naive conceptions of teaching and with different theories about teaching which they might well have been espousing, through activities which bring these together (Crawford & Deer, 1993; Lerman, 1997). It would engage with the personal transitions in becoming a teacher, in terms of developing an identity as a person in that profession and with purposes appropriate to that role, by enabling them to constitute through articulation different ways of being, as a teacher.

In those mathematics teacher education projects which are successful, in terms of the participants perceiving that their beliefs about mathematics and teaching have changed, and where this seems to be borne out in studies of their teaching, it seems to me that we can talk of the teachers having developed their identities as teachers. The goals of the course or project have become their goals, either through their own desire to progress in their career, feel better about their teaching or improve the learning experiences of their students, or because the have taken on the values of the project and the researchers or tutors running the project. The situations of research can be *productive* of new elements of identities, or perhaps new identities, for the teachers. Some situations are particularly fruitful in teacher development, such as setting up on-going communities of teachers, or some of the projects I mentioned at the start of this paper. Where they are not successful (for example, Frykholm, 1999) we may talk of students' identities as teachers not having developed. Thus, so many preservice teacher education courses engage with students' identities as students on courses, and the same with the teachers in other situations to which Cooney and his colleagues refer, and do not impinge on their identities as teachers. As I have mentioned here, Crawford & Deer (1993) offer one way of forcing that engagement, using an activity theory approach, and there are others. My concern is to argue for a focus on identities and the settings in which those can change, as a way of conceptualising mathematics teacher development. "Teaching is more difficult than learning; for only he who can truly learn—and as long as he can do it—can truly teach" (Heidegger, in Krell, 1993, p. 254).

REFERENCES

Bartolini Bussi, M. G. (1996). Mathematical discussion and perspective drawing in primary school. *Educational Studies in Mathematics, 31*(1-2), 11-41.

Boaler, J. (1997). Unpublished paper, King's College, London.

Brown, C., Cooney, T. A., & Jones, D. (1990). Mathematics teacher education. In W. R. Houston (Ed.), *Handbook of Research on Teacher Education* (639-656). New York: Macmillan.

Brown, C. A., Stein, M. K., & Forman, E. A. (1996). Assisting teachers and students to reform the mathematics classroom. *Educational Studies in Mathematics, 31*(1-2), 63-93.

Carr, W. & Kemmis, S. (1986). Becoming critical: Education, knowledge and action research. Lewes: Falmer.

Cobb, P., Wood, T., & Yackel, E. (1990). Classrooms as learning environments for teachers and researcher. In R. B. Davis, C. A. Maher, & N. Noddings (Eds.), Constructivist views on the teaching and learning of mathematics. *Journal for Research in Mathematics Education Monograph No. 4*, (pp. 125-146). Reston, VA: National Council of Teachers of Mathematics.

Cooney, T. (1985). A beginning teacher's view of problem solving. *Journal for Research in Mathematics Education, 16*, 324-336.

Crawford, K. (1994). *Vygotsky in school: The implications of Vygotskian approaches to activity, learning and development.* Paper presented at First International Conference "L. S. Vygotsky and School," Eureka Free University, Moscow.

Crawford, K. & Deer, E. (1993). Do we practise what we preach?: Putting policy into practise in teacher education. *South Pacific Journal of Teacher Education 21*(2), 111-121.

Ellsworth, E. (1989). Why doesn't this feel empowering? Working through the repressive myths of critical pedagogy. *Harvard Educational Review, 59*(3), 297-324.

Ensor, P. (1999). *A study of the recontextualising of pedagogic practices from a South African University preservice mathematics teacher education course by seven beginning secondary mathematics teachers.* Unpublished doctoral dissertation, University of London.

Ernest, P. (1989). The impact of beliefs on the teaching of mathematics. In P. Ernest (Ed.), *Mathematics teaching: The state of the art* (pp. 249-254). Lewes: Falmer.

Even, R. (1990). Subject matter knowledge for teaching and the case of functions. *Educational Studies in Mathematics, 21*, 521-544.

Even, R., Tirosh, D. & Markovits, Z. (1996). Teacher subject matter knowledge and pedagogical content knowledge: Research and development. In L. Puig & A. Gutiérrez (Eds.), *Proceedings of Twentieth Meeting of the International Group for the Psychology of Mathematics Education, 1*, (119-134). Valencia, Spain.

Fennema, E. & Nelson, B. S. (Eds.). (1997). *Mathematics teachers in transition*. Mahwah, NJ: Lawrence Erlbaum Associates.

Fennema, E., Franke, M. L., Carpenter, T. P., & Carey, D. A. (1993). Using children's mathematical knowledge in instruction. *American Educational Research Journal, 30*, 555-583.

Frykholm, J. A. (1999). The impact of reform: Challenges for mathematics teacher preparation. *Journal of Mathematics Teacher Education, 2*(1), 79-105.

Fullan, M. & Hargreaves, A. (Eds.). (1992). *Teacher development and educational change*. London: Falmer Press.

Gattegno, C. (1987). The science of education: Part 1. Theoretical considerations. New York: Educational Solutions.

Gattuso, L. (1994). What happens when robots have feelings? In S. Lerman (Ed.), *Cultural perspectives on the mathematics classroom* (pp. 99-114), Dordrecht: Kluwer.

Grant, T. J., Hiebert, J. & Wearne, D. (1998). Observing and teaching reform-minded lessons: What do teachers see? *Journal of Mathematics Teacher Education, 1*(2), 217-236.

Guskey, T. R. (1986). Staff development and the process of teacher change. *Educational Researcher, 15*(5), 5-12.

Heaton, R. M. & Lambert, M. (1993). Learning to hear voices: Inventing a new pedagogy of teacher education. In D. K. Cohen, M. W. McLaughlin, & J. E. Talbert (Eds.), *Teaching for understanding* (pp. 43-83). San Francisco: Jossey-Bass Publishers.

Jaworski, B. (1998). Mathematics teacher research: Process, practice and the development of teaching. *Journal of Mathematics Teacher Education, 1*(1), 3-31.

Klein, M. (1997a). Looking again at the 'supportive' environment of constructivist pedagogy: An example from preservice teacher education in mathematics. *Journal of Education for Teaching, 23*(3), 276-292.

Klein, M. (1997b). Constructivist practice in preservice teacher education in mathematics: Aboriginal and Torres Strait islander voices heard yet silenced. *Equity & Excellence in Education, 30*(1), 65-71.

Krell, D. F. (1993). *Martin Heidegger: Basic writings from 'being and time' (1927) to 'the task of thinking' (1964)* (Revised edition). London: Routledge.

Lave, J. (1988). *Cognition in practice: Mind, mathematics and culture in everyday life*. Cambridge: Cambridge University Press.

Lave, J. (1996). Teaching, as learning, in practice. *Mind, Culture & Activity, 3*(3), 149-164.

Lave, J. (1997). The culture of acquisition and the practice of understanding. In D. Kirshner & J. A. Whitson (Eds.), *Situated cognition: Social, semiotic and psychological perspectives* (pp. 17-35). Mahwah, NJ: Lawrence Erlbaum.

Lave, J. & Wenger, E. (1991). *Situated learning: Legitimate peripheral participation*. New York: Cambridge University Press.

Leont'ev, A. N. (1978). *Activity, consciousness and personality*. Eaglewood Cliffs, NJ: Prentice Hall.

Lerman, S. (1983). Problem-aolving or knowledge-centred: The Influence of philosophy on mathematics teaching. *International Journal of Mathematical Education in Science and Technology, 14*(1), 59–66.

Lerman, S. (1986). *Alternative views of the nature of mathematics and their possible influence on the teaching of mathematics*. Unpublished doctoral dissertation, University of London.

Lerman, S. (1990). Alternative perspectives of the nature of mathematics and their influence on the teaching of mathematics. *British Educational Research Journal, 16*(1), 53-61.

Lerman, S. (1994). Reflective practice. In B. Jaworski & A. Watson (Eds.), *Mentoring in the education of mathematics teachers* (pp. 52-64). London: Falmer Press.

Lerman, S. (1996). Intersubjectivity in mathematics learning: A challenge to the radical constructivist paradigm? *Journal for Research in Mathematics Education, 27*(2), 133-150.

Lerman, S. (1997). The psychology of mathematics teacher learning: In search of theory. In E. Pehkonen (Ed.), *Proceedings of the Twenty-First Meeting of the International Group for the Psychology of Mathematics Education, 3*, 200-207. Lahti, Finland.

Lerman, S. (1998). A moment in the zoom of a lens: Towards a discursive psychology of mathematics teaching and learning. In A. Olivier & K. Newstead (Eds.), *Proceedings of the Twenty-Second*

Annual Meeting of the International Group for the Psychology of Mathematics Education, 1, 66-81. Stellenbosch, South Africa.

Lerman, S. (2000a). A case of interpretations of *social*: A response to Steffe and Thompson. *Journal for Research in Mathematics Education. 31*(2), 210-227.

Lerman, S. (2000b). The social turn in mathematics education research. In J. Boaler (Ed.), *Multiple Perspectives on Mathematics Teaching and Learning.* (pp. 19-44) Westport, CT: Ablex.

Mason, J. (1998). Enabling teachers to be real teachers: Necessary levels of awareness and structure of attention. *Journal of Mathematics Teacher Education, 1*(3), 243-267.

Parker, S. (1997). *Reflective teaching in the postmodern world.* Buckingham: Open University Press.

Pehkonen, E. & Törner, G. (1996). Mathematical beliefs and different aspects of their meaning. *International Reviews on Mathematical Education (ZDM), 28*(4), 101-108.

Perry, W. G. (1970). *Forms of intellectual and ethical development in the college years.* New York: Holt, Rinehart & Winston.

da Ponte, J. P. (1994). Knowledge, beliefs and conceptions in mathematics teaching and learning. In L. Bazzini (Ed.), *Proceedings of the Fifth International Conference on Systematic Co-operation between Theory and Practice in Mathematics Education* (p. 169-177). Universita degli Studi di Pavia

Post, T. R., Ward, W. H., & Willson, V. L. (1977). Teachers', principals' and university faculties' views of mathematics learning and instruction as measured by a mathematics inventory. *Journal for Research in Mathematics Education, 8*(5), 332-344.

Schifter, D. (1998). Learning mathematics for teaching: From a teachers' seminar to the classroom. *Journal of Mathematics Teacher Education, 1*(1), 55-87.

Schifter, D. (Ed.) (1995). *What's happening in math class? Reconstructing professional identities: Volume 2.* New York: Teacher's College Press.

Shulman, L. (1986). Those who understand: Knowledge growth in teaching. *Educational Researcher, 15*(2), 4-14.

Shulman, L. (1987). Knowledge and teaching: Foundations of the new reform. *Harvard Educational Review, 57*(1), 1-14.

Simon, M.A. (1995). Reconstructing mathematical pedagogy from a constructivist perspective. *Journal for Research in Mathematics Education, 26*(2), 114–145.

Simon, M. A. & Schifter, D. (1991). Towards a constructivist perspective: An intervention study of mathematics teacher development. *Educational Studies in Mathematics, 22.* 309-331.

Sowder, J., Armstrong, B., Lamon, S., Simon, M., Sowder, L., & Thompson, A. (1998) .Educating teachers to teach multiplicative structures in the middle grades. *Journal of Mathematics Teacher Education, 1*(2), 127-155.

Steffe, L. P. (1991). The constructivist teaching experiment: Illustrations and implications. In E. von Glasersfeld (Ed.), *Radical constructivism in mathematics education* (pp. 177-194). Boston: Kluwer Academic Publishers.

Steffe, L.P. & D'Ambrosio, B. (1995). Toward a working model of constructivist teaching. *Journal for Research in Mathematics Education, 26*(2), 146–159.

Steffe, L. P. & Thompson, P. W. (2000). Interaction or intersubjectivity? A reply to Lerman. *Journal for Research in Mathematics Education, 31*(2), 191-209.

Steffe, L.P. & Weigel, H. (1994). Cognitive play and mathematical learning in computer microworlds. *Educational Studies in Mathematics, 26*, 111–134.

Stein, M. K. & Brown, C. A. (1997). Teacher learning in a social context: Social interaction as a source of significant teacher change in mathematics. In E. Fennema, & B. S. Nelson (Eds.), *Mathematics teachers in transition.* Mahwah, NJ: Lawrence Erlbaum Associates.

Tharp, R. & Gallimore, R. (1988). *Rousing minds to life: Teaching, learning and schooling in social context.* Cambridge: Cambridge University Press.

Thompson, A. G. (1982). *Teachers' conceptions of mathematics: Three case studies.* Unpublished doctoral dissertation, University of Georgia, Athens, USA.

Thompson, A. G. (1984). The relationship of teachers' conceptions of mathematics and mathematics teaching to instructional practice. *Educational Studies in Mathematics, 15*(2), 105-127.

Thompson, A. G. (1992). Teachers' beliefs and conceptions: A synthesis of the research. In D. A. Grouws (Ed.), *Handbook of research on mathematics teaching and learning.* (pp. 127-146). New York: Macmillan.

Vygotsky, L. (1978). *Mind in society.* Cambridge, MA: Harvard University Press.

Vygotsky, L. (1986). *Thought and language* (A. Kozulin, Trans. and Ed.). Cambridge, MA: MIT Press.

Walkerdine V. (1984). Developmental psychology and the child-centred pedagogy. In J. Henriques, W. Hollway, C. Urwin, C. Venn, & V. Walkerdine (Eds.), *Changing the subject* (pp. 153-202). London: Methuen.

Wilson, M. & Goldenberg, M. P. (1998). Some conceptions are difficult to change: One middle school teacher's struggle. *Journal of Mathematics Teacher Education, 1*(3), 269-293.

Centre for Mathematics Education
Faculty of Humanities and Social Science
South Bank University
103 Borough Road
London SE1 0AA
United Kingdom

JOÃO PEDRO DA PONTE

INVESTIGATING MATHEMATICS AND LEARNING TO TEACH MATHEMATICS

ABSTRACT. This paper deals with an idea that plays an increasing role in teaching and in teacher education—investigating as a powerful paradigm of knowledge construction. Investigations may be carried out both in learning mathematics and in learning how to teach mathematics at preservice and inservice levels. I look into investigations in mathematics and in the mathematics curriculum, pointing out some issues that teachers face proposing them in the classroom. Then, I discuss teacher education and professional development, stressing the value of investigations about practice as a means of developing knowledge. I conclude with examples of work, done by preservice and inservice teachers and by teams of teachers and researchers focusing on pupils' investigative work in mathematics classes, that illustrate the educational value of this activity and discuss the roles of the teacher.

1. PUPILS INVESTIGATING MATHEMATICS

Pupils learn mathematics doing investigations. Why is it so? Mathematics, on the one hand, is the logical and deductive subject depicted in the works of Euclid and Bourbaki. On the other hand, it involves features that come very close to the natural sciences: observation, experimentation, induction, analogy, and plausible reasoning (Kline, 1970; Mason, Burton, & Stacey, 1982; Poincaré, 1908; Pólya, 1945). Instead of establishing an irreducible conflict between these two sides of mathematics, one may ask how they can complement each other in the learning process. The inductive side is essential to creating new knowledge, and the deductive side is necessary for organizing it and deciding what is valid and what is not. Both the professional mathematician and the young pupil may get curious, raising questions to themselves about the properties of mathematical objects and seeking to validate their answers.

There is a parallel between the activity of the research mathematician and the activity of the pupil in the classroom. Of course, there are differences between the knowledge held by both, their degree of specialization, the time they spend, and their relation with the subject. However, their problem-solving activity is of a similar nature. Hadamard (1945), a well-know mathematician, refers to this, for example:

> Between the work of the pupil that tries to solve a problem in geometry or algebra and a work of invention [by the mathematician] one can say that there is only a difference of degree, a difference of level, both works being of a similar nature (p. 104).

In mathematics education, Ernest (1991) holds a similar view. He considers all mathematics learners as mathematics creators and argues that productive pupils'

F.-L. Lin & T. J. Cooney (Eds.) Making Sense of Mathematics Teacher Education, 53—72.
© 2001 *Kluwer Academic Publishers. Printed in the Netherlands.*

problem solving and problem posing parallels the mathematicians' activity: "They do not differ qualitatively" (p. 283). Pólya (1962-65/1981) also stresses that pupils must have the opportunity to experiment several aspects of the mathematical activity. Based on examples of research problems, he shows that the teacher can create conditions so that pupils develop creative and independent work.

Investigative work by pupils receives significant attention in the mathematics curriculum of several countries, either explicitly or implicitly. For example, the French curriculum for the first year of secondary school underlines the importance of making the pupils experience scientific activity, referring to the discovery process as follows:

> [The aim is] to accustom pupils to the scientific activity and to promote the acquisition of methods: the mathematics class is first of all a place of discovery, of exploring situations, of reflection and debate about the strategies employed and the results achieved, of synthesis that yield some clear ideas and essential methods, indicating the respective value. (Ministère de l'Education Nationale, de la Recherche et de la Technologie, 1997, p. 16)

The English curriculum includes aspects directly related to investigative work in one of its main areas ("using and applying mathematics"). It states, for example, that pupils at Key Stage 2 must
- understand and investigate general statements;
- search for patterns in their results;
- make general statements of their own, based on evidence they have produced;
- explain their reasoning (DFE, 1997).

The Portuguese curriculum speaks about exploration, research activities, and conjecturing by pupils. It includes specific suggestions for carrying out this kind of work. It states, for example, that the use of graphic calculators enables secondary school pupils "to carry out mathematical experiences, formulate and test conjectures" (Ministério da Educação, 1997, p. 11) and indicates that "in the study of families of functions pupils may undertake small investigations" (p. 20).

In the USA, there is no national curriculum. However, influential documents such as NCTM's (1991) *Professional Standards* state that "the very essence of studying mathematics is itself an exercise in exploring, conjecturing, examining and testing" (p. 95). The more recent *Standards 2000* draft (NCTM, 1998) emphasizes the role of conjecturing and indicates that pupils can investigate mathematics objects. This document says that "at all levels, all branches of mathematics provide opportunities of reasoning and conjecture..." (p. 83) and "students at all grade levels can engage—in age-level-appropriate ways—in the kind of systematic thinking, conjecturing, and marshaling of evidence that are precursors to formal mathematical argumentation" (p. 80).

As mathematical activities, investigations and problem solving are very close and many people use these terms interchangeably. Although both notions refer to complex mathematical processes and point towards problematic activity, I suggest that they also involve some differences. Problems may be more structured or more open. They may refer to purely mathematical situations or real-life contexts. In most cases, the conditions and the questions are clearly framed from the outset and are presented ready-made to the pupil. A mathematical investigation stresses mathematical processes such as searching regularities, formulating, testing, justifying and proving conjectures, reflecting, and generalizing. When one starts working on an investigation, the question and the conditions are usually not completely clear and making them more precise is the first part of the work. That is, investigations involve an essential phase of problem posing by the pupil—something that in problem solving is usually done by the teacher. However, investigations go much beyond simple problem posing and involve testing conjectures, proving, and generalizing. Here we have several examples[i]:

> Consider triangles with integer sides. There are 3 triangles with perimeter 12 units. Investigate.

> Investigate the properties of the powers $(1+i)^n$ where i is the imaginary unit. Contrast them with the properties of the powers a^n of real numbers.

> Study the properties of the function defined in **R** by
>
> $$y = ax^n + bx^{n-1}$$
>
> when n is odd and when n is even.

The terminology used by educators regarding investigations varies significantly from time to time, from country to country, and even from author to author (see Pehkonen, 1997; Ruthveen, this volume; Sullivan, this volume). Whatever the labeling used, this kind of task enables pupils to become involved in the activity from the very beginning. Designing strategies, generalizing results, establishing relations among concepts and areas of mathematics, systematizing ideas and outcomes, there are multiple opportunities for creative and significant work during an investigation. The challenge for current educational systems is to make such experiences accessible, not just to a few, but to all pupils who must have opportunities to engage in:

- identifying and initiating their own problems for investigation;
- expressing their own ideas and developing them in solving problems;
- testing their ideas and hypotheses against relevant experiences;
- rationally defending their own ideas and conclusions and submitting the ideas of others to a reasoned criticism. (Love, 1988, p. 260)

2. THE TEACHER AND THE INVESTIGATION CLASS

Let us look at some of the issues that the teacher faces in planning and conducting investigative work in the classroom.

Selecting and designing investigative situations for the classroom is the first issue. Investigations, if they are to be taken seriously, must be part of the mathematics curriculum and relate to the objectives, topics, working methods, and assessment schemes. The possibilities of the teacher heavily depend on the emphasis that investigations are given in the official curriculum. However, teachers have a fundamental role in interpreting this curriculum and adapting it to their particular circumstances. Selecting tasks, establishing objectives, and defining class operation modes need to take into account pupils' characteristics and the class context. Critical factors to consider are the age range, pupils' mathematics development, and their previous experience in investigations.

A mathematics investigation may begin in different ways. However, some situations are more promising than others. A high concern with certain objectives can lead the teacher to construct tasks that are too structured, that pupils tend to face as recipes to follow through and not as investigations whose questions they must define. The following words of Ollerton (1994) express the attention one should put in the choice of tasks:

An important part of my planning is concerned in finding tasks that:
- are a suitable starter for everyone in the class to work on;
- provide rich opportunities for many developments;
- cause a variety of content skills to be worked on;
- create opportunities for students to explore ideas and ask questions;
- support different types of teacher interventions ranging from asking questions to explaining and telling;
- learners can take over more responsibility for developing;
- will have a variety of outcomes, some of which may be unexpected;
- enable content to be processed;
- draw upon 'real' cross-curricular type contexts, such as using information from a newspaper periodical, or problem-solving contexts;
- wherever possible have a practical beginning in order to provide concrete experiences from which abstractions can be made. (p. 64)

In a similar line of thinking, Lampert (1990) draws our attention to what she regards as the main criterion in the selection of a problem. For her, problems must encourage all pupils to make and test conjectures that the whole class will discuss. The situations that she presents to pupils intend to promote their progression towards more complex and abstract mathematics ideas, or, in her words, to create a "stage of zig-zag between inductive observation and deductive generalization, that Lakatos and Pólya see as characteristics of mathematical activity" (p. 39).

Investigations may arise in a natural way when working in many mathematics topics and allow pupils to use the concepts, representations, ideas, and procedures that they already know. The activity of pupils in an investigation, particular and unique, may originate new questions, follow uncommon paths, and end up relating to many mathematical topics. The teacher needs to find an equilibrium point between orderly following of the planned sequence of questions and valuing unforeseen spin-offs from pupils' investigations that may further promote their mathematical development.

After deciding on the task, there is still some planning to do. This includes making decisions regarding time, class organization and management, and assessment. How long shall the class work in this? Will the pupils work individually, in small groups or as a whole class? How will the pupils get feedback for the work done? Such decisions depend on the task presented, on the curriculum and context constraints, and on the objectives valued by the teacher. Creating, reformulating, and refining suitable tasks require time and an investigative attitude. In doing so, the teacher participates in the process of curriculum construction—formulating objectives, methodologies and strategies, and reformulating them by reflecting on practice.

Usually, carrying out investigative work involves three basic stages: starting the activity, developing it, and a final discussion and summing up (Chapman, 1997; Christiansen & Walther, 1986; Mason, 1991). At the start of the activity, the teacher's aim is to involve the pupils in the task. During the activity, the teacher supports them as they pose questions, represent the information given, formulate and test conjectures, and justify them. In the final phase, the teacher wants to know at which conclusions the pupils arrived, how they justify them, and what implications they suggest. The teacher needs to create a favorable environment for learning, stimulate the communication between pupils, and assume a variety of roles to favor their learning.

Starting the activity is a critical process. Behind a polished and neat question, there is much thinking that one cannot immediately grasp—just as the published work of the mathematician does not reveal the advances and the drawbacks it suffered. It is not reasonable to assume that pupils will view the questions necessarily in the same ways as those who generated them. As Mason (1978) says, "the pupil is not in the same state as the originator [of the question]" (p. 45). This author stresses that "a question is just words with a question mark" (1991, p. 16). That is, a question by itself cannot generate an investigation. The situation that the teacher creates needs to be recreated as a question by the pupil. Moreover, the teacher must consistently reveal an investigative attitude in class to have a positive influence on the curiosity of the pupils.

During the activity, the teacher has to pay attention to the development of pupils' work. The support that is to be granted, helping them overcome difficulties or make a richer investigation, is another complex aspect of the teacher's activity. Saying too much tends to kill the challenge and increases pupils' dependence. Saying too little may be highly frustrating and make pupils move off-task. In addition, the reflection of the pupils about the work done is extremely important in an investigation and the teacher needs to stimulate that. Dealing successfully with these problems requires a lot of experience and sensitivity. Teachers may use questions that stimulate pupils' thinking. However, the need for their orientation must decrease as pupils become more familiar with this type of activity.

Jaworski (1994) reports a study that considered the challenges that this approach raises to the teacher. One of these is the "didactic tension" described in these words of John Mason:

> The *more* explicit I am about the behavior I wish my pupils to display, the more likely it is that they will display the behavior without recourse to the understanding which the behavior is meant to indicate; that is the more they will take the *form* for the substance... The *less* explicit I am about my aims and expectations about the behavior I wish my pupils to display, the less likely they are to notice what is (or might be) going on, the less likely they are to see the point, to encounter what was intended, or to realize what it was all about (Mason, 1988, cited in Jaworski, 1994, p. 180)

Jaworski indicates that she observed this tension in some teachers who participated in her study. They "were reluctant to *tell* students the facts that they wanted them to know; yet were unhappy when those facts did not emerge through the investigation" (p. 207).

One of the great objectives of investigations is leading pupils up gradual levels of generalization and abstraction. In consequence, the justification of conjectures is an important aspect of the work and its degree of formalization should depend on the mathematics level of the pupils. The teacher must point out to them the need for becoming convinced and convincing the others of the value of their arguments (Mason, 1991).

Several authors emphasize that pupils must end the activity with a discussion, indicating that without it the value of the investigation may be lost (Christiansen & Walther, 1986; Crockroft, 1982). Usually, in this phase, the pupils (or groups of pupils) indicate their strategies, results, and justifications; the teacher assumes a function of moderator, stimulating them to question the assertions of their colleagues. Thus, the development of pupils' ability to communicate and argue mathematically is a main objective of this phase of the work.

If pupils are to feel authenticity in this process, it is necessary that the teacher demonstrates a high investigative spirit. Pupils will only be able to understand what it means to do mathematics if they have an opportunity to observe genuine mathematics behavior. In an investigation, it is not possible to foresee what will happen—and the teacher has to show how to deal with that in practice. Therefore, great flexibility is required in conducting this type of work.

The teacher needs significant knowledge and competencies to do investigative work in the classroom—regarding the nature of these activities, possible strategies and tools, the pupils' most common difficulties, and the way to lead the classroom dynamics. This takes us, naturally, to consider the role of teacher education.

3. INVESTIGATING IN TEACHER EDUCATION

Let me begin this section on teacher education and professional development with two comments. First, we must have a clear notion of the possibilities and limits of teacher education. As Perrenoud (1993) says: "teacher education can only influence teachers' practices within given conditions and within certain limits" (p. 93). Second, teacher education must support teachers' professional development. That is, teachers' professional learning is a process that involves multiple stages, is always incomplete, and where teachers are the main actors.

In a classic essay, Lesne (1984) contrasts several models for teacher education, according to their pedagogical nature and associated socialization processes. The first model, transmission teacher education, corresponds to a normative orientation. The teacher is considered an object of socialization, that is, a social product. The second, incitative teacher education, follows a personal orientation. The teacher is considered the subject of the socialization process, determining him/herself, and actively adapting to different social roles. The third, appropriative teacher education, is centered on the social insertion of the individual. The teacher is regarded as an agent of socialization, simultaneously being defined by the circumstances and defining them. Another author, Ferry (1987), also considers diverse theoretical models for teacher education. He is not so concerned with the intentions, educational devices, structure of objectives, or nature of the contents, but mostly with the type of processes and the educational dynamics. He distinguishes three main models of teacher education: centered on acquisitions, centered on experimentation, and centered on analysis.

In order to lead investigative lessons successfully, teachers need knowledge and competencies, which they must improve constantly, reflecting on the work done. Recently, the idea of the reflective teacher became a pervasive topic in discussions about teacher education. Schön (1983), one of the authors that has considered this question, underlines reflecting in action and on action as two distinctive aspects of competent professionals.

3.1 Professional Development

There is a close relationship between teachers' professional development and personal and organizational development. António Nóvoa (1991) underlines the importance of valuing the person (and his/her experience) and the profession (and its knowledge). He argues that personal development is necessary to stimulate a critical-reflexive perspective that provides the basis for autonomous thought. This author criticizes the practices of inservice education directed towards individual teachers, that favor the isolation and reinforce an image of teachers as transmitters of external knowledge. Nóvoa endorses the practices that take as reference the collective dimensions and indicates that inservice education must stimulate teachers to value what they know, working from theoretical and conceptual points of view. He considers that teachers need to solve problematic situations, emphasizing the role of investigative and collective networks, conjugating clinical with inquiry-oriented teacher education. Nóvoa also underlines the importance of organizational development. For him, it is necessary to change the contexts where teachers act. Teacher education becomes a permanent process, integrated in the daily life of teachers and schools. He underlines the importance of participation, indicating that teachers must be active protagonists in the conception, implementation, and evaluation of teacher education as well as the need for a new culture in teacher education, bringing together schools and teacher education institutions, in the framework of "positive partnerships" (p. 30).

We can draw several contrasts between teacher education and professional development (Ponte, 1998). First, teacher education is strongly associated with the idea of attending "courses," while professional development occurs through multiple forms, including courses, projects, sharing of experiences, readings, reflections, and so forth. Second, teacher education follows an outside-in movement, aiming for the teacher to assimilate ready-made knowledge and information, while professional development is inside out, leaving the basic decisions regarding the questions to consider, the projects to undertake, and the ways of carrying them out to the teacher. Third, teacher education mostly attends to teachers' deficiencies, and professional development stresses the teachers' potential. Fourth, teacher education is usually compartmentalized in subjects or disciplines, while professional development implies the teacher as a whole embracing cognitive, affective, and relational dimensions. Finally, teacher education usually starts from theory and frequently does not leave theory, whereas professional development may consider both theory and practice.

Professional development stresses the combination of formal and informal processes. The teacher is no longer an object but becomes the subject of the learning process. Attention is given to knowledge and cognitive aspects, but also to affective and relational issues. The aim is not "normalization" but promotion of the individuality of each teacher (Hargreaves, 1998).

Teacher education can be viewed in a logic different from the transmission of a body of knowledge or the training specific skills. In fact, there is no insuperable incompatibility between professional development and teacher education. Teacher education may favor the professional development of the teacher, as it can, through its "hidden curriculum," contribute to reduce his/her creativity, self-confidence, autonomy, and sense of professional responsibility. Teachers who want to develop professionally and personally need to take advantage of the educational opportunities that address their necessities and objectives.

3.2 The Difficult Relationship Between Didactics and Teacher Education

Teacher education at all levels (preservice, inservice, and specialist education) has to take into account the processes of professional development, their rhythms and dynamics. Professional development involves the gradual maturing of the potentialities of each teacher, the construction of new knowing, and bears the mark of the underlying social and collective contexts. On the other hand, didactics has essential contributions to make to the professional activity of the teacher. It suggests useful concepts for understanding educational situations and supplies resources for professional practice (in particular, to conduct pupils' investigative work).

Ignoring the contributions of didactics is to put aside a set of powerful perspectives for education and a set of basic concepts to analyze and intervene in situations of practice. It means wasting an important capital of experience and research, that one could use to the benefit of the pupil. Ignoring the nature of the teachers' processes of professional development leads to designing teacher education programs of the "transmission" type, imposing concepts, practices, and theories that teachers do not need or that they regard without interest. However, that is common in much teacher education (preservice and inservice) that is done all around the world.

The problem consists, then, in combining didactics with professional development. How can we use the perspectives and results of the first without opposing the nature of the processes of the second? This problem is impossible apparently. It concerns movements that go in opposing directions, one inside out and the other outside in.

This problem may have many solutions, if we take into account the appropriate time scales. In other terms, we need to identify the specific contribution of each formative moment to the development of the teacher—remembering that teacher education can not achieve everything one would like, much less in a short period.

People learn from their activity and from reflection on their activity (Bishop & Goffree, 1986; Christiansen & Walther, 1986). Pupils learn mathematics working on mathematics tasks that they consider important and worthwhile. They learn by speaking with their colleagues and reflecting on their reasoning and results. Pupils learn sciences, French, history, or geography in a similar way. In addition, teachers and teacher candidates learn from their activity and from their reflection on activity—carried out in contexts of practice within a well-defined professional culture. Teachers' professional knowledge emerges through their participation in educational practices (Crawford & Adler, 1996; Lerman, this volume). The object of the activity of the teacher is not mathematics, French, history, or geography but the activity of the pupils in educational tasks. That is, teachers (and preservice teachers) learn by processes similar to pupils'; what is different is the basic object of their activity.

Activity, reflection, and cultural participation are important in learning, but deep learning requires a strong involvement from the learner. We can achieve it through investigative activities, because:

- investigations develop the ability to deal with complex problem-solving issues, mobilizing our knowledge in flexible and integrated ways;
- only understanding our own learning, investigating it, can we understand the learning processes of our pupils; and
- investigations provide a working paradigm that constitutes a reference for the reflecting teacher. (Ponte, 1999)

This importance of practice and investigation on practice is also stressed by researchers such as Cooney and Krainer (1996) and Lampert and Ball (1998). However, practice and investigation, only by themselves, are not enough. It is necessary to know in what ways they can play an important role in teacher education.

In an investigation, we may deal with a theoretical problem. Some phenomenon or issue may intrigue us. Working on them may lead to an increase in our knowledge. Other investigations, usually termed as action-research, may emerge from concrete difficulties of practice. Working on them, we strive to· change the situation and to obtain better results. To use Ferry's terms, problem-oriented investigations promote the development of analytical abilities and action-research activities promote the experimentation of new approaches. Both require us to start defining the objectives and designing a working plan to reach them. Just as the investigative work in mathematics is important for pupils' learning, the investigative work regarding professional questions is also necessary for the professional development of teachers.

In both cases, we start defining a problem or an objective. We elaborate a detailed working plan. That plan is carried out and its results are evaluated. From that evaluation, many ideas for new inquiries may appear. There is a strong parallel between the investigation process—in mathematics and in mathematics education—and the process of mathematics problem solving, as considered by Pólya (1945):

Stages	Resolution of a problem, according to Pólya	Investigation and action research
1	Understanding the problem	Characterizing the problem-situation
2	Designing a plan	Designing a plan
3	Carrying out the plan	Carrying out the plan
4	Looking back	Reflecting on the work carried out and identifying new questions for investigation

Closely related to the idea of investigation is the idea of project, a typical context for Lesne's appropriative teacher education. In a project, a teacher, or a group of teachers, identify an objective regarded as important and develop a set of activities to reach it. It can be greater or smaller and more or less ambitious. In any case, the actors are the essential protagonists, and they both are transformed by the process they live and contribute to the transformation of the involving situation.

As Jean-Pierre Boutinet (1996) says, in a project there is a strong demand of unity between conception and execution. It has to consider the singularity of the situation, living permanently between theory and practice, dealing with complexity and uncertainty. It stands between the individual logic and the collective logic, whose management is always difficult, and between success and failure. In a project, failure is always ahead, and success depends not on the ability of preventing failure but on the ability of overcoming it.

An investigation, action-research, or project requires us to start characterizing the problem or the problem-situation that we want to address well. This done, it is necessary to design a working plan, defining the activities to carry out, the instruments to use, the calendar to follow, the resources to mobilize, and the role of diverse people who will participate in the work. This is followed by a phase of execution of the plan, correcting the trajectory when necessary. Finally, one has to evaluate the reach of the work carried through, reflecting on the process and the product, and to identify new questions for further investigation.

4. PRESERVICE TEACHER EDUCATION: INVESTIGATING INVESTIGATIONS

This perspective informs preservice teacher education in my institution. Part of the preservice program is a yearlong *practicum* carried out in a school. Student teachers work in groups and often choose a topic for a project. A group of four student teachers[ii] addressed the potential of mathematical investigations in mathematics teaching.

First, they reviewed the literature on mathematical investigations, in order to gather arguments for using these activities and to collect information about how to conduct them. They developed their own working approach and created instruments to assess pupils and to collect data to support their reflection on the activity. In a final report, they describe the experimentation of these activities as "case studies" and end up with conclusions about what they learned in this project (Esteves, Santos, Ramos, & Roque, 1996).

These student teachers considered it quite important that pupils reflect on their work and on their conclusions. Therefore, they asked pupils to answer a questionnaire. They collected pupils' most significant answers in terms of content, difficulties, and language. They presented these answers in overhead transparencies and discussed them with the whole class, aiming to clarify ideas, improve pupils' form of expression (mathematical or not), and improve their performance in future activities.

Here is an example of an analytic geometry task proposed to 10th grade pupils during the 3rd quarter. The pupils already knew the notion of vector and vector operations. They worked in groups of 4 to 5 and it was the seventh time that they were doing an investigation.

Collinear vectors

Definition: Two vectors are collinear if they have the same direction.
Investigate if there is any relation among the coordinates of collinear vectors.

(grid paper provided)

The following description concerns one class led by one of the student teachers. She initiated the activity handing out a worksheet. Then, she read the definition and asked a pupil to come to the blackboard and give an example and a counter-example of vectors satisfying the definition.

Then the pupils started working in groups. The following excerpt of a conversation that went on between the teacher and a group of pupils provides an idea of the nature of the interactions taking place:

Teacher But these two are collinear... and these two also... and these... are not collinear with these.

Pupils They all are!

Teacher Then is there some relation between the coordinates of these two with the coordinates of these two?

Pupils Yes, they are different!

Teacher They are different?... For example?...

Pupil 2 Then the coordinates are different and then they [the vectors] are collinear.

Teacher OK! So, when vectors have different coordinates, what happens?

Pupil 5 They are collinear!

Teacher They are always? Vectors with different coordinates are always collinear? It is that what you find? If it is what you find, verify it!

(Esteves et al., p. 34)

In the end of the lesson, the teacher collected pupils' work and analyzed it. She found it useful to write some suggestions in their papers so that in the first 15 minutes of the next lesson the slower groups could arrive at more conclusions by themselves.

In the discussion, the teacher started asking the groups to show their conclusions and reasoning, registering them on the blackboard. Later, with the aid of the pupils, she systematized their answers in one sentence: "two vectors **u** and **v** are collinear when **u** = kv, with k a real number."

A group of pupils wrote in the questionnaire:

> We concluded that a vector is collinear to another vector when both coordinates are multiplied by the same number, either positive, negative, or zero. In this last case, the result is always the null vector that may take any direction, and therefore is always collinear to any vector. Thus, mathematically, **u** = kv. (Esteves et al., p. 39)

In the opinion of the pupils, the discussion is important because: "it helps to assemble the ideas of all pupils, clarifying them... and is also useful to dissipate [our] doubts..." and "we have an opportunity to argue, which helps us to understand things better" (p. 40).

These student teachers conclude their report saying that:

> The work that we carried out during this school year made us consider that investigation activities are as stimulating for the pupils as they are for us. This is because we think that this approach is a "true mathematical activity" and develop abilities, attitudes, and values that other pedagogical strategies do not develop so efficiently. (Esteves et al., p. 47)

5. INSERVICE TEACHER EDUCATION: TEACHER NARRATIVES

Next, I present an example of a narrative reflection of an inservice teacher—Irene Segurado—concerning an investigation class. It was carried out in an action-research project that went on from 1995 to 1997, aiming to study the professional knowledge needed to carry out these activities in the classroom. The members of the project team promoted investigative lessons with 10-14 year old pupils. Those lessons were the basis for discussions and the production of narratives on the lived experiences. In project meetings, the team also discussed theoretical issues regarding investigations, lesson dynamics, teachers' professional knowledge, and using narratives in educational research. A first version of a narrative written by Irene was subject to further discussion and analysis, from which more refined versions were developed.

An all-class investigation[iii]

> The task that I presented to my 5th graders concerns the multiples of a number, the topic that I was teaching. I planned that they would work in small groups, as usual in this type of activity. The task is the following:
> - write in columns the 20 first multiples of 5.
> - look at the digits in the units and tens. Do you find some regularities?
> - investigate what happens with the multiples of 4 and 6.
> - investigate for other numbers.
>
> When I entered the classroom, I noted that the pupils were rather agitated, perhaps due to the beautiful day outside or to the proximity of the holidays.

The organization of the material in pupils' desks and the change in places necessary for group work could lead to an even bigger agitation. To not make this problem worse I decided to keep them in their places.

I decided to control the situation immediately. I placed myself in front of the blackboard, asked for the multiples of 5, and registered them on the board.

I questioned pupils if there was something interesting and curious with the units and tens. Tatiana, raising her arm, answered readily: *the number of the units is always 0 or 5*, which was accepted by her colleagues, echoing in the room: *it is always 0; 5, 0; 5...*

And...? —I stimulated them.

The tens digit repeats itself 0-0, 1-1, 2-2; 3-3... said Octávio, with a happy expression.

I was marking these two statements in the blackboard, with colored chalk, so that they could all verify its truth when Carlos, with a certain agitation, interrupted me. *I discovered another thing... Can I go to the blackboard to explain it?* I asked him to wait a little in order to finish what I was doing. He accepted, but communicated his discovery to the nearby colleagues ....

I was pleased, since my expectations had already been exceeded. I asked them to investigate what happens with the multiples of 4, that I placed in a column next to the multiples of 5 .... Quickly, almost all pupils answered in chorus: *they always finish in 0, 4, 8, 2, and 6.* They still discovered that: *they always finish in an even number, the tens happen again 2 times, 3 times, alternatively, the number of tens that repeat three times are always pair and those that repeat two times are always odd.*

The pupils, who were more passive in the beginning, were livening up with the discoveries of the colleagues and became more outspoken, showing great enthusiasm in the search of regularities.

We had discovered all the regularities that I had previously found in my planning and after some moments of fruitless search, I considered that we could move to investigate what happens with the multiples of 6. I wrote them next to the multiples of four—for no special reason, but simply not to lose time in erasing the blackboard.

0	0	0
5	4	6
10	8	12
15	12	18
20	16	24
25	20	30
30	24	36
35	28	42
40	32	48
45	36	54
50	40	60
55	44	66
60	48	72

65	52	78
70	56	84
75	60	90
80	64	96
85	68	102
90	72	108
95	76	114

The discoveries now appeared in batches and there was no pupil who would not pledge in giving a contribution. That made it difficult for me, sometimes, to record and to systematize:

The units are always 0, 6, 2, 8 and 4.

The units are always a number pair.

The tens do not repeat from 5 to 5.

I was breaking their enthusiasm: *Easy! Let us verify if what your colleague said is true; Attention! Look! Look at what an interesting thing your colleague discovered!* ...

Sónia suddenly affirmed: *They are the same numbers as in the multiples of 4.* Even before this statement made any sense to me, Vânia had already declared: *They are in another order.* I perceived that they were comparing the multiples of 4 and 6, and I explained that to the class.

Both start in zero, said Pedro who today was clearly awake.

The other numbers are in contrast, reported Ana.

There are multiples of 4 that are also multiples of 6.

The multiples of 6 from 12 on, are alternatively also multiple of 4....

The discoveries now came purring as cherries, one behind the other, exceeding all my expectations about the answers that the pupils would give. I had not foreseen comparing multiples of different numbers, because I never placed them next to each other. Therefore, I lived their discoveries with enormous enthusiasm. A more astute pupil observed: *The teacher is very happy with us, aren't you?* And I was!

The records made on the blackboard provided a new approach to the task. Moreover, working with the whole class enabled the contribution of each pupil to be grasped immediately by all colleagues, leading to more discoveries.

For me, group work is the best way to have pupils working on investigations. Small group work allows us to attain objectives that can hardly be reached with individual or all-class work: cooperation, teamwork, and organization. It also enables reflecting on the others' ideas, explaining and verifying their reasoning. However, carrying out an investigation with the whole class (an experience that I had for the first time), allowed for a widening of the discoveries. The strategy used by a pupil, for a given discovery, was used by a larger number of colleagues to generate new discoveries. This strategy also allowed the pupils to assume their interventions individually, which is quite important for the educational process. This task, perhaps because it dealt with the investigation of simple regularities, fully resulted in a whole class lesson far beyond my most optimistic expectations.

6. EDUCATIONAL RESEARCH: TEACHER'S ROLES IN INVESTIGATION CLASSES

A third example concerns a research study aiming to characterize the roles of the teacher when pupils carry out mathematical investigations (for detail see Ponte, Oliveira, Brunheira, Varandas, & Ferreira, 1998). This work was done in the assumption that to conduct classroom activities, teachers need special professional knowledge, know how, and experience. Moreover, it considered that doing new types of tasks in the classroom requires the personal construction of new principles and routines.

This study was carried out by a collaborative team of teachers and researchers using a qualitative-based methodology[iv]. It analyzed selected episodes concerning the start, when the teacher presents a task to the class, the development of the investigation, with the pupils working in small groups, and the final discussion, where pupils present their results and all the class, together with the teacher, does a general evaluation of the work carried out.

Data collection involved audio and video records and field notes. The classes were conducted by three teachers from the project. Some of these classes were observed by other project members. In other cases, the teacher also collected images and sounds. The analysis of data involved several stages including (a) transcribing audio and video records; (b) selecting episodes to study, from the transcripts; (c) applying a system of categories to the transcripts (and sometimes re-viewing the video records of the episode); (d) refining the analysis, through discussion of a document produced in the previous stage; (e) making a cross-analysis of the several previous analyses; and (f) analyzing items of the previous step, to identify and characterize teachers' roles.

The study presents diverse roles of the teacher in conducting pupils' investigative work. They concern teachers' professional knowledge, including their mathematical knowledge (in particular, regarding the task), and their didactic knowledge (concerning the organization of the work and the conduction of pupils' activity):

1. *Challenge pupils.* The teacher, in the beginning and during the work, proposes questions that pupils can find challenging, for which they do not have an immediate response, arousing their mathematical curiosity.
2. *Support pupils.* During the development of an investigation, the teacher supports pupils' progress, considering the mathematical exploration of the task and the management of the didactic situation, promoting a balanced participation of the pupils in the activity.
3. *Evaluate pupils' progress.* During the activity, the teacher collects information to know if pupils understand the task, if they are formulating questions and conjectures, if they are testing them, if they justify their results, or if they have difficulties and, if so, what their origin is.

4. *Think mathematically*. New mathematical questions can always arise, especially if the situation is truly open and the teacher may become involved in reasoning mathematically with pupils.

5. *Supply and recall information*. The teacher has to provide useful information to pupils, helping them to remember important ideas, to understand mathematical concepts, and important forms of representation.

6. *Promote pupils' reflection*. The teacher has to assure that pupils relate the work they are doing with known ideas and develop their understanding of mathematics.

These different roles can be systematized in the following diagram:

Mathematics strand

4. To think mathematically (to investigate/to establish connections)

Didactics strand	1. To challenge 2. To support 3. To evaluate	5. To provide information	6. To encourage reflection

When selecting, adapting or elaborating the investigation to propose to pupils, the teacher needs to think mathematically. Therefore, the mathematical reasoning of the teacher (previous to the lesson) assumes a basic importance. However, questions, conjectures, and arguments considered by pupils can lead the teacher, during the lesson, to consider new aspects of the task, requiring additional mathematical reasoning. Continuing the investigation, the mathematical reasoning of the teacher develops in an analogous way to the mathematical reasoning of pupils—placing questions, formulating conjectures, making tests, and validating results, the typical processes of an investigation. Moreover, during the lesson, there are also frequent opportunities to establish relationships between the work in progress and other mathematics or extra-mathematics concepts—which require the teacher to hold a mathematics culture and ability to decide what connections to establish. By doing investigative activity in the classroom, the teacher constitutes a genuine mathematical model for his/her pupils (Lampert, 1990; Mason, 1991). This concerns teacher's role 4, to think mathematically.

The remaining roles assume a didactic nature. Before the lesson starts the teacher establishes the agenda, makes decisions concerning curricular priorities, the actual wording of the task, and the form of presenting it to pupils, as well as the type of class organization. During the lesson, the teacher moves between two poles: one concerns the curriculum, that marks the objectives (aims) to reach, while the other concerns the activity, witht respects to the actions (means), that are carried out to reach those objectives. The learning objectives involve two dimensions (Christiansen and Walther, 1986) that are always there, explicitly or implicitly. The first one concerns the mathematics contents, leading the teacher to explain a concept, to remember a notion, or to establish direct links with other ideas or mathematics or extra-mathematics representations—role 5, to give information. Here we find one of the "classic" roles of the teacher that, as Lampert (1990) indicates, can be carried out in a substantially different way, contextualized and integrated in the accomplishment of significant activity. Instead of assuming this work alone, the teacher can try to get the pupils to participate actively, helping to explain a concept to their colleagues, remembering ideas, representations, and procedures already studied. The second dimension concerns understanding what it is to learn, what mathematics is, and what it is to think mathematically. This dimension introduces another level of activity, evaluating, and commenting on the work done and the new ideas that emerge. We find another basic role of the teacher here—role 6, to promote the reflection—stressed, for example, by Bishop and Goffree (1986).

The actions that the teacher can use to reach the intended objectives are essentially expressed by the three basic roles: (1), to challenge, (2) to support, and (3) to evaluate. These roles are connected to the logic of the development of any activity. The teacher challenges the pupils with situations and questions in order to involve them in investigative work. The teacher supports them, asking questions, making comments, or providing suggestions. The teacher also tries to evaluate the progresses already done and possible difficulties, collecting information, and, based on that, decides to continue, to modify some aspects of the work, or to move to another phase of the activity.

The two strands, mathematics and didactics, are not independent of each other. On the contrary, they cross each other, as the previous picture suggests and as Shulman (1986) underlines. All the didactic work carried out by the teacher requires an understanding of the task and its mathematical connections. The most specific aspect of the activity of the mathematics teacher, as a teacher of a discipline, is supporting the development of mathematical thought, before, during, and after the lesson. However, the educational role of the teacher has other sides besides mathematics—it depends equally on the way the teacher faces education, curriculum, pupils' learning, and the profession. Five of the roles are placed in this interconnection. Thinking mathematically is not. It can be started off by pupils' questions, comments, or affirmations, but concerns the mathematics being of the teacher.

7. CONCLUSION

The investigation paradigm is a good framework to discuss pupils' work in the classroom as well as teachers' activity and professional development. Investigation processes are at the heart of the mathematical activity and, when experienced with authenticity, naturally enable pupils to have a stimulating relationship with mathematics. Investigations about teaching constitute a powerful framework for professional development, providing a bridge between theory and practice, bringing together what we are learning in mathematics education about mathematics learning and teaching and what we are learning in teacher education about professional development. We saw an example of an investigation in preservice teaching, when a group of student teachers collected information on carrying out this type of lesson, designed and made investigation lessons, gathered, compiled and analyzed data, and drew their conclusions about its value. We saw a rather different example in an action-research project, when an experienced teacher conducted a lesson changing her usual way of work and reflected on its implications for future activities. We saw yet another example of a more formal investigation on this type of work, aiming to identify different teacher's roles. Scholars such as Goffree and Oonk (this volume) and Lampert and Ball (1998) also favor the idea that investigations, in mathematics as well as in teacher education, supply a useful framework for fostering pupils' learning process and teachers' professional development.

Investigations may mean different things for different people. As personal experiences, they can be lived in rather different ways. In fact, investigatory work involves a variety of interpretations in different parts of the mathematics education community. In this paper, I stressed a view of investigations that emphasize its problematic nature and its openness, less structured than usual problem solving tasks. The role of the teacher regarding this activity also allow for a range of interpretations from the "sage on the stage" to the "guide on the side." However, whatever the case, learning is a central focus for pupils and teachers involved in this process.

An investigation involves several phases and is connected to the idea of project. However, it is essential that the form of investigations is not used to shadow what it is more important—its content. An activity is not an investigation just because it involves a revision of literature, the conception and application of instruments such as questionnaires, videos, or interviews, and a final report. The essential in an investigation is that it starts formulating genuine and interesting questions and that a careful process is designed to find some type of response. It is the value of the questions and the appropriateness of the answering process that are the basic marks of an investigative work.

Investigations about practice may be nurtured by collaborative activity involving educators and teachers within a research culture (Jaworski, this volume). Investigative activities can arise from initiative of the practicing teacher or in teacher education programs. They also can arise spontaneously during a lesson or in professional development. Finding devices, working ways and situations that favor this activity, and studying its conditions of success are important tasks for present day mathematics education.

REFERENCES

Bishop, A., & Goffree, F. (1986). Classroom organization and dynamics. In B. Christiansen, A. G. Howson, & M. Otte (Eds.), *Perspectives on mathematics education* (pp. 309-365). Dordrecht: Reidel.

Boutinet, J.-P. (1990). *Anthropologie du project*. Paris: Presses Universitaires de France.

Chapman, O. (1997). Metaphors in the teaching of mathematical problem solving. *Educational Studies in Mathematics, 32*(3), 201-228.

Christiansen, B., & Walther, G. (1986). Task and activity. In B. Christiansen, A. G. Howson, & M. Otte (Eds.), *Perspectives on mathematics education* (pp. 243-307). Dordrecht: Reidel.

Cooney, T. J., & Krainer, K. (1996). Inservice mathematics teacher education: The importance of listening. In A. J. Bishop, K. Clements, C. Keitel, J. Kilpatrick, & C. Laborde (Eds.), *International handbook of mathematics education* (pp. 1155-1185). Dordrecht: Kluwer.

Crawford, K., & Adler, J. (1996). Teachers as researchers in mathematics education. In A. J. Bishop, K. Clements, C. Keitel, J. Kilpatrick, & C. Laborde (Eds.), *International handbook of mathematics education* (pp. 1187-1205). Dordrecht: Kluwer.

Cockcroft, W. H. (1982). *Mathematics counts*. London: HMSO.

DFE (1997). *Mathematics in the national curriculum*. London: DFE e Welsh Office.

Ernest, P. (1991). *The philosophy of mathematics education*. London: Falmer.

Esteves, A. C., Santos, C., Ramos, C., & Roque, C. (1996). *Aprender... investigando*. DEFCUL, Unpublished report.

Ferry, G. (1987). *Le traject de la formation*. Paris: Dunod.

Gofree, F., & Oonk, W. (This volume). When real practice can be (digitally) represented in colleges of education. In T. J. Cooney & F. L. Lin (Eds.) *Making sense of mathematics teacher education*. Dordrecht: Kluwer.

Hadamard, J. (1945). *Psychology of invention in the mathematical field*. Princeton, NJ: Princeton University Press.

Hargreaves, A. (1998). *Os professores em tempos de mudança: O trabalho e a cultura dos professores na idade pos-moderna*. Lisboa: McGraw Hill.

Jaworski, B. (1994). *Investigating mathematics teaching: A constructivist inquiry*. London: Falmer.

Jaworski, B. (This volume). Developing mathematics teaching: Teachers, teacher educators and researchers as co-learners. In T. J. Cooney & F. L. Lin (Eds.) *Making sense of mathematics teacher education*. Dordrecht: Kluwer.

Kline, M. (1970). Logic versus pedagogy. *American Mathematical Monthly, 77,* 264-282.

Lampert, M. (1990). When the problem is not the question and the solution is not the answer: Mathematical knowing and teaching. *American Educational Research Journal, 27*(1), 29-63.

Lampert, M., & Ball, D. L. (1998). *Teaching, multimedia, and mathematics*. New York, NY: Teachers College Press.

Lerman, S. (1989). Investigations: Where to now? In P. Ernest (Ed.), *Mathematics teaching: The state of the art* (pp. 73-80). London: Falmer.

Lerman, S. (This volume). A review of research perspectives on mathematics teacher education. In T. J. Cooney & F. L. Lin (Eds.), *Making sense of mathematics teacher education*. Dordrecht: Kluwer.

Lesne, M. (1984). *Trabalho pedagógico e formação de adultos*. Lisboa: Fundação Calouste Gulbenkian.

Love, E. (1988). Evaluating mathematical activity. In D. Pimm (Ed.), *Mathematics, teachers, and children: A reader* (pp. 249-262). London: Hodder & Stoughton.

Mason, J. (1978). On investigations. *Mathematics Teaching, 84,* 43-47.

Mason, J. (1991). Mathematical problem solving: Open, closed and exploratory in the UK. *ZDM, 91*(1), 14-19.

Mason, J., Burton, L., & Stacey, K. (1982). *Thinking mathematically*. London: Addison-Wesley.

Ministère de l'Education Nationale, de la Recherche et de la Technologie (1997). *Programmes de mathématiques*. Paris: MENRT.

Ministério da Educação (1997). *Matemática: Programas*. Lisboa: Ministério da Educação, Departamento do Ensino Secundário.

NCTM (1991). *Professional standards for teaching mathematics*. Reston, VA: NCTM.

NCTM (1998). *Principles and standards for school mathematics: Working draft*. Reston, VA: NCTM.

Nóvoa, A. (1991). *Concepções e práticas de formação contínua de professores*. Congress Formação de Professores: Realidades e Perspectivas, Universidade de Aveiro.

Ollerton, M. (1994). Contexts and strategies for learning mathematics. In M. Selinger (Ed.), *Teaching mathematics* (pp. 63-72). London: Routledge.

Pehkonen, E. (Ed.). (1997). *Use of open-ended problems in mathematics classroom*. Helsinki: Department of Teacher Education, University of Helsinki.

Perrenoud, P. (1993). *Práticas pedagógicas, profissão docente e formação: Perspectivas sociológicas*. Lisboa: D. Quixote.

Poincaré, H. (1908). L' invention en mathématiques. *Bulletin de l'Institut Géneral de Psychologie, 3*.

Pólya, G. (1945). *How to solve it: A new aspect of mathematical method*. Princeton, NJ: Princeton University Press.

Pólya, G. (1981). *Mathematical discovery* (originally published 1962/1965). New York, NY: Wiley.

Ponte, J. P. (1999). Didácticas específicas e construção do conhecimento profissional. In J. Tavares, A. Pereira, A. P. Pedro, & H. A. Sá (Eds.), *Investigar e formar em educação: Actas do IV Congresso da SPCE* (pp. 59-72). Porto: SPCE.

Ponte, J. P. (1998). Da formação ao desenvolvimento profissional. In *Actas do ProfMat 98* (pp. 27-44). Lisboa: APM.

Ponte, J. P., Oliveira, H., Brunheira, L., Varandas, J. M., & Ferreira, C. (1998). O trabalho do professor numa aula de investigação matemática. *Quadrante, 7*(2), 41-70.

Ponte, J. P., Oliveira, H., Cunha, H., & Segurado, I. (1998). *Histórias de investigações matemáticas.* Lisboa: IIE.

Ruthveen, K. (This volume). Mathematics teaching, teacher education and educational research. In T. J. Cooney & F. L. Lin (Eds.), *Making sense of mathematics teacher education.* Dordrecht: Kluwer.

Sullivan, P. (This volume). Thinking teaching: Seeing an active role for the mathematics teacher. In T. J. Cooney & F. L. Lin (Eds.), *Making sense of mathematics teacher education.* Dordrecht: Kluwer.

Schön, D. A. (1983). *The reflective practitioner: How professionals think in action.* New York, NY: Basic Books.

Shulman, L. S. (1986). Those who understand: Knowledge growth in teaching. *Educational Researcher, 15*(2), 4-14.

Departamento de Educação e Centro de Investigação em Educação
Faculdade de Ciências da Universidade de Lisboa

---

[i] The first task is from *SMILE Investigations,* in Lerman, 1989, p. 77.

[ii] Ana Cristina Esteves, Cláudia Santos, Cristina Ramos and Cristina Roque—school year of 1995-96.

[iii] Abridged from Ponte, Oliveira, Segurado, & Cunha (1988).

[iv] This team, that included J. P. Ponte, H. Oliveira, L. Brunheira, J. M. Varandas, and C. Ferreira, was part of the Project MPT-Mathematics for All (1995-99).

DINA TIROSH, RUTH STAVY, AND PESSIA TSAMIR

USING THE INTUITIVE RULES THEORY AS A BASIS FOR EDUCATING TEACHERS

ABSTRACT. In this chapter we illustrate how the explanatory and predictive power of the Intuitive Rules Theory can be used to plan instructional sequences that help students overcome the negative effects of intuitive rules on their work in mathematics and science. We then describe a research-based seminar we developed for raising mathematics and science teachers' awareness of the role of intuitive rules in students' thinking and to encourage them to take this knowledge into consideration when planning instruction. Finally, we discuss some initial impressions regarding the impact of the seminar on teachers' actual teaching.

It is widely accepted that awareness of and knowledge about students' ways of thinking significantly contribute to teaching. Therefore, enhancing prospective and in-service teachers' familiarity with students' conceptions has become a major aim of many prospective teacher education and in-service professional development projects (Cooney, 1999; Fenemma, Carpenter, Franke, Levi, Jacobs, & Empson, 1996; Schifter, 1998; Sowder, Armstrong, Lamon, Simon, Sowder, & Thompson, 1998). Furthermore, several studies have shown that participation in projects focusing on children's conceptions promotes teachers' ability to make instructional decisions that are appropriate to the mathematical needs of their students (for example, Fennema, et al., 1996). These projects have, as a rule, attempted to familiarize teachers with research-based models of students' mathematical conceptions related to specific mathematical topics. The models were based on research which aimed for detailed description of particular alternative concepts and reasoning.

Like many other professional development projects, we strongly believe that enhancing teachers' acquaintance with students' ways of thinking is an important aim. Toward this end, we have chosen to familiarize teachers who participate in professional development teacher programs in our department with the Intuitive Rules Theory. This theory can be used as an organized, general framework to assist teachers in their attempts to understand and predict childrens' responses to a wide variety of mathematical and scientific tasks. In this chapter we briefly describe and discuss the Intuitive Rules Theory. We then present some related, educational implications, and describe how knowledge about the Intuitive Rules Theory can be used in in-service teacher education.

1. THE INTUITIVE RULES THEORY

In our work in mathematics and science education, we have observed that students react in similar ways to a wide variety of conceptually non-related tasks which differ with regard either to their content area and/or to the reasoning they required, but share some common, external features. We have so far identified four types of responses, two relate to comparison tasks (*More A-more B* and *Same A-same B*) and two to subdivision tasks (*Everything comes to an end* and *Everything can be divided*). This part of the chapter briefly describes and discusses these four, intuitive rules.

1.1 Intuitive Rules Related to Comparison Tasks

More A- more B
Consider the following, two tasks:
1. Two matchboxes, one full of sand and the other empty, are held at the same height above the ground, in the same manner. They are both dropped at a specific instant.
    Will the matchboxes hit the ground at the same time? If not, which will hit the ground first?
2. Consider the following two line segments:

    A ——————— B

    C ——————— D

    In your opinion, is the number of points in line segment CD smaller than/equal to/greater than/ the number of points in line segment AB? Explain your answer.

With respect to the first task, research shows that a common, incorrect response is that the heavier matchbox will be the first to hit the ground (Champagne, Klopfer, & Anderson, 1979; Gunstone & White, 1981). This response is often interpreted as evidence of an alternative conception of free-fall according to which the falling time of an object is directly related to its weight. We interpret this response as an instance of the intuitive rule *More A (weight) - more B (speed)*.

With respect to the second task, a common response is that "The longer line segment, CD, contains more points than the shorter line segment, AB, as it contains all points in line segment AB and additional ones" (Tirosh, 1991). This response was interpreted as an evidence of an application of students' ideas of finite sets to infinite ones. Within the Intuitive Rules Theory, we interpret this response as an application of the intuitive rule *More A - more B*. We argue that here, much like in the previous case, subjects are impressed by salient, irrelevant information (for example, the differences in length) and consequently respond in line with the intuitive rule *More A (longer segment) - more B (more points)*.

Responses of the type *More A - more B* are observed in students' answers to many comparison tasks, including classical, Piagetian conservation tasks (conservation of number, area, weight, volume, matter, etc.); tasks related to intensive quantities (density, temperature, concentration, and so on) and other tasks (for example, free-fall, infinite sets). In all these tasks, two objects (or two systems), which differ in a certain, salient quantity A are described ($A_1 > A_2$). The student is then asked to compare the two objects (or systems) with respect to another quantity B ($B_1 = B_2$ or $B_1 < B_2$). In all these cases, a substantial number of students respond inadequately according to the rule *More A* (the salient quantity)- *more B* (the quantity in question), claiming that $B_1 > B_2$. We interpret these responses as evolving from a common source, namely the intuitive rule *More A- more B*. We suggest that students' responses to such tasks are determined by the specific, external characteristics of the task, which activate the intuitive rule, and not necessarily by students' ideas about the task's specific content or concepts.

Same A- same B

Consider the following tasks:

1. On March 1 a store lowered its prices by 10%. On March 10 it raised its prices by 10% over the sale price. How did the March 10 prices compare with the prices before the sale?"

2. The Carmel family has two children, and the Levin family has four children.
   Is the probability that the Carmels have one son and one daughter larger than/equal to/smaller than/ the probability that the Levins have two sons and two daughters? Explain your choice.

3. Take two identical rectangular (non-square) sheets of papers (Sheet 1 and Sheet 2):
   - Rotate one sheet (sheet 2) by 90°.
   a. Is the area of Sheet 1 equal to/greater than/smaller than/ the area of Sheet 2?
   - Fold each sheet (as shown in the drawing). You get two cylinders: Cylinder 1 and Cylinder 2.
   b. Is the volume of Cylinder 1 equal to/larger than/smaller than/ the volume of Cylinder 2?

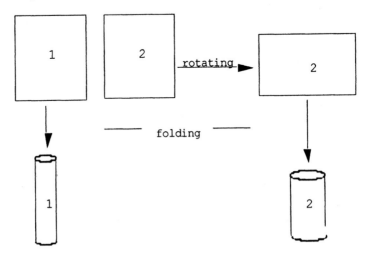

Research shows that a common incorrect response to the first task is that the March 10 prices and the prices before the sale are the same. This claim is based on students' observation that the rise and the reduction are 10% percent each. In the context of students' conceptions of percentages, such a response is often interpreted as evidence of their failure to understand that percentages cannot be compared without taking into account to what they refer (van den Heuvel-Panhuizen, 1994). But clearly, this response is of the type *Same A (same percent)- same B (same amount of money)*

A common, incorrect response to the second task is that the probability that the Carmels have one son and one daughter is equal to the probability that the Levins have two sons and two daughters. Here, the correct answer could be reached by calculating the ratio between the number of successful events in each family (one son-one daughter in the Carmels, two sons-two daughters in the Levins) and the number of all possible combinations of sons and daughters in each of these families. The corresponding ratios are 1:2 for the Carmels and 3:8 for the Levins. Thus, the probability that the Carmels have one son and one daughter is greater than the probability that there are two daughters and two sons in the Levins. However, many students, even those who had studied probability, claimed that "the ratio is the same (1:2), therefore the probability is the same". Clearly, this response is of the type *Same A (ratio) - same B (probability)*.

Regarding the third question, we expected, in line with the rule *Same A- same B*, that when students start to conserve the area and know that the areas are equal they will start arguing that "same area -same volume". Research shows that indeed, almost all those who conserved the area incorrectly claimed that the volumes of the two cylinders are equal (Stavy & Tirosh, 2000). Some of them explained that "the volume of the two cylinders is the same because they are made from identical sheets of paper," or, similarly, that "the volumes of the two cylinders are the same because the areas of the sheets are the same." This response is, clearly, of the type *Same A (area, paper) – same B (volume)*.

In these comparison tasks the two objects or systems to be compared were equal in respect to one quantity A ($A_1=A_2$) but different in respect to another quantity B ($B_1 \neq B_2$). In some of the tasks, the equality in quantity A was directly given (for example, 10%). In other cases, the equality in quantity A could be logically derived (through the schemes of conservation or proportionality). A common incorrect response to all these tasks, regardless of the content domain, was *Same A-same B*. We regard these responses as specific instances of the use of this intuitive rule.

1.2 *Intuitive Rules Related to Subdivision Tasks*

Consider the following, two tasks:
1. Consider the line segment AB. Add to this line segment another line segment, half the size of this one, as illustrated in the drawing below. Again, add to this line segment another line segment, half the size of the previously added one. Continue adding in the same way.

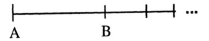

A   B

Will this process come to an end? Yes/ No. Explain your answer.

2. A teaspoon of sugar is put into a cup of water and stirred well into it. Half of the sugar water is poured out, then half a cup of water is added to the cup and is mixed thoroughly with the remaining sugar water. This process is executed again: Half of the sugar water is poured out, half a cup of water is added, etc. This process is repeated.

Is it possible to reach a stage at which no sugar at all will be found in the cup? Yes/No. Explain your answer.

These and other successive division tasks were traditionally used to investigate students' conceptions in mathematics and in science. In mathematics, successive division tasks were used to examine students' conceptions of one of the main concepts in the field - infinity (Fischbein, Tirosh, & Hess, 1979; Nunez, 1991; Tall, 1981). In the physical sciences, successive division of material objects tasks were used to investigate students' conceptions of matter as particulate (Carey, 1992; Egozi, 1993; Pfundt, 1981; Stern & Mevarech, 1991). Research shows that young students (Grades 5- 7) provide finite responses to successive division tasks involving both mathematical and material objects, claiming, in line with one intuitive rule, that *Everything comes to an end.* The older students, who become aware that subdivision processes might continue endlessly, tend to provide infinite responses to both the mathematical and material object successive division tasks, claiming, in line with the other intuitive rule, that *Everything can be divided.*

We have so far pointed out that students tend to give the same type of response to scientifically unrelated tasks. We asked ourselves: What do those tasks that elicit the same type of response have in common?

The *commonalties in the tasks that elicit the same type of response are in the external features of the tasks and not in their scientific content.* It seems that certain task features that activate a related, specific intuitive rule often determine students' responses. The intuitive rules have the characteristics of intuitive thinking, as the responses seem self-evident (subjects perceived statements they make on the basis of these rules as being true and in need of no further justification). These rules are used with great confidence and perseverance (often they persist in spite of formal learning that contradicts them). Moreover, they have attributes of globality (subjects tend to apply them to diverse situations) and coerciveness (alternatives often are excluded as unacceptable) (Fischbein, 1987).

2. EDUCATIONAL IMPLICATIONS OF THE INTUITIVE RULES THEORY

As stated before, the Intuitive Rules Theory enables teachers to explain and foresee students' responses to specific tasks. The explanatory and predictive powers of this theory can be used to plan instruction aimed at helping students overcome the negative effects of the intuitive rules on their responses. Teachers can be educated about ways of using intuitive rules in various teaching strategies, including teaching by analogy (for example, Clement, 1993), and conflict teaching (for example, Piaget, 1980).

Both the teaching by analogy and the conflict teaching approaches exploit a situation in which students correctly solve one problem (the anchoring task) but incorrectly solve another scientifically similar problem (the target task). This situation, where students make contradictory judgments to externally different but essentially similar tasks, enables teachers to use the intuitively correct judgment related to one situation to explain the other. This can be achieved in different ways, two of which will be described here. The first consists of presenting students first with the anchoring task to activate a correct response, followed by the target task, assuming that the similarity between the tasks will trigger a correct response to the target task as well (teaching by analogy). In the second approach the target task is introduced first; then the anchoring task is presented. The teacher attempts to raise the students' awareness that although the two tasks are essentially similar, their responses are contradictory. The teacher encourages the students to reconsider their response to the first task (the conflict teaching approach).

Teachers can be encouraged to use the Intuitive Rules Theory to construct sequences of instruction in line with each of these approaches. Within the Intuitive Rules Theory, an anchoring task is defined as a task to which a correct response is in accordance with an intuitive rule. Students are therefore expected to solve the task correctly. The target task is a task to which a response that accords with an intuitive rule contradicts the correct response.

The teaching by analogy approach has been proven to be effective in helping students overcome the impacts of the intuitive rules in various contexts, one of which was that of comparing vertical angles. Tsamir, Tirosh & Stavy (1997) has shown that when vertical angles were presented with equally drawn length of arms (see Figure 1), practically all students in all grade levels gave correct, equal-angle responses.

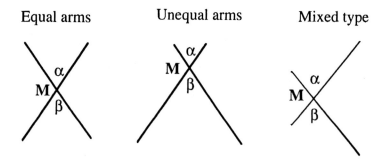

| Equal arms | Unequal arms | Mixed type |

Figure 1. Students' comparisons of vertical angles

However, when the vertical angles were drawn with different lengths of arms (see Figure 1), the percentages of students who responded that these angles were equal were substantially lower than those in the previous task. A substantial number of students argued that angle β was larger. This claim was accompanied by the explanation "β is larger because its lines are longer." This explanation is in line with the intuitive rule *More A - more B*.

In teaching by analogy, the drawing of vertical angles with equal arms was used as an anchoring task. Then, the mixed-typed representation (see Figure 1: Mixed type) was created, in front of the student, by lengthening the upper-right arm of angle α and the lower-right arm of angle β. This representation served as a bridging task. The mixed-typed representation was then rotated by 90^0 to obtain an unequal representation of vertical angles - the target task. This series of tasks, starting with an anchoring one, then going through the bridging one, to the target task, significantly improved students' responses to the target task.

Several studies have shown that the conflict teaching approach is also effective in helping students overcome the impacts of the intuitive rules (e.g., Myers, 1998; Segal, 2000; Ronen, 2000). We shall describe two studies that used the conflict teaching approach.

Tirosh and Tsamir (1996) used knowledge about the effects of the intuitive rules on students' responses to comparison-of-infinite-set tasks to improve their responses to such tasks. They first presented students with the following task:

Consider the two infinite sets:

{1, 2, 3, 4,...} {1, 4, 9, 16,...}

Is the number of elements in these sets the same? If not, which set contains more elements? Why?

As expected, most students in Grades 10 to 12, argued incorrectly in line with the intuitive rule *More A- more B*, that the set {1, 2, 3, 4,...} contains more elements because it contains all the elements in the set {1, 4, 9, 16,...} and some other elements as well. Then, students were offered the same problem, presented in the following way:

Consider two infinite sets:

$\{1, \quad 2, \ 3, \ 4 \,,...\}$
$\{1^2, \quad 2^2, 3^2, 4^2 \,,...\}$

Is the number of elements in these sets the same? If not, which set contains more elements? Why?

This specific representation encouraged students to realize that it is possible to match each element in the first set with a corresponding element in the second set (for instance, 1 with 1^2, 2 with 2^2, and, in general, n is matched with n^2). Students consequently correctly concluded that these two sets have the same number of elements. Each student was then asked to examine his/her answers to the two representations of this task, and was encouraged to notice their identity. Tirosh and Tsamir (1996) reported that the use of the conflict approach, in this case, resulted in improvement in students' responses to the first task.

Dembo, Levin, and Sigler (1997) studied students' conceptions of area and perimeter. They presented students aged 12-18 with a given geometrical figure, then transformed it, in front of the subject, into another figure, changing the area but keeping the perimeter the same. The students were then asked to compare the areas of the two figures (for instance, a square was transformed into a diamond, a circle into an ellipse). Dembo, et al. (1997) reported that many of the students in these grade levels claimed that "same perimeter-same area". Clearly, this response is in line with the intuitive rule *Same A - same B*.

Dembo et al. (1997) asked students to imagine what would happen to the respective areas of two shapes (square and circle) if the transformations were taken to their extremes. The experimenter said "Try to imagine me continuing the actions that changed this shape into another [square into diamond and circle into ellipse]. What will happen: Will the area remain the same, will it increase or decrease?" Dembo et al. (1997) hypothesized that imagining the end state in which the area became zero would elicit the idea that the area must be decreasing throughout the transformation, and that this conclusion would clash with the incorrect response that the area remains equal throughout the transformation. They found that students confronted with this conflict situation significantly outperformed the control group, namely, responses of the type *Same A – same B* were less frequent in the experimental group.

The application of the two teaching approaches that were described here (teaching by analogy and the conflict teaching) is based on knowledge about the effects of the intuitive rules on students' responses to externally different but essentially similar tasks. In the cases described above, the applications of these approaches resulted in suppressing the effects of the intuitive rules and, consequently, in an increment in correct responses. Clearly, formal explanations, proofs, definitions, and other aspects of the relevant scientific framework should follow each and every such intervention. Such formal knowledge may assist students in controlling the effects of the intuitive rules.

3. THE INTUITIVE RULES THEORY SEMINAR

Teachers could use the Intuitive Rules Theory for various purposes, one of which (constructing meaningful sequences of instruction) was demonstrated in the previous part of this chapter. In our opinion, it is important to raise mathematics and science teachers' awareness of the role of the intuitive rules in students' thinking and to encourage them to take this knowledge into consideration when planning instruction.

For this purpose, we developed a research-based seminar on the Intuitive Rules Theory for mathematics and science in-service middle and high school teachers. The seminar consists of three main parts: introduction to the Intuitive Rules Theory, educational implications of this theory, and individual micro-studies. The first part of this seminar is devoted to the introduction of the Intuitive Rules Theory and the common effects of each of the intuitive rules on students' responses. Each rule is presented via exemplary tasks. Participants are asked to respond to each task and then predict possible, common students' responses. In many cases, participants' own responses are affected by the intuitive rules, thus providing them with an opportunity to directly experience the coercive effects of the intuitive rules. Participants are asked to look for the common structure of typical students' responses to the tasks (e.g. *More A – more B*; *Same A – same B*) and for the commonalties in the external features of the tasks. The intuitive rules are then defined and participants are asked to read several, related articles (for example, Stavy & Tirosh, 1996; Stavy & Tirosh, 2000; Tirosh & Stavy, 1996; Tirosh & Stavy, 1999).

The second part of the course presents possible educational implications of the Intuitive Rules Theory. We discuss the teaching by analogy and the conflict teaching approaches. Specific examples of research that make use of these two methods, in the context of the intuitive rules, are presented and critically discussed. Again, several reading assignments are given (e.g., Stavy & Berkovitz, 1980; Tirosh, Stavy, & Aboulafia, 1998; Tirosh, Stavy, & Cohen, 1998; Tirosh & Tsamir, 1996).

The third part of the course consists of involving the in-service teachers in micro-studies related to the Intuitive Rules Theory. Each in-service teacher is asked to select a topic related to the Intuitive Rules Theory and to define specific research questions. Three types of studies are suggested: 1) *Validation of a known intuitive rule*. Here, in-service teachers are encouraged to suggest instances in which a previously defined intuitive rule is expected to be expressed, and test their predictions; 2) *Identification of new, intuitive rules*. In-service teachers are encouraged to look for common student responses to conceptually non-related tasks, to identify common, external features of these tasks, to define a new related, intuitive rule , and to test their prediction regarding this rule; 3) *Development and assessment of interventions aimed at suppressing the effects of the intuitive rules*. In-service teachers could develop and test the effectiveness of an intervention which uses the analogy or conflict approaches or any other method to help their students overcome the impacts of an intuitive rule in a specific content area, or in several content areas.

After selecting a topic and defining specific research questions, each in-service teacher looks for relevant literature (for example, publications related to the Intuitive Rules Theory, students' specific alternative conceptions, and intervention studies). Research instruments are then developed and other decisions related to the methodology are made. All members of the group, including the authors, meet weekly. Some meetings are devoted to group discussions on the research questions and the methodologies. Revisions are made in light of these discussions and preliminary, small-scale trials are carried out. Each in-service teacher presents his proposal to the entire group, considers the participants' comments, administers the instruments, and collects data. The analyses of the collected data are done in cooperation with several in-service teachers, and the results are presented to the entire class. Finally, each in-service teacher writes a small paper on his micro-study.

The impact of such a seminar on in-service teachers' knowledge of the Intuitive Rules Theory and its effects on their actual teaching has not yet systematically been studied. Initial impressions were gathered from several interviews with some participants in the seminar. They were asked if and how their acquaintance with the Intuitive Rules Theory affected their instruction. These participants pointed out that awareness of the intuitive rules is important for teachers and that such awareness strongly affected their instruction. They mentioned that acquaintance with the Intuitive Rules Theory raised their sensitivity to students' incorrect responses, provided them with tools to make sense of these responses and understand their sources, and directed their related reactions. Moreover, they used their knowledge about the intuitive rules to re-examine their previous instruction and to design new ways of teaching. Some of them even exposed their students to the Intuitive Rules Theory. Here we shall provide few quotations from three interviews.

SL, an experienced mathematics and physics high school teacher, related her growing awareness of the effects of the intuitive rules on her and her students' responses:

> SL: I heard from you about the intuitive rules and was not sure that these rules affect my own or my students' responses. However, I became more sensitive to such responses and was surprised to find out that in every single topic and almost in each lesson, many of my students' responses were of the type *Same A - same B* and *More A - more B*.

In her response, SL described how she used her knowledge about the Intuitive Rules Theory in teaching projectile motion. She predicted that students would argue, in line with the intuitive rule "More A - more B," that "the longer the distance, the longer the time." Based on this prediction, she developed a lesson in which she used a cognitive conflict approach:

> SL: When teaching projectile motion, I started with a demonstration: I used two identical balls that were simultaneously released from the same apparatus, V_0 of one of these balls was zero, and the second was horizontally projected with $V_0 > 0$. I asked the class to predict, before the demonstration, if the two balls would reach the ground at the same time or not, and if not which ball would reach the ground first. About 50% of the class predicted that the first ball would be the first one to hit the ground, because "the longer the distance, the longer time..." . Then the demonstration was carried out, and my students were surprised to see the results. This enabled me to emphasize that the first and the second balls indeed hit the ground together, and that falling time is determined only by the height.

SL was one of the teachers who decided to expose her students to the Intuitive Rules Theory. She explained that students' awareness of the role of the intuitive rules in their thinking could be used to encourage critical thinking:

> SL: I believe that such awareness could serve as a "red light," namely, as a tool for them to identify responses of the type *More A - more B*, *Same A-same B* and to start questioning their validity. My goal, as a teacher, is to encourage my students to critically examine their responses and to test whether these responses are in line with the situation and with the formal frameworks. I believe that awareness of the role of the intuitive rules in their thinking could be used as a tool to promote such behavior.

The second interviewee, MM, is an experienced mathematics and physics teacher. He revised his instruction, in line with the Intuitive Rules Theory, using a conflict teaching approach:

> MM: Instead of presenting the materials as such, I tend to open the instruction related to a specific topic by choosing problems which have the potential to activate a certain, incorrect response, in line with an intuitive rule. Then, the students are asked to predict the answer, and, as expected, at least some of them will answer incorrectly (e.g., *More – more* or *Same - same*). Then, we do an experiment (or calculation) that bears out the correct answer. My students are faced with the fact that their initial answers were incorrect. We then discuss the formal explanation.

PT, an experienced mathematics teacher, described in the interviews how she implemented her knowledge about the intuitive rules theory in her instruction, using the teaching by analogy approach.

> *PT:* Sometimes, I draw an analogy between a given task and daily life situations to convince my students that their responses are incorrect. Often, I start teaching a given topic with examples, for which the intuitive rules lead to a correct response, i.e., supporting the scientific related knowledge. Later, I present examples for which the use of this rule leads to incorrect responses, thereby showing the boundaries of the application of this rule.

PT added that teachers should be aware of the intuitive rules and their possible impact on students' responses. They should understand that the intuitive rules are the sources of many of the difficulties students' have in understanding certain topics. They should know how to design instruction which takes into consideration the role of the intuitive rules and how to react to related, incorrect responses. PT made it clear that she does not explicitly talk about the intuitive rules with her high-school students. However, she clarified that in her opinion, introducing the intuitive rules to teachers, is a must.

These three interviewees, and other interviews as well, suggest that acquaintance with the Intuitive Rules Theory affects instruction. The interviewees clearly stated that the Intuitive Rules Theory is "a must" for teachers. The issue of exposing their own students to the Intuitive Rules Theory was also addressed, and different opinions were expressed.

4. DISCUSSION

In this chapter we described an in-service teacher education course which uses a specific theory about students' ways of thinking, the Intuitive Rules Theory, as a means to help teachers understand students' responses to mathematical and scientific tasks. We described two specific sequences of instruction that are used often in mathematics and science education: the teaching by analogy and conflict teaching approaches.

Many educators advocate the use of one or both of these approaches (Driver, 1994; Fischbein, 1987). However, a main difficulty in constructing sequences of instruction in line with these two approaches is finding examples of anchoring and targets tasks. The Intuitive Rules Theory, due to its predictive power, provides a general tool to assist teachers to identify tasks to be used for each specific purpose.

An important aim of teacher education is to provide teachers with general tools for analyzing instructional tasks and for determining which of these are expected to be easy and which will probably be more difficult for their students. The Intuitive Rules Theory provides teachers with such a general tool. However, introducing this general tool is not enough. Teacher education programs should raise and discuss the various factors to be taken into account when choosing a certain teaching strategy. When considering the choice between teaching by analogy and the conflict teaching approach, teachers should be made aware of the learning implications of using each. An instructional sequence that uses an analogy can be planned in such a way that students will be led to realize that the target task demands a response similar to that given to an anchoring task, although without them becoming aware of possible contradictions in their responses. As such, the method does not require them to realize that "something is wrong," or to actively participate in criticizing their responses. In the conflict teaching approach, students are made aware of the contradiction in their judgments and of the need to resolve this contradiction. There is a danger that students may lose their self-confidence or regress to making incorrect judgments. Preparing teachers for understanding the advantages and disadvantages of each of these strategies for specific situations with specific students or groups of students is, therefore, an important aspect of any teacher education program.

At the beginning of this chapter we mentioned the general consensus that teachers' awareness of students' ways of thinking contributes to teaching. We also mentioned that many teacher education projects are aimed at enhancing teachers' familiarity with students' alternative conceptions. The Intuitive Rules Theory provides an essentially different explanation to students' incorrect responses. The essential claim of the Intuitive Rules Theory is that human responses to given tasks are affected by a small number of intuitive rules (or schemes) activated by irrelevant external features of the tasks. It seems, therefore, that students' incorrect responses do not necessarily originate from alternative conceptions or ideas but from an uncontrolled application of certain intuitive rules. In light of the strong impact of these intuitive rules on students' responses, the importance of enhancing students' critical thinking is evident. It follows that in teacher education it is essential to emphasize that students should be encouraged not to rely on the external features of the tasks, but to critically examine their intuitive responses.

REFERENCES

Carey, S. (1992). The origin and evaluation of everyday concepts. In R.N. Giere (Ed.), *Minnesota Studies in the Philosophy of Science, 15* (pp. 89-128). Minneapolis: University of Minnesota Press.

Champagne, A.B., Klopfer, L.E., & Anderson, J.H. (1979). *Factors influencing the learning of classical mechanics.* (Research report). Pittsburgh: LRDC, University of Pittsburgh.

Clement, J. (1993). Using bridging analogies and anchoring intuitions to deal with students' preconceptions in physics. Journal of Research in Science Teaching, 30, 1241-1257.

Cooney, T. (1999). Conceptualizing teachers' ways of thinking. *Educational Studies in Mathematics, 38,* 163-187.

Dembo, Y., Levin, I., & Siegler, R. S. (1997). A comparison of the geometric reasoning of students attending Israeli ultraorthodox and mainstream schools. *Developmental Psychology, 33*(1), 92-103.

Driver, R. (1994). *Making a sense of secondary science.* London: Routledge.

Egozi, R. (1993). *Subdivision processes in science and mathematics.* Unpublished master's thesis(in Hebrew), Tel-Aviv University, Israel.

Fennema, E., Carpenter, T. P., Franke, M., L. Levi, L., Jacobs, V. R., & Empson, S. B. (1996). A longitudinal study of learning to use children's thinking in mathematics instruction. *Journal for Research in Mathematics Education, 27,* 403-434.

Fischbein, E. (1987). *Intuition in science and mathematics: An educational approach.* Dordrecht, Netherlands: Reidel.

Fischbein, E., Tirosh, P. & Hess, P. (1979). The intuition of infinity. *Educational Studies in Mathematics, 12,* 491-512.

Gunstone, R.F., & White, R.T. (1981). Understanding of gravity. *Science Education, 65,* 291-299.

Myers, S. (1998). Effects of conceptual conflict on using the intuitive rule "More A-more B" in 8th grade students. Unpublished master's thesis (in Hebrew), Tel-Aviv University, Israel.

Nunez R. (1991). A 3-dimension conceptual space of transformations for the study of the intuition of infinity in plane geometry. *Proceedings of the Fifteen Conference for the Psychology of Mathematics Education* (Vol. 3, pp. 362-368). Assisi, Italy.

Pfundt, H. (1981). Pre-instructional conception about substances and transformation of substances. In W. Jung, H. Pfundt, & C. V. Rhonock (Eds.), *Problems concerning students' representation of physics and chemistry knowledge* (pp. 320-341). Ludwigsburg: Frankfurt University.

Piaget, J. (1980). *Experiments in contradiction.* Chicago: University of Chicago Press.

Ronen, I. (2000). *The intuitive rule "Same A – Same B": The case of overgeneralization of the conservation scheme.* Unpublished doctoral dissertation (in Hebrew), Tel-Aviv University, Israel.

Schifter, D. (1998). Learning mathematics for teaching: From a teachers' seminar to the classroom. *Journal of Mathematics Teacher Education, 1,* 55-87.

Segal, N. (2000). *Exploring the role of cognitive conflict in conservation task: The case of "same A – same B".* Unpublished master's thesis (in Hebrew), Tel-Aviv University, Israel.

Sowder, J., Armstrong, B., Lamon, S., Simon, M., Sowder, L., & Thompson, A. (1998). Educating Teachers to Teach Multiplicative Structures in the Middle Grades. *Journal of Mathematics Teacher Education, 1*(2), 127-155.

Stavy, R., & Berkovitz, B. (1980). Cognitive conflict as a basis for teaching quantitative aspects of the concept of temperature. *Science Education, 64,* 679-692.

Stavy, R., & Tirosh, D. (1996). Intuitive rules in mathematics and science: The case of "The more of A the more of B". *International Journal of Science Education, 18* (6), 653-667.

Stavy, R., & Tirosh, D. (2000). *How students (mis-)understand science and mathematics: Intuitive rules.* New York: Teachers College Press.

Stern, E., & Mevarech, Z.R. (1991). *When familiar context does not facilitate mathematical understanding.* Unpublished manuscript. Max Planck Institute, Germany.

Tall, D. O. (1981). Intuition of infinity. *Mathematics in School, 10* (3), 30-33.

Tirosh, D. (1991). The role of students' intuitions of infinity in teaching the Cantorian theory. In D. Tall (Ed.), *Advanced mathematical thinking* (pp. 199-214). Dordrecht, Holland: Kluwer Academic.

Tirosh, D., & Stavy, R. (1996). Intuitive rules in science and mathematics: The case of "Everything can be divided by two." *International Journal of Science Education, 18* (6), 669-683.

Tirosh, D., & Stavy, R. (1999). Intuitive rules: A way to explain and predict students' reasoning. *Educational Studies in Mathematics, 38,* 51-66.

Tirosh, D., Stavy, R., & Aboulafia, M. (1998). Is it possible to confine the application of the intuitive rule: Subdivision process can always be repeated? *International Journal of Mathematics Education in Science and Technology, 29*(6), 813-825.

Tirosh, D., Stavy, R., & Cohen, S. (1998). Cognitive conflict and intuitive rules. *International Journal of Science Education, 20* (10), 1257-1269.

Tirosh, D., & Tsamir, P. (1996). The role of representations in students' intuitive thinking about infinity. *International Journal of Mathematics Education in Science and Technology, 27* (1), 33-40.

Tsamir, P., Tirosh, D., & Stavy, R. (1997). Intuitive rules and comparison tasks: The grasp of vertical angles. *Proceedings of the First Mediterranean Conference: Mathematics, Education and Applications* (pp. 298-304). Nicosia, Cyprus.

Van den Heuvel-Panhuizen, M. (1994). Improvement of (didactic) assessment by improvements of problems: An attempt with respect to percentages. *Educational Studies in Mathematics, 27,* 341-372.

School of Education
Tel Aviv University

COLETTE LABORDE

THE USE OF NEW TECHNOLOGIES AS A VEHICLE FOR RESTRUCTURING TEACHERS' MATHEMATICS

ABSTRACT. The process of introducing technology into mathematics teaching provides not only a window of opportunity through which we can consider teachers' beliefs about mathematics but also act as a catalyst for teachers to restructure their mathematics. The chapter describes the evolution of experiences of a team of teachers involved in a project of writing teaching sequences based on the use of the software Cabri-geometry. It attempts to analyse how the role of technology in the tasks evolved and to reveal the various sources of difficulties that teachers encountered relative to their beliefs and conceptions about mathematics and its teaching.

1. INTRODUCTION OF TECHNOLOGY IN THE TEACHING SYSTEM

Teaching often has been modelled as a complex system made of several elements, mutually interacting around three poles: the teacher, the students, and content knowledge. In this model, it is assumed that the teaching system is subject to several constraints (time, societal choices regarding curriculum, inner structure of the mathematical domain of knowledge, conceptions and ideas of students,...) and that it evolves from one equilibrium state to another one by the making of choices. Some choices are made by society; others dealing with the syllabi and some aspects of the curricula, are made by the noosphere. Within the set of constraints imposed by choices external to the classroom, the teacher also has to make decisions based on choices. Some of these choices are partly implicit, and teachers may even be unaware of them. We consider that teacher education would benefit from a better knowledge of possible choices at the disposal of teachers, from a better understanding of the various types of conceptions underlying these choices.

A perturbation caused to the functioning of a system may reveal some tacit or hidden aspects of the system that allow comparison of the functioning of the system in a regular phase and in an unstable phase. The reactions of the system to the perturbation give another source of evidence. The study carried out by Wilson and Goldenberg (1998) about one teacher's local theories was based on this same idea of using the opportunity of a context of changes in the teacher's practice for gaining knowledge about the teacher's conceptions of mathematics and mathematics teaching. We recognise this "struggle" for changes as a perturbation in the normal course of teachers' practice.

In the present situation, introducing the use of technology in mathematics teaching may be viewed as a perturbation for several reasons:

F.-L. Lin & T. J. Cooney (Eds.) Making Sense of Mathematics Teacher Education, 87—109.
© 2001 Kluwer Academic Publishers. Printed in the Netherlands.

- current teachers usually have not been taught how to teach mathematics with an integrated use of technology; but the use of technology requires new competencies on the teachers' part (Boero, Dapueto, & Parenti, 1996);
- the widespread use of technology in teaching has not been achieved, and the usual school culture does not give room to advanced technology such as software programs or symbolic and geometric calculators (Cooney & Krainer, 1996).

This paper reports on a writing project of computer-based teaching scenarios for high school students (15- to 16-year-olds) in mathematics developed by a team of teachers who volunteered to participate in the project. By scenario, we mean a teaching sequence carefully designed with learning goals which are made explicit before the experimentation. The writing of a scenario also includes the writing of observations made during its experimentation and advice about the management of the class for teachers who would like to use the scenario. A scenario is innovative teaching with explicit intentions, not a controlled teaching in which the design of the teaching sequence is based on choices and prior analysis of possible students strategies.

The teachers of the team experimented with these scenarios in their own classrooms and modified them during the three years of the project. The aim of the project[1] was to study the conditions of the integration of advanced technology in mathematics teaching. One of the starting assumptions of the project is that a process of integration is a long-term process depending on several factors. Some of these factors play an important role. Let us mention two of them: the features of the computer environment; and the tacit hypotheses and beliefs of the teacher about learning.

The reasoning as to why the analysis of the choices made by the teachers in writing the scenarios may act as a window on their own epistemology is as follows. In this study, we aim to investigate the reactions of teachers in an unusual situation for them, created by the introduction of technology into teaching. In a way, teachers experience a new, problematic situation similar to the situations that teachers would like their students to experience (Cooney & Krainer, 1996, p.1168). Just as it is for students, this situation not only is a good way of revealing the teachers' conceptions but also contributes to teachers' change.

2. THE DESIGN OF COMPUTER-BASED TEACHING SCENARIOS: A SHORT DESCRIPTION OF THE PROJECT

Experimental teaching sequences were designed by four mathematics teachers and discussed in the team involved in the project, which also included a physics teacher, researchers in mathematics education, and computer scientists involved in the development of software for mathematics teaching.

The observation of the behaviours of the students and the management of the classroom also led to the modification of the scenarios during the three years of the project. Some scenarios have given rise to two or three different versions. For each scenario, an introduction presenting the aims of the scenario was written by the author. The observation of the class working on the scenario also gave rise to written comments[ii].

The scenarios are based on the use of Cabri-geometry (software version and application of the TI 92). Cabri-geometry is a dynamic geometry computer environment in which the user can construct geometrical diagrams. Diagrams result from a sequence of primitives expressed in geometrical terms chosen by the user from menus. When an element of such a diagram is dragged by means of the mouse, the diagram is modified, preserving all geometric relations used in its construction (For a more precise description of Cabri-geometry see Laborde, 1995; Hölzl, 1996; Jones, 1997). These artificial realities could be compared to entities of the real world: It is as if they react to the manipulations of the user by following the laws of geometry, just as material objects react by following the laws of physics. A crucial feature of these realities is their quasi-independence of the user as soon as they have been created. When the user drags one element of the diagram, this latter is modified according to the geometrical way it has been constructed, and not to the wishes of the user.

The students were given a TI 92 for the entire academic year. This allowed them the use of it at home, and not only for geometry. Students also worked on computers in the computer lab of the school for some activities, during part of the maths hours. The fact that essentially the same dynamic geometry program was available in both environments (computer and calculator) allowed this double use of technology. The availability of the geometry application on a handheld device certainly contributed to its integration in several aspects: The students could decide on their own to use it, and the teacher could give homework or class assignments to be done on the TI 92 (the files saved on the TI 92 were easily transferred and collected on the calculator of the teacher). Topics addressed by the scenarios were: configurations, vectors, geometrical transformations, in particular dilation and translation.

It must be stressed that these students were not involved in a mathematics oriented class. At this level of schooling the classes gather all students independently of their achievement in any subject matter. The choice of a major is made on the following year when students are 16 to 17 years old.

The team consisted of four teachers with various profiles:

- two experienced teachers very familiar with the use of technology in mathematics teaching and with research in mathematics education (Even though they were familiar with the use of technology, it was for them the first time that they integrated it in their teaching of geometry to this extent; the availability of the TI 92 for each student probably contributed to their decision to enter the project.);
- a novice teacher who was experienced in computer science (He was a former engineer.);
- an experienced teacher who was a novice at using advanced technology in mathematics teaching.

3. QUESTIONS AND METHODOLOGY

The aim of the present report is
  i.   to reconstruct the choices of the teachers underlying the design of teaching sequences based on the use of technology and their evolution;
  ii.   from these choices to infer their conceptions about the nature of mathematical activities and about learning mathematics: What should students learn and how should they learn ?

Of course, we primarily expected to have access to teachers' conceptions about the role of technology in learning mathematics and in particular how they conceived the nature of mathematical activity when mediated by technology. Nevertheless, we assumed that it should be possible in a second step to infer some elements about their epistemology concerning mathematics teaching and learning from their conceptions about the use of technology.

The method we used is first based on the analysis of the evolution of the design choices of each teacher. Of course, we also assumed that discussing in a team and interacting probably would affect the conceptions of the teachers over time. So we had to take into account that the "teachers' epistemology" we intend to reconstruct is not actually fixed and is subject to changes. Nevertheless, we planned to observe differences in changes; some teachers might resist more than others against some changes. Second, we attempted to contrast choices in the design of scenarios of the different teachers with respect to their experience in teaching and in using technology.

The first version of a scenario was designed by a single teacher who experimented it in his/her class. In some cases, it was discussed in the team before being experimented and slightly changed, but this was not always done. The meeting of the team took place once a month and it occasionally happened that between two meetings a teacher discovered an opportunity (that he did not expect) of using Cabri for a specific part of the curriculum which could not be postponed in the course of the teaching. Since the scenarios were not deeply modified if their first version was discussed, we consider as a first version, any version written before being experimented. It is interesting to note that a real discussion took place only after experimentation in the class, perhaps because the team was heterogeneous in terms of experience and the experienced teachers in both domains did not want to impose a priori their opinions. After a scenario was experimented, they could argue by means of elements coming from the observation of the classroom.

We call second version a version modified by the teacher himself or another teacher after being experimented in class. Of course, this second version was also experimented in class. Subsequent versions could appear, as in the case of the scenario called "Dilation." The project lasted three years, but some scenarios are still used with modifications by the teachers, members of the project. The fact that scenarios are continuously modified is part of the integration process of technology.

The first and second versions of scenarios will be mainly discussed below. More precisely, we will analyse the evolution of the choices of the teachers dealing with the following aspects:

- the kind of computer based tasks they designed in their teaching scenarios, and in particular the role played by technology in the task;
- the distribution of tasks between the paper-and-pencil environment and the technology environment: What kind of tasks were given in each of those environments?;
- the kind of knowledge they tried to introduce: To what extent was it affected by technology?

4. EVOLUTION OF THE FIRST VERSIONS WRITTEN BY NOVICE TEACHERS

We can distinguish two kinds of scenarios in the first versions written by novice teachers:
- the versions written at the beginning of the project, when they had interacted only a little with the rest of the team;
- the versions written after six months or more.

4.1 First Versions at the Very Beginning of the Project

The two teachers who were inexperienced, the one in using technology, the other one in teaching, had similar reactions in that they both proposed activities that were not fully part of the usual curriculum.

The novice in teaching, but expert in computer science, designed several small activities based on various facilities of the TI 92. It was as if he wanted to show to his students the huge range of possibilities of the calculator without going deeper in the use of one of them: programming activities, plotting functions, equations of straight lines.... Each activity was independent of the other. He also used the software Cabri-geometry in the computer room again in independent activities, which were situated at the borderline of the curriculum or are usually done as exercises.

For example, he asked the students to construct, with Cabri, the centroid, the orthocenter, and the center of the circumscribed circle of a triangle and to observe that the three points are collinear (Euler line). Or, he asked the students to measure each angle of a convex polygon, to calculate the sum , to drag a vertex and to repeat the same sequence of actions. One of those activities shows very well how much he did not want to integrate the software into the mathematical activity. He asked the students to construct the figure displayed below (Figure1), in which M is a variable point of segment AB.

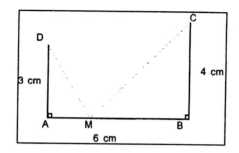

Figure 1. Construction showing M as a variable point of segment AB

He asked the students to measure MC and MD for several values of AM. Then, as it is usually done in paper-and pencil-environment, he asked the students to study the function MC+MD by making a table of values and drawing the graph. He never mentioned the possibility of obtaining this graph with Cabri as a locus, which was a good reason to connect geometry with calculus, nor offered possible feedback to the hand computations made by students. The software was mainly used as an *amplifier* for visualising properties, but not really the source of the tasks given to the students, nor as a *tool for solving the task.*

The experienced teacher, who was novice in using technology, transformed a long problem she found in a book which was aimed at fostering the joint use of several geometrical properties and objects (loci, transformations, ellipse) and which was not especially designed for a computer-based environment. It was conceived as a problem for checking whether the students are able to use various notions in a long problem. The teacher somehow modified the problem by introducing the tasks of constructing rhombuses by imposing, in one of the questions, the free points, and in another question the trajectory of one vertex of the rhombus. She kept the questions of determining the loci, but in an explicit way asked the students to first obtain the locus with Cabri, second conjecture the nature of the locus, and third provide a written proof.

Both teachers in the first step did not use technology for introducing new mathematical notions; they limited the use of technology to. some sessions rather independent of the teaching content. In both cases, the visual power of technology was used, but mainly for seeing and conjecturing, not for experimenting with the aim to better understand the mathematical situation. Using the words of Pea (1985), we would say that in this kind of use for visualisation, technology was just an *amplifier* and *not a reorganiser.*

However, it is worth noting that the experienced teacher designed tasks which could not be done in a paper-and-pencil environment: construction tasks of dynamic diagrams with imposed trajectories for some elements of the figure. She was very explicit about this aim; in her comment for the booklet, she wrote that the problem aimed to show to the students that a geometrical object is not static but changing by preserving its internal geometrical relations (Laborde 1995). She stated that it is a good way to make students aware of the functional aspects of geometrical relations.

We interpret this behaviour as a change subsequent to the perturbation caused by technology, which affected the nature of the tasks she gave. This change is linked to the conception she had about the nature of a geometrical object. Paradoxically, the teacher expert in technology did not change the nature of tasks he gave, while the novice in technology did so partly, perhaps because as an experienced teacher she had time to become aware that students experience difficulties in viewing geometrical objects as functions of other objects.

4.2 First Versions After Some Months in the Project

The teacher who was expert in technology but novice in teaching did not really change the scenarios he wrote over time. They were mainly short and dealing with topics independent of the progression in the class. This was not the case for the experienced teacher who was novice in technology. After some time, she decided to write a scenario for introducing students of tenth grade (15- to 16-year-olds), to the new notion of dilation as a point transformation defined by using vectors.

This scenario often called for immediate visual observations and generalisation by inductive reasoning. The need for proof was less important than in a paper-and-pencil environment. It gave a great role to measuring. For example, the very first activity of the scenario was the following:

I. Definition of a new transformation
In Cabri mark a point I; by means of the tool Polygon create any quadrilateral ABCD as you want.
1. Edit 3 as a number.
Construct the image of ABCD by using the tool Dilation in the following way: designate successively the quadrilateral, point I and number 3.
Label A', B', C' and D' the corresponding vertices of the new quadrilateral which has been obtained.
Compare   vectors IA and IA';
        vectors IB and IB';
        vectors AB and A' B';
        vectors BC and B' C';
        the area of ABCD and the one of A' B' C' D'.
Which equality is valid for vectors IA and IA'? IB and IB'?
2. Modify number 3 into −0.5 and answer again questions of activity 1.
Do several trials by modifying the position of I and then of point A.

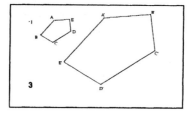

Figure 2. Version 1 of activity 1 of scenario Dilation

The activity called only for discrete measuring and did not use the animation facility of the numerical display of the ratio. From question 1 to question 2, students had only to change the ratio and had to repeat the same comparisons, and it is only after these two trials that they were asked to drag a vertex of the quadrilateral and the dilation centre. Cabri was used more as a *provider of several static diagrams than as a provider of a variable diagram.* After this activity, the definition of a dilation with centre I and ratio k (vector IM' = k vector I) was given, followed by some exercises of writing vector equalities defining the image of a point through a given dilation, done independently of any use of the software.

Next, in part II, students were asked again to draw a polygon and to observe the images of the polygon through dilations with centre a fixed point and various ratios, which they had to change in a discrete way. Then they were asked to generalise by giving a condition on the ratio for obtaining a smaller (with respect to a larger) image, or an image having the same (with respect to one having a different) orientation. Obviously, the use of the drag mode was very little prompted in those activities. The software was mainly used to provide a great number of dilations and to facilitate a conjecture about a general rule, which students were asked to generalise by induction, without proving it. Then, a nearly complete proof was given to students, who only had to fill some blanks left in some vector equalities of the proof. What emerged from those activities is *the strong guidance* of the students, the *weak use of the software, the absence of autonomous experimentation* on the part of the students.

A second striking feature of the scenario was the systematic repetition of the same construction task: the construction in Cabri, then in a paper-and-pencil environment. When asked by the other teachers why she wanted this repetition, the teacher explained that the students had to do the construction in paper and pencil to really understand it. She believed that students understood that the image of a straight line is a straight line only if they construct it by hand with a straightedge. The fact that a straightedge is also an instrument was completely without relevance for her. It was as if she viewed working in paper and pencil as context free and purely abstract.

We interpret these design choices of the teacher as coming from the belief that working with technology is good for enlarging the imagery, intuition, and concrete examples associated with mathematical concepts, but that the real mathematical work should be disconnected from any context and instrument and that a paper-and-pencil environment provided this absence of context.

5. CONTRASTING WITH A REWRITING OF THE SCENARIO DILATION BY ANOTHER TEACHER

The following year, one of the experienced teachers modified the first version of the scenario Dilation. As an example of the modifications, let us mention Activity 1 (Figure 2) as it was changed (Figure 3).

Study of a new transformation, Dilation
In the toolbox Transformation of Cabri, in addition to reflection and point symmetry, there is the tool Dilation. You will study this transformation.
Create a point I; edit a number k by using 2.5 as the starting value; by means of the tool Polygon, create a quadrilateral ABCD and construct its image through the dilation with centre I and ratio k (tool Dilation, designate the quadrilateral, then centre I and number k). Characterise the obtained image.
(Do not hesitate to drag polygon ABCD, points A, B, C, and D, centre I, and to modify number k; do not forget that you can display measures with tool Distance and length and that a calculator is available within Cabri).
Give to k a negative value (choose in a first step – 0.5) and complete the previous characterisation (do not hesitate to vary k again).

Figure 3. Version 2 of activity 1 of scenario Dilation

Version 2 condensed in only one activity the two activities of version 1. In contrast to version 1, it gives a central place to dragging and does not ask students to perform discrete measures. Version 2 gives more autonomy to students in the observation. The text mentions only a range of possible tools to be used. Version 2 is more open-ended and simultaneously prompts students to make more extensive use of available tools. This is confirmed by the other activities of the revised scenario: use of the tool Locus to explore the set of images of a point belonging to a polygon; use of Point symmetry to determine the centre and the ratio of a dilation, vectors, grid, system of axes, equation of a line... Version 2 also eliminated the repetition of the same tasks in both environments.

The revision of scenario Dilation by an experienced teacher in both teaching and use of technology focussed on both a greater integration of Cabri in the task and a greater autonomy of students, in particular, in the exploration phase. The increased number of tools to be used requires, of course, a high command of these tools by students and thus a long-term use of Cabri. In terms of perturbations, it is as if both novice teachers did not dare change too much their teaching and gave small, and not interrelated, activities with a weak intervention of software. Their choices minimised the changes implied by the use of technology, whereas the revised version took into account the perturbations and changed the tasks in a deeper way.

6. EVOLUTION OF THE ROLE OF TECHNOLOGY IN THE TASKS FOR EXPERIENCED TEACHERS

Numerous research papers (Hoelzl, 1996; Jones, 1997; Noss and Hoyles, 1996) stress how the context shapes the students' solution strategies when they are faced with a problem. Sharing this point of view, we also claim that the problem itself is shaped by the context. Features of a computer environment may play a crucial role on the type of task the students have to solve, thus affecting the possible strategies and the cognitive outcome of the task (Laborde, 1995).

As stated above, the scenarios written by novice teachers gave a restricted place to the intervention of the software. It was mainly used for visualising.

6.1 Enlarging the Range of Tools for Exploration

The experienced teachers extended the use of the software to favour a larger and more autonomous exploration phase by students, as shown above (Figure 3) on one example. It has to be noted that the students did not immediately fully use the Cabri tools for exploration. It was only after one year that, for example the teachers gave to students the hint of using Trace for giving evidence of an invariant point. For example, in the first version of scenario Vectors (Figure 2), one of the experienced teachers did not use this possibility in the study of the sum of two vectors. It is only in version 2 that he gave the following activity:

> Let there be two points A and B. Let there be a point M and vectors MA and MB. With Cabri construct the vector MC which is the vector with origin M and is the sum of vectors MA and MB. Apply the tool Trace to MC and make M vary. What do you observe ? Justify your observation. Use this to obtain C without using the Cabri tool Sum of vectors.

One can see easily that vector MC is permanently passing through an invariant point which seems to be the midpoint of AB (Figure 4.)

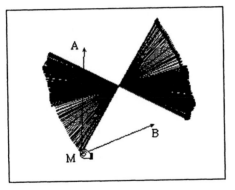

Figure 4. Version 2 vectors activity

The use of Trace was successfully reapplied on their own by students in other exploring activities.

In the latter use of Trace, the visualisation provided by technology is the source of a mathematical question. An interaction between visualisation and mathematical knowledge may also be used to support reasoning, as in the following activity, which teachers planned to introduce in version 3 of the scenario Vectors:

> Create three points A, B, and C and triangle ABC. Create any point M. With Cabri, construct the vector MD with origin M, which is the sum of vectors MA and MB. Then construct vector MS which is the sum of vectors MC and MD. By dragging M find the position of M such that vector MS is vector 0. Characterise this position in triangle ABC. (Figure 5).

By dragging M, it is possible to observe that vector MS = vector 0 when vector MC is opposite to vector MD. This observation is easy to be interpreted by a vector equality and thus justified from vector MS = vector MC + vector MD. Then, geometrically interpreting vector MC = - vector MD leads to the fact that M is the midpoint of C and D. But vector MC is the sum of vectors MB and MA and hence equal to 2 vector MI where I is the midpoint of AB (see Figure 4 example above). M is situated from C at two thirds of segment CI (Figure 6). In this reasoning, there is a back-and-forth process between what is seen on the screen and theoretical knowledge in mathematics. Technology is scaffolding the elaboration of the solution process.

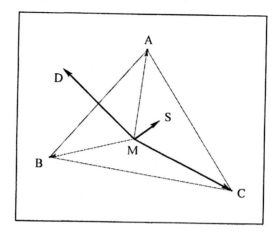

Figure 5. Activity planned for version 3 of scenario Vectors

We consider that in this latter use, technology affects reasoning in a deeper way. It is not by chance that even experienced teachers in using Cabri did not favour this opportunity in the first versions of scenarios. It requires a deeper knowledge of technology, a greater experience of solving problems with Cabri, and possibly also a change in the nature of mathematical activity which is not necessarily accepted by teachers.

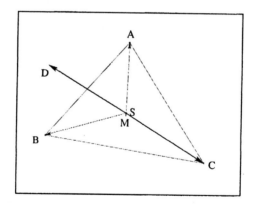

Figure 6. Vector MS = vector 0, vector MC = -vector MD

6.2 New Kinds of Tasks

The later versions of experienced teachers introduced two new kinds of tasks giving another role to technology in their scenarios:

- tasks in which the environment allows efficient strategies which are not possible to perform in a paper-and-pencil environment;
- tasks raised by the computer context, for example, tasks which can be carried out only in the computer environment.

Tasks allowing new solving strategies. The following is an example of the first kind of tasks in the scenario Vectors: "Construct a triangle ABC from the given points B, C, and G the centroid of triangle ABC." A can be constructed as satisfying the vectorial relation:

vector GA + vector GB + vector GC = vector 0. (1)

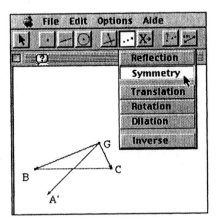

Figure 7. Construction of the image of A' through a point symmetry around G

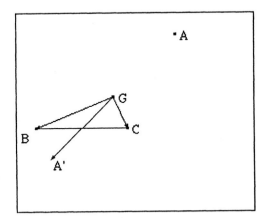

Figure 8. Result of the construction

A is constructed as the symmetrical point with respect to G of the endpoint of the vector sum of the two vectors GB and GC (Figures 7 and 8).

Cabri contributes to linking the algebraic aspects of vectors to the geometrical aspects. Relation (1) is restricted in paper-and-pencil environment to algebraic calculations, whereas in Cabri it also receives a geometrical meaning since it is a tool of construction. It offers a new connection in the conceptual field of vectors (Vergnaud, 1991) or in the *web* of vectors (Noss & Hoyles, 1996).

Tasks making sense only in the environment. The second kind of tasks involves mainly two categories of tasks:

- the "black box" situations
- the prediction tasks

In the black box situations, the students are given a diagram on the screen of the computer and they are asked questions about it. This kind of situation was used in our scenarios for introducing new transformations. A point P and its image P' through the unknown transformation were given to the students. They could move P and observe the subsequent effect on P'. Students were asked to find the properties of the unknown transformation by means of this black box. In such a task, students must ask themselves questions about the transformation: Does it preserve collinearity? Does it preserve distance? Does it have invariant points?

Cabri can be used to design experiments and get empirical answers. For example, one may redefine P as belonging to any given straight line and obtain the image of this line as the Locus of P' depending on the variable point P. This requires the use of two specific tools of Cabri: Redefinition and Locus. It presupposes that the students not only master their use, but also decide to use them. This decision actually involves mathematical knowledge: the fact that the image of a figure is the set of images of points of a figure; this is often completely implicit in our curricula but it presents a conceptual cut (even an obstacle probably from both cognitive and didactical origin) with the view of a figure as an entity and not as a set of points.

Displayed below are diagrams in which the unknown transformation is an affine symmetry. By redefining P as a point on a line, it is possible to see that the image of a straight line seems to be a line; by redefining P as a point on a circle, it becomes obvious that the image of a circle is not a circle (Jahn, 1998).

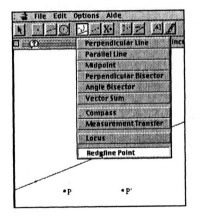

Figure 9. Redefining the given point P

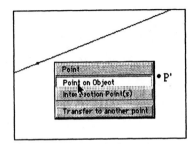

Figure 10. ... as a point on ...

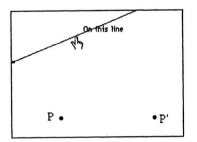

Figure 11. ... a line

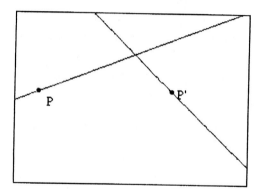

Figure 12. Locus of P' when P is moving on a line

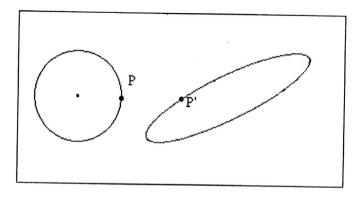

Figure 13. Locus of P' when P is moving on a circle

Such a task offers a very different point of view on the notion of geometrical transformation. Instead of studying the effects of a known transformation, students are asked to characterise the transformation by means of its properties. Of course, this may be an attractive task only if some exotic transformations, and not only the usual ones, are given to students for investigation. Theorems of invariance receive a new meaning in this kind of task: they are tools for identifying the category to which the unknown transformation belongs. An effect of this kind of task is that students may understand the purpose of studying all these theorems about invariant elements of transformations. The invariance properties become remarkable phenomena instead of being the routine.

Although the experienced teachers already were familiar with these kinds of tasks, they introduced them in the process of writing scenarios only late in this project. This shows that it takes time to integrate already known kinds of tasks into new topics. It is not just a question of applying a given task, but of reconsidering mathematics involved in the notion to be taught using the perspective of a black box task. Let us comment this latter claim on one example.

Dilation was introduced as a black box only in version 3 after vivid discussions between a researcher and one of the experienced teachers. P and its image P ' through an unknown transformation (actually a dilation with ratio 1.5) were displayed on the screen. It was possible to drag P anywhere in the screen. It was a proposal of the researcher that the teacher hesitated to accept. After he decided to accept and wrote himself a sequence of activities introducing dilation as an unknown transformation, he carried out this sequence in his own class. He was impressed by the success of his students who used more tools of the software that he would have thought. On their own, the students used Trace, Locus, and Redefinition.

The teacher was used to designing black boxes for exploring properties of figures, but he was reluctant to extend this to properties of transformations (second order properties). From his point of view, it seemed too complex for students. From that point on, the teacher became very confident in this type of task for studying transformations and recommended it warmly to other teachers. It seems that the reluctance he expressed was due to his belief that the task was too demanding in terms of use of software and conceptual reasoning from the students. What we assumed before starting the study, related to the positive effect of a dialectical link to be constructed between the new experiences of teachers and those of their students, has been achieved on this particular point. The teacher really appreciated the new type of situation only after having experimented it with students. This type of situation "challenged his beliefs" (in terms of Cooney & Krainer, 1996, p.1168) about the kind of problems he could propose and, as such, was the source of change in his practice.

6.3 The Reference to Technology in Synthesis Phases

It is only during the second year of the project that one of the experienced teachers included technology in the synthesis phases of his teaching. He started pointing out knowledge not only by referring to mathematics but also to some related aspects of Cabri. This is illustrated in the scenario Vectors.

The notion of direction of a vector is not easy for students to understand. There is a paradox that this notion is understood as soon as the notion of vector is acquired, but to acquire the notion of vector the students need to understand the notion of direction. The use of the two kinds of pointers in Cabri showed the students that when the vector is moved by the usual pointer, its coordinates remain unchanged, while they are changed when the vector is rotated by the pointer Rotate although its norm is unchanged. So the teacher introduced the Cabri property, "The coordinates of a vector are modified by the Rotate pointer," which lead to the usual property "The coordinates of a vector depend on the direction of the vector." The pointer of Cabri played a *mediation role* in Vygotskian terms.

7. EVOLUTION OF THE ROLE GIVEN TO TECHNOLOGY BY THE TEACHERS

7.1 Stages in the Evolution

From the analysis of the written scenarios, we could sketch a gradation in the extent of integration of technology into teaching:

- scarce use of technology for activities not really related to the teaching content: It may happen that teachers use computers for creating sessions for open problem solving, three or four times during the year, but these sessions are not part of the course and no reference is made to these sessions during the ordinary lessons;
- use of computers for activities including previously introduced notions: The computer offers opportunities for "hands on" sessions in which students are more autonomous, but the notions which are objects of teaching have been introduced in an usual way in a paper and pencil environment;
- the teacher introduces mathematical content through technology and not only using technology on previously introduced mathematical notions: This implies that reference situations based on technology are created which may strongly affect the meaning of these notions;
- tasks are given which favour an interplay between theoretical knowledge and instrumental knowledge: The use of technology is intrinsically linked to the mathematical task;
- avoiding inflation of time because of technology: Rather than requiring that everything be constructed with the computer by students, instead seeking critical tasks with technology;
- in addition to content introduced through technology, the teacher "institutionalises" the notions to be memorised by referring to some elements of the computer environment.

It is clear that the latter ways of integrating computers require a long-term use of technology. There must be no need for the teacher to repeat how to use such-or-such a command.

This gradation results directly from our observations of the evolution of the teachers during the project. However, it is also supported by several reports coming from experimental teaching with technology or research about integrating technology in mathematics teaching.

Bottino and Furinghetti (1998) report about two teachers trying on their own to integrate the use of software in mathematics teaching. It is important to note that they were experienced mathematics teachers, competent in the classroom use of computers. Both teachers used technology for enriching topics previously taught and not for creating new scenarios. One of the teachers even advocated strongly the necessity of first developing the topics without the computer, since otherwise students may not have a real understanding of what has taken place. Heid (1995) even claims that technology can be considered by teachers as threatening their own knowledge of mathematics.

The introduction of technology for the new introduction of mathematical notion requires both a certain view of mathematical learning (see below § VIII) and a deep change about the way of considering the mathematical notions. Perturbation is minimised when technology is used only to assist the usual way of presenting the notions. This gradation can be also related to the distinction made by Pea (1985): In the first two steps of the gradation technology is rather used as an amplifier. It is only in the subsequent steps that it contributes to the reorganisation of the mathematical content knowledge by linking it intrinsically to technology: The meaning of mathematical knowledge is constructed through technology.

7.2 Overcoming the Perturbation

The more technology was integrated into the scenarios, the more time teachers needed. Versions 2 or 3 of the scenarios were dramatically time consuming. It is a quite usual phenomenon that any kind of teaching innovation provokes inflation of time. Schneider (1999) reported on teaching about logarithms and exponentials based on the use of the TI 92, which took 40 hours of teaching time instead of the usual nine hours.

Guin and Trouche (1999) claimed that the cognitive reorganisation mentioned by Pea cannot take place without a complete reorganisation of study time, since observation and confrontation of results by groups takes more time. They give examples of interplay between different kinds of student work in teaching that integrated the use of Derive on the TI 92: work with technology and work without technology; work of one student demonstrating in front of the classroom; work in groups; long-term problems which have to be solved outside the classroom. They add that such a reorganisation of time and work requires the teacher to have a thorough knowledge of the calculator and to play various roles according to the type of work given to the students. In our project, the interaction between the tools provided by Cabri like Trace (§VI.1) and the mathematical task was not integrated at the beginning of the scenarios but after teachers could see the pedagogical use of these tools.

We consider that this flexibility of the teacher with respect to his/her role in the classroom can only be the result of a long-term adaptation process of the teacher. It has very often been claimed that technology changes the role of the teacher, from a teacher-directed style to one of guiding and helping students (Farrel, 1996). But completely integrating technology into the teaching seems to require not simply a change of role but the ability to play different roles and to switch from one role to another one.

We could observe in our project this introduction over time of various roles played by the teacher. The inflation of time due to a great number of open tasks with technology led the teachers, after one or two years, to choose the tasks involving technology, seeking simple, critical, computer-based tasks likely to be very efficient in terms of learning, and to have less recourse to lengthy and open tasks.

The teachers also attempted to find an optimal balance between what is demonstrated by the teacher on the LCD display and what is done by students, between what is ready made and given on the calculators to students and what has to be done by the students with the software. After two years, the teachers preferred to give a ready-made macro-construction of the multiplication of a vector by a number to be explored and interpreted, rather than to be constructed by the students themselves. One may have the impression that teachers decided to move to a teaching model in which the student activity is following the teacher demonstration and which would give a restricted place to student autonomy and knowledge construction. This is not at all the case. As in a paper-and-pencil environment in which it is impossible to ask students to reconstruct all mathematics by well-chosen tasks, the teachers decided to select carefully the critical steps in knowledge construction in which students had to play the major role. The teachers were aware that they had too greatly increased their demands on students and that they had to analyse in depth those demands in order to select the most decisive in terms of learning. The use of the LCD display also contributed to make knowledge socially shared among the students.

After some time teachers decided to give homework requiring the use of technology. It not only solved some time problems, but also gave a more institutional status to the use of technology for the students.

We can assume that technology will penetrate the classroom more and more, and that teachers should be able to develop this flexibility. Preservice teacher education should certainly contribute to the learning of such flexibility, or at least make the students teachers aware of it.

Upon examination of the changes that occurred over the last three years, it seems that the use of technology became a more usual and ordinary element of the classroom, less spectacular, calling for less complex tasks, but involved in more events of the school activities of the student, possibly beyond the class. As a result, assessment in the classroom in the last year included tasks in computer-based environments.

8. LEARNING HYPOTHESES : EPISTEMOLOGICAL BELIEFS

In this project, the introduction of technology turned out to provoke different kinds of reactions from the teachers and to give rise to unstable teaching scenarios, subject to numerous changes. We will comment on two phenomena and propose to link them with the beliefs of teachers about learning.

8.1 An Epistemological View of Geometry

One of the teachers did not rely on computer-based activities for the learning of geometry, and in addition to computer activities proposed similar paper-and-pencil tasks without being aware that sometimes a paper-and-pencil task is less demanding in terms of knowledge and involves perceptive strategies rather than strategies based on theoretical properties.

We interpret this behaviour as being linked to the conception of a paper-and-pencil environment as not being a context. Knowing how to perform something in a paper-and-pencil environment would be, for this teacher, the affirmation of a decontextualised knowledge. Noss and Hoyles (1996, p. 48) propose an alternative view of abstraction as not necessarily linked to decontextualisation and "as a process of connection rather than ascension." They add that the "situated, the activity based, the experiential can contain within it the seeds for something more general" (p.49).

Another reason for such a behaviour may be also explained by the institutional context. Even if all kinds of calculators are allowed in our French national evaluation, all tasks are given in a paper-and-pencil environment. The teacher stays within this context to be sure that students are able to perform the tasks in this latter environment. It means that she was not confident that students learned something general from the tasks in a technological environment, which is very close to the first interpretation of her behaviour.

8.2 The Complexification of Tasks

The experienced teachers were willing to integrate technology into the tasks they gave. It should be noted that it took time for them to carry out a real integration of technology in the tasks they designed. But integrating technology gave rise to numerous and complex tasks: Instead of teaching vectors for two weeks, it took two months! Why this increase of demands from the teacher? Again, this may be interpreted as the uncertainty of the teacher about the learning allowed by tasks they provided. In order to be sure that students learned something from this new kind of task, the teachers increased the level of complexity.

Only an analysis of each task in terms of conceptual demands and a long-term observation of the behaviours of students may bring some assurance about their potential for learning. This cannot be done in a short time and by an isolated teacher. It requires teamwork. The other key aspect of our project is the change of the teacher during the project, confirming all observations made by similar studies about teachers (for example, Wilson & Goldenberg, 1998; Schneider, 1999). But our project required time and its impact was quite limited: four teachers involved in a three-year project. To what extent is it possible to stimulate such a change on a large scale through preservice or inservice teacher education?

This is the reason why we call for the development of research on technology-based teaching of mathematics. We need empirical studies for collecting data and analysing the type of complexity teachers are faced with when introducing technologies in their teaching. Our wish would be to see such "teaching/learning" situations for teachers developed in the world for the purpose of gaining more experience in this domain and to use them in teacher education.

REFERENCES

Boero, P., Dapueto, C., & Parenti, L. (1996). Didactics of mathematics and the professional knowledge of teachers. In A. Bishop, et al. (Eds.), *International Handbook of Mathematics Education* (Part 2, pp.1097-1121). Dordrecht: Kluwer Academic.

Boero, P. M., Dapueto C., & Parenti L. (1996). Didactic of Mathematics and the Professional Knowledge of Teachers. In A. Bishop, K. Clements, C. Keitel, J. Kilpatrick, C. Laborde (Eds.), *International Handbook of Mathematics Education,*(Part two, pp.1097-1211). Dordrecht: Kluwer Academic..

Bottino, R. M. & Furinghetti F. (1998). The computer in mathematics teaching: Scenes from the classroom. In D. Tinsley D. & D. Johnson (Eds.), *Information and Communications Technologies in School Mathematics* (pp.131-139). London: Chapman & Hall.

Cooney, T. & Krainer, K. (1996). Inservice mathematics teacher education: The importance of listening. In A. Bishop, K. Clements, C. Keitel, J. Kilpatrick, C. Laborde (Eds.), *International Handbook of Mathematics Education* (Part two, pp.1155-1185). Dordrecht: Kluwer Academic.

Farrel, A. (1996). Roles and behaviours in technology-integrated precalculus classrooms. *Journal of Mathematical Behaviour, 15*, 35-53.

Guin, D. & Trouche, L. (1999). The complex process of converting tools into mathematical instruments: The case of calculators *International Journal of Computers for Mathematical Learning, 3*(3), 195-227.

Heid, K. (1995). The interplay of mathematical understandings: Facility with a computer algebra program and the learning of mathematics. *Proceedings of the 17th annual meeting of the North American Chapter of PME* (pp. 221-225). Colombus, OH.

Hoelzl, R (1996). How does 'dragging' affect the learning of geometry? *International Journal of Computers for Mathematical Learning, 1*(2), 169-187.

Jahn, A.P (1998). *Des transformations de figure aux transformations ponctuelles: étude d'une séquence d'enseignement avec Cabri-géomètre*. Thèse de l'Université Joseph Fourier, Grenoble.

Jones, K (1997). Children learning to specify geometrical relationships using a dynamic geometry package. In E. Pehkonen (Ed.), *Proceedings of the 21st Conference of the International Group for the Psychology of Mathematics Education, 3*, 121-128. Helsinki, Finland.

Laborde, C. (1995). Designing tasks for learning geometry in a computer-based environment. In L. Burton & B. Jaworski (Eds.), *Technology in Mathematics Teaching - a bridge between teaching and learning* (pp.35-68). London: Chartwell-Bratt.

Noss, R. & Hoyles, C. (1996). *Windows on mathematical meanings - Learning cultures and computers*. Dordrecht: Kluwer Academic.

Pea, R. (1985). Beyond amplification: Using the computer to reorganise mental functioning. *Educational Psychologist, 20*(4), 167-182.

Schneider, E. (1999). Mathematische bildung trotz und mit dem TI 92. In G. Kadunz, G. Ossimitz, W. Peschek, E. Schneider, B. Winkelmann (Eds.), *Mathematische bildung und neue technologien* (pp.287-294). Leipzig: B.G. Teubner.

Vergnaud, G. (1991). La theorie des champs conceptuels. *Recherches en didactique des mathematiques, 10*(2.3), 133-169.

Wilson, M. & Goldenberg, P. (1998). Some Conceptions are difficult to change: One middle school mathematics teacher's struggle. *Journal of Mathematics Teacher Education, 1*(3), 269-293.

University Joseph Fourier and Institute of Teacher Education
Grenoble
France

NOTES

[i] It was funded by the Region Rhone Alpes (1994-1997) and the National Institute for Pedagogical Research (INRP) of France. The title of the project is : "Conception et evaluation de scenarios

d'enseignement avec Cabri-geometre" (Design and assessment of teaching scenarios with Cabri-geometry).

[ii] The scenarios, their presentation, and their comments are published in two booklets (1997 and 1998) available at Laboratoire Leibniz-IMAG.

FRED GOFFREE AND WIL OONK

DIGITIZING REAL TEACHING PRACTICE FOR TEACHER EDUCATION PROGRAMMES: THE MILE APPROACH

ABSTRACT. This chapter will give readers insight into the potential of using information technology in primary school mathematics teacher education. The emphasis will be placed on describing the possibilities that are available to teacher education students, the underlying theoretical orientation, and the perspective of finding a promising approach to some all too familiar problems in teacher education. The technology involved will not be discussed. The illustrations are taken from both the (digitally recorded) primary school teaching environment and the colleges of education, in which student teachers investigated this environment during the first two years of the MILE project in the Netherlands. This took place in pilot projects at 15 colleges during the 1997-1998 school year. One of these pilot projects focused on the case of two teacher education students of the Amsterdam College of Higher Professional Education, who were tutored by Wil Oonk. This is referred to below as the D&H case.

1. TEACHER EDUCATION

To be able to place the information in this chapter in its proper perspective, it may be necessary to have some knowledge of Dutch primary school teacher education (see Goffree & Oonk, 1999). The training of primary school mathematics teachers, which takes place in the Netherlands in colleges of education of institutes for higher vocational education, essentially involves teaching pre-service teachers (pedagogical) content knowledge and pedagogics and providing them with the opportunity to do interrelated fieldwork in primary schools. The pre-service teachers then process the information they acquire and their experiences actively, reflectively, and constructively. Similarly to many other countries in the western world, a phenomenon currently taking place in the Netherlands is that attention to content and pedagogical content knowledge in the curricula of colleges of education is being drastically reduced in favour of general professional teaching skills. In our opinion, the causes of this can be found in the education curricula of the past, in which isolated attention to school subjects (disciplines) produced an incoherent and fragmented form of teacher education. This was augmented by the unfamiliarity of policy-makers and general curriculum developers with the high standards required of primary school mathematics teachers and, even more so, with the role that "mathematics" as a school subject can play in learning general teaching skills. The possibilities of incorporating a digital representation of real-time mathematics teaching practice into teacher education programmes means that many

I wonder if that is still true

F.-L. Lin & T. J. Cooney (Eds.) Making Sense of Mathematics Teacher Education, 111—145.

misunderstandings and wrongful assumptions that have been made in this respect can be cleared up.

To justify our claims, it will, however, be necessary to outline the background theory in addition to providing our views on the use of the digital learning environment. Furthermore, the results of evaluation studies on the work floor (the colleges of education) have to be included. In this chapter, all three elements will be discussed.

2. SEVEN THEORETICAL ORIENTATIONS

With respect to the conceptual elaborations, we will focus on the 7 theoretical orientations that served to inspire the designers of the learning environment in both the way it was shaped and its use by pre-service teachers.

It should come as no surprise that the development work for MILE, which is what we will call this digital learning environment from now on, is a continuation of the developmental research that has acquired international esteem through the Freudenthal Institute. This applies not only to the method in which designing and researching cyclically alternate in the work field (Gravemeijer,1995), but also to the content that is described in the aforementioned article (Goffree & Oonk, 1999) in both models for the teacher education programme ("Wiskobas" from 1979 and "National Task Force'" from 1998).

The second orientation concerns the concept of practical knowledge, which was introduced by Elbaz in 1983 and has since been interpreted and expanded in many ways. Donald Schön has provided the third source of inspiration. His book, *The Reflective Practitioner*, has sparked new ideas in many people, including the designers of learning environments for teacher education programmes. "Practical knowledge" and "reflective practice" are to all intents and purposes two ideas that have shaken the world of teacher educators. There is an immense number of publications in both areas. The nature of (practical) knowledge in research of teaching was mapped out around 1994 (Fenstermacher, 1994). This is less true of our fourth orientation—the narratives in teaching, learning, and learning to teach. It would seem that people's beliefs in these areas are gradually becoming established (McEwan & Egan, 1995). This is, however, somewhat limited compared with the latter two orientations and that which follows. Orientation number 5 concerns the idea of knowledge construction related to the socio-constructivist approach as described in the work of Paul Cobb, who in turn drew his inspiration from Kilpatrick (1987) and Schoenfeld (1987). The work of Lampert and Ball (1998) still has an especially large impact on MILE. Because of their efforts, the idea of "investigating real practice in order to learn from practice" has become a key issue. The above orientations not only indicate how we understand the acquisition of knowledge, but also what we mean by the term knowledge itself. In the rest of this chapter, that view on knowledge also displays post-structural features. (Delandshere & Petrosky, 1994). Lastly, we would like to mention the work of Allan Tough (1971) on teaching adults. We are reminded of his adult learning projects, when we think of the pre-service teachers who carried out MILE investigations based on their own research questions.

3.   POINT OF DEPARTURE IN TEACHING PRACTICE

The availability of digitized real teaching practice has made it possible to give teacher education programmes a concrete, real-life basis. For educators in the Netherlands, this has led to a significant U-turn in the way they think about education programmes. Similarly to most of their colleagues in other countries, they were accustomed to using the "theory," whatever it may mean, as their starting point in drawing up curricula for pre-service teachers and for educating them. Additionally, in many school-based teacher education curricula and related discussions (Zeichner, 1981; Tabachnick & Zeichner, 1991), which to this very day have enriched thoughts regarding teacher education, assuming actual practice as the underlying principle has a different character than taking the (digitized) MILE practice as a starting point. It should be noted that when teacher educators (especially in the Netherlands) discuss "the practice of teaching." they may mean the fieldwork their students completed during the training. The activities of the teacher education students has a strong affective character in the first instance (Fenstermacher (1994) uses terms like intentions, desires, frustrations, aspirations, disappointments and surprises), whereas in the second—the digitized practice of MILE—the cognitive element dominates. But amongst the users of MILE, there are still educators who adhere to the old point of departure. This is, of course, still a viable approach, but it strips the new learning environment of one of its essential features. An aspect of this is that the (constructed) knowledge acquired by the students in MILE has different characteristics than was previously the case. It is, amongst other things, by definition reflective and is not experienced as a uniform truth from the word go. The significance that students attach to, and the way they value, the (practical) knowledge they acquire is also likely to be different when working with MILE. The backgrounds and possibilities of MILE described above place well-known bottlenecks in present-day teacher education programmes in a new perspective. The much discussed gap between theory and practice, the doubts concerning learning from practice in schools and the resistance of teacher education students to reflection may, in our opinion, eventually disappear if MILE is fully integrated into the Teacher Education Curriculum.
     In the following sections, these points will be discussed in more detail.

4.   MAKING PRACTICAL KNOWLEDGE AVAILABLE FOR TEACHER EDUCATION STUDENTS

4.1   Knowledge: Acquisition and Application

In general, the curricula of teacher education courses contain the knowledge that students are deemed to learn mainly in the condensed form of summaries and lists of facts, arguments, rules, and principles. These are furthermore essentially fabrications in what Bruner (1986) refers to as the logico-scientific mode of thought: "There are two modes of cognitive functioning, two modes of thought, each providing distinctive ways of ordering experience, of constructing reality. The two (though complementary) are irreducible to one another." Both modes of thinking, of "knowing how," differ on many points: the way in which knowledge is acquired, what it consists of, how it is arranged, what is accepted as "truth," the line of thought that students follow, how theories are proved empirically, where persuasive arguments come from, the link with real-life situations, and the way in which students master this form of expertise (the type of knowledge acquisition).

In teacher education programmes, there is furthermore hardly any time to design useful conceptual schemata. Reference structures in which new knowledge can be arranged and "stored" can be only rarely created, and reflection, for example, for the purpose of establishing a relationship between theory and practice, is virtually impossible. This is also due to the large geographical distance between theory in college and the practice in classrooms.

Epistemology of professional knowledge. Whoever regards teacher education in terms of knowledge, knowledge acquisition, and knowledge application will not escape the impression that the epistemology of teachers' professional knowledge is a neglected aspect of the programme. If theory assumes the form described by Bruner as "logico-scientific," and if education programmes are dominated by this sort of theoretical knowledge, it would seem obvious that pre-service teachers (who moreover come from a school environment where knowledge and theory have effectively the same meaning) acquire a way of knowing that is characterized by as dualistic and regarded as "absolute knowing" by Baxter Magdola (see Cooney's chapter). In addition, how are teacher education students supposed to reach the third level of reflective thinking as a matter of course using this organization (structure) of the professional knowledge base, if it is recognized that knowledge is contextual as argued by King and Kitchener (as is refered to in Cooney's chapter). Looked at in this way, it seems that throughout the past century, we have continually put a great deal of effort into maintaining the gap in teacher education between theory and practice. In this respect, it should be remarked that this does not apply to in-service teacher education. The work of Jaworski, Cobb and Krainer in this book shows, for example, that (action) research of their own practice can bring teachers into contact with "theory" in an especially natural way and in line with their own requirements. However, this type of practice that has a large degree of teacher involvement is not available for pre-service teachers.

Technical rationality. In this context, it is particularly relevant to observe that technical rationality (Schön, 1983) dominates the view on knowledge and theory outlined above and that it enjoyed a great deal of support at the time of the "Teacher's Thinking" studies. In short, the idea was that teaching consisted of the application of theoretical knowledge. People searched for the way in which teaching experts did this. It took a long time for them to realize that it did not work like this in classrooms. The idea of the reflective practitioner and Elbaz's study of the English teacher Sara, in which the concept of "practical knowledge" was launched in teaching research, saw the light of day in the same year—1983.

Since Elbaz (1983), practical knowledge has, however, differentiated into various dimensions and there has been a shift in people's insights into its characteristics.

4.2 Practice Knowledge and Practical Knowledge

Following on from the Dutch educationalist, N. Verloop (1991), we have tried to capture the specific character and the different dimensions of the term "practice knowledge," which by definition includes "personal," "practical," "experimental," "content," "pedagogical content," "curriculum," "subjective," "case," and "strategic" knowledge. All these concepts have therefore been used in a different context in various research projects. In our search for a comprehensive term for the complicated structure of forces that drive a teacher during his or her career, these all support the assertion that "practice knowledge" cannot be described in one dimension. This is because practice knowledge has a personal dimension; it has a user's side, is related to practical experience, concerns the subject matter, the teaching methodology, knowledge of the curriculum and textbooks, is coloured by individual beliefs, is supplemented by cases from real teaching practice, and has something that helps teachers make the right decisions under difficult circumstances.

In addition to that, "practice knowledge" we generally see in the context of pre-service teacher education where familiarisation with "real teaching practice" has a different character than in the case of in-service courses. The distinction between "formal knowledge" and "practical knowledge" (Fenstermacher, 1994) in teacher education is not as easy to make as it is for in-service teachers. The integration of practical and formal knowledge will be expressed in reflective conversations and theoretical reflections. It will also become apparent that we are not satisfied with the term "practice knowledge" as a combination of the terms "knowledge" and "practice."

Educative power. Since "knowledge" is not paramount in every dimension, we are convinced that using this term is inadequate in conveying what we actually mean. Jaworski uses, following on from Cooney, the term "power"—mathematical power as a capability to solve mathematical problems, pedagogical power as a capability to solve pedagogical problems in and possibly outside the classroom. Jaworski also refers to "educative power," a concept that is used by Lampert in a certain sense to indicate that her real teaching practice on laser disc requires further processing in order to become "educative" (Lampert & Ball, 1998).

Nor are "power" and "capability" exactly the terms we are looking for to replace "knowledge". They can, however, be used here in addition to the previously named characteristics to illustrate the complexity of the phenomenon which until now has been referred to as practical knowledge.

Narrative. For the time being, we will carry on using "practice knowledge." By nature, practice knowledge is context-dependent and has to be gained from real teaching practice. Because of this, it is stored and committed to memory in the form of narratives that precipitate a somewhat personal, commonly idiosyncratic organization of knowledge.

Practice knowledge is, according to Gudmundsdottir (1995), "a narrative way of knowing." In this respect, the term "narrative" indicates that there is a story-telling and personal aspect to the acquisition of knowledge that also contains an element of personal experience and individual interpretation. Whoever reads the stories of the teachers (for example, Jackson, 1968; Lortie, 1975; Holt, 1964; Jalongo & Isenberg, 1995) will recognize all these elements and will especially notice the distinction between this mode of thought and thinking in which "propositions are remarkably economic in form (...) are decontextualized, stripped down to their essentials, devoid of detail, emotion, or ambience." (Bruner, 1986).

Reflective practice. It would seem that practice knowledge has potential for teacher education programmes. There are, however, also inherent disadvantages in its use. Practice knowledge may be what gives a professional teacher's actions quality (content, form, direction, result), but with the exception of the actions themselves and sometimes their results, nothing can be seen of what is going on in the mind of the teacher (knowledge, power, capability). Practice knowledge is tacit, but, what is worse, the actual teacher is in many cases unaware of it. The research in the field of beliefs, for instance, is very clear about this. Even the values, as beliefs in action (see Bishop's chapter) do not reveal what is really behind the actions. This is the problem for teacher education programmes. The practice knowledge is present, particularly its application, but it is not explicitly discussed by educators and their student teachers. The educator is capable of discerning what gives the actions of a teacher quality because, in his observations and interpretations, he is guided by his expertise, whereas a teacher education student examines teaching practice with the objective of acquiring expertise. How can a junior teacher education student escape from the grip of this "learning paradox"? Should we perhaps return to a point of departure in theory? We do not think so and, in the following section, we will also attempt to answer Lampert's question of how a real teaching environment can be "educative" for pre-service teachers. MILE will now be described as well—its substance, organization, and possible uses. Because MILE represents real teaching practice, it must be a source of practice knowledge in the sense that has just been described. Practice knowledge is in fact a classic example of "situated cognition," which is an additional challenge to the view of "situated learning" (Herrington, Herrington, Sparrow, & Oliver., 1998), because extracting the cognition from the situation requires a (significant) effort. MILE has internal possibilities for revealing the practice knowledge from teaching situations, but the external role played by an expert (an "educator as a reflective practitioner") is indispensable, because teaching practice needs to be coupled to theory at suitable moments in the learning process of pre-service teachers.

By calling the "educator" a "reflective practitioner," we are retracing the steps of Donald Schön. How are we to understand the work of the educator from Schön's standpoint? In his 1983 study, Schön does not discuss an educator or even a teacher. The first practitioner who shows his reflective practice is the architect, Quist, as he reviews the work of his student, Petra. A school building has to be designed in a hilly landscape. Petra has brought some rough drawings with her, but has to admit that she is stuck. Quist looks at her sketches and is inspired to start working himself, reflectively and thinking out loud. Schön's title for this chapter is "Design as a reflective conversation with the situation." The situation provides the material to start work. The reflective conversation shows what is going on in the head of the designer and reveals what drives him as a reflective practitioner in more than one dimension. This is also how we would like to see a teacher educator who investigates MILE with his student teachers. The question now arises of what are the "situations" and what are the "reflective conversations" in this case.

4.3   The Situations

As previously mentioned, we regard real teaching practice as a source of practical knowledge. The teacher educator makes this source accessible to his pre-service teachers. What does this mean? If we follow Quist in his studio, we see him demonstrate his approach in the design of the school. And doing this he creates a learning environment for Petra, his student. What does the educator do for his teacher education students? This can be regarded as follows he transforms real teaching practice taken from a real life classroom situation into a learning environment for his students. The (representation of) actual practice is "the situation" or the designer's raw material and it can take on various forms - teachers' stories, case studies, critical incidents, videos, teacher education students' fieldwork and multimedia representations. In the following example, we are thinking of a multimedia representation.

An example. Suppose the educator and his student teachers have just been looking into how teacher Paul in grade 5 introduces and tutors problem-oriented group work on percentages. What the educator and his students watched together (approximately ten minutes of teaching) is "the situation," the raw material that has to be processed. In the video fragment, you see the teacher who is, for example, giving out worksheets, asking the children to read the first assignment, letting one pupil read out loud, then asking the whole class what the problem is about, allowing the pupils to speak, and then asking some questions. The last questions are: "Does everybody know what the problem is?" and "Are all the groups ready to start work?" The camera then zooms in on one group. Paul is walking through the classroom; his voice can be heard now and then. He also comes to the group that has been zoomed in on and asks a few questions and responds to the pupils' answers. The video fragment ends before the evaluation of the problem by the whole class takes place.

4.4   The Reflective Conversation

This is the educator's material, "the situation." He now starts working with it reflectively and creates a rich learning environment for his students in the sense meant by Lampert & Ball: "The context of the opportunity—multimedia records of practice—must be coupled with fruitful means of interacting with that context in order for the experience to be educative." The situation (a recording of real practice) is transformed into a learning environment. Just like Quist, the architect, he can—without interruption and without interrupting— think out loud and, if he wants, the "situation" can be stopped, rewound, or wound on ahead to a "future event." By interpreting this teaching fragment as the result of practice knowledge, he shows simultaneously how you can learn from practice, what steers his thoughts, which angles of approach appear to be successful, points of attention that make further reflection necessary (sometimes, theoretical reflection spontaneously occurs— see 4), and last but not least, he expresses that the answers to many of the issues that have been raised are only conjectures and are open for discussion. The result is a case study. The students will later do the same thing when they investigate MILE to collect more information so as to be able to answer a particular question raised in teaching practice or to test a hypothesis.

In addition to his expertise, the educator shows, perhaps between the lines in his reflective conversation, his personal views on mathematics education and his opinion and appreciation of knowledge in general and practice knowledge in particular. Furthermore, he places emphases and makes choices, first in selecting Mile situations and then in choosing an approach for his reflective conversation. This is done from the need to introduce the teacher education students to critical knowledge, as he views them with the fragments presented. Teachers diverge at this point and Mile offers the possibility for every teacher educator to provide the students with a learning environment that is influenced by their ideas and experiences with "actual practice." However, the danger that these students can be manipulated in this manner by their teacher educator is not entirely inconceivable. Fortunately, there is always another discourse in which students can filter through the information presented (ideally in the form of conjectures and questions).

The teacher educator can furthermore assume different roles in this work.

4.5   Three Roles

The problem solver. When considering pedagogic power and its relationship with the creation of a fruitful working climate, Cooney characterizes in his chapter the work of a mathematics teacher in a secondary school as that of a problem solver. In the reflective conversation with a given situation, the educator draws attention to mathematical, didactic, and pedagogic problems that may or may not be seen, dealt with, or solved by the teacher in question. In addition, he looks for the pedagogic power that could be dictating the teacher's actions or the power that may be missing. It might also be possible to reveal any problems of an organizational or, when the children come into the picture, social/emotional nature (Steinbring, 1998).

The educational designer. This is how many people see the mathematics teaching profession (Wittmann, 1995). In this case, the "teacher-in-action" is studied from an angle of approach which includes an examination of the material he uses; how this is adapted for his pupils; the build-up and preparation for his lesson; the set-up of the learning environment; and, on a smaller scale, the architecture of his explanation, and so forth. An educator who has participated in development projects or design teams will be able to apply his expertise in different areas that lie beyond the scope of one lesson.

The investigator. In this role, the educator searches reflectively for specific information in teaching practice. For example, "Can I find out how the teacher, Paul, manages to maintain a good atmosphere in the classroom?"; or "What can I find out about the pupil, Lorenzo, who was noticeable in the basic skills test for the way in which he used the bars of Cuisenaire?" (Markusse, 2000). In this role, the educator distances himself to a certain extent from the teacher when he is following his actions, but places himself in the same position when he wants to follow the learning process of one or more pupils. As an investigator, the educator can also assume the role of an action researcher of his own practical experience. Although a simplified and comparatively safe situation to work from, this digitized practice has the obvious drawback that it cannot be changed. In this case, the reflective conversation will involve signalling investigation-related questions, considering the possibilities of finding information in the given situation, formulating and testing hypotheses, and so forth. (Jaworski, 1998) and (Krainer, 1999).

This is all we want to say at this juncture about the inspiration of Schön. It is high time to look more closely at MILE, which does, after all, provide "the situations" that are used in "the reflective conversation" to reveal practice knowledge.

4.6   MILE as a Collection of Situations

The MILE learning environment (Dolk, Faes, Goffree, Hermsen, & Oonk,1996) is still under development. The most recent version 1.0.0 was installed at all colleges of education (teacher education) in the Netherlands in April and May 1999 on the existing local networks. Version 1.0.0 consists of a core of approximately 42 GB of video clips of real teaching practice and was made by recording 25 interrelated mathematics lessons in grade 2, five in grade 5, and (a year later) five lessons in grade 6 (with 3 video cameras). The lessons were then mounted to one track and placed in categories (divided into teaching fragments). These fragments were considered as small, independently meaningful narratives that together follow the events of an entire lesson. The texts that go with the video clips (short descriptions of the factual content) can be searched through with full text retrieval. The pupils' written material and the teachers' logbooks have also been made available and incorporated into the organized video records.

The MILE developers like to speak of "real teaching practice" to indicate that the programme represents the reality of the educational setting in more ways than fieldwork does. Naturally, Mile has its shortcomings compared to working in the school with actual children and the smell of chalk in the air. Those using the learning environment agree that this representation of practice allows three different research approaches, indicated in the didactic triad model: teacher educator, student, and curriculum material. "Triangulation" (Smaling,1987; Paulien Meijer,1999) as a research methodology aims to map out the reality observed as well as possible, and the three-sided approach to Mile situations offers the possibility to compensate for an overly personal interpretation of one of the perspectives through the correction by another. What remains, however, is that the teacher educator can reveal his personal preferences, during his reflective conversations, from all three perspectives. A variety of these preferences surfaced in the 15 pilot projects mentioned, particularly in the selection of certain Mile fragments. More remarkable were the similarities, and not the differences, in the lists of the most popular fragments. (Goffree, 1998).

The work in MILE, which is described in this chapter, took place with a prototype of the learning environment, in which the technical possibilities and the size of the recorded lessons were still somewhat limited (version 0.0.1). This meant, for example, that the teachers' logbooks and the pupils' material were not available at this stage, and that at some colleges the pioneering students had to work with a stack of CD-ROMS that had to be placed in the CD-ROM drive according to somewhat cryptic software instructions. The students did have access to the database, which they could use to look through all the descriptions of the video clips (after double clicking on a title, the appropriate clip appeared on screen). They could also use a search engine that looked up key words used in the descriptions of the video clips and later in the transcripts of the lessons.

The search engine results are presented as a list of relevant video clip descriptions. If there is a large number of clips matching the search parameters, the students have to select the most relevant ones themselves. In doing this, the students' investigation-related questions mirror the descriptions/search parameters they enter. The descriptions therefore have a double function in that they are used for searching and selecting material.

5. THE CASE OF PAUL: A REFLECTIVE CONVERSATION WITH A SITUATION IN MILE

In the case study described below, we will see how the educator holds a reflective conversation on a teaching situation in MILE. The situation is a 3-minute video clip of the first of a series of five lessons in grade 6 that Paul, the teacher, gives on percentages.

5.1 Episode 1: An Assignment for the Pupils

The situation [MILE]. Paul has just introduced the problem. The mayor of the city of Rommeldam, who has to give permission for a large jumble sale to be held within the next 12 months, is very worried about the large number of visitors that can be expected. This is because it has already been fairly busy this year—a fact that can be seen from the number of occupied spaces in the large car park on the edge of town. The pupils are asked to help the mayor think through his problem. They have been given a recent aerial photograph (worksheet) of the car park, which has enough spaces for 4,000 cars. On the worksheet, it can be seen that not all the spaces are being used. Paul asks some introductory questions and allows the children to answer ("What can you say about it?" "What have you noticed?"). He then gives the children an assignment: "Estimate how many spaces are not being used; try to do it on your own first and then discuss how you should do this in your groups." Paul does not talk about percentages yet at this point. He walks through the class and stops at Jeffrey's group. Jeffrey is prompted to say how he would do this, but instead he answers straight away, "3,000 cars in the car park." Paul does not go into this and he repeats, "Discuss together how you should go about doing this." He wants the children to think about the method they should use and wants them to make a plan of approach together.

We interrupt the video of Paul and his class for a short while to give the educator the opportunity to voice his ideas on the pupils' assignment.

Reflective conversation with the situation. Teacher educator (as a designer and a mathematics problem solver): The children are busy with the worksheet. Before I watch any further, I first want to know what exactly they are working with, what is their assignment and what can be seen on the so-called aerial photograph. Furthermore, I want to do the sums involved myself. The photo appears to be a drawing of a very detailed map of the car park. It is a rectangle built up of four equal quarters. Because the quarters are all the same size, it seems that the designer of the worksheet wanted to make things easy for himself. What should I do? The question on the worksheet reads: "The police have to estimate how many visitors came by car and make a report for the mayor. Estimate this number yourself and explain how you worked out your answer." I therefore have to estimate the fraction of the car park that is occupied; or in this case, it would probably be better to estimate the fraction of the car park that is unoccupied, since this is the smaller of the two. I do not have to count everything because I am making an estimate. This means I only have to count a quarter— one of the four smaller rectangles. If I look at how many empty spaces there are divided over all the rows, I feel that it is safe to say that on average 15 of the 124 spaces are unoccupied. This is about an eighth. It is a pity that there are not that many spaces— I have counted more than estimated. The fraction of spaces that are occupied is therefore 7/8 or 87.5%. This is equal to 3,500 cars. With an average of 4 people per car (a generous estimate to be on the safe side), this means there are therefore 14,000 visitors at that moment. This is how I would do the sum. Now let's see what happens next.

5.2 Episode 2: Group Work with Dennis, Jessica, Julien and Tanja

The situation [MILE]. In the fragment, a group of pupils consisting of Dennis, Jessica, Julien and Tanja start working on the problem. Julien and Tanja are the first children who make contact with each other. Julien whispers to Tanja that it is not necessary to count all the cars; it looks as if Julien is only counting the empty spaces. Dennis has been looking around for a while and then suddenly puts his finger up. In the background, Paul's voice can be heard. He encourages the children to work together effectively, to listen to and to help each other. He does not react to Dennis' finger, which is still raised, but he comes near the group. Dennis then stops holding up his finger and says to the other children in the group, "I reckon, uh...." Paul reacts immediately with, "Exactly, Dennis," and continues on to another group.

Dennis now apparently feels more certain, he takes control and suggests to the group that they should estimate the number of cars in each row. Julien remarks that it would be difficult to estimate how many cars there are per row because there are a lot of cars in some rows and only a few in others. However, Dennis perseveres. He has discovered the symmetry of the figure and explains to the others that you only have to look at one quarter. Does he still have doubts about his discovery? He holds up his finger again. This time, he receives confirmation from Paul. "You've discovered something that you can definitely use!" Dennis then gives each member of the group a task— they each have to count four rows. "Only count the blank spaces," Julien says to Tanja, who still does not really seem to understand what has to be done. A little later, they are all concentrating on counting. Julien and Dennis consult together now and then. Tanja sometimes adds to what Dennis says and asks him questions. Jessica counts busily and does not take part in the group discussion. After a while, Dennis asks the others to write down their results. Paul can be heard in the background saying, "You don't have to count exactly— it's an approximation."

Reflective conversation with the situation. The teacher educator (as an investigator theorizing-on-action, and again as a designer): When I look at this group I see all kinds of images that have been frequently described and analysed in group dynamics. The collaboration in the group is also familiar. I would like to see the whole fragment again so I can go through it step by step. Just look at Dennis. He turns out to be a genuine group leader. He is task-oriented and does not work very much on a social/emotional level. He takes the initiative, hands out tasks, and works with his group to reach a suitable result. He radiates certainty, but on one occasion, he has to seek confirmation from Paul, the class teacher. The conversations in the group mainly take place between the two boys, Dennis and Julien. Tanja asks questions now and then or adds to Dennis' remarks. Jessica does not say anything throughout the scene we have seen and just carefully counts the rows she has been allotted. Am I seeing the same differences here between boys and girls in maths classes that are shown in the research in this area? I remember that girls seem to prefer exact sums instead of guesswork and want security in a safe class atmosphere. (Van den Heuvel-Panhuizen & Vermeer, 1999).

In group work, we make a distinction between co-operative learning (Slavin, 1985) and collaborative learning (Bereiter & Scardamalia, 1992). Paul's style of tutoring is mainly concentrated on the first form. He adopts a remote attitude. He instructs the pupils in general terms and tells them to listen to each other and to discuss how they should solve the problem. He does not start assessing the way the pupils work together. The added value of his approach (open questions, remote attitude) is that he makes the pupils think and encourages them to work together in independent groups.

Working together in groups has received a great deal of attention in educational literature. The question of how, for example, mutual dependence can be established in a group is also interesting.

As a teacher, you also have to know something about the interaction in collaborative or cooperative groups. When groups are working on mathematical problems, there are always two types of interaction— social and cognitive. How does social interaction influence the cognitive process? Heinz Steinbring has recently published an interesting article (1998) on this topic.

Another thing I noticed about this group is that hardly any of the pupils estimate. Julien is the only one who makes remarks that seem to indicate that he is doing this. I suspect that Dennis, who handed out the tasks, is partly to blame for this. On the other hand, material factors can also play a role in this.

The drawing of the car park map does not exactly encourage the children to make estimations. Amongst other things, this is because of the limited number of empty spaces, the degree of detail of the map (all the car park spaces are given in the drawing), and the four equal quarters. When I solved the problem myself just now, I saw what would probably go wrong. If I had to make a worksheet like this, I would do it differently with not so many details and more empty spaces so that it would visually encourage the children to make estimations. Perhaps I would make one large worksheet and hang it on the board in front of the class. This would be the best way of making the groups discuss making estimates separately. What do you think about it? How would a boy like Dennis show his leadership abilities if this were the situation? Is my supposition about his influence on the group correct? Perhaps a follow-up investigation in MILE could bring us further in this respect.

End of the reflective conversation. It may be an effective method for starting a reflective discourse.

As mentioned previously, the teacher educator reveals his preferences during the reflective conversation. In the example above, he directed his attention to the group exercise and more closely addressed the following subjects: group dynamics, boys and girls, co-operation, estimation and material factors. In the context of these subjects, he could make a connection between the (local) practical knowledge and the available formal knowledge (theory), based on the practical situation given and on the assumption that the students would be able to acquire the critical practice knowledge. This sets the course for working professionally with groups.

6.   MILE AS A REPRESENTATION OF REAL TEACHING PRACTICE

6.1 Contents

What do we mean by "real teaching practice" in the context of Schön's reflective conversation? To answer this question, we need to find out what "the real teaching practice" should contain so it can be a fertile basis for reflective conversations, particularly in order to create, from a given situation, a rich learning environment for pre-service teachers for the construction of practice knowledge.

In addition to the lessons on video tape, the scanned work of the pupils, and the teachers' logbooks, MILE also includes recordings of transfer conversations between two teachers of grade 2; interviews with the teachers (before the lessons) and with several pupils (after the lessons); talks with parents about their children; a parent evening; a team meeting; an introduction given by the headmaster, in which he talks about the school and the school population; and a recording of the *Sinterklaasfeest* (Santa Claus festivities celebrated in the Netherlands on the fifth of December) that the whole school took part in together.

SLE and MILE. It is the (narrative) organization of the digital material contained in the teaching fragments (called "clips" from a technical and "narratives" from an educational point of view) that distinguishes MILE as a learning environment for future teachers from its source of inspiration— the SLE (Student Learning Environment) of the University of Michigan (Lampert & Ball, 1998). We should remark here that splitting up the video clips into narratives, which together tell the whole story of a lesson or a series of lessons, has received a different meaning in the course of the experiments with students. Initially, the developers of MILE assumed that a given video clip would contain enough information on its own for a student who had found it using the search engine. At present, each given clip is regarded as being no more than a point of entry to MILE at a suitable moment in a lesson. The requested information can take students to a "point" in MILE and they can attempt to find what they are looking for near this point.

In the SLE, students have different ways of accessing data. They can search for information by looking through the pupils' work, the teacher's logbook and the lesson plan, or directly by looking at the videos.

If we compare both representations of real teaching practice (SLE and MILE) as learning environments, we see the following obvious differences:

	SLE	MILE
Method	open approach	focused approach
Environment	natural design	constructed design
The start of an investigation	impulsive approach	reflective approach
Methodology	no specific methodology for investigative work	use of a specific methodology
Links to theory	"theory" is only externally available	"theory" can also be accessed from within
How is the material accessed	by always stepping in through a total overview	material can also be accessed by entering specific details

Authenticity. However, if a comparison is made on the basis of the criteria that are set for a good case study of teacher education (Herrington et al, 1998; Barnett, 1998), the main difference between both environments is the "authentic activities" they should encourage. What exactly is meant by authentic activities? Herrington and his co-authors define them as activities that could take place in the classroom. This is an essential point of attention for educators and concerns the naturalness of a learning environment. However, teacher education students are often required to carry out preliminary work in order to penetrate through to the (authentic) activities in the given representation of teaching practice. This leaves us with the question of whether we should mark these preliminary activities as "spurious" in the sense that they do not help student teachers in learning their profession. The authenticity of the environment obviously also depends on the users. There is a large difference between pre-service and in-service teachers in this respect. What Barnett (1998), for example, has her in-service teachers do with the selected material cannot be done by pre-service teachers. Take, for instance, the relationship with Cognitive Flexibility Theory (Spiro, Coulson, Feltovich, & Anderson, 1988). The ill-structured domains with the wicked problems to be solved come very close to the "dilemma management" put forward by Lampert (1985). In cases like this, the participants learn that theoretical knowledge does not offer a solution in every real life situation and that "strategic knowledge," in other words, knowing how to cope with dilemmas, has to be applied if necessary. We believe that MILE contains a number of these situations, but we also think that junior pre-service teachers do not need to be immediately discouraged by them. "Authentic" is therefore not just dependent on the target group, it is also a subject of programmatical attention. MILE contains, furthermore, many situations that, sometimes when interrelated, can produce a tailor-made case study. Barnett's idea of this type of case study ("A case ... frames an instance of experience that often includes a subjective analysis of what happened from a participant's point of view.") comes close to Schön's reflective conversation with the situation. (see also Richert, 1991). However, to be perfectly clear, even with a reflective conversation in which the practice knowledge, or even the educative power of the teacher is explicitly revealed, the learning environment that we see embodied in MILE is still not complete. In this respect, the activities of teacher education students must be further evaluated. We will return to this point later.

Solving the learning paradox in teacher education. We will now briefly return to the learning paradox in teaching junior teacher education students, who have to be able to extract practice knowledge from the real teaching practice in MILE without having the necessary foreknowledge.

Fortunately, MILE itself offers a solution. Until now, we have used "narrative" as an idea for organizing the environment of MILE (video clips as narratives) and as a manifestation of practice knowledge (the way of narrative knowing). Both meanings are combined in MILE. This does not, however, remove the fact that the practice knowledge is usually concealed from MILE investigators. Yet, thankfully, there are situations in MILE where this is different. After all, "narrative" can also be regarded as a vehicle for communicating practice knowledge (Pendlebury, 1995). Using this assumption, a teacher education student can observe an "explicit formulation" of "practice knowledge" if he/she is given the opportunity to listen to the conversations of teachers talking about their work. This becomes more interesting and more specific when the teachers discuss recent experiences with their common pupils. In a sense, these conversations between the two teachers can be considered as reflective conversations as well, because the teachers, when having these conversations, reflect on their own teaching as their "situation" and try to explain why things happened and what their underlying thoughts were and their motivation for doing the things they did. What is there left for an educator to do in situations where practice knowledge is fully tacit and the teachers in MILE create a learning environment by themselves for their future colleagues?

6.2 Transfer Conversations

Such a conversation can be witnessed, for example, in MILE, grade 2 (18 November 1996).

Willie: Last week, I did task 36. I started with dictating sums and a speed test (sums like 9 – 5 =). There were three surprising non-starters: John, who made 10 mistakes, Wendy, 6 mistakes and Chantal 11. She doesn't seem to be all that happy at the moment. After that, I went on with the tiles on a schoolyard and I put twelve tiles on the magnetic board. The children were divided into groups of two and given 12 small tiles as well. I then asked them to make a rectangle-shaped yard with the tiles in their group and after that, I discussed the possibilities 3 x 4 and 4 x 3.

Minke: Did they also have tiles themselves?

Willie: Yes. The small ones without a magnet. Furthermore they used of course the tile-yards in their workbooks.

Minke: We agreed to use two colours, in order to emphasize the multiplication structure by giving different colours to the small groups. I am anxious to know what happened.

Willie: I am afraid that using the tiles as well as colouring the tile-yards doesn't support the idea of multiplication sufficiently. Moving the tiles around to reshape the rectangle is a bit confusing for the children. And particularly the language you need to explain what you are doing, is difficult to understand for most of them. And if you have colours to make a distinction, for example with 7 x 2, you take for each pair of tiles a different colour, you break through the unity.

I have also thought about doing something with cutting, but I didn't think it would work out. Because, well, everything gets mixed up, or you have to draw a really big figure....

Revealing tacit knowledge. This "professional" conversation reveals a substantial amount of practice knowledge. The transfer forms a suitable moment to go into the details of practice knowledge with junior teacher education students. In his reflective conversation with the situation (= the transfer conversation between both teachers) given in the example below, the educator gives his interpretation of "abilities" of the respective teachers.

Willie shows that she is familiar with the phenomenon of multiplication, that she knows that the rectangle model can be used to form a bridge between the children's intuitive ideas (about counting, counting with jumps, short counting, repeated adding-up) and formal mathematics, in which multiplication is placed at a higher level than addition and subtraction and that multiplication has to comply with specific rules. During this lesson, she brings to the children's attention one of these rules: the commutative law. She does this with a didactic method that is characterized by the use of manipulatives (tiles and rectangles), guided re-invention, and collaborative work in small groups. Working at this concrete level takes place in a daily life context (tiles on a schoolyard) that the children know and is organized in such a way that the children are induced to work in pairs. Willie shows that she knows her pupils from their performance and that she can use this knowledge to anticipate the difficulties they may experience.

She also knows the possibilities and impossibilities of using concrete manipulatives to give the children insight into the structure of multiplication. She senses and sees when the children become confused and imagines what the children will think of her explanation. For explaining things, she has different approaches in her repertoire and she consciously chooses the approach that seems to her to be the best in the given situation.

Furthermore, she pays attention to the linguistic problems that are dominantly present in this class with a large proportion of non-Dutch native children (Surinam, Netherlands Antilles, Turkey, Morocco, and China). She knows the importance of putting her actions and thoughts into words and takes this knowledge into account during the lesson.

Dimensions. In short, many dimensions of (contextualized) "practice knowledge" are made apparent in this brief extract from the transfer conversation that took place on November 18: the subject matter, the manipulatives and their use, the pupils, the didactic approach, the observations, the interpretations and decisions.

6.3 Interviews

There is also another way of finding out about the practice knowledge of the teachers in MILE. Before each lesson, they were asked to talk about what they had planned for the coming lesson. This "interview" was also recorded on video and is available in MILE. It should be clear that, so short before the lesson, the teachers openly discussed the subject matter, the tasks, the problems they expected, the pupils who needed additional attention, the didactic work form, the manipulatives they wanted to use, and the organization of the lesson. In some cases, the teachers also explained their motives and occasionally reviewed the previous lesson.

A remark made by one of the pre-service teachers in the investigation shows that she recognises the true value of the information contained in these interviews:

> Of the three types of video (transfer, interview, mandarin lesson), the interview made the most impression on me. It was like looking in the head of the teacher and finding out secret information.

From the fragments in MILE discussed above, the reader might get a general impression of situations in which practice knowledge is explicitly manifested. It has, however, previously been remarked that most practice knowledge is implicitly or tacitly present. In order to make this knowledge accessible to teacher education students, we have adopted an approach similar to the one developed at the University of Michigan (Lampert & Ball, 1998). The students at the School of Education in Ann Arbor investigate real teaching practice so as to learn from (and about) it.

7. INVESTIGATING REAL TEACHING PRACTICE

7.1 Learning by Investigation

We now have a representation of real practice on a scale that can be compared with hundreds of case studies and which forms a source of mainly tacit practice knowledge. By combining this with our ideas of reflective practice and narrative knowing, which we can use to penetrate through to the practice knowledge, and our contention that pre-service teachers develop professionally on the basis of their own reflective activities, which also have a constructive character and in which teaching practice is continually visible, we should now ask how we can transform the given environment into a (rich) learning environment for teacher education students on the basis of our aforementioned ideas and convictions.

In the framework of their MATH project, Lampert and Ball (1998) asked the same question and arrived at the statement: "Professional growth by investigating real teaching, discussing hot issues in context, and reporting reflectively." Over a period of five years, they furthermore allowed 200 teacher education students to carry out, either individually or together in small groups, 68 "investigation projects" in the SLE. In addition, their study based on the theme of "investigating the investigations" identifies a number of conditions that learning environments have to satisfy. The most important of these is that students should be helped in preparing and starting their investigations. Subsequently, during their investigation projects, they should receive coaching from an expert in at least four areas: (1) technology, (2) research, (3) knowledge of what can be found in the environment, and (4) the normal expertise provided by an educator of primary school mathematics teachers. Over the aforementioned period, it also became clear, of course, that the knowledge of teacher education students, in particular their beliefs, attitudes, and conceptions with respect to mathematics as well as their individual learning, researching, and teaching experience, could not be ignored. From the discussion of one of the investigations ("Patricia"), it transpires that the strongest learning effects take place in the areas of beliefs and attitude. Lampert and Ball put it this way:

> She is no longer an outsider in Deborah's class, she is no longer on the outside looking in, with no empathy. On the contrary, it seems that she is better able to project herself in the role of the teacher and the pupil. And she shows a different approach to practice, one which is now more investigative.

The experiments in MILE produced similar results. We acquired additional information because the investigations in MILE took place, more so than in the SLE, in the context of didactic theory and because the organization of the learning environment and the availability of a search engine induced a specific research approach.

7.2 Promoting Teacher Education Students' Investigations

What was done in the previously mentioned case study projects—the prior selection of "suitable" cases (what is suitable?) by experts (who is the expert?) —is no longer needed in multimedia environments. If students master some basic technical and methodological skills, they can explore teaching practice on their own, creating their own case studies and initiating their own discussions, provided that they have sufficient foreknowledge to circumvent the learning paradox (p.15).

Preparation. This certainly applies to MILE, which can be regarded as a collection of case studies; each investigative journey in MILE constitutes a case study in itself. In the 15 pilot projects, each study in MILE started with a (re)search problem that was subsequently divided into smaller search questions. Each search question involved thinking up key words that could be used to put the search engine to work. After a whole group of students has first become acquainted with the technical aspects and the contents of MILE, a moment comes when they, often collaborating in small groups, think up a specific research direction and hypothesis they want to test.

Point of departure. The interesting thing about this is that the point of departure that is chosen by the teacher educator for collective research can significantly affect the research direction and the questions the students want to answer. If, for example, a MILE teacher is the centre of attention when students first become acquainted with MILE, the investigations they plan will in most cases also focus on the teacher. The same thing applies to attention to pupils, group work, and assessment. A prospective tutor in MILE therefore knows what he has to do in this respect.

Students' questions. In addition to a general overview of what MILE has to offer as a representation of real teaching practice and the skill to use the technology involved, a teacher education student must have a good research question. The education experiments with MILE in the 15 teacher education colleges in the Netherlands provided several interesting research questions/hypotheses that the students thought up themselves. The ensuing investigative journeys in MILE formed, as previously stated, more or less complete case studies in themselves, each one illustrating a number of dimensions of practice knowledge. For example:

1. What is in the textbooks currently in use about differentiation and how is this dealt with in the class of both teachers in grade 2?
2. When is the use of MAB material recommended in the textbooks in use and how do you see this in practice?
3. How is the number line used?
4. How can the children use the manipulatives (MAB, money, reckon rack, egg boxes)?
5. What are the advantages of the various teaching aids for doing calculations up to one hundred?
6. Which specific manipulative can you use at a given moment when you notice that a child is having a particular mathematics problem?
7. What is a rich learning environment for a child in mathematics education?
8. How do you achieve cooperation during maths lessons?
9. How do children arrive at specific solutions?
10. To what extent does the use of the board influence the children?
11. How does Paul, the teacher in grade 5, build up his lessons? Which situation does he take into account in the beginning and what does he want to achieve?

If the above questions are examined more closely, it can be seen that they contain a number of differences in the possibilities they offer for actual investigations. Those people who know something of the contents of MILE will immediately see interesting case studies emerging from specific questions. Mile case studies certainly have a different character from the studies based on written cases, but the underlying principles (active, learning by investigation) and objective (skills acquisition based on real-life activities from the teacher) are quite similar. In a few cases, similar approaches from the teacher educator and/or the students may arise. (Richert, 1994 and Barnett, 1998).

7.3 The Case of Frank and Linda

This also occurred in the case of Frank and Linda, who planned to study the interaction in small groups. Frank and Linda are two students whose investigation took them to the "ill-structured" domain (of percentages and proportions). They studied the grade 5 lesson, in which Paul starts working in a problem-oriented way wanting to let his pupils collaborate in small groups.

Before the two teacher education students started working together, they explored the learning environment with their whole group. Whilst doing this, they learnt the techniques involved and gained insight into the contents and the possibilities for research. The educator designed a sort of practical lesson for this called "Viewing Guide." After working in MILE for a whole day followed by a group evaluation, Frank and Linda started their own investigation. They first looked into the interaction in the groups, but decided on the advice of their teacher educator to focus on a smaller area of study—the behaviour displayed by a gifted pupil when he/she has to work with others in a small group. There is a small section of their report below (Goffree, 1998). It starts with the first "derived" research question, which the students call "learning question."

> Learning question 1: Choose a random group and look to see whether it contains a gifted pupil. Why do you think this pupil is gifted? If you cannot find one, choose another group.

> Whilst looking at random for a video clip and the related follow-up, we came across a clip in which Vincent S (according to the teacher a high achiever in maths) clearly indicates that he does not agree with his group. We thought that this was the type of clip we had been looking for and we decided to continue with Vincent S as the gifted pupil we needed for our investigation.

> We look at a clip taken from somewhere in the beginning of lesson 2. Sum 5 (see Figure 1) is being discussed. Paul asks the children whether they can start work in the groups. Vincent: "No, because you do not know how much coffee is in the pot." Because of this question, the class agrees that a full pot is enough for the whole cinema audience.

> We look at the follow-up: the group starts work, Jessica counts the squares and Vincent, irritated, says "80!" We both agree that he sounded really annoyed.

> We look further. Until Paul comes, Vincent does not mix with the others and when Paul asks whether things are working out in the group, Vincent tells him that you have to subtract a 1/4 part from both and that 61 people want coffee, but the pot is 3/4 full. He does not use percentages. When the teacher later says, "The problem is about the number of cups you can get out of the pot," Vincent replies, "Only 60." While the rest still think there is enough coffee in the pot, Vincent has worked out precisely that 75% of 80 = 60 is not enough

5 ☞ Enough coffee?

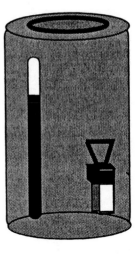

Figure 1. From the workbook: Map of cinema and gauge

for the 61 people who want coffee. He almost says this literally: "61 people want coffee... I don't think that can be right." The rest of this clip provides valuable information for the next learning question; because of Vincent's astute remarks and the effortless way he knows the answers.

Learning question 2: Look for a video clip in which our group starts working on a problem together. What does the gifted pupil do while the group is working out the answer? Describe his behaviour and any typical remarks.

We look at the following section of the clip. Paul has walked away and the pupils now have to formulate their answer. Vincent says again that he does not think there is enough coffee. Andrew says that 71 squares are black, but Vincent does not agree with him. Andrew says that you have to count the black squares, but Vincent explains to him that it is easier to count the white squares and subtract this number from 80. He explains this in great detail: first take ten away and then 9, which leaves 61. While he is explaining this to Andrew, a lot of the other children in the group are listening. Andrew does not accept this from Vincent and says again "71 black squares." Vincent disagrees very peacefully.

After this, Andrew starts to count them, "Oh yes, there are 61." Vincent does not react to this with anything like "I told you so, but you wouldn't believe me." The group continues to talk about it for a while. Ruben thinks that there is enough coffee. Vincent says once more that he does not think so. The rest still think, after making a few jokes (not about Vincent or anything in particular), that there is enough. Vincent then writes something down and the lesson finishes. End of clip.

Conclusion: Vincent clearly wants to explain what he thinks, he is prepared to do this patiently and is not pushy in the sense having to prove he is right at all costs. He is quiet and sure of himself.

Learning question 3: Try to find out whether this behaviour (from learning question 2) is typical for him ...

It could be argued that Frank and Linda open up the case study "Vincent, a gifted pupil." The teacher educator helped them focus on the issue, after which they worked together on the basis of their own practical wisdom, inspired by the records of teaching practice and tutored at a distance by the teacher educator by means of e-mail "annotations." This fundamentally means that they got to know Vincent better as a pupil through their investigations. They also acquired knowledge about interaction during group work and especially how this takes place when the group contains a high achiever in mathematics. Furthermore, both the search for material and the ensuing reflection were not all that easy —just like in a "real" classroom.

The pilot projects mentioned, involving the case of Frank and Linda, asked the question as to which image of actual practice the student would form through the self-selected Mile fragments. This view could be recreated by taking stock of the fragments that were viewed. It is clear that the contributions of an entire group (in this case, six students conducting research in three pairs) offered a reasonable view of 5th grade mathematics. But the contributions per pair offered a rather incomplete image, as the Frank and Linda's work demonstrates. Apparently, students can get a warped or incomplete image of the practice – based on individual choices and perhaps opinions – presented during open research, where the teacher educator does not put forth any guiding preferences.

7.4   A Cyclic Investigation Process

Students in colleges of education in the Netherlands have neither the attitude nor the technology to investigate teaching practice systematically. With the preparatory education, for example for the University of Michigan, students are more likely to have a better attitude and approach towards research. This is, for instance, expressed in the previously mentioned case study about Patricia (Lampert & Ball, 1998).

With this "practice" knowledge about prospective teachers in the Netherlands and the awareness that "action research" in the framework of "teachers as researchers" and "in-service education" is usefully applied (Jaworski, 1998) and (Krainer, 1999), Oonk accurately mapped out the learning process of two students, Dieneke and Hayet, in his explorative study (see the D&H case, 9.2, a part of "the pioneers project"). The objective was to find a suitable methodology for Dutch student teachers, which would support them in investigating teaching practice in MILE and in which attention would remain concentrated on the essentials. Oonk's study (1999) revealed three building blocks of the learning process.

The learning process of the students is characterized by peaks in knowledge construction. The process is initiated and kept in momentum by the investigations in MILE. However, actual learning and the motivation to learn was brought about in the discussions about the issues that were raised during the investigation process. In short, the learning process consists of investigation, discussion, and knowledge construction.

The investigative work of the students, which was carried out in close cooperation with the teacher educator, may have produced a usable systematic that is related to the cyclic procedure of action research, but which, because of the technology involved (searching through digital practice), has its own unique character. This observation made it possible to regard the total investigation process as a succession of nine independent, but interrelated, cycles. To illustrate this, the fourth cycle is given below.

This was preceded by three cycles in which the students under careful supervision started their investigative work and became more familiar with the medium and how to use it. In addition to this, on the basis of the first video clips and the discussions that these produced, they became motivated to review the perspective of their investigations. It was in the fourth cycle that their research plans became concrete.

Cycle 4 "What about Dumb August? A limited number of clips."

4.1 Motivation

The reason for starting this cycle was found in one of the "Stories" (a publication of Oonk's observations during the recording) about teacher Minke playing "Dumb August". The students found this story in the previous meeting and now they go back to it. Their curiosity has been aroused and they want to know more about it.

4.2 Search plan

"What do we want to see? What type of subject matter do the teachers use with the Dumb August technique? Are there sums that are particularly suitable for this technique?"

4.3 Search

They think up the following search words: <u>Dumb August</u>, <u>elicitation</u> or <u>provocation</u> and <u>conflict</u>. The first two come from Oonk's "Stories"; the last one (conflict) was found by browsing through the index of the study book in use. They find a large amount of video clip descriptions. They subsequently use another 17 search words, which they take from the descriptions of previous fragments. This is of little help; one additional fragment is found.

4.4 Selection

Three clip descriptions are left over:

1. The teacher plays Dumb August: Finding the place of 94 somewhere on the number line in front of the classroom. Using the pointer. Where to stop? There?
2. The teacher, using the pointer, is looking for 32. She deliberately pauses on 42. Minke plays Dumb August …
3. Chantal helps. Minke feigns ignorance and lets Chantal repeat what she said.

They decide to look at all three remaining clips.

4.5 Observation

D&H look at the videos from three different perspectives:

- The subject matter. Which subject matter is suitable for this approach?
- The pupils. What are the effects of the Dumb August method on the pupils? Which pupils are called up?
- The teacher. How does Minke present the material?

One week later, the whole workgroup observe the videos, but this time as part of a half-hour lesson (to get a good impression of the context). This causes D&H to amend their search question to: To what extent does the didactic approach of the teacher involve the children in the lesson?

4.6 Reflection

The collective discussion leads to (more) depth. They see more and think ahead.

Dieneke: "We once again notice that Minke knows how to involve the class in the lesson. Dumb August is instrumental in this, but Minke's open questions and the way she builds the tension are also essential." Hayet writes an extensive reflection entitled "Questions for Dumb August." It is about making mistakes (Why does Minke do this?), class culture and Minke's didactic repertoire.

4.7 Evaluation (statements):

"If you do not want to work in MILE at any great length, these three videos will be sufficient."

"You need the whole context of a lesson to find a video clip interesting."

About observing: "It was useful to discuss our different viewing perspectives."

"How should we proceed? ... With the subject involvement' or should we leave it?"

"MILE is addictive, we want to have therapy to get off it."

4.8 Follow-up

Hayet comes up with an idea for the follow-up. "Let's make a 'film for discussion'!" Dieneke works it out.

According to Oonk, a research cycle consists of 8 sections: motivation/a reason to start, search plan, search, selection, observation, reflection, evaluation, and reasons for a new start. In follow-up studies, Oonk would like to find out whether a systematic approach to research based on these steps will help students to become "good" investigators of teaching.

7.5 Discourse and Collective Competence

The nature of the learning environment is determined by the way in which students participate in it. In MILE and in the SLE, students learn by investigating teaching practice. Their investigation process can be considered as the *vehicle of their learning process.*

The discourse appears to be the *motor of the learning process.* Observations in Michigan and the Netherlands prove the validity of the statement: "It all happens in the discourse." What is meant by "it"? This can, amongst other things, be understood as the emergence of new insight, finding new reasons to search further, the impetus for choosing a theoretical line of approach or to start theorizing. The discussions observed in the D&H case have the characteristics of "reflective discourse" (Cobb, McClain, & Whitenack, 1997). Here, we consider the reflective discourse to be a socio-constructive adaptation of Schön's reflective conversation.

We regard discourse amongst teacher education students and the educator in MILE as an extension of both views and as a conversation on a professional level between teachers who are working as action researchers to improve the quality of their education. In these (team) meetings between teachers, the participants use the team's collective competence, which is occasionally augmented by interjections from the expert. The expert can, for example, be a schools inspector, a supervisor, or a parent. However, in theory people should use the collective competence of the whole community, which represents the publicly accessible body of knowledge. Colleges of education provide for the latter. In these institutes of higher education, the study and application of "theory" in a "real life situation" is an important part of teacher education programmes.

Sometimes the discourse between teachers in a school team has an exceptional character, if it takes place in the context of a school self-evaluation, for example. An attempt is made to arrive at well-founded decisions and conclusions regarding the quality of education offered. At that point, the content of the discussion is linked to school policy. The discourse then also develops a socio-political component. That this applies not only to school team meetings, but also in the discourse of prospective teachers, became apparent when the teacher students from the Normal University of Taipei entered into a discussion, motivated by a Mile visit, in which the "interaction in the realistic mathematics lesson" was addressed during a team meeting at one of the schools. This is an example of young, motivated Taiwanese teacher students discussing the policy of implementing a new approach to mathematics education!

In MILE, theory is discussed via "theoretical reflections." This is the subject of the next section.

8. THE NATURE, THE ROLE, AND THE NECESSITY OF THEORETICAL REFLECTIONS

In the Netherlands, recent developments in the curriculum for teacher education have led to a transparent model (Goffree & Oonk, 1999). In principle, it applies to a broad view of school subjects, where a school subject is much more than mere subject matter. It is what the teacher does and thinks and acts; it is what the pupils experience, do, ask, construct, learn, and so forth; it is also what happens in the classroom, the contents of the teacher's logbooks and the pupils' exercise books, what the textbook shows and how pupils experience the tasks it contains, the tests and results and conclusions it is based on, what the teachers tell the parents and what the parents tell and ask the teacher, how they (can) become partners in mathematics education, and so on. In all "modesty" we could say that the school subject mathematics is characterized by what has been recorded in the creation of MILE.

We have previously outlined how these real teaching situations and the practice knowledge that they contain can be made accessible for teacher education students. An issue that has only recently been addressed is theory and how it can contribute to the professionalization of teaching and the way in which it is portrayed in teacher education programmes. Since its inception, teacher education has been an arena in which practice and theory compete for hegemony. The continual hope of teacher educators has been to bring about "the integration of theory and practice." It is only since information technology created the possibility to conduct a safe and comprehensive investigation and study into real practice in teacher education that it seems that their aspirations will become reality.

In MILE, promising results have been achieved in this respect. However, as we have previously remarked, teacher education has been radically changed by the introduction of digitized practice. Educators used to start from theory when working with teacher education students. This is not only what happened in the traditional approach, but with selecting case studies as well. Usually, theory also dominates the videos of teaching practice. Theory is examined by giving direction to observations and accentuating interpretations.

Digitizing real teaching practice has opened it up for reflective investigation. In the "reflective conversations" outlined above (see the cases of Paul and D&H), it was shown how "theory" can be portrayed as a reflection of practice in an extremely natural way. This touches on an essential aspect of the expertise of the educator—being able to "intertwine the investigation of practice with the examination and development of theory," as Lampert and Ball (1998) put it.

8.1 Intertwining Practice and Theory

This "intertwining" took place in the MATH project mainly when coaching students. The case of "Patricia Portland" shows how the teacher education student is led by her educator from specific practice situations in the SLE to "the big issues" of pedagogic and educational theory. In MILE, attempts to do this are undertaken via the reflective conversations right from the start. We refer to those cases in which existing theoretical knowledge is applied to the practical situation in one way or another as theoretical reflection. It should be clear that the "situations" in MILE (and other representations of real practice) distinguish themselves by the vast amount of "latent theory" they contain. In addition to this, there are different variations to the way in which theoretical knowledge is involved in actual practice.

Before we give an overview of these we will go into the envisaged results of theoretical reflection with students. An essential aspect is that theory becomes an integrated part of a student's practice knowledge. But how do we achieve this?

8.2 Introducing Theory-on-Practice

We will look into a specific teaching practice situation, for example the episode in which Paul explores the model of the fractions strip with the children. The lesson is about percentages. The children start with global estimates first using the context of the power check and then the coffee pot. Paul has made a sliding strip (Figure 2) for the lesson that can demonstrate any given sum with fractions (percentages) to the class.

Figure 2. Paul with sliding strip

The strip can be used to represent a (battery) power check and a glass gauge on a coffee pot. A reflective conversation about this situation focuses first on what happens during the lesson, gives meaning to the term *model*, accentuates the fact that this is the first time this subject has been presented, and asks why the class carries on making estimations for such a long time. The reflective practitioner could then ask what the significance is of the chosen context, probably related to the way in which the pupils respond or do not respond. At this moment, the use of theoretical knowledge is demonstrated. Theory gives the educator the ability to see further and to explain what he sees happen. Theory, as students will probably understand it, has, however, remained implicit until this point. This can change if the educator builds an intermezzo into his reflection and says something, for example, about the reasons behind the use of models in mathematics education, research of the number line and the perspective of the "two-scaled number line" that Paul undoubtedly had in mind. Yet, the educator could also talk about "interaction" while doing a classical exercise or about the significance of making estimates at the start of a course on percentages. Who determines what will be discussed? The educator is the initiator in response to what the teacher education students bring forward. This means that the type of reflective conversation with the situation referred to here is part of a reflective discourse "about the situation," and in addition, constitutes a good reason for starting the discourse.

We asked how we could introduce theory in the practice knowledge of the student. This is possible with the aforementioned example. Our hypothesis is that theory (for example about models) is understood by the students in the context of the fragment of Paul's lesson. They subsequently also learn theory by discussing Paul's work with the sliding fractions strip and, without doubt, from parts of the reflective discourse. We believe that practice knowledge can thus become a narrative way of thinking and that the view that practice knowledge is context-dependent knowledge will acquire concrete significance in teacher education.

9. STUDENT TEACHERS' CONSTRUCTION OF PRACTICE KNOWLEDGE

9.1 Levels of Knowledge Construction

In paragraph 7.4, we reported about the MILE pilot project in Amsterdam, tutored by Wil Oonk. His study of the investigation process of two student teachers revealed several moments of knowledge construction. The analysis of the process has provided insight in knowledge construction at four different levels.

How can you observe the construction of practice knowledge? Since the research does not extend to the fieldwork of teacher education students, where practice knowledge in action could have been observed, we will have to rely on the reflective notes of the students and their comments during the discussions.

We observed the following four levels.

Assimilation of practice knowledge. Firstly, knowledge can be "taken over" from the teachers in MILE. This concerns expanding the student teacher's own didactic repertoire through assimilation of the "practice knowledge" contained in MILE. Assimilation occurs if the student teacher indicates that he/she would like to implement the knowledge of the MILE teacher without any restrictions for his/her own purposes. This often involves more a takeover of pedagogic/didactic actions in a specific situation than the knowledge these actions are based on,

Adaptation and accommodation of practice knowledge. Users of MILE can also modify the repertoire of the MILE teacher to suit their own purposes; they expand their own repertoire by modifying the MILE teacher's. This is adaptation, the second level of knowledge construction. It can occur, for example, when the explanation of a MILE teacher is critically examined and then changed according to personal views.

The knowledge construction on the second level can have a greater impact on the student, especially if the student has to adjust his/her personal opinions or beliefs. In this case, something changes in the cognitive/affective structure that we refer to here as practice knowledge. For this reason, this is called accommodation.

We suspect that the nature of the knowledge on the level of accommodation has some of the same characteristics as what Perry calls relativism. The knowledge on the first level that is actually constructed on the authority of the "model teacher" will have more characteristics of Perry's "dualism."

Integrating theory. The student teachers display an even higher level of knowledge construction when they establish (new) links between the events in MILE and the related theory. In this case, they might (re)consider didactic insights and points of view. They ask themselves a number of questions about the observed situation in MILE and make links with what they find in the literature. The educator has a crucial task in this respect. He has responded positively to the questions posed by the student teachers. Through theoretical reflections about the given real practice situation, "intertwining the investigation of practice with the examination and development of theory" (section 4), he puts them on the track of explanatory theory, which is understood and remembered in the context of a scene in MILE. This is usually in the form of a story of the events that took place in MILE and is therefore narrative.

Theorizing. The highest level of knowledge construction manifests itself when the investigators in MILE design their own local theories. They build up certain ideas about causes and consequences through the observation and interpretation of fragments they find themselves. The ensuing discourse can have a specific theoretical orientation and provide the motivation for follow-up investigations. In this way, people start theorizing and may even form theory on a local level.

The case of Dieneke and Hayet given below especially illuminates this highest level of knowledge construction.

9.2   The Case of Dieneke and Hayet

Introduction. MILE became the work area of two bright teacher education students, Dieneke and Hayet, from the Amsterdam College of Higher Professional Education (*Educatieve Faculteit Amsterdam*) from 16 May to 27 June 1997. They were the first student teachers who made their investigation in MILE. They only had ten CD-ROMs of lessons in grade 2 to work with. The subject matter in grade 2 includes calculating to one hundred and the multiplication tables. The lessons in question were given by Minke and Willie, two teachers whom we met previously in Secion 6 during their "transfer conversation." The student teachers investigated the teaching practice of Minke and Willie together with their tutor (educator), Wil Oonk. This took place in the framework of their final dissertation. The group had 15 two-hour meetings; in eight of these the tutor was also present.

The original case study was concerned with the whole process. The part of the study described here took place during two of the meetings. During their investigation in MILE, Dieneke and Hayet constructed knowledge on all four of the aforementioned levels; in this section the fourth level of knowledge construction, theorizing, is illustrated. We will follow the student teachers from the moment that their investigative work focuses on a teacher who uses a "model" to support the transition from concrete to mental action.

The situation. During the aforementioned search in MILE, D&H find a fragment of the lesson in which one of the teachers in grade 5, Willie, introduces the 5-times table. In the ten minutes that preceded this video clip of the lesson, Willie told the children a story about mandarins that she bought at the market. On the teacher's desk, there is a basket with bags each containing 5 mandarins. The pupils take turns to lay one or more bags next to each other and then the whole class has to think up the multiplication ("sums" says the teacher) that goes with the number of bags that have been placed together. Willie writes the multiplication tasks on the board: 2 x 5, 4 x 5, 8 x 5 and 9 x 5. Some of the children know the products and answer straight away, others use easy doubling or (repeated) counting.

On the left of the board next to the sums that Willie is writing, a row of bags has been drawn with an (empty) number line underneath (see Figure 3).

Figure 3. Willie in front of the board

The video clip that D&H have selected starts at the moment when Willie begins to use the drawings on the board. She points to the row of bags drawn on the board and says that the real mandarins will no longer be in the classroom the next day. She asks several questions to focus the class on the subject ("How many bags are there?" (10) and "How many mandarins are there in each bag?" (5). While she is doing this, she writes "5" in each bag on the board. She then points to the number line underneath and says, "Let's agree to make jumps of five on this number line. Let's go through it now, shall we?" The whole group then "sings" the row of multiplication products from 5 to 50. Lastly, nine children are allowed to take turns to name one of the multiplication products in the correct order, which Willie writes on the number line. The video then ends, having lasted approximately 5 minutes.

9.3   The Reflective Discourse

The first statement. After Dieneke and Hayet selected and discussed the "Willie and the mandarins" video clip. Dieneke noted:

> What is there to see exactly? Willie uses an awkward transition to move from concrete to mental action. We wonder whether the children can understand it and remark on her approach. If we had to re-enact the situation ourselves, we would have hung the bags on the number line before demonstrating the jump from five to ten; or we would have drawn connecting lines between each bag and the corresponding point on the number line. In our opinion, this would make it easier for the children to see the connection. Hayet and I have made the following statement related to this video: if the transition from concrete to mental action does not take place in sufficiently small and logical steps, the (material and mental) actions will remain separated from each other. The main objective is, however, to couple these actions together....

Theoretical reflection. The tutor (WO) goes into this point with extensive (and electronic) theoretical reflections. He takes the opportunity to make the student teachers aware of the distinction between (mechanistic) "step-by-step" and realistic didactics in which properly raising learning levels is considered and encouraged. In this context, he also focuses on theoretical views about different levels in subject matter and learning processes applied to the architecture of the various learning strands in mathematics courses (Treffers & De Moor, 1990; Goffree, 1994; Gravemeijer, 1995).

Theorizing about practice. The students become interested in this material. Hayet responds directly to the e-mail sent by WO. She has become aware that the practice situations in MILE shed new light on the theory that she learnt at teacher education college.

> I always found current theory difficult, but I am only now aware of how little of it actually got through to me. During exams, this was not a problem; I always knew which "list" I had to have. Now you have to link it to practical experience....

She does not, however, just make this observation. She realizes that MILE contains information that you cannot find in textbooks or teachers' guides. In other words, she becomes interested in (tacit) practical knowledge.

> When looking at the way Minke and Willie and the children interact, we are mainly interested in the aspects that you cannot find in textbooks or teachers' guides (latent practical knowledge). How do Minke and Willie see whether pupils receive (enough) support from material and models? How do they observe learning processes and moments when pupils raise their level? If you can observe and name these things (as a MILE spectator), it will increase your skill to take advantage of similar situations in real teaching practice?

In her reaction to the problem of concrete and mental actions, she shows that she realizes the practical value of theory.

> In my opinion, "the abstract level" means formal mathematics. The phrase "mental actions with material" does contain the word mental but it does not belong on that abstract level, it should be placed on the concrete—material level. Actions with material are performed "in your head" (it is not a physical action), but they are concrete, or in other words, conceivable and meaningful....

She becomes aware that the terms *concrete, abstract,* and *formal* put her on the wrong track. The "lists" and summaries of (action) levels that she learnt, lead her to start thinking in terms of a logical progression in building up pupils' learning levels.

> It unconsciously reinforced thinking in successive steps. This chain of thought can also be explained in that subjects at school (seem to) be in line with the developments of the average pupil. And the more globally you look, the more logical it seems that certain learning levels should follow on from each other. For example, it seemed obvious to us that mental actions (with manipulatives) should take place after a period of working physically with manipulatives....

She then goes back to the "theory" about taking "small logical steps," which she developed together with Dieneke:

> After reconsideration, the idea of small steps perished. With "logical," we meant especially interconnectivity: meaningful actions with manipulatives because there is, for example, a clear analogy with a situation in the world as perceived by the pupils' and an isomorph with the formal sum....

Revision of personal theory. In the next meeting, the "reflective discourse" between D, H, and WO was continued and they looked purposefully for video clips that supported arguments or confirmed assumptions. Reflecting and theorizing in the way outlined above, leads indirectly to a revision of the statement previously formulated by D and H. The reason for this is a video clip in which Fadoua shows that thinking of egg boxes helps her interpret 43 as 40 (four egg boxes) + 3 (separate eggs).

After the meeting, Dieneke writes the following about this point:

> This statement applies to small logical steps, raising pupils' levels and direct support. Support and raising pupils' levels are after all very similar concepts. The concrete material is first used as support and when pupils let go of it by not only looking at it anymore and just thinking about it, their level rises. Manipulatives always help and support, provided you introduce them properly. If you do not do this, they are only extra ballast and lead to confusion. The clip "Think of egg boxes" is a good example of this, since Minke had not referred to them before and 'suddenly' introduced them without making the small logical step towards them....

Reflection. This shows that the student teachers have acquired new theoretical insights. In our opinion, this is the pinnacle of their knowledge construction. The practical situations in MILE motivate them to make statements about the actions of the teacher and the pupils' learning processes. After thinking about one statement and with the support of the theoretical reflection of the educator, the student teachers are led to new insights and subsequently to revising that same statement. We characterize this process as theorizing and in our opinion, it is a step further than Schön's "theory in action."

10. DISCUSSION

Making sense of teaching means that teaching practice has to be taken seriously in teacher education. Amongst other things, this means that, in teacher education programmes, (a large amount of) time has to be spent on learning to understand what happens in "real teaching practice." A primary school teacher education college that takes teaching practice seriously also makes it a central part of the curriculum, which in turn means that teaching practice can be used as a broad-based starting point for learning to teach. It should be remarked that with "teaching practice," teacher educators immediately think of what their students experience during their fieldwork. The teaching practice of student teachers is everything they experience while doing fieldwork—in the classroom and amongst the children in that classroom. This produces two problems—even with all its diversity, "teaching practice" alone does not suffice for educating teachers, and teaching practice as it takes place in classrooms is not really accessible for the purposes of study and reflective discourse amongst teacher education students (Cohen, 1998).

Teaching practice can also be represented in teacher education programmes, for example, with stories, cases, videos, and also by records of practice, organized in a multimedia environment. Such an environment gives a teacher education college a digital representation of real teaching and means that teaching practice can be chosen as a point of departure for the courses the college provides. As a result of this, acquired practice knowledge becomes a narrative way of knowing and can reach the level of reflective knowledge. The acquisition of this knowledge, which is regarded as an active and constructive process, occurs by means of in-depth and focused investigations of teaching practice. This investigation process can be understood as the vehicle of the learning process. The discourse amongst teacher education students, sometimes improved by the theoretical reflections of the educator, appears to be the motor of the learning process. The moments of knowledge construction form the high points in the learning process and are sometimes remembered as peak experiences.

The results of the 15 pilot studies conducted in the Netherlands and the 68 investigations completed by the University of Michigan in the US have fostered the expectation that problems that have confronted teacher educators and their students during the 20th century can be tackled in the 21st century because of the availability of a digital representation of teaching practice and the use of information technology in studying it. This will serve to solve the irreconcilable differences between theory and practice enabling student teachers to learn from previously inaccessible real teaching situations and help them acquire practice knowledge, which they can reconstruct as reflective knowledge.

In the MILE project, an environment/digital representation of teaching practice is being developed for Dutch primary school mathematics teacher education. At present, nearly all the 40 Colleges of Education in the Netherlands have access to the material, which consists of 65 GB records of practice, on local networks. This chapter was written on the basis of the results of 15 pilot projects and the considerations that were made in developing the environment.

Some questions still have to be answered, such as how to establish a useful link between the fieldwork of teacher education students and their investigations and discourses in MILE. In addition, we need to find out how we can best help educators put into effect this major reversal of ideas that starting from teaching practice and holding theoretical reflections require of them.

REFERENCES

Barnett, C. S. (1998). Mathematics case methods project. *Journal of Mathematics Teacher Education, 1*, (349-356).

Bereiter, C. & Scardamalia, M. (1992). An architecture for collaborative knowledge building. In De Corte, Linn, Mandel, & Verschaffel (Eds.), *Computer based LE and problem solving* (Nato ASI series 1992).

Bruner, J. (1986). *Actual minds, possible words.* Cambridge, MA: Havard University Press.

Cobb, P., McClain, K., & Whitenack, J.(1997). Reflective discourse and collective reflection. *Journal for Research in Mathematics Education, 28*(3).

Cohen, D. (1998). Experience and education: Learning to teach. In Lampert, M. & Loewenberg Ball, D. (Eds.), *Teaching, Multimedia, and Mathematics, investigations of real practice.* New York: Teachers College Press.

Delandshere, G. & Petrosky, A.R. (1994). Capturing teachers' knowledge: performance assessment. a) and post-structuralist epistemology; 6) From a post-structuralist perspective; c) and post-structuralism; d) None of the above. *Educational Researcher, 11*(18).

Dolk, M., Faes, W., Goffree, F., Hermsen, H., & Oonk, W. (1996). *A multimedial interactive learning environment for (future) primary school teachers with content for primary mathematics teachers education programs.* Utrecht: MILE-reeks, publicatie 1, Freudenthal Instituut/NVORWO.

Elbaz, F. (1983). *Teacher thinking: A study of practical knowledge.* London: Croom Helm.

Fenstermacher, G.D. (1994). The Knower and the known: The nature of knowledge in research on teaching. In L. Darling-Hammond (Ed.), *Review of Research on Teaching, 20*,1-54.

Goffree, F. (1994). *Wiskunde & didactiek, deel 1.* Groningen: Wolters-Noordhoff.

Goffree, F. (1998). *MILE op de werkvloer.* MILE-reeks nr 8. Utrecht: Freudenthal Instituut.

Goffree, F. & Oonk, W. (1999). Educating primary school mathematics teachers in the Netherlands: Back to the classroom. *Journal of Mathematics Teacher Education Education, 2* (2), 207-214.

Gravemeijer, K. (1995). *Developing realistic mathematics education.* Utrecht: Freudenthal Instituut.

Gudmundsdottir, S. (1995). The narrative nature of pedagogical content knowledge. In H. McEwan & K. Egan (Eds.), *Narrative in teaching, learning and, research.* (pp. 24-38). New York: Teachers College, Columbia University.

Herrington, A., Herrington, J., Sparrow, L., & Oliver, R. (1998). Learning to teach and assess mathematics using multimedia: A teacher development project. *Journal of Mathematics Teacher Education, 1* (1), 189-112.

Holt, J. (1964). *How children fail.* New York: Pitman Publishing Company.

Jackson, P.W. (1968). *Life in classrooms.* New York: Holt, Rinehart, & Winston.

Jalongo, M.R. & J.P. Isenberg. (1995). *Teachers' stories. From personal narrative to professional insight.* San Francisco: Jossey-Bass Publishers.

Jaworski, B. (1998). Mathematics teacher research: Process, practice and the development of teaching. *Journal of Mathematics Teacher Education, 1*(3-31). Netherlands: Kluwer Academic Publishers.

Kilpatrick, J. (1987). What construction might be in mathematics education. In: J.C. Bergeron, N. Hercovics, & C. Kieran (Eds.), *Psychology of mathematics education, PME-XI, Vol. I.* (pp. 3-27).

Krainer, K. (1999). Teacher education and investigations into teacher education: A conference as a learning environment. In K.Krainer & F.Goffree (Eds.), *On research in teacher education. From a study of teaching practices to issues in teacher education.* CERME 1. Forschungsinstitut für Mathematikdidaktik, Osnabrück.

Lampert, M. (1985). How do teachers manage to teach? Perspectives on problems in practice. *Harvard Educational Review, 55* (2).

Lampert, M. & Loewenberg Ball, D. (1998). *Teaching. Multimedia and mathematics. Investigations of real practice.* New York: Teachers College Press.

Lortie, D. C. (1975). *Schoolteacher: A sociological study of teaching.* Chicago: University of Chicago Press.

Markusse, A. (2000). Mile voor tweedejaarsstudenten. Pabo Educatieve Faculteit Amsterdam. *Panamapost, Tijdschrift voor nascholing en onderzoek van het reken-wiskundeonderwijs, 18* (2). Utrecht: Freudenthal Instituut.

McEwan, H & K. Egan, (Eds.) (1995). *Narrative in teaching, learning and, research* (pp. 24-38). New York: Teachers College, Columbia University.

Meijer, P. (1999). *Teachers' practical knowledge. Teaching reading comprehension in secondary education*. Doctoral dissertation, University of Leiden.

Oonk, W. (1999). *Pioniers in MILE. Een exploratief onderzoek*. MILE-reeks nr 9. Utrecht: Freudenthal Instituut.

Pendlebury, S. (1995). Reason and story in wise practice. In H. McEwan & K. Egan, (Eds.), *Narrative in teaching, learning and, research. (pp. 50-68)*. New York: Teachers College, Columbia University.

Richert, A.E. (1991). Case methods and teacher education. Using cases to teach teacher reflection. In B.R. Tabachnick & K. Zeichner. (Eds.), *Issues and practices in inquiry-oriented teacher education*. The Falmer Press: London.

Schoenfeld, A.H. (Ed.). (1987). *Cognitive science and mathematics education*. Hillsdale: Lawrence Erlbaum.

Schön, D. (1983). *The reflective practitioner*. Basic Books, New York.

Slavin, R.E. (1985). An introduction to cooperative learning research. In R. Slavin, S. Sharan, S. Kagan, R. Hertz-Lazarowitz, C. Webb, & R. Schmuck (Eds.), *Learning to cooperate, cooperating to learn* (pp. 5-15). New York: Plenum Press.

Smaling, A. (1987). *Methodologische objectiviteit en kwalitatief onderzoek* (Methodological objectivity and qualitative research). Doctoral dissertation. Lisse, The Netherlands: Swets & Zeitlinger.

Spiro, R.J., Coulson, R.L., Feltovich, P.J., & Anderson, D.K. (1988). Cognitive flexibility theory: Advanced knowledge acquisition in ill-structured domains. In V.Patel (Ed.), *Tenth annual conference of the Cognitive Science Society* (pp. 375-383). Hillsdale, NJ: Lawrence Erlbaum.

Steinbring, H.(1998). Elements of epistemological knowledge for mathematics teachers. *Journal of Mathematics Teacher Education, 1*, (2), 157-189.

Tabachnick, B.R. & Zeichner K. (1991). *Issues and practices in inquiry-oriented teacher education*. The Falmer Press: London

Tough, A. (1971). *The adult's learning projects: A fresh approach to theory and practice in adult learning*. Toronto: Ontario Institute for Studies in Education.

Treffers, A. & E. De Moor (1990). *Proeve van een nationaal programma voor het reken-wiskundeonderwijs op de basisschool, deel 2*. Tilburg: Zwijsen.

Van den Heuvel-Panhuizen, M. & Vermeer, H.J. (1999). *Verschillen tussen meisjes en jongens bij het vak rekenen-wiskunde op de basisschool. Eindrapport MOOJ-onderzoek*. Utrecht: Freudenthal Instituut.

Verloop, N. (1991). *Praktijkkennis van docenten als deel van de onderwijskundige kennisbasis*. Oratie Rijks Universiteit Leiden.

Wittmann, E.Ch. (1995). Mathematics education as a 'design science'. *Educational Studies in Mathematics, 29*, 355-374.

Zeichner, K. (1981). Reflective teaching and field-based experience in teacher education. *Interchange 12*, (4), 1 - 22.

Freudenthal Institute
University of Utrecht
The Netherlands

PETER SULLIVAN AND JUDY MOUSLEY

THINKING TEACHING: SEEING MATHEMATICS TEACHERS AS ACTIVE DECISION MAKERS

ABSTRACT: Many teachers are now incorporating a broader range of strategies into their teaching, including problem solving, investigations and open-ended questions. Among other things, such teaching requires teachers to talk less but to make more decisions. The acknowledgment of this complexity and the centrality of active decision making have implications for teacher education and teacher development, and for the strategies and resources used.

The role of teacher is partly scientific and partly artistic; partly following routines and partly being creative; partly technical and partly professional; partly theoretical and partly practical; partly proactive and partly reactive; and partly principles and partly application. The list can go on. This chapter focuses on the second of each of these bipolars: the artistic, creative, professional, practical, reactive and applied elements of teaching. In other words, the aspects of teaching that require active decision making.

It is recognised that in the classroom too much is happening for teachers to make new decisions in response to every circumstance, and guiding principles, theories, and technical skills are needed to help. Nevertheless, the very complexity that makes routines necessary also requires teachers to be making and remaking decisions in response to circumstances pressing in the classroom. This key teaching role—that of decision maker—is sometimes not fully acknowledged in teacher development programs and even by teachers themselves.

The chapter is in two parts. The first elaborates the nature of complexity of teaching, and describes some factors impacting on one aspect of teaching about which teachers must make active decisions—the choice of tasks. The second attends to ways that teacher development programs can highlight this complexity and so increase awareness among teachers of their decision-making roles and, as an example, describes a particular resource designed for use in teacher education using this complexity as the basis for development experiences for teachers.

1. FACTORS INFLUENCING THE CHOICE OF CLASSROOM TASKS

This part of this chapter summarises some of the aspects of beliefs and constraints that influence teachers' actions, giving the argument that teaching is complex, and so teachers must make active decisions more or less constantly. As an exemplar to illustrate this complexity, this section includes a summary of issues associated with

F.-L. Lin & T. J. Cooney (Eds.) Making Sense of Mathematics Teacher Education, 147—163.
© 2001 *Kluwer Academic Publishers. Printed in the Netherlands.*

the decisions teachers make on the choice of classroom tasks for pupils. A model adapted from Clark and Peterson (1986) elaborates the factors influencing classroom action as follows.

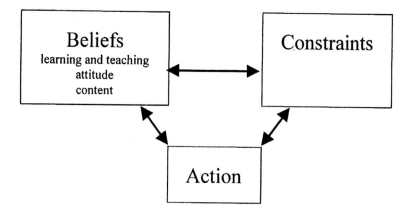

Figure 1. Interactions between beliefs, constraints, and action

1.1 Beliefs About Learning and Teaching

The way that teachers define their role is based on not only their conceptions of learning, but also their beliefs about teaching. These perspectives of learning and teaching underlie both the choice of tasks teachers make and the way in which they use the tasks. For example, some teachers adopt a social constructivist view that Ernest (1994) summarised as recognising that knowing is active, individual, and personal; is based on previously constructed knowledge; is socially negotiated rather than transmitted as fixed; and is sought and expressed through language.

Ernest listed among the pedagogical implications that teachers need to be sensitive to learners' previous constructions; to seek to identify errors and misconceptions; to foster metacognitive techniques; and to acknowledge social contexts of learners and content. Other apparent implications are that experiences that allow learners to think and create for themselves, as well as to have opportunities to discuss their interpretations and develop shared meanings, will be productive. In other words, the learners' active and social construction of concepts is important.

There are also teachers who draw on models of learning and thinking from studies of expertise (e.g., Bransford, Brown, & Cocking, 1999). The argument here is that experts have well-organised, systematic knowledge structured to support understanding, and that students need explicit experiences of a range of mathematical concepts, opportunities to link new knowledge to existing conceptual frameworks, and practice at accessing that information.

Such views also have implications for the ways that teachers see their role. As Lerman (1998) said, "...the metaphor of students as passive recipients of a body of knowledge is terribly limited: so too is the metaphor of students as all-powerful constructors of their own knowledge, and indeed of their own identities" (p. 70). A useful way of thinking about a role for the teacher was proposed by Vygotsky (1978). He described the zone of proximal development to be the "distance between the actual developmental level as determined by independent problem solving and the level of potential development as determined by problem solving under adult guidance or in collaboration with more capable peers" (p. 86).

Cognitive gains are made in sociocultural contexts in which teachers enable learning by drawing learners forward with appropriate activities, including dialogue. "Guided participation necessarily involves subtle communication between people as to what new information is needed or appropriate and how it can be made compatible with current levels of skill and understanding ... (building) bridges from children's current understanding to reach new understanding through processes inherent in communication" (Rogoff, 1991, p. 351). Vygotsky noted that learning is essentially social, and is the process by which children "grow into the intellectual life of those around them" (1978, p. 88) with the assistance of an appropriate learner-focused sequence of ideas and activities.

A similar perspective was suggested by Cobb and McClain (1999) who proposed that teachers should actively consider an "instructional sequence (that) takes the form of a conjectured learning trajectory that culminates with the mathematical ideas that constitute our overall instructional intent" (p. 24). Once again, the teacher has socially-valued endpoints in mind, but starting points are grounded in children's current levels of cognition.

Both the notions of a zone of proximal development and of a learning trajectory define key roles for teachers. These roles are not transmissive, but involve teachers first in considering potential spaces and pathways between children's current understandings and higher levels of knowledge; and then in providing a supportive environment with appropriate activities to enable learners to move forward in their own ways. Both theories identify an active decision-making dimension to those roles, a dimension that links learners' knowledge with social-valued learning objectives.

The contentious issue is how such zone or trajectory can be identified and activated. One metaphor is a climbing wall in an area set up for learning mountain climbing skills and techniques. Commonly, viable pathways are set up with hand and foot holds that are colour coded to indicate difficulty. The particular colour is matched to the degree of challenge, so climbers not only have appropriate challenges but also structured pathways that link starting points with their goals, Most importantly, they have degrees of choice, and they may respond in different productive ways. Not every choice will be productive however—using a hold of just any colour the climb is too easy, and the choice of inappropriate color combinations makes the climb impossible. The pathways and potential objectives have been set up by experts familiar with the skills, techniques, and typical levels of competency, and through the semi-structured environment experts use their knowledge to help climbers to scale more challenging paths than would be possible without this guidance.

The implications for teachers planning mathematical tasks include the need for the purpose of the task to be clear to learners; for the teacher to have a good sense of students' current understandings of concepts and key points to be grasped in moving forward; for teachers to have a sense of appropriate standards as well as particular intentions for the way the pupils may respond to the tasks; and for learners to have some sense of choice and ownership over forms and levels of engagement with the task.

1.2 Beliefs About Attitudes

Another factor that teachers consider in relation to classroom tasks is the attitudes of the pupils. Rather than describing attitudes broadly, we consider the complexity of just one aspect, motivation.

In a review of research on motivation, Middleton and Spanias (1999) identified three key findings. First, it appears that students who are successful are more likely to perceive engagement in mathematics as worthwhile, particularly if the success is attributable to their ability and effort. The perception that lack of success is due to the lack of ability can inhibit students' motivation to learn. This may operate differentially based on gender (e.g., Fennema & Leder, 1990), and culture (e.g., Stigler & Stephenson, 1994).

The second finding is that motivation towards mathematics is developed early, is learned, is stable, but is amenable to influence by teachers. It seems that the same applies to students' conceptions of mathematics and the way it is learned (McDonough, 1998).

Third, assisting students to develop intrinsic motivation toward learning mathematics is superior to providing extrinsic rewards. McComb and Pope (1994) argued that this is particularly important for "hard to reach" students.

Middleton and Spanias (1999) also argued that achievement motivation in mathematics could be effected through careful instructional design. This relates to the Middleton's earlier (1995) research that identified arousal, personal control, and interest as important in determining the motivation of students to undertake particular activities. They concluded that:

> when individuals engage in tasks in which they are motivated intrinsically they tend to exhibit a number of pedagogically desirable behaviours including increased time on task, persistence in the face of failure, more elaborative processing, the monitoring of comprehension, and selection of more difficult tasks, greater creativity and risk taking, selection of deeper and more efficient performance and learning strategies, and choice of activity in the absence of extrinsic reward. (1999, p. 66)

The implications of this are that tasks need to provide opportunities for success, yet also present an appropriate level of challenge and difficulty for students; that increasing students' sense of control, interest, and arousal can help elicit intrinsic motivation; that classroom tasks in which the students choose to participate will be more productive; and that there is a need for consideration of the social context in which the learning takes place.

Clearly, consideration of pupils' motivation alone is very complex. When other effective aspects such as enjoyment, attribution, self-efficacy, persistence, and so on, are taken into account, this increases the scope of the teacher's considerations even further.

1.3 Beliefs About Mathematics as the Focus of the Learning

A further factor contributing to the complexity of teaching is the way the mathematics to be learned is presented. Sullivan (1999) suggested that teachers must consider the relationships between mathematics content and mathematics context, situational content and situational context. The following model might illustrate how these interact:

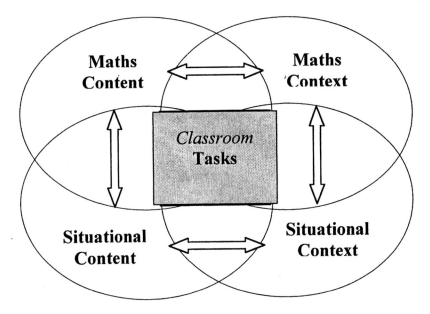

Figure 2. Relationship between aspects of classroom tasks

To clarify the interaction of these components, Sullivan (1999) elaborated these elements for the following problem:

> If each person were to shake hands with each other person in the room once and only once, how many handshakes would take place? (Stacey & Southwell, 1983, p. 38)

The *mathematical content* of this problem is about recognising that there is a pattern, recognising the n(n–1)/2 relationship, manipulating the symbols, substituting, calculating, and like actions.

The *situational content* is about knowing what is a handshake. This issue is perhaps most relevant to those students with different cultural or linguistic backgrounds, and is sometimes overlooked. Even though this context is probably clear enough, consider how it may be viewed by children who may never shake hands, to women who may shake hands less or greet each other in other ways, to Thai people or to Maoris who may at times use other forms of greeting. This perhaps suggests the possibility of multiple interpretations of particular contexts.

The *situational context* is about people in a room, that you do not shake hands with yourself, that a meeting of two hands is counted as one handshake, and that the key variable is the number of people. What normally are referred to as real life contexts are included under this heading.

The *mathematical context* refers to the concept of trial and error, of strategies such as making the problem simpler, and making a table. It includes making links with similar problems such as calculating the number of lines needed to join n points on a circle, the number of different pairs for table tennis chosen from n students, and so on. This latter aspect is really the ultimate focus for mathematical learning and often is blurred by over-attention to either the situational context or the mathematical content.

On the one hand, there is a need for the curriculum, and classroom tasks, to address specific mathematics content explicitly. On the other hand, focusing only on the mathematical content is too narrow. In other words, even though the focus may be on particular concepts, the enacting of these concepts requires attention to generalising, problem solving, creating, linking, and synthesising, as well as to a variety of situations in which the concepts will be applicable. These contextual and situational processes are as much a part of the mathematics curriculum as the specific content.

The implications for classroom tasks are that there are key ideas in mathematics which should form the focus of the mathematics curriculum and classroom tasks, and that the role of the teacher is to frame a program that moves children towards these concepts by extending and building on the mathematical concepts of which the students have understanding. Situational contexts can help give the students access to the mathematics, but these should not be the end goal of the learning experience; nor should they be allowed to blur either the mathematics content or the mathematical context. Providing classroom tasks that allow consideration of each of these aspects is a key element of the teachers' role.

1.4 Constraints on Classroom Processes

In the Clarke and Peterson model considered earlier, opportunities and constraints interact with all of these considerations related to teachers' beliefs about learning, teaching, attitudes, and mathematics.

A framework for considering opportunities and constraints, adapted from Yackel and Cobb (1996), delineates two complementary norms of activity in mathematics classrooms. *Mathematical norms* refer to the principles, generalisations, processes and products which form the basis of the mathematics curriculum and which serve as the tools of so much other learning. *Socio-cultural norms* refer to the usual practices, organisational routines, and modes of communication that impact on the approaches to learning teachers choose, the types of responses they value, their views about legitimacy of knowledge produced, the responsibility of individual learners, and their acceptance of risk-taking and errors. These socio-cultural norms are too often under-emphasised.

It is our contention that participants in mathematics classrooms need to be made aware that they are becoming members of a "community of practice" (Lave, 1988). The community here is not just a group of people, but includes traditional socio-professional expectations, beliefs, tools (including language), physical settings, and patterns of interaction—the socio-cultural norms of mathematics education contexts. The community thus embraces not only the classroom and its participants but (also) the broader social system of teaching and learning in institutions as well as that of using mathematics in schools and the wider society. What counts as valid knowledge in mathematics as well as ways of acting in mathematical environments forms the core of this community, and the mathematical and socio-cultural norms of classrooms interact to convey this information to learners. Students' activities in this learning community make possible not only their own increasing participation in its core activities, but also transformations in their understandings, identities, and future opportunities.

One aspect of the socio-cultural norms is the very real constraints which students naturally impose on the mathematics teacher. It appears that the reaction of students is foremost in the thinking of teachers in planning, during teaching, and in post lesson reviews. Teachers seek to avoid negative student reactions (Shroyer, 1982), to adhere to stated plans (Peterson & Clark, 1978), to minimize risks (Marland, 1986), and to adjust their teaching to the preferred learning style of the students, who exert indirect but real influence over the teacher (Larson, 1983).

Doyle (1986) noted the tendency for this influence of students on teachers tends to be negative and the effects of this negative influence on implementation of mathematical norms. He reported that pupils tended to misbehave during tasks that involved higher-order processes such as understanding, reasoning, and problem formulation because they could not anticipate the response expected by the teacher, and the risk of failure was high. In contrast, students worked efficiently on tasks involving recall of algorithms. Doyle argued that, on the one hand, students tried to reduce their risk of failure by seeking to increase the explicitness of task requirements and to reduce the level of accountability, thereby narrowing the demands of a task. Teachers tended to react by selecting tasks that were familiar and easy.

Desforges and Cockburn (1987) reached similar conclusions. They examined the influence of classrooms processes on mathematics teaching in particular. Among their findings were that students were not interested in each other's opinions and quickly became fidgety during class discussions. Classroom order was seen as a negotiated contract, and teachers were understandably reluctant to threaten the cooperation of students. Children liked the worksheets, which reinforced the teachers' approach. The more the content moved toward unfamiliar work, the more difficult teaching became.

One implication of the choice of classroom tasks is that reducing the censure commonly associated with failure, and therefore the liability associated with risk, is key. This can perhaps be achieved by explicit attention to classroom sociocultural processes, along with consideration of tasks for which the risk is reduced by, for example, allowing the possibility of multiple correct responses. It may also be helpful for teachers to emphasise the way in which discussion contributes to learning for the students, and the way in which they can benefit from hearing the perspectives of their peers. Teachers can encourage children to see mistakes as actions and ideas worth examining and learning from, rather than as objects of derision (Stigler & Hiebert, 1999).

A different but highly relevant aspect of these socio-cultural processes is related to implicit pedagogies associated with teacher pupil interactions, and cultural biases inherent in so called progressive teaching methodologies. As Lerman (1998) commented, classroom discourses both "distribute powerlessness and powerfulness" (p. 76). Zevenbergen (1998) referred to the literature outside mathematics education which has recognised the distinct differences in patterns of language use of socially-disadvantaged students and that of the formal school, but noted that only minimal work on this has been carried out in the field of mathematical learning. Zevenbergen argued that procedural processes can contribute to student disadvantage, and noted that pedagogy often renders invisible cultural norms through which meaning is conveyed. Students from backgrounds in which there are discontinuities between linguistic registers and societal aspirations of home and school have to decode aspects of classroom processes. For children whose cultural norms are similar to those embedded within mainstream pedagogical practice the mathematics is usually more accessible, while the converse is true for those students whose culture does not fit the dominant classroom routines. Zevenbergen proposed that one solution that appears to enable these students to gain access to the lesson content is to make socio-cultural norms of pedagogy explicit to teachers and, through them, also to children.

Although the implications for this are not elaborated here, it is clear that tasks which allow teachers to discuss with pupils the goals and purpose of their activity, can be accessed in a variety of ways, and allow for a wide range of legitimate classroom activity, will facilitate an environment in which the teacher can address these other aspects of socio-cultural processes.

2. CONSIDERING THE COMPLEXITY

This part of the chapter uses considerations related to teachers' choice of particular classroom tasks to illustrate the complexity of teaching. We present the argument that given that teaching is complex and multidimensional, teachers need to be active decision makers who determine their own priorities rather then merely implementing standard directions, plans, and routines.

In summary, in making decisions about mathematical tasks arising from perspectives on learning and teaching, teachers might choose to:
- be sensitive to learners' previous constructions and provide structured pathways to link new knowledge to their previous conceptual frameworks;

- allow practice at accessing knowledge, and foster metacognition that includes identifying errors and misconceptions;
- allow opportunities for learners to think and create in ways that provide rich assessment data; and/or
- exercise leadership of the learning and provide expert advice by focusing explicitly on specific mathematics concepts and key ideas and by including an appropriate level of challenge.

Consideration of social and attitudinal aspects might lead teachers to:

- be more aware of and acknowledge social contexts of mathematics education, including pupils' perspectives of learning and learning environments;
- encourage learners to take responsibility for their learning, and create opportunities to discuss students' goals and purpose of activity;
- increase students' sense of control and choice, interest, and arousal by allowing a range of legitimate activity and by ensuring opportunities for success; and/or
- change the nature of right/wrong as the measure of success and establish a classroom ethos where students can take risks.

Of course, the development of specific strategies for attending to each one of these considerations is problematic. Such characteristics should not be thought of as recipes for good teaching, but as key issues to be considered in the light of the complexity of the classroom milieu.

To put such ideas into context, consider a Year 3 teacher about to teach vertical notation of multiplication. A measurable endpoint of the classroom activities may be to have the children perform the multiplication algorithm with regrouping. The teacher believes it is important for the children to be able perform this process with understanding, and to be able to use it in school and wider social contexts. Limits are set by curriculum documents—the aim is to be able to multiply two digits by one digit.

However, the task is not as clear as it first appears. In many countries, 3 x 4 is thought of in two ways. One interpretation is three groups with four in each group (reflected in language like "three lots of four" and "three fours"). The other is four groups with three in each group (the essence of "three multiplied by four"). In early primary classrooms in Australia and USA (as opposed to Japan and some other countries), teachers use almost exclusively the former idea and language such as "lots," "times," and "groups of." However, when introducing larger numbers and vertical recording are introduced, these teachers make a subtle switch not only in the algorithm, but in the underlying idea. The latter number in any pair generally becomes the multiplier. To add complexity, it is likely that even if a written problem does not have the larger number as the multiplicand, the algorithm will be constructed this way. Thus children who were quite confident in finding the number of sweets if 3 children have 4 sweets might not easily transfer that skill to finding the number of children in 3 buses with 44 children in each. Of course, the commutative law applies, so children are likely to find the right answers; but how well do they understand the basic concepts involved—the different ideas, words and conceptual transitions involved in commutivity of multiplication? Thus the task of planning a learning trajectory that leads to an understanding of the formal multiplication algorithm and ability to use it in everyday contexts becomes quite complex.

Given the elements of complexity requiring consideration listed above, our third grade teacher needs to ask some serious questions, and to respond to these by making decisions.

- What are the key ideas involved, and how are these commonly represented by the children? (For example, how is place value used in the children's thinking as well as spoken and written language?)
- What type of activity will allow each of these to be developed and integrated within this new context?
- How can the purpose of vertical notation best be conveyed to the children?
- What do the children understand and do habitually in relation to multiplication? What words do they generally use, and what actions do these words represent?
- Which number facts are best known so that the need for calculation does not add further complexity?
- Which problems from everyday contexts will be meaningful to the children?
- What are errors and misconceptions common in learners of this concept, and how can these be prevented, or perhaps be drawn on in the teaching and learning processes?
- What freedoms can be allowed in modes of working? (For example, when is repeated addition an appropriate substitution for multiplication?
- Must number facts be known rote, or is slower reasoning to be encouraged?
- Is mental calculation and just writing the solution appropriate? (Which aspects of setting out are negotiable?)
- What should be the role of estimation and/or approximation?
- How can the lesson be structured so that the children have time for reflection on and reporting about their own thinking processes, successes, and difficulties?

All of these questions centre around achievement of mathematical norms; a similar range of socio-cultural aspects could be identified, such as "Should the children work in groups, and if so what social elements need to be considered in the grouping process?"

This is just one example. The teaching of multiplication at Year 3 level is no more or less complex than teaching most other mathematics topics at other levels of primary, secondary, and tertiary mathematics education. The point is that teachers make decisions about such factors more or less constantly.

3.   IDENTIFYING MECHANISMS FOR ADDRESSING COMPLEXITY
WITHIN TEACHER EDUCATION PROGRAMS

With acceptance that teaching is complex, it is possible to acknowledge this complexity as part of teacher education. This can be done in different ways, depending on the model used for describing teacher education. Merseth and Lacey (1993) summarised some different approaches to teacher education. These include:

- an academic orientation that sees the teacher as the transmitter of knowledge and the focus of teacher education as being to increase the knowledge of the teacher;
- a personal development orientation where the focus is to foster self-knowledge in the teacher, who in turn will emphasise that with the pupils;
- a technical orientation that identifies and assesses competence in a range of discrete skills;
- a practical orientation where the emphasis is on thinking, decision making, practice, and the study of particular exemplars; and
- a social or critical approach that sees the teacher as a political actor forming part of a larger stage.

Merseth and Lacey argued for the practical orientation for teacher education and in turn for the use of case methods. Perhaps it is useful to extend this orientation and for teacher education students to study cases within the context of the recognition of complexity. This could include the intensive and intelligent study of practice; the critique of practice both within its own context and within the light of other factors; the establishment of critical reflection; the development of orientations toward looking beyond the obvious and moving beyond merely seeking to describe practice to analysing actions, responses, and pedagogical practices.

Clearly this is a tall order. One tool that can be used to both foster the study of practice and emphasise the importance of the recognition of complexity is the study the dilemmas that teachers face. Explicit focus on dilemmas illustrates both the complexity of practice and the need for strategic decisions. It highlights the tensions and develops an awareness of possibilities, advancing an orientation that seeks practical reconciliation that is appropriate for particular contexts. Such dilemmas are not easily reconciled because they are not open to consistently correct advice: while a decision may be appropriate at one time it will be less useful and even ill-advised in a different context. Most of all, well-informed but on-the-spot teacher decisions are seen as essential and vital aspects of purposeful and successful classroom practice.

The complexity illustrated by the discussion of factors influencing the choice of tasks raises significant dilemmas for teachers in planning and teaching. The dilemmas themselves may provide a way for teacher educators and teachers to address the complexity. Mousley and Sullivan (1997) argued that teacher educators should introduce teachers and prospective teachers to a range of dilemmas they will face in classrooms, to highlight both awareness of specific tensions and the need to seek reconciliation of these to allow effective action.

3.1 Using Classroom Dilemmas in Mathematics Teacher Education

Mousley and Sullivan (1997) described how the consideration of dilemmas is a central principle in their use of technology to provide case study material for education *in* the profession. Teachers face dilemmas constantly: whether to seek to reproduce society or transform it, to foster specific objectives or broad goals, to present mathematics as universal or culturally determined, to privilege communication or allow it to be free, to develop confidence or provoke challenge, and so on.

Other researchers also have found that electronic technologies provide new tools for making professionals aware of problematic situations in all levels of mathematics education. Foley and Schuck (1999) formed part of a teaching team that set up an internet-based facility for teacher education. They posed some classroom discussion starters and asked a number of well-respected mathematics educators and teachers from around the world to respond in writing to these. Not surprisingly, the respondents did not have consistent opinions, and some raised associated dilemmas. Student teachers working in groups used the responses as a starting point for their own theoretical and practical investigations. Foley and Schuck argue that this exercise successfully challenged student teachers' ideas about mathematics and mathematics education, and raised their awareness of the complexities of schooling

Lampert and Ball (1998) noted that students of education rarely have opportunities in schools to replay events in order to examine them through different lenses, to make and test conjectures, to watch development (of ideas, children, and teaching approaches) over time, to discuss with others specific occurrences and assumptions, or to consider alternative responses and courses of action. They demonstrated how a multimedia environment could support the knitting of theory with practice, where "theory" includes published research findings and advice about teaching as well as the grounded theory that can develop through engaging with data. Their research illustrated that knowledge which is constructed in this practice complements, supports, and extends what is learned in the practice of school experience.

Our own research over the past five years has centred on the development of a computer-based resource that facilitates detailed investigation of classroom dilemmas, as is discussed below. The choices are not so much about which poles of the dilemmas to emphasise, or even about determining which poles are compatible with conventional wisdom, but how to use the dilemmas themselves to strengthen both curriculum and pedagogy. Rather than seeing different processes as dichotomous, teachers can become aware of the continua associated with each dilemma and move along these strategically, according to situational factors operating at particular times (see, for example, Berlak & Berlak, 1981). In other words, each pole of a dilemma interplays with its opposite, in a productive and dialectical engagement. In this sense, knowledge about teaching is not so much about knowing which choices are correct, but more about having an acute awareness of possibilities and an ability to make informed, strategic decisions.

Using technology to stimulate consideration of the complexity of teaching. *Learning About Teaching* was a product of a research project that identified the need to use real contexts to facilitate the analysis of teaching (see Mousley, Sullivan & Clements, 1991). Prior to the development of the resource, the project proposed a framework for describing elements of quality mathematics teaching. It used analysis of recent literature and a survey of 200 practitioners, teacher educators and other education professionals from several countries to identify these components (see Sullivan & Mousley, 1994).

Full lessons that exemplified the components of quality mathematics teaching identified were planned, then taught and videotaped. The videotapes were examined using several techniques, including a qualitative analysis of unstructured reviews of the lessons by over 30 experienced teacher educators (see Mousley, Sullivan, & Gervasoni, 1994). Along with other relevant data and readings, they were transferred to CD-ROM disc (Mousley, Sullivan, & Mousley, 1997). An interactive multimedia computer environment was authored to provide flexible access to all aspects of the lessons and to make links between related aspects of the resource.

The decision to use multimedia was made because of its capacity to show many facets of classroom situations and to allow simultaneous features of the classroom interaction to be unpacked. Classrooms are multidimensional and the daily world of the mathematics teacher is a capricious one, but multimedia can give users access to minute features of classroom interaction as well as control over the use of different constructs. We support the claims of Merseth and Lacey (1993) that this has potential for introducing the complexity of pedagogy to novices and experienced teachers alike and that the non linear capability of multimedia allows the use of multiple perspectives as well as opportunities to review situations.

To capture some of this complexity, the *Learning About Teaching* resource links the videotape of a mathematics lesson to other video records such as pre- and post-lesson interviews with the teachers, procedural documents and readings associated with the lessons, graphic representations of data, a full transcript, and so on. This forms an extensive information bank that can be accessed in flexible ways to support detailed analysis of classroom interactions. Indexing allows scenarios to be examined in conjunction with other data, enabling users to focus on specific teaching skills, moments of interaction, selected sets of incidents, sequences of events, links between theory and the pedagogical action presented, particular students' work, and so on.

A key feature of the resource is the extent to which it raises problematic teaching situations, allowing users to become aware that there are dilemmas to be confronted. The basic proposition that underlies the resource is that the study of particular exemplars of quality practice can stimulate reflection on key components of teaching.

Using dilemmas as the basis of the study of teaching. The videotape of the lesson shows a Year 5/6 teacher giving groups of children 24 blocks each, and asking them to design as many buildings as they can. Her instructions confine the buildings to cuboid shapes. The introductory stage of the lesson involves children exploring the properties of a cube individually, and out of this come some important ideas and words, such as *right angles* and *dimensions*. When the lesson moves on to children designing their buildings, the groups of children record their findings in quite different ways. Some discover a formula for volume and express this symbolically, and later use logic to determine how many different cuboids are possible. Others work more comfortably with drawings and longer descriptions of their buildings. During the last half of the lesson, the children share their group strategies and ask each other questions. The children then complete a worksheet, and it is clear that some children use the ideas and language introduced by other groups.

The lesson is successful; but like all lessons it raises many issues, and these are highlighted in the multimedia presentation. For each incident in the lesson, the program asks one or more thought-provoking questions that aim to draw out varied pedagogical beliefs and to stimulate sensitive responses. It is expected that groups of users will investigate and discuss these focus questions. Many of the questions draw attention to particular aspects of the lesson where teacher decision-making is involved, and they are intended to provide a stimulus for deeper reflection on problematic aspects of the task of teaching. The following are some examples of focus questions that appear in different sections of the resource:

Numbers of questions

The teacher asked about 60 questions. Should she take steps to reduce the proportion of her questions and increase the proportion of pupil questions? If so, what steps could be taken?

Teacher education students working on this question generally raise issues of control. They recognise a need for teachers (and particularly student teachers) to feel in control of the learning activities, as well as of the learners, and the power of teacher questioning in maintaining this. However, they also see the need for lessons to attend to learners' questions and for the children to feel a sense of ownership over the forms of interaction. This question also leads to discussion, reading, and writing about the different types purposes of questions (such as challenging, probing) and when it is appropriate to use each. This and more pointed focus questions stimulate debate about whether teachers' questions should be directed to quieter, more reluctant students who are listening attentively, or whether such a strategy can be counter-productive. In such discussions, socio-cultural aspects are relevant; teachers using the resource point out such factors as some children finding challenging questions threatening and some questions such as "Do you think using the blocks would help?" actually being subtle directions, a genre with which some children are not familiar.

Blackboard

In explaining the concept of dimension, the teacher uses a two dimensional diagram on the chalkboard. This has advantages and disadvantages. List these, and suggest some other appropriate strategies.

This question has stimulated discussions about how use of teaching aids sometimes gets in the way of children's conceptual development, as well as who about uses the blackboard and for what purposes. Some student teachers note how the teacher encourages other forms of explanation, and that later in the lesson this is replicated when the children use the board during their explanations while others get a chance to make further comments. One group of student teachers may focus here on the key issue of ways teachers use tools of the trade, including questions of when, who, how, and with what consequences. Another group may concentrate on the teachers' use of terms (such as *breadth* and *depth*) and the gestures she uses to convey meaning as overcoming the limitations of the two-dimensions sketch.

A mathematical concept

> Daniel claims there is a fourth dimension. What are your ideas on this concept? Is this
> an idea that the teacher could have taken further at this stage? Find out how some other
> people would react to this classroom incident. How could you explore this concept with
> older children?

This focus question has been the subject of debates that raise key issues related to socio-constructivist theory. Daniel is asked to explain what he means by "prism", and says "Well it's a dimension ... (the cube) would have three dimensions, and there are others that have three dimensions ... or four dimensions, or maybe even two". The teacher responds to Daniel by saying "Well there's some very interesting ideas there. Does anyone have any ideas to follow on from Daniel's thoughts about prisms?" After another child comments that he does not know what prisms are, the teacher suggests they should leave further discussion about prisms until the next day. This snippet of video raises a host of issues about children's use of mathematical language and about the notions of misconceptions and partial understandings. We have found that experienced primary and secondary teachers react differently to this context. Attention to this situation has also led to consideration of the advantages and disadvantages of a teacher holding to a lesson plan despite fruitful, and perhaps vital, pathways being offered that imply the risk of changing the intended lesson radically. Thus such a snippet raises opportunities for contemplation about teachers' roles in the light of theories such as those of Vygotsky and/or Cobb and McClain, as mentioned above. One group of teachers using *Learning About Teaching* in a professional development session explored the topic of how the targets set in curriculum documents shape teaching and learning activity, and the possibility that teachers' use of the set objectives in effect curtails different or tangential types of learning activity.

In summary, it can be seen that the focus questions have the potential to address a wide range of teaching dilemmas that relate to mathematical norms, socio-cognitive norms, and interactions between these. The dilemmas they raise both illustrate the complexity of teaching and also provide a vehicle for its study.

A further dimension of the potential of focus questions to illustrate dilemmas is the environment in which these are studied. The resource described above is ideal for use by groups of peers. These groups can ideally operate within a framework of a particular focussed study, operating independently of a lecturer or so-called expert. The intention is that the sharing of the experiences between peers helps to raise awareness of the different perspectives, different ways of viewing classroom events and the nature of the complexity of teaching. In other words, it is not about students seeking to find the right way, but rather it is about creating awareness in students that no single right way exists, and that approaches are dependant on multiple factors that are idiosyncratic to a particular context.

4. CONCLUSION

Teaching is complex, and teachers make many significant decisions progressively throughout each lesson. Teacher education should recognise this complexity, and professional development programs can use the complexity as a focus. In the company of colleagues, detailed analysis and consideration of this complexity of situations drawn from classroom practice can both raise awareness of this complexity and suggest alternative modes of resolving such situations. The focus is on acknowledging the teacher as a thinking, decision making, intelligent professional.

We suggest that interactive multimedia is a tool that can be used to develop student teachers' and teachers' understandings of the complexities of mathematics classrooms as well as about the many roles that they can play. It allows moments that have potential for active classroom decision making to be "frozen," discussed, and explored in relation to relevant literature. Thus it facilitates reflective analysis of teaching and debate about alternative possibilities for the resolution of inherent tensions.

REFERENCES

Berlak, A., & Berlak, H. (1981). *Dilemmas of schooling: Teaching and social change.* New York: Methuen.

Bransford, J. B., Brown, A. L., & Cocking, R. R. (Eds.) (1999). *How people learn: Brain, mind, experience, and school.* Washington: Committee on Developments in the Science of Learning, National Research Council.

Cobb, P., & McClain, K. (1999). Supporting teachers' learning in social and institutional contexts. In Fou-Lai Lin (Ed.), *Proceedings of the 1999 International Conference on Mathematics Teacher Education* (pp. 7–77). Taipei, National Taiwan Normal University.

Clark, C. M., & Peterson, P. L. (1986). Teachers' thought processes. In M. C. Wittrock (Ed.), *Handbook of research on teaching* (3rd edition) (pp. 256–296). New York: Macmillan.

Desforges, C., & Cookburn, A. (1987). *Understanding the mathematics teacher: A study of practice in first schools.* London: The Falmer Press.

Doyle, W. (1986). Classroom organisation and management. In M. C. Wittrock (Ed.), *Handbook of research on teaching* (pp. 392–431). New York: Macmillan.

Ernest, P. (1994). Varieties of constructivism: Their metaphors, epistemologies and pedagogical implications. *Hiroshima Journal of Mathematics Education, 2,* 1–14.

Fennema, E., & Leder, G. (Eds.) (1990). *Mathematics and gender.* New York: Teachers College Press.

Foley, G., & Schuck, S. (February, 1999). *Locating discussion about maths in virtual space: Grounding it in reality.* Paper presented at the Initial Teacher Education Forum "Showcasing excellence in initial teacher education and schooling," RMIT University, Melbourne.

Lampert, M., & Ball, D. L. (1998). *Teaching, multimedia, and mathematics: Investigations of real practice.* The Practitioner Inquiry Series. New York: Teachers College Press.

Larson, S. (1983). Paradoxes in teaching. *Instructional Science, 12,* 355–365.

Lave, J. (1988). *Cognition in practice: Mind, mathematics and culture in everyday life.* Cambridge: Cambridge University Press.

Lerman, S. (1998). A moment in the zoom of a lens: Towards a discursive psychology of mathematics teaching and learning. In A. Olivier & K. Newstead (Eds.), *Proceedings of the 22nd Conference of the International Group for the Psychology of Mathematics Education* (vol. 1, pp. 66–81). Stellenbosch, South Africa: PME.

Marland, P. (1986). Models of teachers' interactive thinking. *Elementary School Journal, 87*(2), 209–226.

McComb, B. L., & Pope, J. E. (1994). *Motivating hard to reach students.* Washington: American Psychological Association.

McDonough, A. (1998). Young children's beliefs about the nature of mathematics. In A. Olivier & K. Newstead (Eds.), *Proceedings of the 22nd Conference of the International Group for the Psychology of Mathematics Education* (vol. 3, pp. 263–270). Stellenbosch, South Africa: PME.

Merseth, K. K., & Lacey, C. A. (1993). Weaving stronger fabric: The pedagogical promise of hypermedia and case methods in teacher education. *Teacher and Teacher Education, 9* (3), 283–299.

Middleton, J. A. (1995). A study of intrinsic motivation in the mathematics classroom: A personal construct approach. *Journal for Research in Mathematics Education, 26* (3), 254–279.

Middleton, J. A., & Spanais, P. A. (1999). Motivation for achievement in mathematics: Findings, generalisations and criticisms of the research. *Journal for Research in Mathematics Education, 30* (1), 65–88.

Mousley, J., & Sullivan, P. (1997). Dilemmas in the professional education of mathematics teachers. In E. Pekhonnen (Ed.), *Proceedings of the 21st Conference of the International Group for the Psychology of Mathematics Education* (pp. 131–147). Lahti, Finland: PME.

Mousley, J., Sullivan, P., & Clements, M. A. (July, 1991). *The perceptions which student teachers have of teaching practices in classrooms observed during field experience.* Paper presented at the thirteenth annual conference of the Mathematics Education Lecturers Association, Perth.

Mousley, J., Sullivan, P., & Gervasoni, A. (1994). The analysis of teaching: Constraints in lesson description and critique. In G. Bell, B. Wright, N. Leeson, & J. Geake (Eds.), *Challenges in mathematics education: Constraints on construction* (pp. 437–444). Lismore: MERGA.

Mousley, J., Sullivan, P., & Mousley, P. (1997). *Learning about teaching.* Reston, VA: NCTM.

Peterson, P. L., & Clarke, C. M. (1978). Teachers' reports of their cognitive processes during teaching. *American Educational Research Journal, 15,* 555–565.

Rogoff, B. (1991). Social interaction as apprenticeship in thinking: Guided participation in spatial planning. In L. B. Resnick, J. M. Levine, & S. D. Teasley (Eds.), *Perspectives in socially shared cognition* (pp. 349–364). Washington, CD: American Psychological Association.

Stacey, K., & Southwell, B. (1983). *Teacher tactics for problem solving.* Canberra: Curriculum Development Centre.

Shroyer, J.C. (1982). Critical moments in the teaching of mathematics. What makes teaching difficult? *Dissertation Abstracts International, 42A,* 3485.

Stigler, J. W., & Hiebert, J. (1999). *The teaching gap: Best ideas from the world's teachers for improving education in the classroom.* New York: The Free Press.

Stigler. J. W., & Stephenson, H. W. (1994). *The learning gap: Why our schools are failing and what we can learn from Japanese and Chinese education.* New York: Simon and Schuster.

Sullivan, P. (1999). Seeking a rationale for particular classroom tasks and activity. In J. Truran and K. Truran (Eds.), *Proceedings of the 22nd annual Conference of the Mathematics Education Research Group of Australasia* (pp. 15–29). Adelaide: MERGA.

Sullivan, P., & Mousley, J. (1994). Quality mathematics teaching: Describing some key components. *Mathematics Education Research Journal. 6*(1), 4–22.

Vygotsky, V. (1978). *Mind in society.* Boston, MA: Harvard University Press.

Yackel, E., & Cobb, P. (1996). Sociomathematical norms, argumentation, and autonomy in mathematics. *Journal for Research in Mathematics Education, 27,* 458–477.

Zevenbergen, R. (1998). Language, mathematics and social disadvantage: A Bourdieuian analysis of cultural capital in mathematics education. In C. Kanes, M. Goos, & E. Warren (Eds.), *Teaching mathematics in new times. Proceedings of the 21st annual Conference of the Mathematics Education Research Group of Australasia* (pp. 716–722). Gold Coast: MERGA.

Peter Sullivan
Australian Catholic University
p.sullivan@patrick.acu.edu.au

Judy Mousley
Deakin University
judym@deakin.edu.au

KENNETH RUTHVEN

MATHEMATICS TEACHING, TEACHER EDUCATION, AND EDUCATIONAL RESEARCH:

DEVELOPING "PRACTICAL THEORISING" IN INITIAL TEACHER EDUCATION

ABSTRACT. This chapter will consider the relevance of research ideas and processes to teacher education and classroom teaching through the example of the postgraduate pre-service training course for secondary mathematics teachers to which I contribute. First, however, this example will be situated within the wider context of the English educational system.

1. CONTINUING CONTROVERSY OVER EDUCATIONAL RESEARCH AND TEACHER EDUCATION

In England, the central purposes of educational research and teacher education are not fundamentally contested. Educational research is a means to develop a greater understanding of the conditions and processes of teaching and learning, with a view to improving them. Teacher education is a means to help teachers develop their professional understanding and skill, so as to maintain and improve the quality of teaching and learning. In short, educational research and teacher education are seen as means of educational improvement. But what constitutes improvement, and how it can be brought about, are controversial. Rightly or wrongly—and inevitably the story is more complex than such simple evaluations allow—continuing changes in the organisation of teacher education, and forthcoming changes in the organisation of educational research, have arisen from a public perception and a political conviction that what were intended as *means* have become *ends* in themselves.

Educational research and teacher education have been accused of turning in on themselves, mesmerised by an endlessly recursive process of reflection and theorisation. Consequently, the charge is that, when they do engage with the practice of teaching and learning, they do so in unduly idealised terms. That, on the one hand, a *theory-into-practice* model encourages advocacy of exemplary models of teaching, without adequate analysis of their fitness for purpose under typical classroom conditions. That, on the other hand, when divergences and tensions emerge between ideal models and actual practice, *theory-into-practice* tends to become *theory-is-better-than-practice,* as these differences are construed unreflectively in terms that are critical of practice and practitioners.

F.-L. Lin & T. J. Cooney (Eds.) Making Sense of Mathematics Teacher Education, 165—183.
© 2001 *Kluwer Academic Publishers. Printed in the Netherlands.*

It has to be said that this same charge of idealism could be levelled with even more devastating force against recent governments. In their eagerness to effect their versions of educational improvement, they have proved ready to issue ever more directive— and no less idealized— models for teaching and teacher education, accompanied by systems of inspection and evaluation which hold teachers and teacher educators to regular and often punitive account against the detail of these models. This has produced a culture of strategic compliance in all sectors of the system, so that, once again, means have become frozen into ends.

A significant issue, which has tended to get lost in the increasingly heated and often polarised debate accompanying the reform of teacher education and educational research in England, is the absence of a shared professional culture embracing researchers, teacher educators, policy-makers and practitioners[i]. One of the more measured contributions to the debate has pointed out that:

> The overall message... from practitioners is that most educational research does not impinge much on policy or practice, and if it does so, it is likely to be in an *ad hoc* and individual way. This is partly a result of the complex web of influences that affect the development of policy and practice. It may also be a product of research not being done on the right issues or in the right way. Additionally, it reflects a lack of interest and understanding of research among policy-makers and practitioners, the absence of a capacity to assimilate research findings, and an insufficiently evidence-based policy formation and development system in the field of education. (Hillage, Pearson, Anderson, & Tamkin, 1998, p.xi)

2. CURRENTS OF THINKING AND REFORM IN INITIAL TEACHER EDUCATION

Initial teacher education provides a good example of the imperative tone adopted by central government. The most recent regulations comprise 138 close-packed pages (Department for Education and Employment [DfEE], 1998). The "Standards" which new teachers must meet in order to qualify, contain over 100 performance criteria, organised at five levels of heading and subheading. Most of these competences are worthy, if taken as heuristics indicating aspects of professional capability deserving of development. As presented, however, they convey an image of teaching— and of learning to teach— as a largely unproblematic matter. There are occasional hints that teachers need to exercise judgement; in "selecting," in "exploiting opportunities," in "using appropriately"; but no sense of the need to balance priorities, to entertain doubts, to cope with uncertainty.

What is entirely missing from this view of professional capability and of professional learning is the dimension which has served as the traditional argument for university involvement in initial teacher education. As summarised by Alexander:

> Learning to teach must be a continual process of hypothesis testing framed by detailed analysis of the values and practical constraints fundamental to teaching. The 'theory' for teacher education should therefore incorporate (i) speculative theory (ii) the findings of empirical research (iii) the craft knowledge of practising teachers, but none should be presented as having prescriptive implications for practice: instead students should be

encouraged to approach their own practice with the intention of testing hypothetical principles drawn from the consideration of different types of knowledge. (Alexander, 1984, p.146)

However, it has to be said that we have much evidence of how difficult it has proved to achieve this ideal of "practical theorising" within teacher education. The "endemic problems" identified by McIntyre (1988, 1990) include:

- Educational theorising is often experienced as largely irrelevant to the tasks facing student teachers in schools;
- There is often little opportunity to try out in schools even the practical advice given in university;
- Little value is generally attached to the observation of experienced teachers, and little learning apparently results;
- Little help is given to student teachers in critically examining the range of practice they observe in schools;
- Much of student teachers' learning about teaching is a semi-conscious trial-and-error kind of learning;
- What largely determines each student teacher's learning about teaching is his or her own individual agenda of concerns.

Student teachers, then, find themselves moving between contrasting worlds of university and school. However, an assumption is often made that the creation of a common culture enveloping both worlds is feasible and desirable. McIntyre dissents, arguing that the roles of university-based and school-based teacher educators need to be clearly differentiated to take account of the particular expertise that they are able to bring by virtue of other aspects of their work.

> The jobs which [university lecturers] have to do.... both require and allow them to concern themselves with [particular] kinds of knowledge... of good practice nationally and internationally, of research evidence, of different theoretical positions and their implications.... Their university positions also require and allow them to concern themselves with appropriate academic... criteria in judging the validity and value of claims to knowledge.... The work of mentors and other schoolteachers, on the other hand, enables and requires them to give priority attention to what is practical, what is feasible, socially acceptable and effective... within the specific contexts within which they work. In these circumstances, it would be very surprising indeed if the same ideas for thinking about teaching and learning tended to seem valuable to both schoolteachers and university [lecturers] or if the same norms of good practice were generally upheld by these two groups... The implicit model underlying most initial teacher education programmes... is that there *ought* to be a straightforward theory-into-practice continuity between the ideas discussed and approved in university contexts and those practised and approved in school contexts. (McIntyre, 1990, pp. 25-26)

A new opportunity to explore such issues has come from reforms which have required pre-service courses to become increasingly school-based, and which have transferred resources from universities to schools to enable this to happen. Indeed, the ambitious goal has been to create "partnership" in which responsibility is shared between university and collaborating schools for all aspects of initial teacher education programmes.

Traditionally within the English system, it was university-based lecturers who were seen as "teacher educators." During the periods of "teaching practice" that student teachers spent in schools, they were— in the official view— supervised by these university-based lecturers through periodic— but still relatively occasional— visits to observe their teaching and offer them guidance. Yet, in practice, and often without recognition, serving teachers within schools frequently played a far more significant part in advising student teachers. And, in some important respects, these teachers were better equipped to do so. They knew and understood the school context; they themselves taught the classes concerned, and knew the pupils in them; they understood the way in which teaching was organised within the school, and the resources available to support it; and— perhaps most important— they were able to draw directly on a craft knowledge which had established some kind of fitness-for-purpose in that context.

Within the new partnership arrangements, this expertise is acknowledged, and teachers take on the title and extended role of "mentor," as school-based teacher educators. Quite naturally, however, the priority of schools and teachers has remained with what they see as their primary task of educating school-age pupils; and they continue to be under enormous pressure from other government reforms affecting these core activities. Acting as school-based teacher educators remains a marginal role; and so, initially, schools and teachers tended to continue to construe it in the familiar terms of "supervision" of "practice."

In developing the Cambridge course, such consideration led to an initial agenda focused on those school-based components in which mentors were directly involved, and to which they felt a strong commitment. A paper, written in the early years of the partnership, reports how working closely with mentors enabled us to identify ways in which they could better help students to develop practical capability through a more extended, structured and supported pattern of school experience.

> At its best, the school-based approach allows students to be accepted within a school community; to feel valued and to have some stake in that community; with a corresponding shift in perceptions of the student role and patterns of school support. Students gain immeasurably from the opportunity to learn and develop through working closely and collaboratively with talented mentors; with a high quality of support and guidance, and sensitive matching of professional assignments and advice to personal needs and development. (Ruthven, 1994, p. 119)

Building partnership is hard when the partners have few opportunities to meet together face to face. This reflects the stretched— and continually reducing— resources allocated to teacher education. Lecturers and mentors meet only occasionally, and there is continuing change in school personnel. Nevertheless, over time, the partnership has become more veritable, and it has proved possible to start exploring a fuller integration of university-based and school-based work, to advance a common agenda of grounding the acquisition of practical capability in the development of thoughtful practice. It is on this agenda, and, in particular, on the role of ideas and processes from research in pursuing it, that the remainder of this chapter will focus.

3. SUPPORTING PRACTICAL THEORISING THROUGH PROFESSIONAL EXERCISES

At the heart of this issue is the way in which mentors and students tended to see training as comprising "theory" in the university, and "practice" in the school. Not that "theory" necessarily carried pejorative connotations. As Meredith found:

> Trainees predominantly reject [a] common sense [view of professional knowledge as restricted to] craft knowledge...; they need theory as background information to support practice... [However] over time trainees become increasingly uncertain about the nature of educational theory, seen as an ideal located in the [university] and contrasted with the reality of school. (Meredith, 1996, pp. 213-214)

It was against this background that the idea of "professional exercises" was developed. The majority of students' university-based work is carried out over a 12-week period at the start of their 36-week course. Over this term, students spend three days a week in the university, participating in workshops led by lecturers and studying independently. They spend the remaining two days per week working in pairs, each pair attached to the mathematics department of a local secondary school. There they are supported by a mentor who, as well as working with each student in his or her classroom, organises a programme of wider school experience, and is allotted one hour per week to plan and debrief classroom work and to discuss students' work on the professional exercises.

As agreed with mentors, and presented to students, the purpose of the professional exercises[ii] is to help students develop:

> an effective classroom practice, grounded in a critical understanding of mathematics teaching. The required tasks provide opportunities... to learn from school observation, experience and practice; from discussion with... mentor, fellow trainees and subject lecturers; and from thoughtful scrutiny of teaching materials, professional guidelines and research reports; above all, from the insights into mathematics teaching which become available when all these resources are brought together intelligently.

Students are required to present a written report on each professional exercise, providing evidence both of their growing practical capability and of their developing thinking about practice. The submission of a written report is an issue that deserves some consideration. Prospective mathematics teachers may not be confident about preparing such reports, although this is a skill which will become increasingly important as they make their way in the profession. Perhaps more important, though, having to write about an issue appears to encourage students to reflect more deeply on it, and to organise their thoughts more carefully than if they are simply asked to speak to it. So too does the fact that the file of exercises is assessed. This is another delicate issue. It does seem to result in the exercises being prioritised by all parties. For example, it encourages mentors to ensure that students have access to particular experiences, and to discuss those experiences—and the issues at stake— with them.

On the other hand, the assessed file creates some anxieties amongst students. This is more than just the business of writing reports. How are students to know what it means to "satisfactorily complete" the file? To address these concerns, they have the option of submitting one or two exercises at an early stage to receive detailed feedback on them. They can also get informal feedback on other exercises, notably during— and as a follow up to— working sessions in the university. Another important function of feedback is to encourage students to see the reports as a genuine opportunity to reflect on ideas and evidence, not as a piece of formal assessment detached from their professional learning, and not as a matter of strategic compliance with a received university position. As a party to this persuasion, it is, of course, difficult for me to offer a wholly detached perspective on how successful it is. Nevertheless, evidence from the reports themselves, and from student evaluations, does offer some encouragement, as will emerge in due course.

Two university-based sessions are set aside to support work on each exercise. An introductory session sets an agenda: typically eliciting and discussing what students already know and think about the issue, and relating this to different currents in professional thinking. Usually, in the course of this, illustrative examples are proposed and considered; relevant resources are identified; the brief for the professional exercise is discussed and clarified; and something is said about the items of further reading, if these have not already been referred to earlier in the session. Some weeks later, a working session allows students to present and discuss their work-in-progress. This gives them insight into practice across a range of schools, not just their own, and allows key issues to be identified and discussed. The example of the professional exercise entitled *Investigational work in school mathematics* will serve to illustrate this approach— in particular, to bring out the way in which it draws on ideas from, and processes of, research.

4. RESEARCH-BASED PERSPECTIVES ON MATHEMATICAL INVESTIGATION

Something of the ideas and issues which are considered in the university-based sessions can perhaps best be conveyed by reviewing the examples and readings to which students are referred.

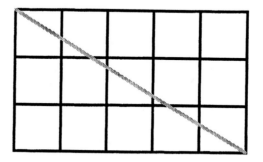

Figure 1. Rectangular grid with diagonal

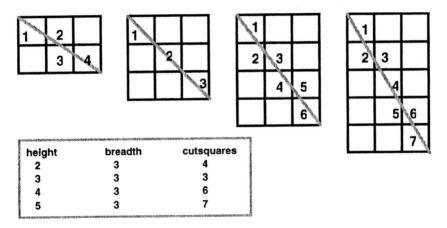

height	breadth	cutsquares
2	3	4
3	3	3
4	3	6
5	3	7

Figure 2. Approach through numeric pattern

The classic work on investigations is *Starting Points* (Banwell, Saunders, & Tahta, 1972) which proposes a wide range of mathematical situations lending themselves to exploration, and provides examples and analyses of pupils' work in an investigative style. The main example which the book uses to illustrate this style concerns rectangular grids on which a diagonal has been drawn (see Figure 1). The question is: on such a rectangular grid, how many squares does the diagonal pass through? A range of approaches is discussed, including those which exploit the numeric patterns which can be generated by systematically varying the dimensions of the grid and tabulating results (as in Figure 2); and those which focus on the visual pattern created as the diagonal passes from square to square (as in Figure 3).

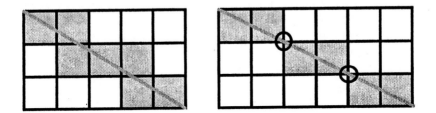

Figure 3. Approach through visual pattern

The central educational case for investigations such as these is that they give pupils opportunities:
- to develop skills of mathematical enquiry and argument;
- to consolidate understanding of standard mathematical ideas already met through their use in unfamiliar situations;
- to encounter new situations and form new ideas which can then be used to support the development of standard mathematics.

It was through the influence of the Cockcroft Report that the idea of "investigational work" came into the mainstream of secondary school mathematics in England. The relevant section of Cockcroft acknowledged that the idea of investigation was often associated with projects of the type described above, but argued that:

> At the most fundamental level, and perhaps most frequently, [investigations] should start in response to pupils' questions, perhaps during exposition by the teacher or as a result of a piece of work which is in progress or has just been completed. The essential condition for work of this kind is that the teacher must be willing to pursue the matter when a pupil asks "could we have..." or "what would have happened if... ." (Cockcroft, 1982, p. 74)

Many schools took up investigations only when it became an examination requirement that their pupils present investigative coursework for assessment. Brown (1991) draws attention to the resulting danger of coursework investigations being treated as a process of assessment, quite distinct from learning. However, the main value of this article for our students is that Brown goes on to carefully describe a sequence of lessons in which pupils tackled a topic investigatively; trying, in the course of this account, to answer many of the questions that trouble teachers: how to launch an investigation; when to intervene in pupils' work, and how; how much time to set aside for different stages; how to cope with pupil absences; how to encourage pupils to share their findings; how to help pupils organise and summarise their work; how to draw the different paths of an investigation together and to a close.

In practice, however, investigations have become institutionalised in a rather rigid way in many schools, and this has become a matter of debate within the profession. We are fortunate in England in having a teachers' journal, *Mathematics Teaching,* in which such issues are discussed, and one of our aims is to introduce our students to these "professional conversations." Hewitt describes five lessons, all starting from different open mathematical situations lending themselves to investigation. However he is disappointed by the way in which all seem to reduce to a process of generating numerical data and spotting a pattern in it:

> Despite the fact that in each of these lessons children were well motivated and involved in mathematics, I am saddened because the children ended up doing a similar activity irrespective of the initial mathematical situation. Is the diversity and richness of the mathematics curriculum being reduced to a series of spotting number patterns from tables? (Hewitt, 1992, p. 6-7)

Two issues of the journal later, and a reply from Andrews appears. He argues that we know nothing of the circumstances under which the reported lessons took place, and ought to consider how knowing something of these might change our judgement:

> We do not know what the intentions of the different teachers were for their different lessons. We do not know anything about the skills of either the children or the teachers involved. We know nothing about the pupils' or the teachers' previous experience. We know nothing of the context of the lessons discussed ... [T]eachers behave according to the context in which they work, and change, if it is to be achieved, usually comes slowly. (Andrews, 1993: 21)

Of course, none of these publications are research papers in the narrowly conventional sense. However, they represent a form of "popular research," involving careful observation of exemplary cases and systematic reflection on them, drawing on the authors' expertise as teachers, teacher educators and researchers. Such writing is readily accessible to students at this stage in their professional learning, but it also provides a springboard for their proceeding to more demanding material. To encourage this, we also refer students to more mainstream research papers—typically more quasi-experiential than quasi-experimental— which offer further insight into the intellectual and professional context of an exercise.

Coe and Ruthven (1994) examine investigation as a foundation for proof. Major ideas about proof in mathematics education are reviewed as a prelude to reporting a study of pupils who had recently completed a module on problem-solving, investigation and proof within a widely-used innovative course. The study examines— on the basis of their coursework— the kind of argumentative strategies that pupils employed, and— on the basis of interviews with them— their thinking about these strategies. What emerges is a predominance of "empirical" strategies, based on forming and testing rules and patterns by generating numeric data.

Askew (1996), drawing on a national evaluation, shows clearly how primary and secondary teachers have tended to interpret the national curriculum component of "using and applying mathematics" in very different ways: primary teachers tending to emphasise "relevant" or "practical" mathematics; secondary, the "stand alone" investigation. The paper highlights the "genetic fallacy" by which policy-makers assume that the intentions of policy documents are coherent and clear, while teachers struggle to interpret them.

5. STUDENTS' SCHOOL-BASED WORK ON MATHEMATICAL INVESTIGATION

The professional exercise on mathematical investigation asks students to make careful summaries of at least three classroom episodes or lessons typical of the investigational work they have observed or taught during their school experience. Their report is to consist of these summaries, together with a critical examination of the contribution of investigational work to pupils' learning of mathematics, in the light of the different ideas and evidence they have available to them.

From the student reports, it is clear that gaining opportunities to observe or carry out investigational work remains difficult in some schools. Jack, for example, wrote:

> In my Term 1 school, lessons including investigational work were rather sparse, although I finally managed to observe several classes.... . However, with limited time available both for the [pupils]'[iii] work and discussion there was less actual investigation than I would have liked.

One beneficial effect of the exercise, then, is simply to ensure that students gain such opportunities. Virtually all are able both to observe an experienced teacher leading an investigation and to lead one themselves.

Two examples will capture the variety of experience which students have in leading an investigation themselves.

Jack reports an investigation on tessellations carried out with first-year secondary pupils, employing cardboard cutouts in the shape of regular polygons with sides of identical length. In the first phase, pupils were set the more structured task of trying to form tessellations with each type of shape, recording their results in a table (exemplified by the pupils' work shown in Figure 4). (Note, in passing, the potential for such an example to be used, by mentor or lecturer, to concretise later discussions with students about developing pupils' approaches to recording and checking their results: the use of "0" in the "no. round a point" column, in cases where tessellation "doesn't work"; the use of "=" in the final column; and the incongruous presence of 180º in the "angle" column.)

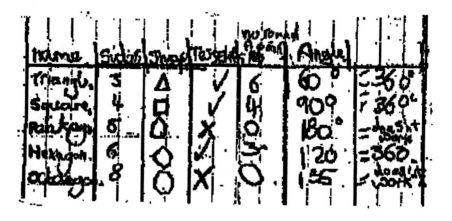

Figure 4. Pupil's table for a tessellations task

Jack's comments show that he is thinking about how appropriate support for pupils can underpin opportunities to explore:

> [This] was a closed question, but it did allow difficulties to be addressed before the more open second part. I was pleased that one group started looking for non-regular tessellations before I asked them to, a perfect example of someone extending the original problem.

> All the [pupils] finished this task successfully... . Interestingly, the group that had originally had the most difficulty grasping the task had already noticed that it was possible to make a tessellation using two octagons and one square.

In the second phase, pupils were invited to find tessellations involving any two different shapes. Jack notes different strategies adopted by pupils, and recognises his preconceptions, giving pupils latitude to pursue their own ideas:

> Some groups concentrated on finding which combination of polygons fitted around a vertex, and some groups on general tessellations (some of which were semi-regular as I had intended, but many of which were irregular).

Looking back on the investigation, Jack comes to realise the value of scheduling investigative work so that it can be related to the wider mathematical agenda being pursued with a class. He also recognises the value of carrying through an investigation to the stage where ideas and results are organised, compared, and codified.

> While this investigation worked quite well, it would have benefited from several changes:

> It would have been better if it could have been done after the [pupils] had worked on angles — they might then have worked out for themselves that shapes only fit around a point if the angles sum to 360° — or I could have used it as more of an introduction to angles.

> It really needed more time for the [pupils] to work, to make their work systematic and for their results to be collected and shared amongst the rest of the group.

[handwritten margin note: Seems to always boil down to time]

However, students do not always have such productive experiences. Kathy reports an investigation, planned with her student pair and the class teacher. The small class of lower-attaining pupils was divided into two groups, each group to work with one student, with the class teacher having general oversight. This was a thoughtful strategy on the part of the class teacher, aimed at reducing the managerial demands on the students. However, the way in which the students were briefed to teach the two groups produced an unfortunate situation. The class teacher wanted the lesson to lead into the Pythagorean triangle relation, with Kathy using a more exploratory approach with the "top" half of the class, while her colleague pursued a more directed approach with the remainder.

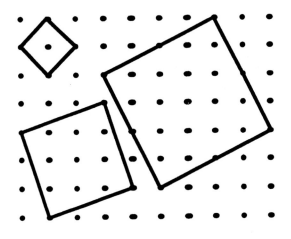

Figure 5. Tilted squares

The five pupils that Kathy was working with were asked, first, to work out the area of "tilted squares," drawn on "square dotty paper" (see Figure 5); and then, to find a way of relating the area of each square to the properties of its lower edge. Kathy reports:

> [The pupils] made some progress but by the end of the lesson we had not even finished
> the investigation let alone consolidate[d] and present[ed] to the rest of the class. The
> problems in this investigation were [that]: pupils were demotivated and had a very short
> attention [span]; as a consequence pupils spent the majority of their time chatting,
> messing around and generally avoiding their work; pupils had their own ideas on how to
> find the areas of squares and wouldn't listen to any other ideas or guidance... . Pupils
> were quite unwilling to try out other ideas and were adamant that their ideas were
> correct (which they were not). When I presented them with the correct method for
> finding the area they could follow an example through with me (although reluctantly)
> but could not do any others by themselves.

One can understand how— in the pressure of the moment, and following the example of the class teacher— Kathy did not see how her insistence on a particular method might be contributing to the pupils' demotivation, and countering the spirit of investigation. Her evaluation concludes with alternative possibilities:

> Due to the low level of ability across the group I feel that it would have been more
> beneficial to either:
>
> • Spend more time on the tilted squares investigation with much more discussion
>   and hopefully less guidance...; or
>
> • Compromise. Is it worth investigating a subject at the risk of confusing the
>   pupils...? Would a more textbook-based approach have been a safer option?

This is the kind of situation which it is important for the mentor to pick up and talk through constructively with students in the weekly meeting. Equally— if volunteered by the student(s) concerned and sensitively handled— it can lead to profitable discussion in a later university-based working session. Finally— in suitably anonymised form— examples such as those of Jack and Kathy can become a very valuable resource, both in the professional development of mentors and in working with later cohorts of students.

6. STUDENTS' CRITICAL EXAMINATION OF MATHEMATICAL INVESTIGATION

How, then, are such experiences reflected in students' critical examination of the contribution of investigation to pupils' learning? Let us return to Jack. He identifies some strengths of investigative work:

> By involving [pupils] in investigative work, they can be given opportunities to apply
> their knowledge and skills to unfamiliar problems, providing practice, challenge and
> motivation.... . Investigation can incorporate many mathematical ideas that may not be
> explicitly taught, such as mathematical modelling, organisation and communication of
> ideas, pattern spotting (not just number patterns), and justification (or proof). The fact
> that many investigations are easily solved through algebra might be a way this topic's
> importance can be brought to [pupils]' attention.

But he then notes some important qualifying factors:

> However, it should also be noted that many of these ideas can also be covered without
> requiring any investigation... . Probably the greatest difficulty in relation to
> investigational work is time. It is all very well the Cockcroft Report saying "Nor should

an interesting line of thought be curtailed because 'there is no time'...", but the pressure of public examinations and the size of the corresponding syllabi is bound to affect teachers' ability to allocate time for such work.

In addition, Jack shows developing awareness of the conditions necessary for investigations to achieve their broader goals.

> I noticed in both of my investigations that I needed more time to let the [pupils] do their own work. I also realise that producing a worthwhile investigation is a very different task for [pupils] of different abilities - unless one is very careful lower ability [pupils] will need more directions, making the work more closed than open.

Despite her difficult classroom experience, Kathy, too, is alert to the way in which investigations can be so tightly structured as to lose their key qualities. She now sees the possibilities of alternative approaches, as well as greater pupil autonomy. At the same time, she recognises the constraints and pressures which can lead towards tighter structuring. Referring to another investigation observed at the school, she asks:

> Isn't this activity really teacher exposition dressed up as practical work — reduced to one where there were right and wrong answers, with no creativity possible in the solution, or do pupils need this much guidance so as they can actually obtain the correct results and thus feel they've achieved something? I found that with [Tilted squares] I was giving the pupils as many hints as possible without actually saying how to do the particular activity. The pupils, used to being told exactly what to do and so [not having] the confidence to just strike out on a path and risk being wrong, stumbled around in the dark without guidance.... The problem of time constraint overlaps this. If you have only one lesson in which to investigate, you will want the pupils to reach the 'answer' and so benefit from the activity, hence a certain amount of the work is bound to be teacher led, even if only via directed questions.

An important factor, enabling her to take a more detached view of her school experience, was an opportunity to observe a masterclass targeted at higher-attaining pupils, held at the university as part of another programme:

> [This] had a [longer] timescale and so was able to let the pupils explore at their own rate. No pressure was put on them to arrive at a formula immediately and therefore they needed less guidance. Due to the fact that these were talented young mathematicians who were used to investigative work, they had the confidence to work on their own ideas, seeing being stuck as a challenge rather than a pitfall. Unfortunately, this can account for why investigation can be quite an exclusive activity.

Many of the students' comments reveal the salience of ability constructs in their thinking about teaching and learning. This important issue is followed up through course sessions which look at strategies for supporting pupils who are experiencing difficulties or lacking motivation.

Some students achieve notable insight, given that they complete this assignment during the first term of their training. Louise notes how an activity with which she assisted the class teacher could have been varied, perhaps to better effect:

> The contribution to pupils' learning does not depend on how many results are obtained from an investigation... fewer tiles could have been used which would have evoked the same idea, possibly more quickly, given the same answer, but would have also freed some time for their extensions.

Similarly Louise contextualises a rather highly structured investigation carried out with a first year class which has just entered the school, by comparing it with one conducted with an older class, relating contrasting characteristics to the stage of the pupils concerned, and to progression in their capacity to manage the investigative process for themselves:

> Take... the intentionally small, question-led, multi-purpose [investigation] completed in one lesson [with a first year class]... . Not only did it achieve the overall intention for pupils to start learning the skill of a systematic approach and increase their mathematical awareness, but it served as an enjoyable way through which to include some algebra and to either remind them of, or introduce them to some other important terms such as perimeter and area. Guided... by the structured worksheet they were able to progress at their own level of ability, a necessity for this distinctly mixed-ability class... As pupils mature so their personal strategies develop. The way, manner and style in which the [third year] class had approached their more lengthy investigation... clearly showed how this learning process was coming to fruition. The investigation itself and the teacher's approach of letting them, after initial discussion, extend their own investigation for homework, allowed much more scope, seemingly aeons apart from the experience with the [first year] class.

7. STUDENTS' EVALUATION OF THE PROFESSIONAL EXERCISES

What do the students themselves make of the professional exercises? An evaluation of the first term of the course is carried out by a mentor who visits the university to meet the students to discuss the written comments they have already prepared in response to an agenda which includes the issue of the professional exercises.

There is a general view that the exercises encourage "thinking" focused on "issues" and "aspects" of teaching:

> Made us think about a range of topics/issues that may have been ignored/passed over hadn't we done them.

> Helps us analyse the lessons. Enables us to think about what we should be looking for.

> Made you think about issues in the classroom.

> A good mix of assignments which promote the thinking of the different aspects involved in mathematics teaching.

> Encourages thinking in depth about subjects and the theory behind practices in the classroom.

This year, however, one newly introduced exercise was criticised by students, in a way which indicates the kind of "relevance" which other exercises are perceived to have. This exercise on *School mathematics as a tool in school science* asks students to work with a colleague training to teach science to identify a topic— at any level of the secondary science curriculum— which incorporates the use of mathematical ideas and skills. The assignment asks students to report on how pupils are expected to use mathematics within work on the scientific topic; to compare the handling— and positioning— of these ideas and skills within the mathematics and science curricula; and to examine how productive links might be made between pupils' experience within mathematics and science lessons. Unlike the other exercises, however, this one requires no direct link to classroom teaching actually observed or carried out by students, (because it was anticipated that practical constraints might make this difficult to organise in many schools within the limited period of time available). This lack of direct connection to classroom teaching, combined with the weak relationship between mathematics and science teaching in schools, had a significant influence on students' perceptions of the exercise.

> School science assignment was interesting: I get the impression there is a them and us attitude within schools.

> The school science assignment was hard to do because we saw little or no links in school between maths and science.

> I failed to see the relevance of the Maths as a tool in school science assignment, as much as the others.

> We are all aware of maths/science links. Assignment hasn't helped my teaching.

> Science assignment seemed barely relevant.

This assignment, then, was seen as less "relevant" because it did not relate to the task of mathematics teaching as experienced by students, and as construed by the teachers they were working with. This well illustrates how tightly focused a learning agenda the school-based, competence-directed aspect of the training encourages students to set. It also suggests that the exercise— and its embedding in school experience—need to be redesigned to create a more successful dialogue between university and school contributions. We will have to review this with mentors.

This example also illustrates how, in designing the professional exercises, account has to be taken of what it is realistic for a mentor to organise under normal school circumstances, and within the time envelope available for school experience during the first term of the course. A small number of student comments reflect the difficulty that a few continue to experience in carrying out some of the exercises:

> It was hard to make one's teaching exactly relevant. Sometimes the assignments didn't exactly fit what happened in school.

> Sometimes it was difficult to write certain assignments when the school wasn't particularly strong on technology or didn't do much investigative work.

> Assignments were very rigid and caused some difficulty when subjects were not observed or covered in schools.

The general tenor of student comments on the readings associated with the professional exercises is that they are "helpful" and "useful," but— as one might expect— some students favour the shorter pieces, more directly located in classroom experience, such as those from *Mathematics Teaching*.

> Readings were helpful and perhaps not enough of them.

How much "practical" reading do preservice teachers experience?

Readings were generally useful and gave plenty of background information about topics.

The readings were helpful. There were not too many and the majority I found very useful.

The readings were predominantly useful, such as [*Mathematics Teaching* examples].

Some of the readings are very lengthy and only sporadically relevant.

Students are positive about the feedback they receive on drafts of their assignments. It is clearly important to them, not just in allaying anxieties about meeting assessment expectations, but in helping to focus their attention on important issues for learning:

Feedback was detailed and constructive.

The feedback was helpful and gave good informative points.

Feedback was useful to focus assignments on important points and show the type of content expected.

Feedback was very beneficial since it put you on the right track and smoothed out problems.

Feedback was very good to judge whether we were writing at the correct level and what particular points we need to think about.

Some students request model examples of the kind of assignment expected. Providing such models would, of course, inhibit students from thinking issues through for themselves. Perhaps, however, the lateral solution would be to harness this motivation, by dropping the *School mathematics as a tool in school science* exercise, but making previous reports on it available to students as model assignments!

8. PROFESSIONAL EXERCISES, PRACTICAL THEORISING, AND PEDAGOGICAL LEARNING

To what extent, then, do the professional exercises promote the development of thoughtful practice as well as practical capability? Do they address what McIntyre saw as the "endemic problems" of pre-service teacher education? Do they lead students to engage in the "practical theorising" envisaged by Alexander?

As noted earlier, this approach certainly helps students to gain experience of different aspects of pedagogical practice, including some— such as investigational work and the use of technology— which are relatively underdeveloped in many schools. Where such aspects are more developed, students are also able to benefit from access to the craft knowledge of mentors and class teachers, gained through discussion linked to observation of, and cooperation with, these experienced teachers. Where such aspects are less developed, however, students must depend more on other sources, such as student peers, university lecturers, and professional resources. This is an important limitation. Nevertheless, such alternative sources do provide access to ideas which can help students to shape their own classroom practice and critically examine it alongside the practice which they are able to observe.

Moreover, the professional exercises appear to play a part— alongside the national performance standards— in setting a common— and broader— agenda for pedagogical learning, overlaying the immediate concerns and interests of students and the teachers with whom they work. Where exercises are clearly focused on the task of mathematics teaching as construed by students and teachers, they do seem to encourage engagement with— and appreciation of— forms of practical theorising. First, concepts drawn from scholarship in mathematics education provide new resources, of potential value in making sense of school practice. Second, reflection on school observation and experience provides opportunities for students to "fill out" such concepts, and to appraise them in action. Finally, as such concepts— and their associated language— start to take on clearer shape for students, and to be used more confidently and purposively by them, they can become tools for deeper analysis of classroom practice. In this way, pedagogical learning can move beyond "semi-conscious trial-and-error."

There is still much scope for improvement in the use of these professional exercises; notably, through finding ways to sustain closer working contact between lecturers in the university, mentors in schools, and students as they move between the two. Here, one hope is that the current drive to expand information and communications technology provision in schools may open up new possibilities for more direct collaboration through electronic conferencing. Equally, there is the perennial danger of means becoming ends; vigilance is required to ensure that the exercises are actually supporting students' development as teachers and not degenerating into mere paper assignments. Nevertheless, on the strength of their positive evaluation both by students and by government inspectors, they do seem to provide a modest pointer to one way in which research ideas and research processes can be brought to play an important part in the professional learning of teachers from the very earliest stage of their careers; and to a model of informed, analytic professionalism which students can carry forward into their work as teachers.

In this "practical theorising" approach, ideas, methods and findings from research are granted no privileged status. They must "prove" their practical value in giving insight into teaching and learning processes, and in supporting the improvement of classroom practice. Equally, a generous view is taken of what constitutes "research"; the priority is that ideas, methods and findings should be attuned to the professional situation in which students and mentors are working. This takes us back to the wider debate about the relevance and impact of educational research. Boero, Dapueto, & Parenti have pointed to the decreasing involvement of leading research schools in pedagogical and didactical analysis and development of the type on which the work reported here depends:

> Fewer and fewer results of the 'innovative patterns' type are considered as outstanding 'research outcomes', worth publishing by important journals. And even in many...

international meetings... the introduction of innovations takes place in poster sessions.
(Boero, Dapueto, & Parenti, 1996. p. 1108)

Perhaps, one important implication of this case is that— for the purposes of teacher education— we need to take a broad view of what can be valued as research. Different methods of research, different kinds of rigour, different styles of reporting are fit— and cost-effective— for different purposes. Indeed, this very chapter exemplifies a form of practitioner case discussion which I believe can make a modest, but worthwhile, contribution to professional learning. Although it falls short of some of the standards necessary for a more sustained and systematic piece of research, these can be achieved only at much greater opportunity cost, and arguably without much greater professional benefit. And to whatever standards, the ideas from such a case need to be adapted to changing circumstances or in new settings[iv], and to be kept under review.

Acknowledgements

Particular acknowledgements are due to my colleague, Charlie Gilderdale, who has been a sympathetic partner in exploring the developments described here, and on whose unfailing energy and enthusiasm their implementation has depended. Also to the students following the course, who have helped us better understand their learning -in particular those whose experience and advice is pseudonymously represented here. Thanks also to Fou-Lai Lin, Tom Cooney, and an anonymous reviewer for their helpful comments in preparing the paper for publication. And to the National Science Council of Taiwan for supporting my participation in the International Conference on Mathematics Teacher Education, held in May 1999 at the National Taiwan Normal University, at which an earlier version of this paper was presented.

REFERENCES

Alexander, R.J. (1984). Innovation and continuity in the initial teacher education curriculum. In R.J. Alexander, M. Craft, & J. Lynch (Eds.), *Change in teacher education: Context and provision since Robbins* (pp. 103-160). London: Holt, Rinehart & Winston.

Andrews, P. (1993). Train spotters have feelings too. *Mathematics Teaching, 142,* 20-22.

Askew, M. (1996). Using and applying mathematics in schools: Reading the texts. In D.C. Johnson & A. Millett (Eds.), *Implementing the mathematics national curriculum: Policy, politics and practice* (pp. 99-112). London: Paul Chapman Publishing.

Banwell, C.S., Saunders, K.D., & Tahta, D.G. (1972). *Starting points.* Oxford: Oxford University Press.

Boero, P., Dapueto, C., & Parenti, L. (1996). Didactics of mathematics and the professional knowledge of teachers. In A. Bishop, et al. (Eds.), *International handbook of mathematics education* (pp. 1097-1121). Dordrecht: Kluwer.

Brown, L. (1991). Stewing in your own juice. In D. Pimm & E. Love (Eds.), *Teaching and Learning School Mathematics* (pp. 3-15). London: Hodder & Stoughton.

Cockcroft, W.H. (Ch.) (1982). *Mathematics counts: Report of the Committee of Enquiry into the Teaching of Mathematics in Schools.* London: HMSO.

Coe, R. & Ruthven, K. (1994). Proof practices and constructs of advanced mathematics students, *British Educational Research Journal 20* (1) 41-53.

Department for Education and Employment (1998). *Standards for the award of qualified teacher status.* London: Department for Education and Employment.

Hewitt, D. (1992). Train spotters' paradise, *Mathematics Teaching, 140,* 6-8.

Hillage, J., Pearson, R., Anderson, A., & Tamkin, P. (1998). *Excellence in research on schools.* London: Department for Education and Employment.

McIntyre, D. (1988). Designing a teacher education curriculum from research and theory on teacher knowledge. In J. Calderhead (Ed.), *Teachers' professional learning* (pp. 97-114). Lewes: Falmer.

McIntyre, D. (1990). Ideas and principles guiding the internship scheme. In P. Benton (Ed.). *The Oxford internship scheme: Integration and partnership in initial teacher education* (pp. 17-33). London: Calouste Gulbenkian Foundation.

Meredith, A. (1996). *The construction of knowledge for teaching through apprenticeship training.* Unpublished doctoral dissertation, University of Cambridge, Cambridge.

Ruthven, K. (1994). The school-based training of secondary mathematics teachers: A Cambridge perspective, *Teaching Mathematics and its Applications, 13* (3) 116-119.

Ruthven, K. (1999). Reconstructing professional judgement in mathematics education: From good practice to warranted practice. In C. Hoyles, C. Morgan, & G. Woodhouse (Eds.), *Rethinking the mathematics curriculum* (pp. 203-216). London: Falmer.

Ruthven, K. (in press). Linking researching with teaching: Towards synergy of scholarly and craft knowledge. In L. English (Ed.). *Handbook of international research in mathematics education.* Mahwah, NJ: Lawrence Erlbaum Associates.

University of Cambridge
School of Education

---

[i] I discuss these issues more fully elsewhere (Ruthven, 1999; in press).

[ii] All the information used in this chapter comes from the first term of the 1998/99 academic year.

[iii] As a way of writing more directly, which also reflects the conventional way of referring to people in most of the partner schools, I refer to student teachers as "students" and to the children they are teaching in school as "pupils." For ease of reading, I have altered Jack's references to "students" to read "[pupils]."

[iv] Compare this case, for example, with those reported by Joao Pedro da Ponte earlier in this volume: the same idea of mathematical investigation; but in a different setting; relating to in-service as well as pre-service teacher education; and involving a different relationship between university and schools.

ANNA SFARD AND CAROLYN KIERAN

PREPARING TEACHERS FOR HANDLING STUDENTS' MATHEMATICAL COMMUNICATION: GATHERING KNOWLEDGE AND BUILDING TOOLS

ABSTRACT: The main thesis of this chapter is that to prepare teachers to their new role in the reformed mathematics classroom, we must first understand better the mechanisms of the interactions supposed to take place in these classrooms. Of particular interest are the instances of students' collective problem-solving. The student-to-student classroom interactions are highly recommended for their potential to promote learning, but at the present stage it is not clear what should be the role of the teacher in promoting the realization of this potential. How students' interactions should be investigated, what tools could be used for this purpose and what impact the insights thus gained can have on decisions about the optimal directions in teachers' preparation are the main focus of the discussion that follows.

1. ON THE NEEDS AND OBLIGATIONS OF THE "GUIDE-ON-THE-SIDE"

The reform movement initiated a decade ago by the call for new standards in learning and teaching issued by the North American National Council of Teachers of Mathematics (NCTM, 1989, 1991, 2000) redefined what it means to teach mathematics. The request for change and refinement in the spirit of the NCTM Standards can be heard all around the world these days , and indicates, among other things, a whole new way of thinking about the role of the mathematics teacher. The new definition, in turn, requires a different kind of teacher preparation.

On the face of it, the relation between the new standards of teaching and the principles of teacher education is straightforward: The teachers should prepare themselves to whatever kind of activities they are requested to perform in the "reformed" classroom. In fact, the problem is much more complex than that. First, for all the specifications given in the NCTM Standards, it is still far from clear in what way the preparation for carrying our the new type of classroom activities should be done. Second, and even more seriously, the new activities themselves - their exact shape, the way they should be planned and then implemented, and the manner in which they spur and support students' learning, are not sufficiently understood. Much research is therefore needed if the new standards are to become truly beneficial for the student. For the reasons just presented, the required research cannot be confined to the domain of teacher education and should also tackle the more basic issues of learning in environments promoted by the Standards. In this chapter, we present a project which aimed at these two goals in tandem: It's purpose was to gain a better understanding of new ways of learning while, at the same time,

F.-L. Lin & T. J. Cooney (Eds.) Making Sense of Mathematics Teacher Education, 185—205.
© 2001 *Kluwer Academic Publishers. Printed in the Netherlands.*

offering and testing tools with the help of which teachers would be able to monitor and regulate their own and their students' future activities.

Before turning to the project and its results, let us take a closer look at the problems it addresses. As indicated by some researchers, changes in the domain of teacher education are slow and insufficient, and they lag seriously behind the needs of the reformed classroom. According to some writers, it was evidently unforeseen by the reform planners that their new requests with respect to teachers' positioning in the classroom would catch the teachers unprepared (see e.g. Smith, 1996). Indeed, the field is fraught with problems. The main indication of the ineffectiveness of common methods of preparing teachers is the frequently observed disparity between teachers' explicit opinions and the ways in which the same teachers act in the classroom. The gap between the "espoused" and "enacted" beliefs that can be observed in teachers quite regardless of their age and experience, shows an insufficient impact of both pre-service and in in-service teacher education (see e.g. Frykholm, 1999 and Levenberg, 1998, respectively). In spite of the acute awareness of the need for improvement, and despite all the efforts invested so far, the problem is felt all around the world (for a comparative survey of approaches to teacher preparation in different countries see Comiti & Loewenberg Ball, 1996).

It seems that one of the major reasons for the present ineffectiveness of teacher preparation is our as yet insufficient understanding of the dynamics of learning in the reformed classroom, and our uncertainty with regard to the role of the teacher within this type of learning. At this point we must turn to the principle of a "teaching mathematics through conversation"[i] which is one of those ideas forcefully promoted within the Reform movement that seem to be affecting both the student's learning and the teacher's role in the most profound way. The principle in focus is that learning of mathematics should take place in an interactive setting, that students' collaborative problem solving is the best way to enhance their learning and understanding, and that the teacher should renounce her traditional place in the center of the class to play the role of an unobtrusive helper and navigator. This basic principle is usually interpreted as suggesting that students should spend most of their time in the classroom in almost entirely self-organized team activities. The two prevalent modes of action are therefore *students' group work* and teacher orchestrated *classroom discussion,* whereas the aim of the latter activity is to summarize the results of the former[ii]. Both these situations are characterized by "the theoretical assumption that learning is a constructive process," and this assumption "often leads to the slogan that 'telling is bad' because it deprives students of the opportunity to construct understanding for themselves" (Cobb & Bowers, 1999).

The lack of appropriate preparation for implementing these goals would express itself in teacher's diminished sense of efficacy and in their feeling of being pushed aside and silenced rather than charged with any well-defined new role (Smith, 1996). According to Smith these phenomena indicate the "tension between the traditional foundation of efficacy in teaching mathematics and current reform efforts in mathematics education." His research has shown that the teachers in the new classrooms are losing their once robust sense of being effective and doing their job right. A later study by Levenberg (1998) confirms these findings by demonstrating that the teachers would sometimes feel lost and redundant during the periods of students' team work, and most of them would have no means to deal with the idea of "teacher orchestrated whole-class discussion." In fact, the study has shown that the majority of the in-service interviewees could not even explain the meaning of the latter notion.

I can relate!

Thus, the new teacher's most urgent need is to know how she should handle a "talking class." This, in its turn, implies the need of research on the dynamics of classroom interactions and on the role teachers may or should play in them. So far, only one of the two basic modes of classroom interactions, classroom discussion, is getting a reasonable amount of attention on the part of researchers. A sizable bulk of recent studies (Voigt, 1985, 1994, 1995; Lampert, 1990; Forman, 1996; O'Connors & Michaels, 1993; O'Connor, 1996; Cobb, 1996; Yackel & Cobb, 1996; Rittenhouse, 1998) bring much substantial information on patterns of interaction and rules that govern teacher orchestrated whole-class conversations. This information, although of great value for those who are supposed to teach according to the new standards, is still insufficient. Not enough is known about the mechanisms that govern the other recommended classroom mode: students' group work.[iii] Without the basic understanding of the factors responsible for student's learning in this kind of environment, the teacher has no way to know what her moves should be. Thus, much research is needed before we begin to know how teachers could be prepared for orchestrating this central type of classroom activity.

The need to get an insight into the dynamics of students' interactions and to fathom how these interactions spur – or fail to spur – participants' learning was one of the direct incentives for the analyses presented in this paper. Although originally aimed at some other goals, the project from which our data are taken[iv] gave us an opportunity to examine the assumption, seemingly implicated in the idea of the group work, that the learning is most effective when students interact with each other, and that the teacher may safely renounce her traditional position of the "sage of the stage" and become a discrete "guide on the side" (Davis & Maher, 1997). Thus, in this paper we are dealing with the teacher's role in a seemingly paradoxical way: by considering classroom situations from which the teacher is practically absent (these situations become more and more ubiquitous in today's schools, if not because of the reformer's intentions, then because of the constrains of classroom reality). At the same occasion, we demonstrate a tool with the help of which the teachers might be able to steadily enhance their understanding of these issues and also monitor their own effectiveness as facilitators of these processes. The emphasis on the tool reflects our basic belief on best ways to prepare teachers for their new role in the classroom: Rather than devising ready-made prescriptions for action, the teachers should endow themselves with means for continuous self-improvement; rather than planning what to do, the teachers should acquire tools for self-monitoring and regulation on the one hand, and for better understanding of the students, on the other hand.

2. PREPARING MEANS FOR TEACHER PREPARATION: TAKING A CLOSE LOOK AT A MATHEMATICAL CONVERSATION BETWEEN TWO STUDENTS

2.1 Setting the Scene

The teaching experiment from which our data are taken was designed as an implementation of a certain theoretical model for teaching introductory algebra. The instruction was carried out in the spirit of the reform. Classroom activities were organized as a sequence of intermittent periods of students' group work and whole class discussions. In this paper we will focus on a single pair of students, whom we have every reason to take as representative of many others pairs in this classroom.

The two 13 year old boys, whom we call here Ari and Gur, performed reasonably well on all the tests they were given, and both seemed to be quite happy with our special approach. And yet, a close look at the lengthy transcripts of their interactions throughout 30 meetings in the span of two months eroded our sanguine vision of the experiment and its results. As a matter of fact, the discovery that things were not working exactly the way we would like them to work did not come as a total surprise. A vague sense of something being wrong with Ari and Gur's collaboration at large, and their collaborative learning in particular, already accompanied our regular visits to the classroom and only intensified during our endless sessions with the videotapes. When watching the two boys first with the "naked eye" and then in a more systematic way, we could not escape an impression that not much was happening during the long hours they spent together and that the most effective progress was being made in those situations which were meant as occasions for assessment rather than for learning: the interviews[v]. In contrast to the interview situations, teacher's unplanned interventions during the team-work sessions proved ineffective.

2.2 The Daylight Episode

To get a better sense of what we are talking about, we invite the reader to take a look at a sample of Ari and Gur's interactions. The following episode, taken from the students' second meeting, lasted for a mere 2.5 minutes. During that time, Ari and Gur used the graph presented in the activity sheet presented in Figure 1 to answer the following question: During which period of time did the number of hours of daylight increase most rapidly?

One does not need special tools to notice that the boys had a hard time trying to communicate on the problem in question (see Figure 2). The conversation can be divided into three distinct phases. The episode begins with the a brief segment of *pre-engagement*, when both boys seem preoccupied with their own thoughts rather than with the exchange with the partner; it continues with the period of *engagement* when the students carry on a lively conversation about their respective solutions; and ends in *disengagement*, when the answers are written and the transition is made to

READING CONTINUOUS GRAPHS

The number of hours of daylight on any given day is a function of what day it is in the year and of the latitude of the location. The number of hours of daylight in Alert, NWT (near the North Pole) was recorded every day in 1993. The graph below shows the information.

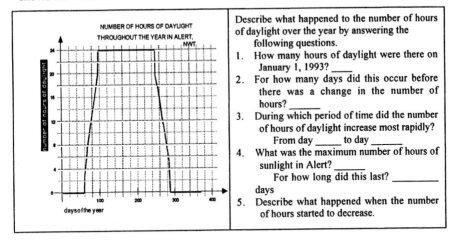

Describe what happened to the number of hours of daylight over the year by answering the following questions.

1. How many hours of daylight were there on January 1, 1993? ____

2. For how many days did this occur before there was a change in the number of hours? _____

3. During which period of time did the number of hours of daylight increase most rapidly? From day ____ to day _____

4. What was the maximum number of hours of sunlight in Alert? _____ For how long did this last? _____ days

5. Describe what happened when the number of hours started to decrease.

Figure 1. Daylight episode: Activity sheet

the next problem on the activity worksheet (see Figure 3). It is notable that in spite of the brevity of the episode, it does include one teacher's intervention. It seems, therefore, that everything is proceeding in accord with the reformers' expectations, except that it does not proceed as well as the reformers seem to have promised.

WHAT IS DONE	WHAT IS SAID
	- 19:14 -
	[1] A: During which period of time did the number of hours of daylight increase most rapidly? From day, to day
	[2] G: Woah.
	[3] A: Increase most rapidly?
[4] "day 60": G. points to (60,0) "to day": G. points to about (290,0)	[4] G: Yes (mumble). From day 60 to day ... 290
	[5] A: From day 60 to
	[6] G: 290. Oh, no, no, no, no. (mumble)
	[7] A: From day 60 to a hundred.
	[8] (here, interruption from the teacher on some other matter)
[9] G. points along the x = 250 line	[9] G: So from day -
	[10] A: During which period of time did the number of hours of daylight increase most rapidly? From day

WHAT IS DONE	WHAT IS SAID
[11] G. points along the x = 100 line	[11] G: one hundred
	[12] A: 60 to 100. From day 60 to 100.
[13] "up here": G. points to (100,24) "to day -": G. goes along upper horizontal line, and down the vertical to arrive at about x=250.	[13] G: Cause, Oh no, no, no no no. Look, look. Up here. It's day 100 to day --- to day
	[14] A: What are you talking about?
	[15] G: 55.
	[16] A: Where?
[17] "here and here": G. points back and forth several times to the extremes of the upper horizontal line, about (100,24) to (250,24)	[17] G: Look, it changed most rapidly in between here and here. You see?
	[18] A: Oh? It's exactly the same.
[19] G. traces the "descent" of the line from x=100 to 0	[19] G: No, because see, it moves up (mumble)
	[20] A: It goes up most rapidly
	[21] G: So it's from day 100
	[22] A: To day 100
[23] G. is still pointing at about 250 on x axis.	[23] G: No, from day 100 to day ---
	[24] A: No, No, No.
	[25] G: 2 hundred and sixty,
	[26] A: That's not how you're supposed to do it.
	[27] G: two hundred and eighty. To day
	[28] A: See, during which time. The time, the period of time has to change rapidly.
	[29] G: Oh. No, it says from day to day what?
[30] A. underlines "time" on G's question sheet.	[30] A: Read the question. During which period of <u>time</u> - time.
[31] G. traces horizontal line at 24 hours	[31] G: Up here, time.
[32] "that didn't change: here A. traces horizontal line at 24 hours. "right here": A. puts pencil mark along graph from y=20 to 24	[32] A: No, but that didn't change, it stayed still, which means it has to be right here,
	[33] G: No
	[34] A: which is about 90
[35] G. traces ascent of graph from 0 to 100	[35] G: Right here
	[36] A: No, right here

WHAT IS DONE	WHAT IS SAID
[37] G. traces a curve along graph from 0 to about 250.	[37] G: You don't get it, do you? If it was like this
	[38] A: Fine, it's from 60 to a hundred, ok?
	[39] G: No.
	[40] A: Yes. I'm writing that.
	[41] G: Why?
	[42] A: We can have different answers.
	[43] G: Why? I don't care.
[44] G. is still pointing around (250,0)	[44] A: What was the maximum number of hours of sunlight in Alert?
	[45] G: To day 250.
	[46] A: 24
	[47] G: Just a sec, just a sec.
	[48] A: 24
	[49] G: 250. I'm telling you, change it. Anyway it doesn't matter.
	22:44

Figure 2. Daylight *episode: Protocol*

Phase	Segment	Nature of activity	
		Ari	Gur
Pre-engagement: Solving separately	[1]-[13]	Solves	Solves
Engagement: Arguing/explaining	[14]-[37]	Argues against Gur's solution and presents his own	Insists on his solution
Disengagement	[38]-[49]	Writes his answer; begins to solve the next problem	Keeps insisting on his solution

Figure 3. The three-phase structure of the Daylight episode

2.3 Overview of Interaction Analysis

To be able to have a deeper insight into the nature of classroom interactions (and this includes student-teacher and student-student interactions) and into the possible reasons for their ineffectiveness, we devised two types of analysis, one of them cognitively oriented and the other aimed at detecting patterns of students' interactions. *Focal* (or *object-level*) *analysis*, which was forged first, and the results of which will not be presented here, has brought an eye-opening close-up at the boys' miscommunication.[vi] And yet, to fathom the nature and the reasons of the problem, we needed an additional way of looking at the interaction. In this presentation, we will focus on this latter approach, which is called *preoccupation* (or *meta-level*) *analysis.*[vii]

Interpersonal communication is an extremely complex phenomenon, in that at any given moment each participant is simultaneously involved in a number of object-level and meta-level activities: in trying to understand the explicit contents of previous utterances and to produce new ones, in monitoring the interaction, in presenting herself to others the way she would like to be seen, in engineering her position within the given group, and so on. These different-level discursive concerns compete for being in focus. As a discourse evolves, participants' attention is moving between channels – between one's own line of thought and those of his or her partners (see Figure 4), and it also winds back and forth between the explicit object of discourse and meta-discursive considerations. All this is true whether we speak about communication between students or between students and teachers.

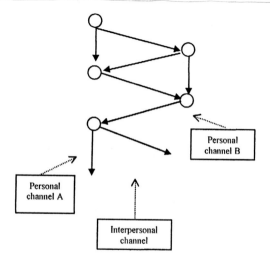

Figure 4. Dialogue as multi-channel communication

Preoccupation analysis deals with the question of how the participants of a conversation move between different channels of communication (private, interpersonal) and different levels (object-level and meta-level). Our principal tool in this analysis is the *interactivity flowchart*. With the help of this special instrument one is able to evaluate the interlocutors' interest in activating different channels and in creating a real dialogue with their partners.

We can look upon consecutive utterances in a discourse as endowed with invisible arrows that relate them to other utterances – those which have already been pronounced and those which are yet to come. These arrows express the participants' meta-discursive wishes: the wish to react to a previous contribution of a partner or the wish to evoke a response in another interlocutor. The organization of these invisible arrows in a conversation would often reveal certain regularities. The recurring forms of reactive and proactive behaviors, in their turn, may help in deciding whether interlocutors are really addressing their partners or, in fact, concentrating on a "conversation with themselves." In our study, interaction analysis was done with the help of a diagram in which the imaginary arrows mentioned above are made visible (see Figure 5). Let us now say a few words about the construction of such interaction flowcharts.

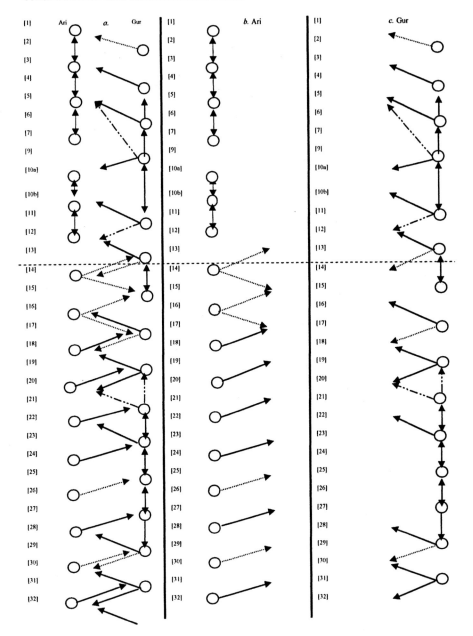

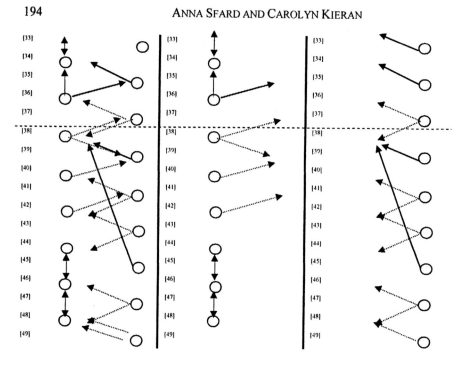

Figure 5. Interaction flowchart: Daylight episode

In the flowchart, the two *personal channels*, namely the respective "parts" of the two boys, are shown in separate columns. The numbers marking the little circles correspond to the numbers of the utterances in the episode transcript. There are two types of arrows that originate in the different utterances (Figure 6):

- *Reactive* arrow (an arrow which points vertically or diagonally backward/upward): this type of arrow expresses the fact that the source utterance is a reaction to the target utterance;
- *Proactive* arrow (an arrow pointing vertically or diagonally forward/downward): this type of arrow symbolizes the fact that the source utterance *invites* a response, so that the following utterance is expected to be a reaction.

The two partial flowcharts present the individual "parts" of Ari and Gur, respectively.[viii]

2.4 *Interactivity Analysis of Daylight Episode*

From the flowcharts we got for the *Daylight* episode (Figure 5) it is quite clear that the interactive behaviors of the two boys differed in a significant way. Let us begin with analyzing Ari's meta-level communicative actions. Because of the unbalanced form of the diagram *b*, the overall impression is that Ari is trying to avoid, or at least minimize, a true bi-directional interaction with Gur. Here are some salient characteristics of his discursive activity that point in this direction.

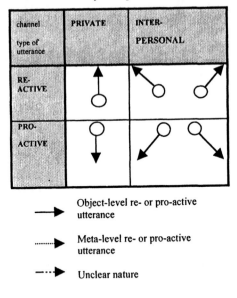

Object-level re- or pro-active utterance

Meta-level re- or pro-active utterance

Unclear nature

Figure 6. Interaction flowchart symbol

Ari's flowchart begins with an integrated stretch of utterances running along his private channel. This long strip of continuous self-talk, corresponding to the pre-engagement phase, shows Ari's preference for working separately, at least for as long as he needs to arrive at the solution of the problem. This phenomenon can be observed twice during the brief episode – see segments [1]-[12] and [44]-[49]. A number of other features of the flowchart in flowchart *b* point in the same direction. Perhaps the most striking of them is its uni-directionality: While there are some reactive arrows, proactive arrows are almost non-existent. Even when in the engagement phase, and evidently trying to correct Gur's solution, Ari limits his utterances to reactions to what Gur says. Sometimes, he simply presents his alternative view. One can say, therefore, that the boy refrains from proactive, response-inviting utterances, evidently not being interested in a prolonged interaction with his partner. We shall sum up by saying that his discursive conduct is *uninitiating*. Moreover, in spite of the prevalence of reactive utterances, Ari's behavior may also be described as *unresponsive*. Indeed, he rarely offers direct fully-fledged answers to Gur's proactive statements. More often than not, Ari turns to Gur only to express his disagreement. It is also quite remarkable that Ari is rather quick, indeed abrupt, in initiating the disengagement phase. Thus, in [40], after only a very brief (and not necessarily very sincere!) attempt to bring the evidently incoherent conversation back into focus, he gives up and turns his attention to a new question. He is also quite adamant in his decision to leave the limping conversation rather than try to make it run again.

Let us turn to Gur now (flowchart c). One glimpse at the arrows originating in Gur's utterances is enough to notice that the boy's interactional behavior is, in a sense, the exact opposite of that of his partner. Indeed, the new flowchart seems rather disintegrated in comparison with the other one, even in the pre-engagement phase. Further, Ari's uni-directional activity stands in striking contrast to the highly interactive, bi-directional behavior of Gur, who "bombards" his partner with proactive statements, and thus displays an *initiating* attitude. The ratio between the numbers of Ari's and Gur's proactive utterances is 3:11! Being obviously determined both to talk and to listen, Gur has a full arsenal of means for sustaining contact and spurring response. Except for extensive gesturing and numerous proactive statements, Gur himself is highly *responsive*. Particularly interesting are his means for signaling attention to his partner's utterances ("Whoa" in [2]), and for drawing attention ("look," etc.). Some of these seem to have no other role than to say "I hear you" and to initiate or sustain an engagement phase.

The different proportions of initiating and reacting activities disclose different needs, attitudes, and expectations of the two interlocutors. For those interested in the two boys' perception of their mutual positioning, the interactive structure of the discourse is particularly revealing. Gur's eloquence, gesturing, and generally highly interactive behavior may create an impression that he is the one who navigates the conversation. A closer look will reveal a rather different picture. Ari uses *interaction curbing* and *camouflaging techniques* to ensure his way in discourse. These techniques are particularly well instantiated in the disengagement phase, [38]-[49]. His disengagement technique is rather impolite, even though Ari tries to camouflage his impatience in many ways (e.g., he speaks in a pleasant tone and justifies his move with the "norm": "We can have different answers" [42]). Being interested much more than Ari in a true communication, Gur finds himself in a somewhat inferior position. Ari's disengagement action, showing his self-assurance and somewhat condescending attitude, makes his partner acutely aware of this uneven positioning. Gur copes with the situation with the help of multifarious *face-saving techniques*. Thus, for example, after he reacts spontaneously to Ari's declaration with a request for explanation , he immediately puts on an indifferent face by saying "I don't care" ([43]). Then, when Ari defiantly makes a move to the next question on the worksheet ([44]), Gur pretends to be still engrossed in the former one ([45]), and still convinced of his being right (while in fact he probably doubts it). Eventually, when in [44]-[48] Ari stubbornly sticks to his private channel, pretending Gur is not there, Gur eventually gives up by offering Ari "friendly" advice ("I am telling you, change it") and concluding with "Anyway, it doesn't matter"([49]).

We may sum up by saying that while Gur is evidently very much concerned with his positioning in the discourse and thus interested in a genuine bi-directional interaction, Ari would rather be left alone. Evidently, Ari is mainly preoccupied with object-level issues (solving the mathematical problem) whereas Gur focuses his attention on the interaction itself. The two boys' respective preoccupations are bound to have a considerable impact on how they manage their private channels and how well they function on the object-level.

2.5 Slope Episode

Contrary to expectations, the conversation with the relatively knowledgeable and successful partner did not spur Gur's progress, and the incoherent discourse clearly did not contribute to his understanding. Was it because the interlocutors were not truly open to the other's thinking, or because they did not have the skills necessary for effective interaction? Probably a little of both. When facing the results of our analysis for the first time, we consoled ourselves with the thought that the problems we identified were local and transitory. We tended to believe that they were simply a matter of the boys' initial lack of adjustment, and that their disappearance was only a matter of time. Thus, when beginning the analysis of a much later episode (Figures 7, 8), we anticipated seeing some substantial changes in the patterns of interaction. Whether our hopes came true the readers may now judge for themselves with the help of the table presenting episode structure (Figure 9) and the interaction flowchart, picturing boys' exchange that took place 20 meetings and 6 weeks later (Figure 10).

TABLES REPRESENTING FUNCTIONS

A function g(x) is partly represented by the table below. Answer the questions in the box.

x	g(x)
0	-5
1	0
2	5
3	10
4	15
5	20

(1) What is g(6)? _____
(2) What is g(10)? _____

(3) The students in grade 7 were asked to write an expression for the function g(x).

Evan wrote $g(x) = 5(x - 1)$
Amy wrote $g(x) = 3(x - 3) + 2(x - 2)$
Stuart wrote $g(x) = 5x - 5$

Who is right? Why?

Figure 7. Slope episode: Activity sheet

WHAT IS DONE	WHAT IS SAID
	- 25:40 -
[1] A. is trying to get the expression from the table	[1] A.: [1a] Wait, how do we find out the slope again? [1b] No, no, no, no. Slope, no, wait, [1c] intercept is negative 5. [1d]Slope
	[2] G.: What are you talking about?
	[3] A.: I'm talking about this. It's 5.
	[4] G.: It doesn't matter if it's on (mumble)
	[5] A.: 5x. Right?
[6] A. has written 5x + -5	[6] G.: What's that?
	[7] A.: It's the formula, so you can figure it out.
	[8] G.: Oh. How'd you get that formula?
[9] to do the next task: find g(6)	[9] A.: and you replace the x by 6.
	[10] G.: Oh. Ok, I
	[11] A.: [11a] Look. Cause the, um the slope, is the zero.

WHAT IS DONE	WHAT IS SAID
	[11b] Ah, no, the intercept is the zero.
	[12] G.: Oh, yeah, yeah, yeah. So you got your
[13] "each": A. points to both columns, indicating that you have to check both	[13] A.: [13a] And then you see how many is in between each, [13b] like from zero to what
"from zero to what": he points to the x column	
[14] the left counterpart of the right-column 0 is 1	[14] G.: And the slope is, so the slope is 1.
[15] "zero": he circles the zero n the x column on G.'s sheet	[15] A.: [15a] Hum? No, the slope, [15b] see you look at zero,
[16] -5 is the f(x) value when x = 0	[16] G.: [16a] Oh that zero, ok. [16b] So the slope is minus 5
	[17] A.: yeah. And
	[18] G.: How are you supposed to get the other ones?
[19] A. first points to x column ("going down by ones"), then the f(x) column ("by fives"), and again to f(x) column ("look here")	[19] A.: [19a] You look how many times it's going down, like we did before. So it's going down by ones. [19b] So then it's easy. This is ah by fives. See, it's going down by ones, so you just look here
	[20] G.: Oh. So it's 5
	[21] A.: yeah. 5x plus
	[22] G.: Negative 5.
	[23] A.: Do you understand?
	[24] G.: [24a] Negative 5. Yeah, yeah, ok. [24b] So what is g 6?
	[25] A.: [25a] 5 times 6 is 30, plus negative 5 is 25. [25b] So we did get it right.
[26] "this column": he points to x column	26] G.: No, but it's - in this column there?
	[27] A.: yeah
	[28] G.: [28a] Oh, then that makes sense. [28b] (writes) It's 30. [28c] What is g 10? ... 40
	[29] A.: 20, ah 40. No, 45.
	[30] G.: No,
	[31] A.: 45
	[32] G.: because 20
	[33] A.: 10 times 5 is 50, minus
[34] he points to the two entries in the last row	[34] G.: Well, 5 is 20, so 10 must have 40
[35] A. circles the 10 in g(10) on G.'s sheet	[35] A.: times 5
	[36] G.: Oh, we do that thing. Ok, just trying to find it.
	[37] A.: yeah
[38] again he points to the last row of the table	[38] G.: Cause I was thinking cause 5 is 20,

WHAT IS DONE	WHAT IS SAID
	[39] A.: It's 45. Yeah
	[40] G.: (mumble) So it's 45.
	- 27:42 -

Figure 8. Slope *episode– the protocol*

A cursory glance at the flowcharts suffices to understand that if there was any change in the patterns of Ari and Gur's interactions, it must have been marginal. The new diagrams are quite similar in their general features to those we saw in the Daylight episode (Figure 9). In fact, certain salient phenomena observed in the first episode reappeared in the second one with an even greater force. Among the constant patterns that repeat themselves in all three episodes (the two Slope sub-episodes and the Daylight episode), let us first note the three-phase overall structure of an interaction, where the relatively restrained Ari, rather than the outgoing Gur, sets the pace. Every new activity starts with the pre-engagement period during which the problem at hand is tackled by the boys separately. Ari will not leave this phase until he has the problem solved. In fact, the boys never really solve problems together. The engagement phase begins only when there is a ready solution or two to discuss. Ari invariably pushes his own solution, refuses to really listen to Gur, and remains unaware of the sources of his partner's mistakes. Gur, in turn, is too keen to save face to persist in questioning his partner. The disengagement, initiated by Ari, always comes quicker than he would like it to happen.

Phase	Sub-episode 1: Finding g(6)			Sub-episode 2: Finding g(10)		
	Seg-ment	Ari	Gur	Seg-ment	Ari	Gur
Pre-engagement: Solving separately	[1]-[5]	Solves	Inquires	[28],[29]	Solves Gets g(10)=45	Solves Gets g(10)=40
Engagement: Arguing/explaining	[2]-[26]	Explains his solution	Inquires about Ari's solution	[30]-[38]	Repeats his solution	Tries to explain his solution
Disengagement	[23]-[28]	Confirms his answer	Says he accepts Ari's answer, but errs in writing it down. Goes to the next problem	[39],[40]	Repeats his answer	Accepts Ari's answer

Figure 9. The structure of the Slope episode

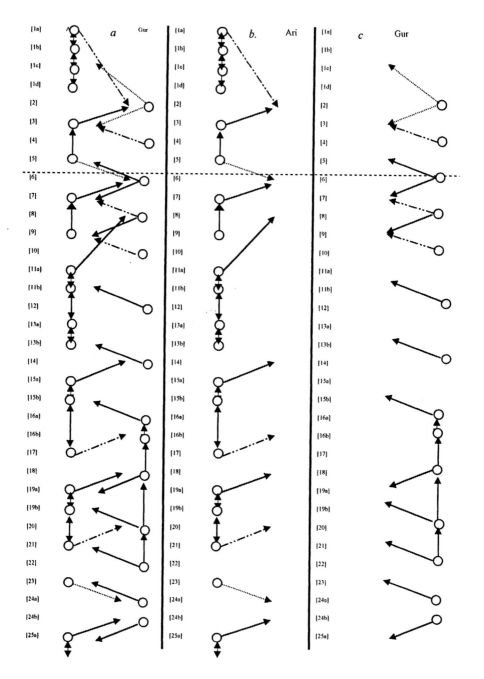

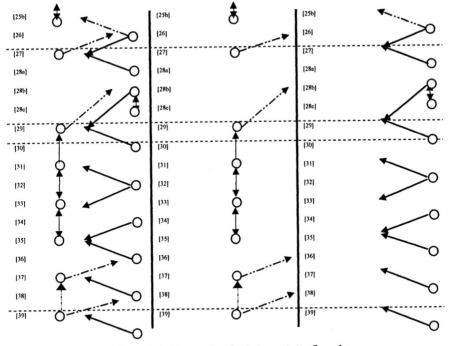

Figure 10. Slope episode: Interactivity flowchart

This brief description of the recurrent scenario makes it clear how unhelpful this collaboration is. It could hardly be otherwise considering Ari's and Gur's differing interests and their imperfect interactive skills. Twenty sessions together did not change much in this respect except, perhaps, pushing each of the boys further in his own direction: Ari became even more effective in protecting his private channel and in preventing any real exchange, and Gur became even more dependent on his interaction with Ari. All this undermined the effectiveness of the boys' interaction, rather than bringing any real improvement.

3. IMPLICATIONS: HOW MATHEMATICS TEACHERS CAN PREPARE THEMSELVES FOR HANDLING THE "TALKING CLASSES"

What has been shown in this paper is but an example of the type of research that seems necessary if we wish to help teachers in preparing themselves for teaching mathematics according to the principles promoted by the reform movement. The study brought a glimpse into a possibly quite common type of interaction between students working together on mathematical problems. This type of information is indispensable for those who are supposed to teach mathematics in the "talking classes" envisioned in NCTM *Standards*. More importantly, the tool of analysis developed for the sake of this study may help in teacher education and in the teachers' subsequent efforts to improve the effectiveness of classroom interactions. Let me elaborate on these two points.

3.1 Learning About the Mechanisms, Advantages, and Disadvantages of the Students' Interaction

To get a sense of the way in which teachers may capitalize on the kind of detailed analysis carried out in this paper, let us take a look on what can be learned from this analysis. The results of the study compel us to conclude that being a Guide-on-the-Side cannot possibly mean either simple refraining from unsolicited intervention or intervening in ways which are not based on some well-thought of, well-defined principles. The interactions between Ari and Gur, sporadically interrupted with teacher's accidental, unsystematic attempts to support their efforts, proved quite unhelpful to either of the boys. The study has therefore demonstrated that contrary to the nowadays popular beliefs, the "more knowledgeable peer" cannot automatically become a good substitution for a teacher. Were Ari's attempts to help Gur ineffective because of the lack of the true willingness or because of the absence of necessary communicative skills? Probably because of both. Our analysis has clearly confirmed what Reddy asserted quite a while ago: "understanding without effort" is but a myth and human communication is subject to the law of entropy (Reddy, 1979). Besides, being a student himself, Ari had no real incentive to share with Gur responsibility for his learning, whereas he did have every reason to feel that he would be better off working alone. And yet, strong motivation is necessary to engage in mathematical conversation and make it work. Such motivation can only be found in teachers – people committed to their students' success and understanding.

Let us make it clear: The bottom line of what we have said so far *is not* that mathematics cannot or should not be learned in an interactive way. Our limited example could not have given rise to such an extreme claim. The only reasonable conclusion of our analysis is that if conversation is to be effective and conducive for learning, the art of communicating *has to be taught*, and that the role of the teacher in making students' learning interactions work is incomparably greater than it has been assumed so far, by default. The exact nature of this role is yet to be investigated. To put it into Smith's (1996) words, "For the current reform to generate deep and lasting changes, teachers must find new foundations for building durable efficacy beliefs that are consistent with reform-based teaching practice".

Our own study has shown, among others, that the reform central character, the Guide-on-the-Side, has yet a long way to go, and many new skills to learn, before she enters the classroom. For example, she should probably get some systematic knowledge on communication. Based on our observations, we were able to come up with a few ideas about the aspects of classroom interactions that should be attended to, and deliberately developed, if the students are to capitalize on mathematical conversation. But this is far from enough. There are great many other questions that must be answered before the teachers may start preparing themselves in a systematic way for the role of the Gide-on-the-Side. One of the most nagging issues is that of the nature, the manner, and the timings of teacher's interactions during students' team work. Our example has demonstrated that when it comes to guiding students' group activities, one cannot always count on teachers' natural instincts. The need of a systematic research and specially designed methods is therefore quite clear. And there are also questions of organizational nature, such as: What are the techniques that could help the teachers to manage the simultaneous work of many different teams, while keeping abreast of their respective advances, monitoring their diverse difficulties, and trying not to overlook any of students' ideas that may be useful in the later whole class discussion? We could go on with the list of problems that remain to be investigated, but we shall stop here, hoping that the general message is now sufficiently clear.

3.2 Using Interactivity Analysis as a Tool for Self-Improvement.

It is noteworthy that our special tools of analysis may also have practical uses as instruments that can be useful both in teacher preparation and in the teaching itself. The teacher who gets ready for orchestrating multifarious exchanges in a mathematics classroom may use the tool to get a deeper insight not only into students' interactions, but also into her own ways of interacting with students. For such a teacher, an analyzed sample of a few episodes in which she communicates with students may have an eye-opening quality. Such analysis would face her with certain recurrent, and possibly unhelpful, patterns in her discursive conduct of which, so far, she might have been completely unaware. One glimpse of a representative sample of classroom discourse may show, for example, whether she really listens to the children or, like Ari, she hears nobody but herself. Once learned, the tool may then assist the teacher during her everyday work as a means of monitoring classroom exchanges and for testing a continuous attempt at communication improvement.

REFERENCES

Booth, S., Wistedt, I., Hallden, O., Martinsson, M., & Marton, F. (1999). Paths of learning – the joint constitution of insights. In L. Burton (Ed.), *Learning mathematics: From Hierarchies to Networks* (pp. 62-82). London: Falmer Press.

Cobb, P. (1996). Accounting for mathematics learning in the social context of the classroom. In C. Alsina., J. M. Alvarez, B. Hodgson, C. Laborde, & A. Perez (Eds.), *8th International Congress of Mathematics Education selected lectures* (pp. 85-99). Sevilla: S.A.E.M. 'THALES'.

Cobb, P. & Bowers, J. (1999). Cognitive and situated learning perspectives in theory and practice. *Educational Researcher, 28(2)*, 4-15.

Comiti, C. & Loewenberg Ball, D. (1996). Preparing teachers to teach mathematics: A comparative perspective. In A. J. Bishop, K. Clements, C. Keitel, J. Kilpatrick, & C. Laborde (Eds.), *International handbook of mathematics education* (pp. 1123-1154). Dordrecht, The Netherlands: Kluwer Academic Publishers.

Davis, R.B. & Maher, C.A. (1997). How students think: The role of representations. In L English, (Ed.), *Mathematical reasoning: Analogies, metaphors, and images* (pp. 339-371). London: Lawrence Erlbaum Associates.

Forman, E. (1996). Forms of participation in classroom practice: Implications for learning mathematics. In P. Nesher, L. Steffe, P. Cobb, G. Goldin, & B. Greer (Eds.), *Theories of mathematical learning* (pp. 115-130). Hillsdale, NJ: Lawrence Erlbaum Associates.

Frykholm, J.A. (1999). The impact of reform: Challenges for mathematics teacher preparation. *Journal of Mathematics Teacher Education, 2(1),* 79-105.

Goos, M. & Galbraith, P. (1996). Do it this way! Metacognitive strategies in collaborative problem solving. *Educational Studies in Mathematics, 30,* 229-260.

Kieran, C. (1994). A functional approach to the introduction of algebra: some pros and cons. In J.P. da Ponte & J. F. Matos (Eds.), *Proceedings of the 18th International Conference for the Psychology of Mathematics Education, (*Vol. 1, pp. 157-175). Lisbon, Portugal: PME Program Committee.

Kieran, C. & Sfard, A. (1999). Seeing through symbols: The case of equivalent expressions. *Focus on Learning Mathematics 21(1),* 1-17.

Lampert, M. (1990). When the problem is not the question and the solution is not the answer: Mathematical knowing and teaching. *American Educational Research Journal, 27(1),* 29-64.

Lampert, M. & Cobb, P. (in press). White Paper on Communication and Language for Standards 2000 Writing Group.

Levenberg, I. (1998). *Mathematics teachers in the process of change.* Unpublished dissertation. Haifa: The University of Haifa.

NCTM (National Council of Teachers of Mathematics) (1989). *Curriculum and evaluation standards for school mathematics.* Reston, VA: NCTM.

NCTM (National Council of Teachers of Mathematics). (1991). *Professional standards for teaching mathematics.* Reston, VA: NCTM.

NCTM (National Council of Teachers of Mathematics) (2000). *Principles and standards for school mathematics.* Reston, VA: NCTM.

O'Connor, M.C. (1996). Managing the intermental: classroom group discussion and the social context of learning. In D. Slobin, J. Gerhardt, A. Kyratzis, & J. Guo (Eds.), *Social interaction, social context, and language* (pp. 495-509). Hillsdale, NJ: Lawrence Erlbaum.

O'Connor, M.C. (1998). Language socialization in the mathematics classroom: Discourse practices and mathematical thinking. In M. Lampert & M. Blunk (Eds.), *Talking mathematics: Studies of teaching and learning in school* (pp. 17-55). New York: Cambridge University Press.

O'Connor, M. C., & Michaels, S. (1996). Shifting participant frameworks: Orchestrating thinking practices in group discussions. In D. Hicks (Ed.), *Discourse, learning, and schooling* (pp. 63-103). New York: Cambridge University Press.

Reddy, M. (1979). The conduit metaphor: A case of frame conflict in our language about language. *Metaphor and thought, Second edition* (pp. 164-201). Cambridge: Cambridge University Press.

Rittenhouse, P.S. (1998). The teacher's role in mathematical conversation: Stepping in and stepping out. In M. Lampert & M. L. Blunk (Eds.), *Talking mathematics in school: Studies of teaching and learning* (pp. 163-189). Cambridge, Mass.: Cambridge University Press.

Saxe, G.B. & Guberman, S.R. (1998). Studying mathematics learning in collective activity. *Learning and Instruction, 8,* 489-501.

Sfard, A. (1991). On the dual nature of mathematical conceptions: reflections on processes and objects as different sides of the same coin. *Educational Studies in Mathematics, 22,* 1-36.

Sfard, A. (2000). Steering (dis)course between metaphors and rigor: Using focal analysis to investigate the emergence of a mathematical object. *Journal for Research in Mathematics Education. 31(3),* 296-327.

Sfard, A. & Kieran, C. (in press). Cognition in interaction: Dissecting students' mathematical communication to see what makes it ineffective. To appear in *Mind, Culture, and Activity.*

Smith, J. P. (1996). Efficacy and teaching mathematics by telling: A challenge for reform. *Journal for Research in Mathematics Education, 27(4),* 387-402.

Stacey, K. & Gooding, A. (1998). Communication and learning in small group discussion. In H. Steinbring, M. Bartolini-Bussi, & A. Sierpinska (Eds.), *Language and communication in mathematics classroom* (pp. 191-206). Reston, VA: The National Council of Teachers of Mathematics.

Voigt, J. (1985). Patterns and routines in classroom interaction. *Recherches en Didactique des Mathematiques, 6(1),* 69-118.

Voigt, J. (1994). Negotiation of mathematical meaning and learning mathematics. *Educational Studies in Mathematics, 26,* 275-298.

Voigt, J. (1995). Thematic patterns of interaction and sociomathematical norms. In P. Cobb & H. Bauersfeld (Eds.), *The emergence of mathematical meaning: Interaction in classroom cultures* (pp. 163-201). Hillsdale, NJ: Lawrence Erlbaum Associates.

Yackel, E. & Cobb, P. (1996). Sociomathematical norms, argumantation, and autonomy in mathematics. *Journal for Research in Mathematics Education. 27(4)*, 58-477.

Anna Sfard
The University of Haifa
Israel

Carolyn Kieran
Universite du Quebec a Montreal
Canada

NOTES

[i] The *Standards* authors speak extensively about the need to give the student opportunities to "speak mathematics":

> "The development of a student's power to use mathematics involves learning the signs, symbols, and terms of mathematics. This is best accomplished in problem situations in which students have an opportunity to read, write, and discuss ideas in which the use of the language of mathematics becomes natural." (NCTM, 1989, p. 6)

The recommendation implies a number of different types of classroom activity: "group and individual assignments; discussion between teacher and students and among students; and exposition by the teacher."

[ii] This later type of activity may be conceptualized and organized in many ways. Names like *cooperative learning* and *collaborative learning* are often used to denote the most popular approaches to students collective work.

[iii] This is not to say that research on students' interaction is nonexistent (see, e.g., Goos & Galbraith (1996); Booth, Wistedt, Hallden, Martinsson, & Marton (1999); Saxe & Guberman (1998); Stacey & Gooding (1998)). And yet, the attention given to the ways students learn together is still rather scarce in comparison with the amount of work invested in teacher-class or teacher-student interaction.

[iv] Conducted in Canada since 1993. For details on the project see Kieran (1994), Kieran & Sfard (1999), and Sfard & Kieran (in press).

[v] This observation was thought provoking since our interviews were designed to be "non- interventional," or at least as "neutral" as possible.

[vi] For details of focal analysis see Sfard & Kieran (in press) and Sfard (2000).

[vii] We limit the scope reluctantly, because the two analyses, focal and preoccupational, are intimately interrelated. Presenting one without the other may be compared to a text from which every other word has been deleted. Still, space limitations leave us no choice. We hope the message will be sufficiently clear in spite of this one-sidedness.

[viii] Drawing an interaction flow chart is, naturally, an interpretive task, and so it is quite likely that charts obtained by different analysts would sometimes differ in a number of details. From our experience, however, the users of the method usually attain a high degree of consensus.

PAUL COBB AND KAY MCCLAIN

AN APPROACH FOR SUPPORTING TEACHERS'
LEARNING IN SOCIAL CONTEXT

ABSTRACT. Our purpose in this chapter is to outline a general approach to collaborating with teachers in order to support the establishment of a professional teaching community. As will become apparent, our goal is to help teachers develop instructional practices in which they induct their students into the ways of reasoning of the discipline by building systematically on their current mathematical activity. We develop the rationale for the approach we propose by describing how our thinking about in-service teacher development has evolved over the last thirteen years or so. To this end, we first revisit work conducted in collaboration with Erna Yackel and Terry Wood between 1986 and 1992 in which we supported the development of American second- and third-grade teachers. In doing so, we tease out aspects of the approach we took that still appear viable and discuss two major lessons that we learned. In the next section of the chapter, we draw on a series of teaching experiments we have conducted over the past seven years in American elementary and middle-school classrooms both to critique our prior work and to develop three further aspects of the approach we propose. We conclude by highlighting broad features of the approach and by locating them in institutional context.

1. GUIDING THE RENEGOTIATION OF CLASSROOM SOCIAL NORMS

1.1 Insights From a Classroom Teaching Experiment

Our initial work with teachers grew out of a year-long teaching experiment that we conducted in an American second-grade classroom with seven-year-old students during the 1986 – 1987 school year. As part of our efforts, we developed a complete set of instructional activities for second-grade mathematics. Our original intent when conducting this experiment was to extend the methodology of the constructivist teaching experiment (Cobb & Steffe, 1983; Steffe, 1983) to the complexity of a public-school classroom. In the constructivist teaching experiment, a researcher works one-on-one with a small number of students for an extended period of time to investigate the *process* by which they reorganize their mathematical thinking. We planned to take a similar approach when conducting the classroom experiment by analyzing individual students' mathematical learning as they interacted with the teacher and their peers. However, incidents that occurred during the first few classroom sessions led us to radically modify our research focus.

Briefly, both we and the second-grade teacher with whom we collaborated expected the students to engage in genuine mathematical discussions in which they explained and justified their mathematical reasoning. However, as a consequence of their prior experiences in school, the students seemed to assume that their role was

F.-L. Lin & T. J. Cooney (Eds.) Making Sense of Mathematics Teacher Education, 207—231.

to infer the responses that the teacher had in mind rather than to articulate their own interpretations. The teacher spontaneously coped with this tension between her own and the students' expectations by initiating a process that we subsequently came to term the renegotiation of classroom social norms (Cobb, Yackel, & Wood, 1989). Examples of social norms that became explicit topics of conversation include explaining and justifying solutions, attempting to make sense of explanations given by others, indicating agreement or disagreement, and questioning alternatives when a conflict in interpretations had become apparent. It was as we attempted to make sense of these observations that the classroom participation structure (Erickson, 1986; Lampert, 1990) and microculture (Bauersfeld, 1988) became a primary focus of our research agenda. This orientation in turn proved useful when we attempted to understand a second unexpected phenomenon that occurred during the teaching experiment.

Although it might seem naive with hindsight, we were surprised at the extent to which the classroom constituted a learning environment for the teacher throughout the year of the experiment (Cobb, Yackel, & Wood, 1991). It is important to note that the teacher's initial concern in the first few weeks of the experiment centered on the establishment of classroom norms that would make it possible for her students to work productively in small groups and to engage in substantive whole-class discussions of their reasoning. The establishment of these norms in turn made it possible for the teacher to attend more directly to the nature of her students' mathematical reasoning. Similarly, the emergence of viable small-group norms made it possible for the teacher to relinquish her traditional responsibility of constantly monitoring the students to ensure that they stayed on task. As a consequence, she was able to interact with her students as they completed instructional activities during small-group work and to focus directly on their explanations during whole-class discussions. As she did so, the teacher repeatedly made observations that led her to question and revise aspects of her practice. Comments that the teacher made shortly after the teaching experiment about what she termed her metamorphosis are consistent with this brief account of her learning. As she describes the process, it was one of gradual evolution rather than of sudden insight and revolutionary change. The implication we drew for our subsequent work with a group of second-grade teachers was that an emphasis on the renegotiation of social norms might initiate a long-term, generative process of change.

1.2 Initial Collaboration With Teachers

In the summer following the teaching experiment, we conducted a week-long session with 25 second-grade teachers and then visited their classrooms every two weeks throughout the school year to provide support. In addition, we organized the teachers into small teaching groups that would meet each week to share observations and to collaboratively plan lessons. As we have noted, our intent in revisiting this work is not to provide a complete description of the approach we took. Instead, we will limit our focus to aspects of the approach that continue to hold promise. The first of these aspects concerns the need for teachers to have reason and motivation to want to change the way they teach mathematics. To this end, the initial discussions we organized during the summer session focused on video-recorded interviews conducted with students who had received traditional instruction. In the interviews, the students were asked to solve two sets of parallel tasks. The tasks in one set were presented in a format that simulated their textbook, whereas the tasks in the other set were designed to draw on the students' pragmatic, out-of-school reasoning. One of the questions we posed to the teachers was to explain why the students solved the two sets of tasks in radically different ways, often resulting in different answers even though the tasks used the same number combinations. The issue that emerged was that of the students' beliefs about mathematics that they develop as a consequence of traditional American instruction. The teachers saw these beliefs as detrimental and thus had a reason to consider revising their instructional practices.[1]

The issue that we then raised with the teachers was that of how students develop these beliefs. This question focused attention on the teachers' current instructional practices and led them to critique both the types of instructional activities they used and the norms established in their classrooms. Against this background, we used video-recordings from the teaching experiment classroom as a basis for discussion. In doing so, we asked the teachers to consider what students had to know and be able to do mathematically in order to be effective in this classroom. In addressing this issue, the teachers developed a rationale for general aspects of the classroom participation structure that was cast in terms of students' mathematical learning.

A further aspect of the summer session that is worth highlighting is our decision to orient activities and discussions towards issues with which the teachers were familiar on the basis of first-hand experience. For example, the video-recordings we used all involved mathematical ideas that the teachers viewed as central to the second-grade curriculum. As a consequence, the episodes we showed from the teaching experiment classroom had face validity for the teachers in that they could recognize points of contact with their current instructional agendas. The remaining activities included time to familiarize the teachers with the instructional sequences we had developed during the teaching experiment. In doing so, we discussed the rationale for the sequencing of the instructional activities with the teachers by focusing on the envisioned course of students' mathematical development. In addition, we also attended to the various ways in which students might solve particular instructional activities by drawing on the video-recordings that the teachers had already viewed. The discussions therefore served as occasions for the teachers to scrutinize aspects of their current instructional practices that had previously seemed beyond question.

The support the teachers received during the school year included bi-weekly classroom visits by a member of the project staff, the weekly planning meetings, and monthly working sessions that we conducted with all 25 teachers. Our purpose in visiting the teachers' classrooms was to address pragmatic concerns and to frame classroom events as paradigm cases in which to discuss the relation between their instructional practices and their students' reasoning. The observations we made during these visits indicated the teachers' development of forms of instructional practice in which materials are used flexibly as a resource was a slower process than we had anticipated. Even by the midpoint of the school year, several of the planning groups struggled with the realization that they could not just work through the instructional activities. This might be dismissed as simply an instance of teachers clinging to an aspect of their traditional instructional practices. However, we came to view it as a limitation of the approach we took in attempting to support the teachers' development. On reflection, we realized that we did not fully appreciate the complexity of instructional practices in which teachers adapt instructional materials to their classroom situations. As a consequence, we had failed to adequately support the teachers' development of the intellectual resources that would enable them to judge how to adapt the instructional materials. Although most of the teachers did come to use the materials flexibly in the latter part of the school year, their development of these relatively sophisticated practices involved largely ad hoc modifications on their part in the absence of systematic support. We will return to this issue when we discuss the approach we would now take when working with teachers. First, however, we discuss two major lessons we learned from this initial collaboration with teachers.

1.3 Lessons Learned

As we have clarified, our collaboration with the second-grade teachers was premised on the assumption that their classrooms would be a primary site of their learning. In making this assumption, we viewed the teachers' learning as situated in that it would be grounded in their interactions with their students. At the same time, however, our conception of the teachers' learning was relatively individualistic in that we were concerned with the learning opportunities that arose for them in their classrooms. It was not until we had worked with the teachers for some time that we began to view the teachers and ourselves as constituting a *professional teaching community*. This in turn led us to question the accounts we had developed of the teachers' learning in that they did not relate changes in their instructional practices to their participation in this community. Elsewhere, we have argued that it is not possible to adequately account for individual students' mathematical learning as it occurs in the classroom without also analyzing the developing mathematical practices of the classroom community (Cobb, Wood, & Yackel, 1993). Similarly, we have come to realize that it is not possible to adequately account for the process of teachers' development without also analyzing the pedagogical community in which they participate. This realization has implications for our approach and orients us to consider the ways of talking and thinking about mathematics teaching that we want to become normative or taken-as-shared in a professional teaching community.

The importance that we now attribute to participation in professional teaching communities might seem questionable given that American teachers typically work in relative isolation from one another with little discussion of or joint reflection on substantive issues relating to the teaching and learning of mathematics (Newman & Associates, 1996; Stigler & Hiebert, 1999). As Jackson (1968) and Goodlad (1983) have observed, teaching in the United States tends to be a highly routinized activity that is scripted in advance and involves few adaptations to students' contributions. Gamoran, Secada, & Marrett (in press) have noted that this routinization obscures the uncertainties of teaching by allowing teachers to proceed without the need to consider possible mismatches between their instructional scripts and students' reasoning. In contrast, the teachers with whom we worked came to view teaching as a complex, dynamic activity in which instruction is informed by ongoing assessments of students' mathematical activity. Gamoran et al. (in press) argue that teachers' recognition of the uncertainties involved in supporting the development of students' mathematical understanding can lead them to collaborate on issues of teaching and learning that arise in their classrooms. This conjecture is consistent with our experience in that the teachers with whom we worked indicated that they saw great value in both the weekly planning meetings and monthly work sessions. A number of other researchers who have collaborated with groups of teachers have reported similar observations (Lehrer & Schauble, 1998; Schifter & Fosnot, 1993; Warren & Rosebery, 1995). It would therefore seem that teachers' participation in a pedagogical community can provide crucial support for their development of instructional practices that are responsive to students' reasoning. This in turn indicates the need for analytical approaches that locate teachers' learning within the social context of both the professional teaching community and their classroom.

The importance of treating teacher change as a communal activity when both planning collaborations with teachers and accounting for their development was the first lesson that we learned. The second lesson was to take account of the institutional settings of the schools in which teachers work. We can clarify the relevance of taking this broader perspective by returning to our initial collaboration with teachers and summarizing events that occurred after we had worked with them for a year. As we have noted, our focus was almost exclusively on changes in the teaching and learning of mathematics in individual classrooms. However, as Dillon (1993) has documented, some members of the governing school board of the school district objected to the changes that were occurring in mathematics instruction. They seemed to assume that it was their right to decide both what mathematics should be taught and how it should be taught. The school board's assumption was reasonable in that, in the past, teachers had typically accepted its pronouncements with little dissent. However, as a consequence of their first year of collaboration with us, the teachers were now able to justify both their new view of mathematical activity in school and their new instructional practices in terms of the quality of their students' learning (Simon, 1993). They therefore believed that they were more qualified than the school board members to make decisions about the learning and teaching of mathematics at the classroom level. Their professionalization can therefore be viewed as distributed in that it involved interrelated changes in the instructional practices they developed while participating in the professional teaching community and in the institutional setting in which they worked.

The implication that we drew from this sequence of events is to attend to what transpires outside classrooms as well as what occurs within them by developing ongoing collaborative relationships with school principals and district administrators (Cole, 1996; Lazerson, McLaughlin, McPherson, & Bailey, 1985; Price & Ball, 1997). In addition, we concluded that it is important to conduct ongoing analyses of the institutional settings in which the teachers work. On the one hand, these analyses can guide attempts to collaborate with principals and administrators. On the other hand, these analyses are crucial in understanding the development of the teachers' classroom practices given the distributed nature of professionalization.

In a companion paper to this chapter, we have discussed several specific constructs that might prove useful when conducting analyses of this type (Cobb & McClain, 1999). Although our primary focus in this chapter is on the classroom as an arena for teachers' learning, we have included this brief discussion of institutional context in order to indicate the broader setting in which the approach we are proposing should be seen as located.

2. INSTRUCTIONAL SEQUENCES AND LEARNING TRAJECTORIES AS A BASIS FOR TEACHER DEVELOPMENT

It should be clear that our strategy for formulating a new approach to teacher development is to take a highly critical stance to our prior work. Our initial collaboration with teachers was in fact reasonably successful when assessed in terms of several criteria. For example, the performance of students in project classrooms on paper-and-pencil instruments designed to assess problem solving and conceptual understanding was significantly superior to that of students in traditional classrooms (Cobb, Yackel & Wood, 1991). In addition, there were no significant differences in the performance of the two groups of students on basic skill tests that were consistent with the goals of traditional instruction. The assessment studies we conducted also indicated that project students had developed more desirable beliefs about and motivations to engage in mathematical activity in school (Cobb, Wood, Yackel, Nicholls, Wheatley, Trigatti, & Perlwitz, 1991). A follow-up study revealed that these differences in mathematical reasoning and in beliefs and motivations held up a year later after project students had received traditional instruction in third-grade (Cobb, Wood, Yackel, & Perlwitz, 1992). Equally important, the professional teaching community has not only sustained itself but has inducted new members into its practices with reasonably impressive results (Wood & Sellars, 1996).

This pattern of findings is generally consistent with those reported by other researchers who have established collaborative relationships with groups of elementary school teachers (CTGV, 1997; Cohen & Hill, 1998; Fennema, Carpenter, Franke, Levi, Jacobs, & Empson, 1996; Lehrer & Schauble, 1998; Little, 1993; Stein, Silver, & Smith, 1998). Encouraging as these results are, we have become aware of further inadequacies of our initial work with teachers as we have reflected on a series of six teaching experiments that we have conducted during the past seven years. These inadequacies concern both the instructional materials we developed and the role of the teacher in proactively supporting students' mathematical development. With hindsight, we now view our initial approach of relying on cognitive models to develop instructional activities as flawed because such an approach cannot in principle yield positive heuristics that can guide the design process (Gravemeijer, 1994). In addition, in our earlier work, we focused on the teacher's role in initiating the renegotiation of classroom social norms but did not go farther by thinking through how the teacher might actively pursue a mathematical agenda in the classroom. We address these two interrelated issues in the following paragraphs by drawing on the teaching experiments we have conducted in recent years to explicate our overall goals for teachers' learning by clarifying what might be involved in teaching mathematics for understanding. We then focus on the role of instructional sequences in supporting teachers' learning and on aspects of the teacher's proactive role in the classroom.

2.1 Teaching for Understanding as the Goal of Teacher Development

The teaching experiments we have conducted during the past seven years have focused on numerical reasoning and measurement in the early elementary grades, and on statistical data analysis in the middle grades. In these experiments, which were conducted in collaboration with Koeno Gravemeijer, we have drawn extensively on the theory of Realistic Mathematics Education developed at the Freudenthal Institute in the Netherlands to produce eight sequences of instructional activities that are aimed at significant mathematical ideas. We have also reflected on our own activity of planning and conducting these experiments to deepen our understanding of what might be involved in pursuing an instructional agenda that aims at mathematical understanding. This is an important aspect of our work because it parallels our goal in our teacher development efforts, that of clarifying end points.

These reflections clarify that one of the initial challenges when preparing for a teaching experiment is to be explicit about the global intent of the planned instructional sequence. In our experience, this task of specifying the overarching mathematical ideas is typically a non-trivial exercise. Once delineated, the overall instructional goals orient the formulation of a conjectured learning trajectory that itself serves as the backdrop against which we make local pedagogical judgments once we begin working in the classroom. This trajectory takes the form of an envisioned developmental route by which students' mathematical activity and discourse might evolve into the ways of understanding that constitute the intent of the sequence. This notion of a learning trajectory, which is taken from Simon (1995), is consistent with Gravemeijer's (1994) analysis of the process of instructional development. In Gravemeijer's account, the developer first carries out an anticipatory thought experiment in which he or she envisions both how the proposed instructional activities might be realized in interaction and what students might learn as they participate in them. As Gravemeijer notes, in conducting this thought experiment, the developer formulates conjectures about both the course of students' mathematical development and the means of supporting it. In other words, the rationale for the instructional sequence takes the form of a conjectured learning trajectory that culminates with the mathematical ideas that constitute our overall instructional intent.

It is important to note that these conjectures about both a learning route and the means of supporting development along it are provisional and are tested and modified on a daily basis as we make local pedagogical judgments in the classroom. At the same time, the conjectured trajectory serves to guide the local decisions that lead to its revision. We can illustrate this process by focusing on the judgments we make when preparing for the daily whole-class discussions that follow individual or small-group work. The purpose of these discussions is not merely to give the students an opportunity to explain their reasoning. Instead, a classroom discussion is justifiable only if mathematically significant issues emerge as topics of conversation. We therefore draw on our observations of individual or small-group activity to identify students whose explanations might give rise to substantive mathematical discussions. At times, we call on one student whereas, on other occasions, whole-class discussions involve the comparison of two or more students' reasoning. In either case, our judgments about the potential significance of the issues that might emerge are made with respect to the conjectured learning trajectory. In other words, an issue is considered to be mathematically significant if it contributes to the realization of our pedagogical agenda. Metaphorically, the learning trajectory might therefore be said to constitute the big picture within which local decisions and judgments are made on a daily basis.

In this way of working in the classroom, the relationship between the learning trajectory and the daily judgments is reflexive. On the one hand, daily decisions and judgments are framed by the learning trajectory. On the other hand, the envisioned learning trajectory itself evolves as a consequence of these local decisions and judgments. Thus, at any point in a teaching experiment, we typically have conjectures about both the course of the students' mathematical development and the means of supporting it. In the weekly project meetings that we hold while an experiment is in progress, the first agenda item is in fact to talk through how mathematical activity and discourse might evolve during the remainder of the experiment. However, this conjectured trajectory itself continually changes as a consequence of local interpretations and judgments. The actual learning trajectory as realized in the classroom can therefore depart quite markedly from that proposed at the outset.

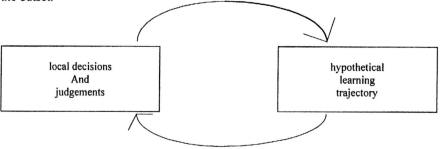

Figure 1. A simplified version of Simon's (1995) teaching cycle

The account we have given of the reflexive relationship between local judgments and the big picture is compatible with Franke, Carpenter, Levis, & Fennema's (1998) analysis of the instructional practices of highly skilled teachers whose goal is to support the development of mathematical understanding. As Franke and her colleagues demonstrate, mathematics teaching for these teachers is a generative activity in the course of which they elaborate and refine their understanding of both their students' thinking and the means of supporting its development. We can further clarify these links between the instructional practices of Franke et al.'s teachers and the process of experimenting in classrooms that we have described by drawing on Simon's (1995) discussion of what he terms the Mathematics Teaching Cycle. This cycle is shown in simplified form in Figure 1.

Simon stresses that the notion of a hypothetical learning trajectory "is meant to underscore the importance of having a goal and rationale for teaching decisions and the hypothetical nature of such thinking" (p.136). At any point, the teacher has a pedagogical agenda and thus a sense of direction. However, this agenda is itself subject to continual modification in the act of teaching. Simon likens this process to that of undertaking a long journey such as sailing around the world.

> You may initially plan the whole journey or only part of it. You set out sailing according to your plan. However, you must constantly adjust because of the conditions that you encounter. You continue to acquire knowledge about sailing, about the current conditions, and about the areas that you wish to visit. You change your plans with respect to the order of your destinations. You modify the length and nature of your visits as a result of interactions with people along the way. You add destinations that prior to the trip were unknown to you. The path that you travel is your [actual] trajectory. The path that you anticipate at any point is your "hypothetical trajectory." (pp. 136-137)

As Simon observes, this way of acting in the classroom involves both a sense of purpose and an openness towards the possibilities offered by students' solutions to instructional activities.

The terms we have used when talking about teaching experiments and that Simon uses to describe his activity as a mathematics teacher both involve the notion of enacting an instructional sequence. As Varela, Thompson, and Rosch (1991) emphasize, the idea of enactment implies that processes are "inextricably linked to histories that are lived, much like paths that exist only as they are laid down by walking" (p. 205). In the case of an instructional sequence, the teacher and students lay down an actual learning trajectory as they interact in the classroom. This, we should stress, does not mean that classroom activities drift aimlessly. At any point, there is both an overall instructional intent and an envisioned means of achieving it. However, both the intent and the conjectured trajectory are subject to continual revision. Thus, to pursue Varela et al.'s metaphor, the path is laid down by walking even though, at each point in the journey, there is some idea of a destination and of a route that might lead there.

This enactivist view can be contrasted with the more traditional notion of *implementing* an instructional sequence. The latter metaphor casts the teacher's role as that of carrying out the plans and intentions of others, whereas the notion of enactment highlights the teacher's (and students') contributions to an instructional sequence as it is realized in the classroom. In addition, an enactivist view brings the teacher's learning to the fore. As Simon (1995) illustrates, teaching can be an occasion to deepen one's understanding of the mathematical ideas that are the focus of classroom discussions, of students' reasoning, and of the means of supporting its development. These same comments apply to researchers who work in classrooms, and in fact constitute the primary reason why we conduct classroom teaching experiments. As a consequence, if we want to continue to use the term implementation, we need to redefine it by treating it as an idea-driven process of adapting instructional sequences developed by others.

It should be clear that our primary reason for drawing on Franke at al.'s and Simon's work is to illustrate that teaching for understanding and classroom-based design research are closely related forms of activity that are motivated by similar concerns and interests. For example, both involve an intensive engagement with students for the purpose of supporting and organizing their mathematical development. This suggests that the various aspects of the teaching experiments that we have described might be able inform the formulation of admittedly ambitious goals for working with teachers. The first of these goals concerns the importance of teachers attempting to make sense of individual students' mathematical interpretations and solutions. This goal is, of course, consistent with the generally accepted view that teaching should be informed by a relatively deep understanding of students' mathematical thinking. A second goal is evident in the comments we have made about the value of locating students' mathematical activity in social context by attending to the nature of the social events in which they participate in the classroom. Elsewhere, we have argued that students' participation in these events constitutes the conditions for the possibility of mathematical learning (Cobb & Yackel, 1996). In the case of whole-class discussions, for example, this focus on social context implies that pedagogical justifications should go beyond general claims about the role of interaction, communication, and discourse in mathematical learning. We have instead indicated that particular classroom discussions should be justified in terms of their contributions to the fulfillment of an evolving instructional agenda as indicated by the mathematical significance of the issues that emerge as topics of conversation.

A third goal that stems from the view of teaching as a generative process of idea-driven adaptation in that of teachers appreciating the pedagogical intent of instructional sequences. This, we should stress, is not a separate "piece of knowledge" that informs pedagogical decision making. Instead, the pedagogical intent involves an envisioned developmental process and thus involves the teacher's understanding of students' mathematical thinking. Further, it involves a relatively deep understanding of the mathematical ideas that constitute the overall instructional goals *in relation to students who are attempting to learn them.* Finally, it involves specific conjectures about how the process of students' mathematical development might proceed in an instructional setting when proactive efforts are made to support their learning.

A detached analysis of the long-term goals we have proposed for working with teachers might dissect them into components corresponding to a psychological theory of students' thinking, a theory about the sociology of the classroom, mathematical knowledge, and a domain-specific instructional theory (i.e., Shulman's pedagogical content knowledge). In our view, such an approach separates pedagogical knowing from the activity of teaching and treats knowledge as a commodity that stands apart from practice. It is precisely this separation that we have tried to resist by focusing on our ways of acting in the classroom. Our primary concern has been with acts of knowing and judging that occur moment by moment as we attempt to support students' mathematical development.

The view of teaching that emerges from this account portrays teachers as professionals who continually modify their instructional agendas even as they use materials developed by others. It therefore transcends the dichotomy between the claims that reform should be fueled almost exclusively by either materials development or by teacher enhancement (Ball & Cohen, 1996). We would again acknowledge that the types of instructional practices we have in mind are ambitious and, perhaps, idealistic. It could be argued for example, that the form of practice we have outlined is unfeasible for any teacher working alone. In the case of a classroom teaching experiment, the entire research team in effect constitutes a collective teacher with some members of the team actually teaching while others observe and analyze classroom events. The demands of this collective activity are, however, balanced by the possibility that the teachers will be able to capitalize on the results of others' learning as represented by instructional sequences and learning trajectories. It is to this issue that we turn next.

2.2 Instructional Sequences as Resources for the Development of Professional Teaching Communities

One of the primary conjectures underlying our proposed approach is that instructional sequences of the sort that we have developed in recent teaching experiments can serve as an important means of supporting the teachers' development of generative instructional practices (cf. Ball & Cohen, 1996; Gearhart, Saxe, Seltzer, et al., 1999; Hiebert & Wearne, 1992). The key point to note is that such sequences are justified in terms of 1) the trajectory of the students' mathematical learning, and 2) the means by which that learning can be supported and organized. This can be contrasted with the standard approach of using traditional experimental data to justify an instructional innovation. In the latter case, teachers know only that the innovation has proven effective elsewhere but do not have an understanding of the underlying ideas that would enable them to adapt the innovation to their own instructional settings. In contrast, a justification cast in terms of learning trajectories offers the possibility that teachers might be able to adapt, test, and modify the instructional sequences in their classrooms. To the extent that they do so, they would cease to be mere consumers of instructional innovations developed by others and would instead contribute to both the improvement of the sequences and the development of the local instructional theories that they embody.

With regard to the specifics of an approach to teacher development that is based on this conjecture about the role of instructional sequences, we would certainly capitalize on the viable aspects of our prior work with the second- and third-grade teachers. For example, we would initially focus on the renegotiation of classroom social norms so that teachers' classrooms might become learning environments for them. In addition, we would support their development of reasons and motivations to want to change their current instructional practices in much the same way as we did in our prior work. Beyond this, we would frame selected teaching experiments as cases both of students' mathematical thinking and of how effective teachers build on that thinking to support and organize the emergence of significant mathematical ideas (cf. Barnett, 1991; Barron & Goldman, 1994; Bowers, Barron & Goldman, 1994; Lampert & Ball, 1990; Schifter, 1990; Franke, et al, 1997). In addition to the instructional activities and associated resources (e.g., computer-based tools used as part of a sequence), the case materials might involve CD-ROMs that are based on video-recordings of classroom sessions, student interviews, and copies of the students' written work. The specific types of activities in which teachers might engage as they investigate these cases could include:

(a) using the instructional activities to conduct mathematical investigations oriented towards the mathematical ideas that constitute the overall intent of the sequences;

(b) using the CD-ROMs to investigate the development of students' reasoning and the means that can be used to support it.

We view investigations of this type as crucial given that, in our prior work, we failed to adequately support the second- and third-grade teachers' development of intellectual resources that would have enabled them to adapt instructional materials flexibly to their particular classroom situations. Our agenda as teachers investigate these cases would be to support their reconstruction of the justifications for the sequences. We conjecture that they might then be in a position to begin to make informed decisions and judgments about how they might adapt the sequences. We would note that this case-based approach is consistent with research which indicates the importance of teachers developing a relatively deep understanding of both the mathematics they are teaching (Thompson & Thompson, 1994, 1996) and of students' reasoning (Carpenter & Fennema, 1992; Cobb, Wood, Yackel, & McNeal, 1992; Fennema, Franke, Carpenter, & Carey, 1993; Knapp & Peterson, 1995; Schifter & Fosnot, 1993; Simon & Schifter, 1991).

Our prior work with teachers has convinced us of the value of providing support for at least one school year. This might involve both classroom visits and periodic seminars. Regardless of the details, the intent would be for teachers to become actively involved in the process of improving and adapting the instructional sequences once they begin to use them as the basis for their instruction. We therefore envision a division of labor between the teachers and the researchers such that the teachers assume primary responsibility for documenting (a) their instructional designs, (b) observations of instruction, and (c) students' learning. The researchers, for their part, would organize the teachers' documentation and distribute syntheses to all participants. It is important to stress that although the teachers and the researchers would have different roles in this proposal, the division of labor that we envision would *not* be based on a distinction between teaching and research (cf. Stigler & Hiebert, 1999). Instead, the teachers would be active agents in a process of continual improvement. To the extent that this occurs, they would contribute to the generation of insights into the teaching and learning of mathematics that are grounded in classroom practice and that are shared with and critiqued by others.

3. ASPECTS OF THE TEACHER'S PROACTIVE ROLE IN PURSUING A MATHEMATICAL AGENDA

In stepping back from the specific proposals we have made thus far, it should be apparent that there are several parallels with the process of preparing for a classroom teaching experiment. For example, we have noted that in planning a teaching experiment we begin by conducting an anticipatory thought experiment in the course of which we develop a conjectured learning trajectory for students' mathematical learning. This trajectory in turn guides the development of instructional activities. In a similar manner, our discussions of the process of teaching mathematics with understanding and of the role of instructional sequences in supporting teachers' learning serve to outline at least a fragment of a conjectured learning trajectory for teacher development that orients decisions about the types of activities in which we might engage them. We attempt to elaborate this trajectory further by identifying issues that we conjecture would constitute productive topics of conversation both for the professional teaching community and for the learning of the participating teachers. The three issues we will discuss are (1) developing norms for mathematical argumentation; (2) ensuring that students' activity remains grounded in the mathematical imagery of the situation they are investigating; and (3) redescribing and notating students' solutions and explanations.

3.1 Norms of Mathematical Argumentation

In focusing specifically on norms for argumentation, it is helpful if we relate the discussion to our prior work on sociomathematical norms (Yackel & Cobb, 1996). Sociomathematical norms differ from general social norms that constitute the classroom participation structure in that they concern the normative aspects of classroom actions and interactions that are specifically mathematical. These norms regulate classroom discourse and influence the learning opportunities that arise for both the students and the teacher. Examples of sociomathematical norms include what counts as a *different* mathematical solution, a *sophisticated* mathematical solution, and an *efficient* mathematical solution (Yackel & Cobb, 1996). These three norms all involve a taken-as-shared sense of when it is appropriate to contribute to a discussion. In contrast, another sociomathematical norm, that of what counts as an *acceptable* mathematical explanation and justification deals with the actual process of making a contribution. Previous analyses of classrooms in which mathematics is taught with understanding indicate that acceptable explanations and justifications typically have to be interpretable in terms of actions on mathematical objects that are experientially real to the listening students (Cobb, Wood, Yackel, & McNeal, 1992). The importance we attribute to sociomathematical norms stems from the contention that students reorganize their specifically mathematical beliefs and values as they participate in and contribute to the renegotiation of these norms (cf. Bowers & Nickerson, 1998; Lampert, 1990; Simon & Blume, 1996; Voigt, 1985). This claim implies that teachers can support their students' development of appropriate dispositions toward mathematics by guiding the negotiation of sociomathematical norms.

Of the sociomathematical norms that we have mentioned, one that we speculate is particularly important for teachers' learning is that of what counts as an acceptable explanation. We have noted that, in the classrooms where mathematics is taught with understanding, acceptable explanations typically have to be interpretable in terms of actions on mathematical objects. Thompson et al. (1994) have pushed the analysis one step further in their research on teachers' thinking by distinguishing between conceptual and calculational orientations in teaching. We have found it useful to extend this distinction by talking about conceptual and calculational classroom discourse (Cobb, Stephan, McClain, & Gravemeijer, in press). It is important to emphasize that calculational discourse does not refer to conversations that focus on the mere procedural manipulation of conventional symbols. Instead, calculational discourse refers to discussions in which the primary topic of conversation is any type of calculational process. As an example, in whole-class discussions of elementary word problems, first-graders typically report a variety of counting and thinking strategy solutions. Discussions that focus on the students' methods are calculational in nature in that they are concerned with the calculational processes the students used to arrive at answers. In the case of a word problem corresponding to $4 + \_ = 11$, for example, the calculational process might involve counting on from four to eleven as well as various thinking strategy methods (e.g., four and six is ten, so four and seven make eleven). As this example makes clear, calculational discourse can involve insight and understanding. Many of the illustrations given in the literature of discourse compatible with current American reform recommendations are in fact calculational in nature.

Calculational discourse can be contrasted with conceptual discourse, in which the reasons for calculating in particular ways also become explicit topics of conversation. Conversations of this type therefore encompass both students' calculational processes and the task interpretations that underlie those ways of calculating. In the case of elementary word problems, the teacher might help students explain how they related the quantities described in the problem statement. For example, in solving a problem corresponding to $4 + \_ = 11$, some students might have included the 4 in the 11, whereas others might have treated them as separate quantities and added them to arrive at an answer of 15. In conceptual discussions, it is these different ways of relating the quantities that would become a focus of discussion in the classroom. Our experience in the recent teaching experiments indicates that discussions in which the teacher judiciously supports students' attempts to articulate their task interpretations can be extremely productive settings for mathematical learning. As the brief example illustrates, students' participation in discussions of this type increases the likelihood that they might come to understand each other's mathematical reasoning. Had the discussion remained purely calculational, students who added 4 and 11 to get the answer of 15 could only have understood other students' explanations by creating a task interpretation that lay behind the calculational method entirely on their own. In contrast, their participation in conceptual discourse provides them with resources that might enable them to reorganize their initial interpretations of the task. It is also important to note that a significant mathematical idea, that of numerical part-whole relations, emerges as an explicit topic of conversation in the example. Our teaching experiment data indicate that, at least in the early and middle grades (ages 6 - 13), most students can learn to give conceptual explanations and to ask others clarifying questions that bear directly on their underlying task interpretations within a few weeks when they receive appropriate support from the teacher.

As this brief discussion of the *proactive* role of the teacher in supporting the development of sociomathematical norms illustrates, the issue for us is not *whether* teachers should be authorities in the classroom. Instead, the issue is that of *how* to express their institutionalized authority in action as they support their students' mathematical learning (Bishop, 1985). Framed in these terms, conversations about episodes from both the project classrooms and the collaborating teachers' classrooms can then serve to highlight the role of the teacher in these negotiations. Elsewhere we have argued that the establishment of sociomathematical norms that concern what counts as a different, sophisticated, and clear explanation are critical in allowing teachers to build on students' contributions as they seek to achieve their pedagogical agendas (McClain & Cobb, 1995). In addition, it is as students participate in the establishment of these norms that they become increasingly autonomous members of the classroom community who can judge the value of their own and others' explanations. Further, it is as students participate in this process that they develop specifically mathematical beliefs and values that constitute the types of mathematical dispositions described in American reform documents (cf. NCTM, 1989, 1991).

3.2 Mathematical Imagery

The second pedagogical issue that we anticipate might give rise to productive conversations is that of the teacher's role in ensuring that students' activity remains grounded in the mathematical imagery of the situations they are investigating. In this regard, we are particularly interested in a process that we call the *folding back* of discourse, wherein mathematical relationships under discussion are redescribed in terms of the specific situations from which they emerge (McClain & Cobb, 1998). We conjecture that individual students' participation in this collective process constitutes a supportive context for them to ground their increasingly sophisticated mathematical activity in situation-specific imagery. This, for us, is an important aspect of mathematics instruction that has understanding as a major priority.

As Thompson (1996) notes, difficulties often arise for students because insufficient attention is given to their images of the settings in which problems ostensibly occur. This often results in students' activity becoming "decoupled" from their interpretations of problem situations. As Thompson observes, the task for students is then to decipher the relationship between conventional notation schemes and "superficial characteristics of a problem statement's linguistic presentation" (1996, pp. 15-16). Thompson also suggests that students' construction of quantitative imagery of the problem scenario is supported by conceptual (as opposed to calculational) discourse in which the focus is on their interpretations of problem situations rather than merely on calculational processes.

Despite these seemingly clear-cut pronouncements, our experience in recent teaching experiments indicates that students' activity can lose its grounding in imagery even when the explicit and consciously pursued goal is to support the growth of understanding. This leads us to conjecture that episodes from teaching experiment classrooms might serve as a means of highlighting a tension that arises between supporting reflective shifts in discourse such that what is said and done itself becomes an explicit topic of conversation, and ensuring that discussions remain grounded in situation-specific imagery. Pirie and Kieren (1989) argue that, in psychological terms, the development of mathematical understanding is a recursive, non-linear phenomenon. In our view, discourse that supports the growth of understanding shares these characteristics. This was the case in the more recent teaching experiments as we strove to ensure that students' mathematical activity was grounded in quantitative imagery of problem scenarios. Discussions of cases that are based on such experiments as well as on incidents in teachers' own classrooms might therefore offer an opportunity for teachers to investigate these phenomena.

3.3 Notating Students' Interpretations and Solutions

The third pedagogical issue that we anticipate might lead to productive discussions is that of the teacher's role in redescribing and notating students' interpretations and solutions. In our view, the teacher's role in supporting the development of ways of symbolizing is integral to the process of supporting students' development of mathematical power in that symbolizations provide a vehicle for reasoning, reflection, and argumentation. Further, we contend that if students are to develop grounded understandings of the meanings and uses of notations and symbolizations introduced by the teacher, it is essential that the ways of symbolizing fit with their current ways of reasoning. This contention implies that ways of symbolizing should be consistent with students' initially informal mathematical activity while at the same time serving as a means of reorganizing that activity (Cognition and Technology Group, at Vanderbilt 1990; Lesh & Akerstrom, 1982; Thompson, 1992). The symbolizations would then constitute a resource that students can use to express, communicate, and reflect on their mathematical activity (Confrey, 1990; Kaput, 1987).

Given these considerations, we see value in discussions in which the teacher's role in supporting shifts in students' reasoning by symbolizing and revoicing their explanations becomes an explicit topic of conversation in professional teaching communities (cf. O'Conner & Michaels, 1995). This aspect of the teacher's role is subtle and, in our experience, involves an inherent tension. On the one hand, in recasting students' explanations, teachers can initiate shifts in their ways of reasoning. On the other hand, there is a danger of imposing ways of symbolizing that do not fit with the students' current understandings. Judgments about the appropriateness of such interventions therefore have to be made against the background of teachers' assessments of their students' reasoning. In our view, it is important that tensions and dilemmas eventually emerge as explicit topics of conversation.

3.4 Summary

Taken together, the three pedagogical issues that we have discussed illustrate the complexity of teaching and the multiple decisions that must be made in any lesson. Simon (1995) alludes to this complexity when he observes that there is an "inherent tension between responding to the students' mathematics and creating purposeful pedagogy based on the teacher's goals for student learning." Our purpose in fleshing out a conjectured trajectory for teachers' learning by discussing three aspects of the teacher's proactive role is not to dismiss such tensions. Instead, our intent is to acknowledge that teaching is, in Lampert's (1990) words, a dilemma-ridden activity, while simultaneously clarifying how it might be possible to help teachers begin to cope with the diverse and sometimes conflicting demands of effective teaching. We therefore do not want to be perceived as offering a prescriptive list of effective techniques that, when employed, will improve students' learning. Instead, our goal has been to identify pedagogically significant issues that might emerge as topics of conversation in much the same way that we prepare for whole-class discussions during classroom teaching experiments by identifying mathematically significant issues that might emerge as topics of conversation. The practical challenge is then to ensure that the pedagogical issues emerge in a way that is experienced as relatively natural by the participating teachers. In this regard, the realization of the conjectured learning trajectory we have outlined gives rise to tensions for mathematics teacher educators that parallel those experienced by teachers as they attempt to achieve their instructional agendas by building on their students' contributions.

4. DISCUSSION

4.1 Teachers' Learning in Social Context

In this paper, we have drawn on both our prior collaboration with teachers and a series of recent teaching experiments to develop an approach for supporting teachers' learning within the social context of a professional teaching community. In doing so, we have assumed that the primary contexts for the teachers' learning involve individually and collectively planning for instruction; interacting with students; and analyzing and reflecting on classroom incidents. In assessing our prior collaboration, we concluded that the approach of attempting to establish an initial basis for communication with teachers by focusing on the renegotiation of classroom social norms continues to be viable. However, we also noted that we failed to support the teachers' development of the intellectual resources that would enable them to pursue a mathematical agenda by adapting instructional materials flexibly to their classroom situations. To address this oversight, we framed the process of planning for and conducting a teaching experiment as a paradigm case in which to clarify what might be involved in teaching for understanding. In doing so, we introduced the notion of a learning trajectory that consists of conjectures about both the possible course of students' mathematical learning and the means of supporting and organizing that learning. We argued that a conjectured trajectory of this type can serve to orient local pedagogical decisions even as the conjectures are modified and revised in light of local decisions. This led us to conclude that an appreciation of the conjectured learning trajectory that captures the pedagogical intent of an instructional sequence is an important intellectual resource when teaching mathematics for understanding. The other intellectual resources we identified included both a relatively deep understanding of the mathematical ideas that constitute the endpoints of an instructional sequence in relation to students who are attempting to learn them, and a proclivity to locate students' mathematical activity in social context by attending to the nature of the social events in which they participate in the classroom.

We built on this discussion of teaching mathematics for understanding by proposing that instructional sequences justified in terms of a conjectured learning trajectory can provide an important means of supporting teachers' as well as students' learning. In making this argument, we described case-based investigations that might make it possible for teachers to reconstruct the justifications for instructional sequences. We then went on to discuss several pedagogical issues that we hope might emerge as topics of conversation within the professional teaching community. These include initiating and guiding the renegotiation of sociomathematical norms; supporting both reflective shifts in classroom discourse and the folding back of discourse; and guiding the emergence of ways of symbolizing and notating. In much the same way that we contend that classroom discussions should be justified in terms of the mathematical issues that emerge as topics of conversation, so these pedagogical issues provide an initial orientation as we attempt to ensure that discussions in professional teaching communities are pedagogically significant.

In addition to making these relatively pragmatic proposals, we also noted a limitation of our prior work that is primarily theoretical in nature. This limitation concerned our failure to relate the changes in the teachers' instructional practices to their participation in the professional teaching community. In this regard, we argued that it is essential to analyze the taken-as-shared ways of talking and thinking about mathematics teaching that emerge in the professional teaching community when accounting for individual teachers' learning. We have attempted to follow our own advice in this chapter by indicating the collaborative nature of teachers' learning and by focusing on the issues that might be addressed by the professional teaching community.

4.2 Teachers' Learning in Institutional Context

An issue that we discussed when critiquing our prior work is that of attending to the institutional settings of the schools in which teachers work. As we noted earlier, we have discussed the institutional context of teachers' learning and the distributed nature of professionalization in a companion paper (Cobb & McClain, 1999). We will therefore limit ourselves to a brief summary of the pragmatic issues that arise from this more encompassing perspective on teacher development. As a starting point, recall that in our previous work conflicts arose between the teachers with whom we collaborated and the governing school board of the school district. The immediate issue was that of who was more qualified to make decisions about how mathematics should be taught and which instructional materials should be used. At a deeper level, the conflict was between two forms of instructional practice that were organized by different overall intentions or motives.[2] The motive of the instructional practices institutionalized in the school district appeared to be competent performance on a relatively limited range of tasks as assessed by teacher-made tests and by a state-mandated test of skills. In contrast, the motive of the instructional practices established within the professional teaching community was mathematical understanding as assessed by teachers' observations of students' reasoning and discourse. Such discrepancies are particularly pressing for those of us who are interested in the sustainability of the instructional practices developed within professional teaching communities. In this regard, Cole (1996) observes that, although it might be possible to nurture novel instructional practices in almost any institutional setting by supplying human and material resources necessary to create appropriate conditions, it often is not possible to sustain those conditions once the resources have been withdrawn.

Our prior collaboration with teachers is atypical in that the teachers have sustained their practices for over ten years. However, this was possible only because the teachers initiated the creation of institutional conditions that were aligned with their focus on student understanding. The pragmatic implication is, of course, to involve administrators, parents, and other stakeholders in activities of the professional teaching communities with the goal of developing more compatible understandings of both instructional goals and the means by which they might be achieved (cf. Lehrer & Shumow, 1997; Price & Ball, 1997). Our previous collaboration with teachers also indicates that it is important to develop ongoing analyses of the organizational conditions in the schools in which they work. In much the same way that skilled teachers adjust their pedagogical agendas as informed by their ongoing assessments of their students' reasoning, so the approach we propose involves developing collaborative relationships with administrators and other stakeholders as informed by ongoing analyses of the institutional settings of their schools. We conjecture that in addition to providing a context for discussion between various stakeholders, these analyses will orient collaborations with teachers towards the building of the organizational capacity of their schools from the outset. The overall intent of such an approach is to bring the instructional goals of professional teaching communities and of the schools in which the participating teachers work into closer alignment. This is essential in that the teachers' instructional practices must come to fit with institutional goals if they are eventually to be sustained by local resources.

Although our interest in the institutional settings in which teachers work is pragmatic, it gives rise to a theoretical challenge that is evident in a bifurcation in the literature on teacher change. One body of scholarship focuses on the role of professional development in supporting changes in teachers' views of their instructional practices and themselves as learners. A second body of scholarship is concerned with the structural or organizational features of schools and with how changes in these conditions can lead to changes in classroom instructional practices. The challenge as we see it is to move beyond these two largely independent lines of work, one oriented towards teachers' learning as they participate in professional teaching communities and the other towards broader policy considerations. To state the issue directly, we need to be able to locate teachers' activity within the institutional setting of their schools when we analyse their classroom instructional practices.

In accounting for the relatively few lasting effects of American school reform efforts, Engestrom (1998) focuses on this same bifurcation. He argues that, on the one hand,

> school reforms have remained at the level of systems and structures, not reaching the daily practices of teaching and learning in classrooms. On the other hand, attempts to change the daily instructional practice have themselves not been particularly effective in the long run either. The dichotomy of systems and structures, on the one hand, and daily practices, on the other hand, may be an important reason for the difficulties. (p. 76).

Engestrom's analysis serves to steer us away from a structural perspective and towards a focus on teachers' activities as they participate in what he terms the taken-for-granted aspects of school life. It therefore indicates a way of locating the teachers' instructional practices within the institutional setting of their schools. At the same time, the specific analytical approach that Engestom goes on to illustrate seems ill-suited to our purposes as mathematics educators because it is framed in content-free terms. We and other mathematics teacher educators are therefore faced with the challenge of developing ideas and constructs that might enable us to relate teachers' instructional practices to the institutional settings of their schools in a relatively seamless manner.

We do not pretend to be able to articulate even a provisional solution to this issue. We can, however, indicate one promising avenue for future research that draws on Wenger's (1998) discussion of communities of practice. One of the strengths of Wenger's analysis is that it brings together theories of social structure (i.e., institutions, norms, and rules) and theories of situated experience without focusing on either social structures in the abstract or the minute choreography of interactions. Instead, the notion of a community of practice that he develops captures structures that are within the scope of people's engagement with the world. In the case of the school, these familiar structures would include the relatively inconspicuous, recurrent, and taken-for-granted aspects of school life that Engestrom describes as characteristic of a mid-level approach. Several recent analyses of mathematics teachers' learning indicate the potential value of taking community of practice as a unit of analysis and locating professional teaching communities within a constellation of interconnected communities that constitute the school (cf. Franke & Kazemi, in press; Stein & Brown, 1997; Stein, Silver, & Smith, 1998). A major thrust of our work in the coming years will also involve exploring these ideas as they relate to mathematics teacher education.

5. CONCLUSION

The issues we have touched on in this paper are relatively broad in scope and range from the micro-level of teachers' learning as they interact with their students to the macro-level of the institutional setting of their work. The breath of these issues indicates the complexity of teacher professional development. Simon (in press) indicates one source of this complexity when he observes that whereas the focus in a classroom teaching experiment is on students' mathematical development, collaborations with teachers are concerned with their pedagogical development as well as their mathematical development. A second source of complexity stems from the realization that teachers develop their instructional practices as they participate in multiple communities. In contrast, it is often possible to limit the focus to a single community, that of the classroom, when accounting for students' mathematical learning. The conjectures we have made and the approach we have outlined in this chapter represent an attempt to come to terms with the first source of complexity while acknowledging the critical importance of the second. As has been the case in prior work, we fully expect that many of these conjectures and ideas will be revised significantly as we continue to engage in collaborative efforts with teachers in an attempt to support the establishment of professional teaching communities.

NOTES

1. Cobb and Yackel (1996) describe a case in which a group of teachers did not view the disconnection between mathematics in school and in out-of-school settings as problematic. Although these teachers did eventually revise their instructional practices, the course of their development differed from that which we discuss in this paper.
2. Our use of the term *motive* is generally consistent with that of activity theorists (e.g., Leont'ev, 1978).

REFERENCES

Ball, D. L., & Cohen, D. K. (1996). Reform by the book: What is--or might be--the role of curriculum materials in teacher learning and instructional reform? *Educational Researcher, 25*(9), 6-8, 14.

Barnett, C. (1991). Building a case-based curriculum to enhance the pedagogical content knowledge of mathematics teachers. *Journal of Teacher Education. 42*(4), 263-271.

Barron, L.C. & Goldman, E.S. (1994). Integrating technology with teacher preparation. In B. Means (Ed.), *Technology and Education Reform.* San Francisco: Jossey-Bass.

Bauersfeld, H. (1988). Interaction, construction, and knowledge: Alternative perspectives for mathematics education. In T. Cooney & D. Grouws (Eds.), *Effective mathematics teaching* (pp. 27-46). Reston, VA: National Council of Teachers of Mathematics and Erlbaum Associates.

Bishop, A. (1985). The social construction of meaning—a significant development for mathematics education? *For the Learning of Mathematics, 5* (1), 24-28.

Bowers, J., Barron, L., & Goldman, E. (1994). An interactive media environment to enhance mathematics teacher education. In J. Willis, B. Robin & D.A. Willis (Eds.), *Technology and Teacher Education Annual* (515-519). Washington, DC: Society for Technology and Teacher Education.

Bowers, J. & Nickerson, S. (1998, April). Documenting the development of a collective conceptual orientation in a college-level mathematics course. Paper presented at the annual meeting of the American Education Research Association, San Diego.

Carpenter, T., & Fennema, E. (1992). Cognitively guided instruction: Building on the knowledge of students and teachers. In W. Secada (Ed.), Curriculum reform: The case of mathematics in the United States. Special issue of *International Journal of Educational Research* (pp. 457-470). Elmsford, NY: Pergamon Press, Inc.

Cobb, P., & McClain, K. (1999, May). *Supporting teachers' learning in social and institutional context.* Paper presented at the 1999 International Conference on Mathematics Teacher Education, Teipei, Taiwan.

Cobb, P. & Steffe, L.P. (1983). The constructivist researcher as teacher and model builder. *Journal for Research in Mathematics Education, 14*, 83-94.

Cobb, P., Stephan, M., McClain, K., & Gravemeijer, K. (in press). Participating in classroom mathematical practices. *Journal of the Learning Sciences.*

Cobb, P., Wood, T., & Yackel, E. (1993). Discourse, mathematical thinking, and classroom practice. In N. Minick, E. Forman, & A. Stone (Eds.), *Education and mind: Institutional, social, and developmental processes* (pp. 91-119). New York: Oxford University Press.

Cobb, P., Wood, T., Yackel, E., & McNeal, B. (1992). Characteristics of classroom mathematics traditions: An interactional analysis. *American Educational Research Journal, 29*, 573-602.

Cobb, P., Wood, T., Yackel, E., Nicholls, J., Wheatley, G., Trigatti, B., & Perlwitz, M. (1991). Assessment of a problem-centered second grade mathematics project. *Journal for Research in Mathematics Education, 22*, 3–29.

Cobb, P., Wood, T., Yackel, E., & Perlwitz (1992). A follow-up assessment of a second-grade problem-centered mathematics project. *Educational Studies in Mathematics, 23*, 483-504.

Cobb, P., & Yackel, E. (1996). Constructivist, emergent, and sociocultural perspectives in the context of developmental research. *Educational Psychologist, 31*, 175-190.

Cobb, P., Yackel, E., & Wood, T. (1989). Young children's emotional acts while doing mathematical problem solving. In D.B. McCleod & V.M. Adams (Eds.), *Affect and mathematical problem solving: A new perspective* (pp. 117-148). New York: Springer-Verlag.

Cobb, P., Yackel, E., & Wood, T. (1991). Curriculum and teacher development: Psychological and anthropological perspectives. In E. Fennema, T. P. Carpenter, & S. J. Lamon (Eds.), *Integrating research on teaching and learning mathematics* (pp. 83-120). Albany, NY: SUNY Press.

Cognition and Technology Group at Vanderbilt (1990). Anchored instruction and its relationship to situated cognition. *Educational Researcher, 19(6)*, 2-10.

Cognition and Technology Group at Vanderbilt (1997). *The Jasper Project: Lessons in Curriculum, instruction, assessment, and professional development.* Mahwah, NJ: Erlbaum.

Cohen, D.K., & Hill, H.C. (1998). *Instructional policy and classroom performance: The mathematics reform in California.* Ann Arbor, MI: University of Michigan.

Cole, M. (1996). *Cultural psychology.* Cambridge, MA: Belknap Press of Harvard University Press.

Confrey, J. (1990). How compatible are radical constructivism, sociocultural approaches, and social constructivism? In L. P. Steffe & J. Gale (Eds.), *Constructivism in education* (pp. 185-225). Hillsdale, NJ: Lawrence Erlbaum Associates.

Dillon, D. R. (1993). The wider social context of innovation in mathematics education. In T. Wood, P. Cobb, E. Yackel, & D. Dillon (Eds.), *Rethinking elementary school mathematics: Insights and issues.* (pp. 71-96.) Journal for Research in Mathematics Education Monograph No. 6. Reston, VA: National Council of Teachers of Mathematics.

Engestrom, Y. (1998). Reorganizing the motivational sphere of classroom culture: An activity theoretical analysis of planning in a teacher team. In F. Seeger, J. Voight & U. Waschescio (Eds.), *The culture of the mathematics classroom* (pp. 76 – 103). New York: Cambridge University Press.

Erickson, F. (1986). Qualitative methods in research on teaching. In M.C. Wittrock (Ed.), *The handbook of research on teaching* (3rd. ed., pp. 119-161). New York: Macmillan.

Fennema, E., Carpenter, T.P., Franke, M.L., Levi, L., Jacobs, V.R., & Empson, S. B. (1996). A longitudinal study of learning to use children's thinking in mathematics instruction. *Journal for Research in Mathematics Education, 27*, 403-434.

Fennema, E., Franke, M. L., Carpenter, T. P., & Carey, D. A. (1993). Using children's mathematical knowledge in instruction. *American Educational Research Journal, 30*, 555-583.

Franke, M.L., Carpenter, T.P., Levi, L., & Fennema, E. (1998, April). *Capturing teachers' generative change: A follow-up study of teachers' professional development in mathematics.* Paper presented at the annual meeting of the American Educational Research Association, San Diego.

Franke, M.L., & Kazemi, E. (in press). Teaching as learning within a community of practice: Characterizing generative growth. In T. Wood, B. Nelson, & J. Warfield (Eds.), *Beyond classical pedagogy in elementary mathematics: The nature of facilitative teaching.* Mahwah, NJ: Lawrence Erlbaum Associates.

Gamoran, A., Secada, W.G., & Marrett, C.B. (in press). The organizational context of teaching and learning: Changing theoretical perspectives. In M.T. Hallinan (Ed.), *Handbook of sociology.*

Gearhart, M, Saxe, G. B., Seltzer, M. Schlackman, J., Fall, R., Ching, C. C., Nasir, N., Bennett, T., Rhine, S., & Sloan, T. (1999). When can educational reforms make a difference? Opportunities to learn fractions in elementary mathematics classrooms. *Journal for Research in Mathematics Education, 30,* 206-315.

Goodlad, J.I. (1983). *A place called school.* New York: McGraw-Hill.

Gravemeijer, K. E. P. (1994). *Developing realistic mathematics education.* Utrecht, Netherlands: CD-ß Press.

Gravemeijer, K. (1994). Educational development and developmental research. *Journal for Research in Mathematics Education, 25*(5), 443-471.

Hiebert, J., & Wearne, D. (1992). Instructional tasks, classroom discourse, and students' learning in second grade arithmetic. *American Educational Research Journal. 30,(2),* 393-425.

Jackson, P. (1968). *Life in Classrooms.* New York: Holt, Rinehart, and Winston.

Kaput, J. J. (1987). *The body in the mind: The bodily basis of reason and imagination.* Chicago: University of Chicago Press.

Knapp, N.F., & Peterson, P. L. (1995.) Teachers' interpretations of "CGI" after four years: Meanings and practices. *Journal for Research in Mathematics Education, 26,* 40-65.

Lampert, M. (1990). When the problem is not the question and the solution is not the answer: Mathematical knowing and teaching. *American Educational Research Journal, 27*(1), 29–63.

Lampert, M. & Ball, D. (1990). *Using hypermedia to support a new pedagogy of teacher education.* Issue Paper 90-5. East Lansing, MI: Michigan State University, National Center for Research on Teacher Education.

Lazerson, M., McLaughlin, J. B., McPherson, B., & Bailey, S. K. (1985). New curriculum, old issues. In *An education of value: The purpose and practices of schools.* (pp. 23-46). Cambridge, England: Cambridge University Press.

Lehrer, R., & Schauble, L. (1998, April). *Developing a community of practice for reform of mathematics and science.* Paper presented at the annual meeting of the American Educational Research Association, San Diego, CA.

Lehrer, R., & Shumow, L. (1997). Aligning the construction zones of parents and teachers for mathematics reform. *Cognition and instruction, 15(1),* 41-83.

Leont'ev, A. N. (1978). *Activity, consciousness, and personality.* Englewood Cliffs, NJ: Prentice Hall.

Lesh, R. & Akerstrom, M. (1982). Applied problem solving: Priorities for mathematics education research. In F. K. Lester & J. Garofalo (Eds.), *Mathematical problem solving: Issues in research.* Philadelphia: Franklin Institute Press.

Little, J.W. (1993). Teachers' professional development in a climate of educational reform. *Educational Evaluation and Policy Analysis, 15,* 129-151.

McClain, K. & Cobb, P. (1995, April). *An analysis of the teacher's proactive role in initiating and guiding the development of productive mathematical discourse.* Paper presented at the annual meeting of the American Educational Research Association, San Francisco, CA.

McClain, K. & Cobb, P. (1998). The role of imagery and discourse in supporting students' mathematical development. In M. Lampert (Ed.) *Mathematical talk and school learning: Where, what, and how* (pp. 56 – 81). New York: Cambridge University Press.

National Council of Teachers of Mathematics. (1989). *Curriculum and evaluation standards for school mathematics.* Reston, VA: NCTM.

National Council of Teachers of Mathematics. (1991). *Professional standards for teaching mathematics.* Reston, VA: NCTM.

Newman & Associates (Eds.). (1996). *Authentic achievement: Restructuring schools for intellectual quality.* San Francisco, CA: Josey-Bass.

O'Connor, M.C. & Michaels, S. (1996). Shifting participant frameworks: Orchestrating thinking practices in group discussions. In D. Hicks (Ed.), *Discourse, Learning, and Schooling* (pp. 63-103). New York: Cambridge University Press.

Pirie, S. & Kieren, T. (1989). A recursive theory of mathematical understanding. *For the learning of mathematics, 9*(3), pp. 7-11.

Price, J. N. & Ball, D. L. (1997). 'There's always another agenda': Marshaling resources for mathematics reform. *Journal of Curriculum Studies, 29(6),* 637-666.

Schifter, D. (1990). Mathematics process as mathematics content: A course for teachers. In G. Booker, P. Cobb, & T. deMendicuti (Eds.), *Proceedings of the 14 annual meeting of the Psychology of Mathematics Education* (pp. 191-198). Mexico City, Mexico.

Schifter, D., & Fosnot, C. T. (1993). Reconstructing mathematics education: Stories of teachers meeting the challenge of reform. New York: Teachers College Press.

Simon, M.A. (in press). Research in mathematics teacher development: The teacher development experiment. In R. Lesh & E. Kelly (Eds.) *New Methodologies in Mathematics and Science Education.* Dordrecht, Netherlands: Kluwer.

Simon, M. A. (1993). Context for change: Themes related to mathematical education reform. In T. Wood, P. Cobb, E. Yackel, & D. Dillon (Eds.), *Rethinking elementary school mathematics: Insights and issues.* (pp. 109-114.) Journal for Research in Mathematics Education Monograph No. 6. Reston, VA: National Council of Teachers of Mathematics.

Simon, M.A. & Blume, G.W. (1996). Justification in the mathematics classroom: A study of prospective elementary teachers. *Journal of Mathematical Behavior, 15,* 3-31.

Simon, M. A. (1995). Reconstructing mathematics pedagogy from a constructivist perspective. *Journal for Research in Mathematics Education, 26,* 114-145.

Simon, M. A., & Schifter, D. (1991). Towards a constructivist perspective: An intervention study of mathematics teacher development. *Educational Studies in Mathematics, 22,* 309-331.

Steffe, L. P. (1983). The teaching experiment methodology in a constructivist research program. In M. Zweng, T. Green, J. Kilpatrick, H. Pollak, & M. Suydam (Eds.), *Proceedings of the Fourth International Congress on Mathematical Education* (pp. 469-471). Boston: Birkhauser.

Stein, M.K. & Brown, C.A. (1997). Teacher learning in a social context: Integrating collaborative and institutional processes with the study of teacher change. In E. Fennema & B. Scott Nelson (Eds.), *Mathematics teachers in transition* (pp. 155 –192). Mahwah, NJ: Lawrence Erlbaum Associates.

Stein, M.K., Silver, E.A., & Smith, M.S. (1998). Mathematics reform and teacher development: A community of practice perspective. In J. Greeno & S. Goldman (Eds.), *Thinking practices: A symposium on mathematics and science learning* (pp. 17–52). Mahwah, N.J.: Erlbaum.

Stigler, J.W., & Hiebert, J. (1999). *The teaching gap.* New York: Free Press.

Tharp, R. G., & Gallimore, R. (1988). *Rousing minds to life.* New York: Cambridge University Press.

Thompson, A. G. (1992). Teachers' beliefs and conceptions: A synthesis of the research. In D. Grouws (Ed.), *Handbook of research on mathematics teaching and learning.* (pp. 127-146). New York: Macmillan.

Thompson, A. G., & Thompson, P. W. (1996). Talking about rates conceptually, part II: Mathematical knowledge for teaching. *Journal for Research in Mathematics Education, 27,* 2-24.

Thompson, A. G., Philipp, R., Thompson, P. W., & Boyd, B. (1994). Calculational and conceptual orientations in teaching mathematics. In *1994 Yearbook of the National Council of Teachers of Mathematics* (pp. 79-92). Reston, VA: National Council of Teachers of Mathematics.

Thompson, P. W., & Thompson, A. G. (1994). Talking about rates conceptually, part I: A teacher's struggle. *Journal for Research in Mathematics Education, 25,* 279-303.

Thompson, P. W. (1992). Notations, principles, and constraints: Contributions to the effective use of concrete manipulatives in elementary education. *Journal for Research in Mathematics Education, 23,* 123-147.

Thompson, P. W. (1996). Imagery and the development of mathematical reasoning. In L. P. Steffe, B. Greer, P. Nesher, & G. Goldin (Eds.), *Theories of learning mathematics.* Hillsdale, NJ: Erlbaum, p. 167-184.

Varela, F.J., Thompson, E., & Rosch, E. (1991). *The embodied mind: Cognitive science and human experience.* Cambridge: MIT Press.

Voigt, J. (1985). Patterns and routines in classroom interaction. *Recherches en Didactique des Mathematiques, 6,* 69-118.

Warren, B., & Rosebery, A. S. (1995). Equity in the future tense: Redefining relationships among teachers, students, and science in linguistic minority classrooms. In W. Secada, E. Fennema, & L. Byrd (Eds.), *New directions in equity for mathematics education.* New York: Cambridge University Press.

Wenger, E. (1998). *Communities of practice.* New York: Cambridge University Press.

Wood, T., & Sellers, P. (1996.) Assessment of a problem-centered mathematics program: Third grade. *Journal for Research in Mathematics Education, 27,* 337-353.

Yackel, E., & Cobb, P. (1996). Sociomathematical norms, argumentation, and autonomy in mathematics. *Journal for Research in Mathematics Education, 27,* 458-477.

Vanderbuilt University
Nashville, TN
U.S.A.

ALAN J. BISHOP

EDUCATING STUDENT TEACHERS ABOUT VALUES IN MATHEMATICS EDUCATION

ABSTRACT. Current recommendations for changing mathematics education ignore the crucial role of values in those changes. Values have also been ignored in research into affective issues and it seems from current research that they are only addressed in implicit ways in the mathematics classroom. This chapter offers an analysis of values in mathematics teaching and develops some frameworks for creating values-related activities with student teachers. It bases these ideas on a current research project based in Australia.

1. CHANGES IN MATHEMATICS EDUCATION AND THE NEED TO ADDRESS VALUES

As we have approached the new century it has been interesting to see the variety of proposals and ideas for improving mathematics teaching being generated. In particular, in the areas of information technology (see Noss & Hoyles, 1996), ethnomathematics (see Barton, 1996; Gerdes, 1995), and critical mathematics education (see Skovsmose, 1994), the role of mathematics teachers is being critically examined. What is of special interest here about these developments, however, is that there is a strong concern both to question, and also to try to change, the values currently being taught. Also, at the 1998 Psychology of Mathematics Education conference in South Africa there was considerable discussion of implicit values in various sessions under the overall theme of the conference which was: *Diversity and Change in Mathematics Education.*

Current developmental policies in many national programs are focused on improving the achievement outcomes of students, and although their statements of intent often mention the encouragement of "desirable" values, the curriculum prescriptions which follow have little to say about their development. For example, the Goals of the Australian school mathematics curriculum have been described as follows (Australian Education Council, 1991):

As a result of learning mathematics in school all students should:

- *realise that mathematics is relevant to them personally and to their community;*
- *gain pleasure from mathematics and appreciate its fascination and power;*
- *realise that mathematics is an activity requiring the observation, representation and application of patterns;*

F.-L. Lin & T. J. Cooney (Eds.) Making Sense of Mathematics Teacher Education, 233—246.
© 2001 *Kluwer Academic Publishers. Printed in the Netherlands.*

- *acquire the mathematical knowledge, ways of thinking and confidence to use mathematics to:*
  - *conduct everyday affairs such as monetary exchanges, planning and organising events, and measuring;*
  - *make individual and collaborative decisions at the personal, civic and vocational levels;*
  - *engage in the mathematical study needed for further education and employment;*
- *develop skills in presenting and interpreting mathematical arguments;*
- *possess sufficient command of mathematical expressions, representations and technology to:*
  - *interpret information (e.g. from a court case, or a media report) in which mathematics is used;*
  - *continue to learn mathematics independently and collaboratively;*
  - *communicate mathematically to a range of audiences; and*
- *appreciate:*
  - *that mathematics is a dynamic field with its roots in many cultures; and*
  - *its relationship to social and technological change.*

It is clear from these statements, which are typical of educational goal statements, even if in this case they are more progressive than usual, that firstly, valuing has entered into their choice, and much negotiating would have gone on before they reached this state. Secondly, they all contain implications for values teaching and for cultivating what we might term "mathematically informed valuing."

However, values teaching in mathematics seems to happen more implicitly than explicitly, and at least one study suggests that there is not necessarily a one-to-one correspondence between what is intended by teachers and what they actually teach (Sosniak, Ethington, & Varelas, 1991). We can certainly assume, therefore, that values teaching inevitably affects the achievement of curricular outcomes, and perhaps those with responsibility for developing state and national curricula in mathematics should be concerned about the poor state of knowledge about the values that are being taught in and through mathematics.

In my experience, there are many teachers who know very little about the values they are teaching in mathematics. I am not, of course, saying that they think that the mathematics they teach has no value for their students. They might not know what values they are teaching, but that it is important and has value is one of the values that they actually are teaching, by merely teaching the subject! They also could be acculturating their students into believing that they are learning mathematics for its benefits as applicable knowledge, or to have pleasure in its finest or most intriguing discoveries or inventions, "for its own sake," or even to train their minds.

The pressure to gain mathematical qualifications means that the more likely version of the value that "Mathematics is important" in most classrooms is now that "Mathematics has importance for all learners *who wish to get on* in our society," given the market driven nature of many current educational programs. But what about the value of "Mathematics has importance for all learners in our society, *because it helps them to understand and critique many of the structures of our society*"? Could that be one of the values also being learnt?

Understanding more about values is the key to generating more possibilities for mathematics education. Sadly, we know very little about the values which mathematics teachers think they are imparting, or how successful they are in imparting them. Nor do we know anything about how teachers and others change the values they are teaching, or even if they are able consciously to do that. We have, however, just started a research project on values, and this chapter builds on various ideas that are developing through the project.[1]

Firstly, there appears to be very little explicit values teaching in mathematics classrooms, and very little explicit addressing of values in the general discourse about mathematics education. Why is this the case? Why do we, as mathematics educators, know so little about values in this context? Is it because much teaching of values is done by modelling, by imitation, and by other implicit rather than explicit methods which we fail to see? If so we have been guilty of a gross oversight. It is likely that implicit values teaching is far more effective than explicit values teaching, which exposes the values so that they can be discussed and attacked more easily. Could it be that it is our oversight which has continued to feed the myth that mathematics is value-free, which in its turn has been a powerful way of protecting the values which it does convey?

This book is about student teachers, and at present there is little knowledge about what values student teachers think they are teaching in mathematics classes, about how aware student teachers are of their own value positions, about how their values affect their teaching, and about how their teaching thereby develops certain values in their students. Values are rarely considered in any discussions about mathematics teaching. A casual question to any student teachers about the values they are teaching in mathematics lessons often produces an answer to the effect that they don't believe they are teaching any. One student commented when asked, that one reason he chose to teach mathematics was so that he didn't have to think about teaching any values, unlike his colleagues who were training to be history, social studies, or science teachers! He shared the widespread belief that mathematics is the most value-free of all school subjects, a belief existing not just among student teachers but also among practising teachers, parents, university mathematicians and employers.

2. WHAT DO WE MEAN BY VALUES IN MATHEMATICS EDUCATION?

How can we best conceptualise values in mathematics education? I believe that firstly it is essential to consider them within the whole socio-cultural framework of education and schooling. Culture has been defined as "an organised system of values which are transmitted to its members both formally and informally" (McConatha & Schnell, 1995, p. 81). Mathematics education as a cultural phenomenon has been well researched over the last twenty years (Bishop, 1988), and it is clear from the work in ethnomathematics in particular that values are an integral part of mathematical knowledge (Barton, 1996; Gerdes, 1995).

The fact is that in the last two decades there has been an increasing awareness of the need to include the social dimension in any definition of our field. This development has come about basically from a desire to make mathematics accessible to more and more people. Governments around the world have realised that in the next century every country needs to ensure that as many of its citizens as possible are as well educated as possible, and particularly in mathematics. Research just cannot provide helpful ideas for the mathematical education of all people in the real educational context if it omits the social dimension.

This dimension is therefore now stimulating research at several different levels, the most important of which are:

- the individual level, concerning the kinds of mathematical practices and knowledge gained by mathematics learners, both inside and outside the classroom;
- the pedagogical level, concerning the many social interactions taking place inside the mathematics classroom;
- the institutional level, concerning the socio-cultural norms within schools and institutions which affect the mathematics teaching in the classrooms;
- the societal level concerning the relationships between mathematics education and political, economic, governmental, and other institutions in the wider society;
- the cultural level, concerning the relationships between mathematics education and the cultural and historical context of the society.

Of interest to us here is that we can imagine that values and valuing enter at every one of those levels. At the individual level, learners have their own preferences and abilities, which predispose them to value certain activities more than others. In the classroom there are values inherent in the negotiation of meanings between teacher and students, and between the students themselves. At the institutional level we enter the small political world of any organisation in which issues, both deep and superficial, engage everyone in value arguments about priorities in determining local curricula, timetables, teaching approaches, and so on. The large political scene is at the societal level, where the powerful institutions of any society determine national and state priorities in terms of curriculum, teacher preparation, teacher accreditation, and so on. Finally, at the cultural level, the very sources of knowledge, beliefs, and language, influence mathematics education in implicit and formative ways.

Another socio-cultural perspective on values is offered by Billett's (1998) analysis of the social genesis of knowledge. This analysis points to the different sources of influence on teachers' values. Billett categorises knowledge at five levels, and below is an indication of how different knowledge at these levels can impinge on and influence teachers' values.

1. *Socio-historic knowledge* factors affect the values underpinning decisions made by both management and teachers. For example, we can find important values ideas in the writings of Apple (1979) and Popkewitz (1997) concerning the historic, ideological purposes of schooling, in those of Cockcroft (1982), Ernest (1992), and Galbraith and Chant (1993) concerning public attitudes towards mathematics and mathematics education, and in AEC (1991) and the Ministry of Education, Victoria (1988) concerning the history of mathematics curriculum frameworks in Australia.

2. *Socio-cultural practice* is described by Billett as historically derived knowledge transformed by cultural needs; goals, techniques, and norms to guide practice; and expectations of transformed socio-historic knowledge. At the institutional level these are manifested by curricular decisions influenced by such factors as: (a) current school management philosophy with respect to educational and social values (*in loco parentis*); (b) State or national curricular frameworks such as the Victorian Curriculum and Standards Framework for mathematics (Board of Studies, 1999); and (c) the ethos of the mathematics faculty or teacher's peer group.

3. *The community of practice in the classroom* is identified by Billett as particular sociocultural practices shaped by a complex of circumstantial social factors (activity systems), and the norms and values which embody them. This community is influenced by: (a) the teachers' goals with respect to and portrayal of mathematical, mathematics educational, and general educational; (b) students' goals and portrayal of learning values (e.g., the didactical contract — Brousseau, 1997), instrumental values (e.g., mathematics as a positional good — Marginson, 1997), and personal values (e.g., acquiescence with or disruption of the teacher's and fellow students' intentions).

4. *Microgenetic development* is interpreted by Billett as individuals' (teachers' and students') moment-by-moment construction of socially derived knowledge, derived through routine and non-routine problem solving. The nature of teaching as a profession is reflected in the *relative* autonomy assumed within the walls of the classroom, where teachers' decisions are constantly being made or revised on the basis of a continuous flow of new information. The instantaneous nature of many decisions is likely to be influenced to a greater or lesser extent by the teacher's internalised sets of values.

5. Billett's last category is *ontogenetic development*, in which he included individuals' personal life histories, socially determined, and which furnish the knowledge with which to interpret stimuli; this development includes participation in multiple overlapping communities. Thus the values teaching in the mathematics classroom would be likely to be influenced by: (a) the teacher's prior experiences of learning mathematics, researching mathematics education, classroom teaching, and using mathematics in other life/workplace experiences; and (b) the students' prior experiences of using and learning mathematics in formal, informal, and non-formal settings — and the relationships, if any, made between in-school and out-of-school mathematics.

A social and cultural perspective on values is crucial to their analysis in mathematics education because valuing is done by people. The symbols, practices, and products of mathematical activity don't have any values in or of themselves. It is people, and the institutions of which they are a part, who place value on them. The research and writing on social and cultural aspects of mathematics education (e.g., Davis & Hersh, 1981, 1986; Joseph, 1991; Wilson, 1986) makes this abundantly clear.

How then can we approach the issue of what are the values we need to consider here, when thinking about teaching and student teaching? The most obvious sources for ideas are the literatures on the affective domain and values education generally. For example, Krathwohl, Bloom, and Masia (1964), in their second taxonomy of educational objectives, put values and valuing clearly within the affective domain, and point also to their deep-seated nature. Raths, Harmin, and Simon (1987) also describe seven criteria for calling something a value:

1.   Choosing freely
2.   Choosing from alternatives
3.   Choosing after thoughtful consideration of the consequences of each alternative
4.   Prizing and cherishing
5.   Affirming
6.   Acting upon choices
7.   Repeating

Although the first three seem to suggest that valuing is always a conscious, cognitive, decision-based matter, the list does indicate some possibilities for activities for the education of student teachers. Generally, these literatures indicate that values education should involve the existence of alternatives, choices and choosing, preferences, and consistency.

Regarding research on the affective domain in mathematics education, it has tended to focus on the two areas of attitudes, and beliefs (e.g., Buxton, 1981; Fasheh, 1982; McLeod, 1992; Thompson, 1992). Indeed, in McLeod's impressive review chapter no specific research on values in mathematics education is to be found. The research on attitudes has generally produced interesting results in that it shows how difficult it is to change attitudes of both teachers and students, although it is well accepted that teachers' attitudes appear to influence those of students. Regarding beliefs, one significant study by Sosniak et al. (1991) showed that teachers could hold what they referred to as "inconsistent" sets of beliefs.

There is clearly a relationship between values, beliefs and attitudes, with the literatures suggesting that values are more deep-seated and personal than attitudes, and less rationalised than beliefs. Beliefs seem to have the nature of propositions about phenomena, e.g. "I believe that girls are just as cognitively capable of high mathematical performance as boys", "I believe that no textbook can replace the human teacher." These propositions are testable in some sense, according to one's experiences, and presumably therefore they are also capable of change if one meets appropriately conflicting evidence.

Values, however seem to be of a different order. As we have seen, valuing is the key activity, from which then patterns of responses can be identified as values. If a teacher continually chooses to present opportunities for investigation, discussion, and debate in her class, we might surmise that she values the ability for logical argument. This "value" might, if the teacher is questioned, lead to her explaining that she values this ability because of her belief that it is fundamental for mathematical development. Which comes first, values or beliefs, is the chicken-and-egg problem. What is certain is that if values are as deep-rooted in us as the literatures suggest, we may not be very aware of them ourselves, and even less-able to describe them to others. The patterns of our behaviour and the consistencies of our responses to situations may only be visible to others. For now, and in our new research project on values in mathematics education, the research team is describing this relationship by the phrase "Values are beliefs in action." Teachers may hold various beliefs, but it is when they are operationalised in their classroom teaching that they become identifiable as values.

3. VALUES IN MATHEMATICS TEACHING

As a result of analysing these different literatures, values in mathematics teaching are conceptualised here as the deep affective qualities which teachers promote and foster through the school subject of mathematics. They, of course, do not do this alone. No teacher is autonomous and as we have seen from the social dimensions described above, there are cultural, societal and institutional factors influencing teachers' decisions about what values to inculcate in the classroom.

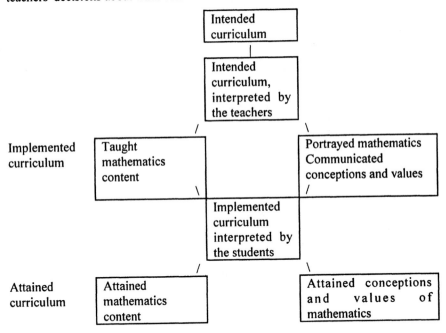

Figure 1. Intended, implemented, and attained curriculum.

Another way to conceptualise the situation is with the aid of the diagram in Figure 1, adapted from Kaleva (1998). Kaleva's research showed the necessity of not just considering the standard three levels of the curriculum—intended, implemented, attained—but also what he referred to as the "interpreted curriculum." This was revealed as a product of the didactical transposition process described by "didactique" theory (Brousseau, 1997) whereby the mathematics of the intended curriculum is interpreted, and valued in particular ways by the teachers, resulting in the implemented curriculum. This, then was revealed not only in terms of mathematical content, but also in terms of what Kaleva called the "portrayed mathematics," involving conceptions and values, portrayed by and through the teaching. This implemented curriculum is then in its turn interpreted by the students, who attain their own curriculum and values.

Our initial analyses reveal that there are three kinds of values which teachers seek to convey: the general educational, the mathematical, and the specifically mathematics educational. For example, when a teacher admonishes a student for cheating in an examination, the values of "honesty" and "good behaviour" derive from the general educational and socialising demands of society. In this case, the values are not especially concerned with, or particularly fostered by, the teaching of mathematics.

However when a teacher proposes and discusses a task such as the following: "Describe and compare three different proofs of the Pythagorean theorem," certain values associated with mathematics are being pursued. In Bishop (1988) and (1991) I argued that the values associated with what can be called Western mathematics could be described as three sets of complementary pairs:

- *Rationalism* involving ideas such as reason, hypothetical reasoning, logical thinking, explanations, abstractions, theories;
- *Objectism* involving ideas such as objectivising, symbolising, concretising, materialism, determinism, atomism;
- *Control* involving ideas such as rules, security, power, prediction, mastery over environment;
- *Progress* involving ideas such as cumulative development of knowledge, generalisation, growth, alternativism, questioning;
- *Openness* involving ideas such as demonstration, facts, verification, universality, individual liberty;
- *Mystery* involving ideas such as dehumanised knowledge, abstractness, wonder, unclear origins, mystique.

These are the values which I argued have been fostered by Western mathematicians over the last centuries, and it is reasonable to expect therefore that these same values will appear in some way in the teaching of that mathematics. In the example above about Pythagoras' theorem, I think the mathematical values of rationalism and openness are being conveyed.

Textbooks can also be considered to be carriers and shapers of values. They are in effect 'text teachers' and are certainly written by people interested in developing certain values and understanding. In a recent study by one of my research students, Wee Tiong Seah (1999), into the values portrayed by textbooks in Australia and in Singapore many interesting points were revealed. His study confirmed my earlier hypothesis (see Bishop, 1988) that in much of the current mathematics teaching there is a predominant emphasis of the mathematical values of:

Objectism	over	Rationalism
Control	over	Progress, and
Mystery	over	Openness

However there are other values being transmitted during teaching which are specifically associated with the norms of the institutions within which mathematics education is formally conducted. For example, at one level, the values implied by the following instructions from the teacher: " Make sure you show all your working in your answers," "Don't just rely on your calculator when doing calculations, try estimating, and then checking your answers," are about "examination-wiseness" and "efficient mathematical behaviour."

At another level, Seah found that the textbooks he analysed strongly encouraged the mathematical educational values of:

Formalist view	over	Activist view of mathematics learning
Instrumental understanding	over	Relational understanding
Specialism	over	Accessibility of mathematics learning
Process	over	Tool aspects in mathematics learning

Suggesting the three pairs of values (rationalism ... mystery) does not imply that teachers carry these as separate dimensions in their heads. Indeed, there is every reason to believe that teachers will, and must, integrate their values into coherent structures, if they are to develop the consistency that we recognise values require. A good example of this is provided by the elementary school teacher Ms Tsen, whose values are reported by Yuh-Chyn Leu (1998) in the previous chapter. The analysis of the interview transcripts of Ms Tsen showed that she held a very coherent set of values underpinned by her Buddhist faith. It is likely that all teachers underpin their values structures with some religious or philosophical faith.

We can then imagine the teacher's value structure as being influential in the following way (see the diagram). It is likely that as teachers become more experienced in their teaching, so a kind of decision schema develops (Bishop, 1976). In this, the teacher's value structure monitors and mediates the on-going teaching situation, constructing options and choices together with criteria for evaluating them. The teacher thus is able to implement the decisions in a consistent manner.

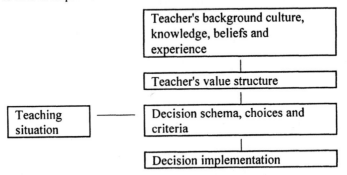

For the purposes of developing further ideas for student teacher training, we need then to consider aspects of teachers' decisions and actions that could reveal their values. Here is a partial list:

Macro level
- Planning and evaluating curriculum and assessment
- Choosing textbooks/electronic teaching aids

- Undertaking one's own professional development

Meso level
- Planning lessons
- Planning and setting assessment tasks, mark schemes
- Developing/accessing tasks and activities
- Making *in situ* pedagogical decisions
- Setting homework
- Grouping students in class
- Organising extension activities, clubs, competitions, camps

Micro level
- Working with individual students or small groups
- Working with individual teachers

4.   VALUES-RELATED ACTIVITIES WITH STUDENT TEACHERS

These actions and the decisions associated with them are the contexts in which the values of mathematics teaching become revealed. Alternatives, choices, preferences, and consistency are, as was said above, the key aspects of values education, and armed with the ideas from the earlier sections we can now move on to consider possible activities with student teachers of mathematics.

Table 1. Framework for Curriculum

	Declared curriculum	De facto curriculum	Potential curriculum
Aims : intended curriculum	What, if anything, teachers and others, say they might do or aim at by way of value-related aspects	What they actually seem to hold as value-related possibilities of their subject	What value aims might be promotable via the teaching of the subject
Means: implemented curriculum	The process and means by which they say these value-aims might be effected	The nature of actual value-related activities, including implicit ones, in this subject area	Value-related teaching activities that might be tried in this subject area
Effects: Attained curriculum	The value effects, if any, they think are being realized through teaching their subject	The actual effects, including hidden ones, being made on pupils' value outlooks, actions and reactions	The value effects that might be attainable under particular teaching conditions

The first area is that of sensitising the students to the whole idea of values in mathematics education. It is likely that they, as with many teachers, do not consider mathematics teachers to be involved with values teaching. Thus activities based on various writings from the history of mathematics literature, together with writings on developments such as ethnomathematics and critical mathematics education, will offer an important educational and philosophical basis for the students own values structures.

A second area would build on the framework offered by Tomlinson and Quinton (1986), as shown by in Table 1 (the column and row titles have been changed here for the sake of clarity).

One can imagine several activities for student teachers that fall in the different cells of columns one and three of this matrix, based on the teachers' action and decision list described above. These activities would surely begin to make them aware of some of the key aspects of values teaching in mathematics. However, column two could be accessed in two ways. Firstly, it would be very instructive to replicate a study like that of Seah (1999), and analyse the different values revealed by textbooks. However, there is no real substitute for their being able to talk about this area together with real teachers. It would be a real opportunity for them to get insight into the very core of mathematics teaching.

The third, and arguably the most important, area of values education for student teachers is to develop values clarification activities in our teacher education programs. Our review of the literatures, and our broad experience of practices in initial-training and in-service courses in mathematics education suggest that there is a particular need for activities which focus on the behavioural aspects of values in mathematics education, such as the choosing, the preferring, the consistency of behaviour, and so on. If values are beliefs in action, then we must build the student teachers' experiences and analyses on the action. They need to clarify their own values and preferences.

A strand of previous research which can be built on is that of "teacher decision-making." My original research work in this area (Bishop, 1976) laid the foundations for other research studies which have demonstrated that a simple documentation of teacher behaviour is not adequate for assisting with development. One also needs also to know why teachers choose to do what they do, what they think they then do, what they appear to do, and what alternatives they can generate. Hence, the emphasis earlier on the values structure and the decision schema.

An important and helpful activity for the student teachers is the analysis of "critical incidents," those incidents which happen in every classroom, and which have a strong effect on the course of the teaching. Critical incident analyses always raise issues about just what makes any incident critical to the sequencing and flow of teaching, about the choices facing teachers at such moments and about the values behind the criteria for choosing the appropriate option at that moment. In my experience of using such material, teachers find it stimulating to engage with and explore in a neutral and supportive environment the complex issues involved. For example, if you were a mathematics teacher and had to deal with this incident, what would you do?

> On returning from the summer holiday you are chatting with the class before getting down to work and you ask if anyone had any interesting presents. One boy said that he had been given a "mathematical game from my uncle's country," which he produced from his bag. He said "It's very interesting and has lots of variations. Can I show you how we play it?"

What would you do?

My favourite incident for provoking serious discussions about values in teaching mathematics is this one, which happened to me many years ago:

> You are working on fractions with a lively class, and you ask them to suggest a fraction that lies between one half and three-quarters. One of the sharper students in the class offers the answer "Two thirds." When you ask how she knows that it lies between the other two fractions, she answers: "Well you can see that on the top the numbers go 1,2,3, and on the bottom they go 2,3,4. The 2 is between the 1 and the 3, and on the bottom the 3 lies between the 2 and the 4, so therefore two thirds must be between the other two fractions!"

What do you respond? What activities could you now develop?

Incidents like these can be very revealing and can help student teachers begin to understand more about their role as mathematics teachers. This is not to say that they will find these activities simple. In fact, they can then begin to see just how complex mathematics teaching is. The start for them in learning this complex practice is to begin to understand themselves. This is true about their learning preferences, about their background mathematical knowledge, about their outside activities, and it is also true about their own values.

These then are the three main areas for developing values education with student teachers. They will, of course, never develop their values completely before beginning on their teaching career. The hope and intention is, however, that at least by sensitising them to values issues, by showing them examples of approaches to mathematics education that differ markedly in the values aimed at, and by helping them clarify their initial values, they will be in a better position to construct a coherent value structure for their own teaching. One assumption, or belief, that we are working on in our research project is that the more teachers understand about their own value positions the better teachers they will be.

5. THE NEED FOR MORE RESEARCH ON VALUES

It always important to argue that there should be more research done, and particularly so here. It is amazing to us that there has been so little research attention paid to values in mathematics teaching, and none related to student teachers' values. It is a difficult area to research, as we are finding out in our project, but that is not the only reason. Plenty of research is done on equally challenging areas. I still think that many people have the feeling that the good thing about mathematics teaching is that it does not have the same kinds of values issues that other subjects have. I would say that those people should pay more attention to what has been happening in research in our field over the last ten years. More and more we can see that values teaching, and values conflicts, are implicitly being either assumed or recognised, but not perhaps by that name. In my view the sooner we have more research focusing on values education in mathematics the better. If we want high quality mathematics teachers to come from our colleges and universities, we need to develop in them a far greater awareness of the highly significant role that values teaching plays.

NOTE

[1] The project is called the Values in Mathematics Project. Other colleagues involved are Phil Clarkson (Australian Catholic University), and Gail FitzSimons and Wee Tiong Seah from Monash University, Melbourne, Australia. More information about the project is available on the Web site http://www.education.monash.edu.au/projects/vamp

REFERENCES

Australian Education Council (1991). *A national statement on Mathematics for Australian schools.* Carlton: Curriculum Corporation.

Apple, M. W. (1979). *Ideology and curriculum.* Oxon: Routledge & Kegan Paul.

Barton, W. (1996). Anthropological perspectives on mathematics and mathematics education. In A.J.Bishop, M.A.Clements, C.Keitel, J.Kilpatrick, & C.Laborde (Eds.), *International handbook of mathematics education* (pp.1035-1053). Dordrecht, Holland: Kluwer

Billett, S. (1998). Transfer and social practice. *Australian & New Zealand Journal of Vocational Education Research, 6*(1), 1-25.

Bishop, A.J. (1976). Decision-making, the intervening variable. *Educational Studies in Mathematics, 7,* 41-47.

Bishop, A. J. (1988). *Mathematical enculturation: A cultural perspective on mathematics education.* Dordrecht: Kluwer.

Bishop, A. J. (1991). Mathematical values in the teaching process. In A. J. Bishop, et al. (Eds.), *Mathematical knowledge: Its growth through teaching* (pp. 195-214). Dordrecht: Kluwer.

Board of Studies. (1999). *Curriculum & Standards Framework II (Draft for consultation).* Melbourne: Author.

Brousseau , G. (1997). *Theory of didactical situations in mathematics (Didactique des mathematiques, 1970-1990)* (N.Balacheff, M.Cooper, R.Sutherland, & V.Warfield, Eds. and Trans.). Dordrecht: Kluwer.

Buxton, L. (1981). *Do you panic about maths?* London: Heinemann.

Cockcroft, W. H. (Chairman). (1982). *Mathematics counts: Report of the Committee of Inquiry into the Teaching of Mathematics in Schools.* London: Her Majesty's Stationery Office.

Davis, P.J. & Hersh, R. (1981). *The mathematical experience.* New York: Penguin.

Davis, P.J. & Hersh, R. (1986). *Descartes' dream.* New York: Penguin.

Ernest, P. (1992, August). *Images of mathematics: A philosophical perspective.* Paper presented at ICME 7, Working Group 21, The public image of mathematics and mathematicians. Québec, Canada.

Ernest, P. (1995). Values, gender and images of mathematics: A philosophical perspective. *International Journal of Mathematical Education in Science and Technology, 26,* 449-462.

Fasheh, M. (1982). Mathematics, culture, and authority. *For the Learning of Mathematics, 3*(2), 2 - 8.

Galbraith, P. L. & Chant, D. (1993). The profession, the public, and school mathematics. In B. Atweh, C. Kanes, M. Carss, & G. Booker (Eds.), *Contexts in mathematics education* (pp. 267-273). Brisbane: Mathematics Education Research Group of Australasia.

Gerdes, P. (1995). *Ethnomathematics and education in Africa.* Sweden: Stockholm University.

Joseph, G.G. (1991). *The crest of the peacock.* London: I.B.Tauris.

Kaleva, W. T. (1998). *The cultural dimension of the mathematics curriculum in Papua New Guinea: Teacher beliefs and practices.* Unpublished doctoral dissertation, Melbourne, Australia: Monash University.

Krathwohl, D.R., Bloom, B.S., & Masia, B.B. (1964). *Taxonomy of educational objectives, the classification of educational goals: Handbook 2: Affective Domain*. New York: Longmans.

Leu, Y.C. (1998) *Values in an elementary mathematics classroom in Taiwan*. Paper presented at the Psychology of Mathematics Education conference, Stellenbosch, South Africa.

Marginson, S. (1997). *Markets in education*. St Leonards, NSW: Allen & Unwin.

McConatha, J. T., & Schnell, F. (1995). The confluence of values: Implications for educational research and policy. *Educational Practice and Theory, 17*(2), 79-83.

McLeod, D. B. (1992). Research on affect in mathematics education: A reconceptualization. In D. A. Grouws (Ed.), *Handbook of research on Mathematics teaching and learning* (pp. 575-596). New York: Macmillan.

Ministry of Education, Victoria. (1988). *The mathematics framework P-10*. Melbourne: Ministry of Education (Schools Division), Victoria.

Noss, R. & Hoyles, C. (1996). *Windows on mathematical meanings: learning cultures and computers*. Dordrecht: Kluwer.

Popkewitz, T. S. (1997). The production of reason and power: Curriculum history and intellectual traditions. *Journal of Curriculum Studies, 29*(2), 131-164.

Raths, L.E., Harmin, M. & Simon, S.B. (1987). Selections from values and teaching. In Carbone, P.F. (Ed.), *Value theory and education* (pp. 198-214). Malabar, USA; Krieger.

Seah, W. T. (1999). Values in Singapore and Victoria lower secondary mathematics textbooks: A preliminary study. In M. A. (Ken) Clements & Y. P. Leong (Eds.), *Cultural and language aspects of science, mathematics, and technical education* (pp. 261-270). Brunei: Universiti Brunei Darussalam.

Skovsmose, O. (1994). *Towards a philosophy of critical Mathematical Education*. Dordrecht: Kluwer.

Sosniak, L. A., Ethington, C. A., & Varelas, M. (1991). Teaching mathematics without a coherent point of view: Findings from the IEA Second International Mathematics Study. *Journal of Curriculum Studies, 23*(2), 119-131.

Thompson, A.G. (1992). Teachers' beliefs and conceptions: A synthesis of the research. In D.Grouws (Ed.), *Handbook of research on mathematics teaching and learning* (pp.127-146). New York: Macmillan.

Tomlinson, P. & Quinton, M. (Eds.). (1986). *Values across the curriculum*. Lewes: The Falmer Press.

Wilson, B.J. (1986). Values in mathematics education. In P.Tomlinson & M.Quinton (Eds.), *Values across the curriculum* (pp. 94-108). Lewes: The Falmer Press.

Monash University
Melbourne, Australia

CHIEN CHIN, YUH-CHYN LEU, AND FOU-LAI LIN

PEDAGOGICAL VALUES, MATHEMATICS TEACHING, AND TEACHER EDUCATION: CASE STUDIES OF TWO EXPERIENCED TEACHERS

ABSTRACT. This chapter addresses the role of values in mathematics teachers' thinking, and the relationship of those values to teachers' classroom practices, in order to examine the assumption raised in Bishop's chapter that the more teachers understand about their own value positions the better teachers they will be. Studying values from two aspects, referred to as social identity and valuing, we explore two mathematics teachers' pedagogical values and the degrees of value clarification and their relation to changes in classroom teaching. We also examine the research questions related to this assumption, such as "How can we explore teachers' values?" and "How can we help teachers understand their own values and the relationship of those values to classroom mathematics teaching?" Some activities that might be useful in initiating mathematics teachers' professional development through value clarification are provided and criteria suggested.

1. THE EDUCATIONAL AND RELIGIOUS CONTEXT IN TAIWAN

The profession of secondary school teachers is subject-oriented in Taiwan. They teach one subject with different classes. However, nearly 90% of elementary school teachers in Taiwan have to teach three subjects on average, such as Mathematics, Mandarin, and Social Studies. Compulsory education in Taiwan starts at 6 years and ends at 15 years. Then, the students take entrance tests for further education, and are streamed into senior high schools, vocational schools, and junior colleges. The 18 year-old students have to take the university entrance test, and about 60% of them pass. Last year, there were less than 8% of the junior high school graduates enrolled in public high reputation schools (CHSEE, 1999); and about 20% of the senior high school graduates went into public universities (CUEE, 1999). In recent years, students have various opportunities for further education, as the multi-entrance programs have been in effect since 1998 for junior high school and university graduates. But, due to both parents' and society's expectations, these two tests are still very competitive for those students who are in the top 30% of each population and supposed to be able to get into the very few high reputation schools and universities.

These tests have become a crucial annual event in the society for the past 40 years. They undoubtedly generate a unique and special *culture of examinations* in the society, reflected in many of the Taiwanese students' school performance results. Consequently, many tests are used for preparing students to pass such examinations,

F.-L. Lin & T. J. Cooney (Eds.) Making Sense of Mathematics Teacher Education, 247—269.
© 2001 *Kluwer Academic Publishers. Printed in the Netherlands.*

and therefore, the aim of primary and secondary education seems to be just concerned with performance on tests.

As most of the residents of Taiwan were immigrants from the southeast of Mainland China, the Taiwanese have similar beliefs to the Chinese, such as *showing respect for the heavens and keeping oneself well*. About a quarter of the Taiwanese are followers of Buddhism (Liou, 1997), in which individual meditation is stressed; the remaining 60% are of multiple folk beliefs associated with Confucianism, Buddhism, Taoism, and various spiritual faiths. For example, the most well known Buddhist organization, Tzu-Chi, has more than one million followers. The Tzu-Chi Teachers Association has more than ten thousand members representing about 5% of the teacher population. The mission of the association is to move Buddhism into the school curricula, to purify the campuses, and to relate school education to society. Buddhism thus has a huge hidden impact on Taiwanese society in general, and on education in particular. As inherited from India, Buddhism has been characterized by different religions in China such as Confucianism and Taoism. Not believing in a supernatural creator representing the universe, Buddhists believe instead in a Buddha who is aware of the natural world, and that anyone who accepts Buddha to live in his/her mind is capable of seeing his/her own mind clearly.

The significant impacts that mathematics teachers' pedagogical beliefs have, either consistent or not, on their classroom instructional practices and their attitudes toward student conceptions, have been well documented. A probable answer to such (in)consistencies in beliefs is considered to be related to teachers' values of mathematics and pedagogy concerning the deeper affective and evaluative qualities that underpin their pedagogical preferences, judgments, and choices. But, what are the salient educational values regarding mathematics and pedagogy that experienced mathematics teachers have? We first describe the educational values of the two teachers, followed by a discussion of how to clarify their values through value clarification approach and its relationship to classroom practices. Finally, some implications of values in mathematics teacher education are discussed.

In this chapter, three issues raised in Bishop's chapter concerning the presentation and interpretation of teachers' values, the possibility of clarifying their own value positions, and the relationship of value clarification and teaching practices, will be elaborated in terms of a case study of two experienced mathematics teachers.

2. TWO TEACHERS' PEDAGOGICAL VALUES

Teachers' educational values about mathematics and pedagogy were investigated in terms of two aspects, firstly relating to Tajfel's (1978, 1981) theories of social identity, and secondly to Raths' (Raths, Harmin, & Simon, 1987) theory of the process of valuing. The case study method with questionnaire survey, interviews, and classroom observations was used to explore two experienced mathematics teachers' (Ming and Hua) values of mathematics and pedagogy. Ming has taught mathematics in a public senior high school for 20 consecutive years since he received a master degree in mathematics. His patterns of teaching were very consistent, revealing salient features. Hua has taught in primary school for 21 years since she graduated from Teachers' college.

The method of *dialogue interview,* including reflective and introspective discussion, and recursive probing procedures, was developed and used in the interviews in which teachers played active roles in the conversation while researchers acted as listeners and inquirers. A set of probes was used in such dialogues, for instance, "What are the most important things you would consider in your teaching? And why?" "What messages do you try to pass to your students through mathematics teaching? And why?" and "For what reasons do you teach mathematics like this?"

Relevant information about the framework of presenting and interpreting the two teachers' pedagogical values are given elsewhere (Chin & Lin, 2000; Leu, 2000).

2.1 Values Underlying Pedagogical Identities: The Case of Ming

During his professional career, Ming has been involved in several projects playing different roles, such as textbook writer, member of the board of national entrance test, teacher of gifted students, and mentor, who was also very much welcomed by the students and colleagues. In other words, he is an expert teacher of mathematics in senior high schools.

The pedagogical values that Ming revealed were represented in terms of five components (Chin & Lin, 1999, p. 50), concerning the social, educational, mathematical, mathematics educational, and pedagogical aspect, a structure used by Tomlinson and Quinton (1986) and modified by Bishop (1999). As a result, the value system of the teacher was represented by a tetrahedron (Chin & Lin, 1999, p.51), consisting of these five components. Two value statements and the relevant values attached to the mathematical and mathematics educational components will be exemplified here. They are "Mathematics is a useful and interesting knowledge" and "Mathematics education is to develop students' knowledge, abilities, and intellect." The remaining three sets of values and values statements have been discussed elsewhere (see Chin & Lin, 1999, 2000).

As far as Ming is concerned, mathematics is presented in an *ideal* and *abstract* form, and yet, it can be applied to a more general and realistic context in practice. He said "mathematics is an *ideal* and *abstract* knowledge for living and practical purposes," "mathematics is a *useful* and *practical* knowledge," and "mathematics is a knowledge for *practical uses.*" An example from mathematical induction can be used to explain these value statements. He used 15 minutes at the beginning of the first lesson to develop certain essential ideas of the concept, for example "activation" and "infinite induction." Using the activity of Hanoi Tower with student practices and manipulations, his purposes were to initiate student interest and motivation in the process of learning such a concept as well as to relate such practices and manipulations to the foundations of the concept. Typically, he used classroom dialogues and practices to develop students' feelings about "how the finite and infinite induction can be right when N increases from 4 to 5 and from finite to infinite?" The rest of the lesson then continued with a second activity, "colors painting," by using similar approach. The teacher therefore suggests that *usefulness, practicality,* and *interests* are three values of mathematical knowledge that the first values statement given above carries.

On the other hand, mathematical *meanings* and *forms* also played an important role in his classroom teaching. However, teachers have to relate both together. According to Ming, as mathematics teachers, "we should let our students realize the connections between the mathematical world and the real world." For Ming, mathematics is all his life, as he expressed,

> Mathematics has influenced me a lot, I use it to *see the world,* to *interpret life,* and to *conceive knowledge.* It's my personal habit to do so, seeing the world from a mathematical point of view, and it has a significant impact on my life and on my teaching.

At the end of second lesson, he then introduced the canonical form of mathematical induction including the well-known two-step process. Because "mathematics needs shared forms for communication, we can exchange our ideas about mathematical concepts through mutual communications by using certain well-known symbols. We have to use mathematical forms and meanings in exchanges." Meanings and fun are all that he will be concerned with in mathematics teaching, in which the forms and symbols are meaningfully sustained through such activities as the Hanoi Tower.

Another value of mathematics for him is a kind of *knowledge for living* and a *product of human civilization.* For Ming, mathematics is in this sense "a kind of knowledge and *a part of human civilization,* therefore, it is used to improve our quality of life, and also relevant to other forms of knowledge." Mathematics is not just formal rules and logical games for students to remember, it is derived from "*the needs of our living and cultural development*" Mathematics is "not something about formal games for students to follow" and it has resulted from " *the social needs of living,* it is very dangerous for us to ignore the sources of the development of mathematical knowledge." Thus, according to his view, students are capable of doing most of school mathematics. For instance, in the activity of Hanoi Tower at the moment N was changing from 4 to 5 a student, who had failed to solve the problem when N equals to 5, raised his hand and said, "Oh! My goodness, you are cheating me. If this is all right then I will say that the process of examination is correct for any natural number, as I can use this similar approach of reasoning for any natural numbers N."

For Ming, the purpose of mathematics education is "to improve students' mathematical *knowledge* and *abilities,* helping them to reason and develop individual *personality* and *intellect.*" He reveals a deep concern for mathematical knowledge and a sense of mathematical abilities, and suggests that the values of mathematics education include *human knowledge, abilities,* and *intellect.* The aim of school education is to teach students the kind of knowledge that is useful in real life, as for him "searching for new knowledge is one of the basic human instincts and abilities." Therefore, knowledge, abilities, and intellect might have enormous impacts on the development of individuals' personalities, as he sees himself as an initiator of such students' knowledge and abilities. He hoped that he could "teach students the knowledge that can be applied in the later stages of education, this knowledge would play the critical role in the development of student personalities." For example, the first two lessons in designing and teaching of mathematical induction through "one metaphor and two manipulative activities" format were used for developing such values for the students. It was through the process of learning from simulated metaphors, trial and error, practice, and finite steps of reasoning that student knowledge, abilities, and intellect might have been built.

The five core pedagogical value statements (Chin & Lin, 2000) located in the *self* phase of the representative framework, are central and the most salient principles for Ming to choose and judge among various pedagogical identifications. When he *thinks* beforehand about his classroom teaching, these statements and the attached values are *re-shaped* into those statements and values related to the intended phase. Using pedagogical reasoning (Brown & Borko, 1992), the teacher then *transforms* these intended value statements and the relevant values into certain teaching activities such as the activity of "Hanoi Tower" (Chin & Lin, 2000), through which his or her intended values are implemented and become explicit in the classroom teaching of mathematics.

2.2   Values as the Products of Valuing: The Case of Hua

When Hua first became our study subject, she had just taken over a new fifth grade class. It was her first time teaching the new mathematics curriculum of elementary school. Before that, Hua had taught the old curriculum for around twenty years. Other than mathematics, she taught Mandarin, Life and Ethics, and other subjects. Hua was a very hard-working teacher and was selected to be a mentor advising an intern teacher. Additionally, she had been elected as an excellent teacher in school in 1997 academic year.

Hua came into contact with Buddhism because of an event involving her daughter. She bought a house in 1992. Her daughter, who was six at that time, had a headache the first day they moved into a new house. Though her daughter went to the doctor for one year, she didn't get any better. Her daughter was always lethargic, crying, and at times insane. She even said things that she wouldn't have said when she was well. Eventually, Hua met a Zen master who helped her solve her daughter's problem. It was this special event that led Hua to Buddhism. From Buddhism, she realized many different viewpoints. For instance, she said,

> Buddhism is actually education but a religion. My life is open in Buddhism. Since I coming into contact with Buddhism, I have felt my teaching is changing. I became happier and happier in my teaching. Teaching is not merely teaching students knowledge in the textbooks. Teaching is teaching students how to behave well. Seen in this way, teaching becomes easier.

Hua's pedagogical values were grouped into four components, relating to the educational, pedagogical, social, and religious aspects respectively. Two value statements and the relevant values attached to the pedagogical and religious components will be exemplified here. They are "Education is to reinstate students' original enlightenment" and "The purpose of mathematical assessment is to know students' learning and to help students' self-correcting in learning and living." The remaining three sets of values have been reported elsewhere (Leu, 2000).

As far as Hua is concerned, mathematics education should stress the relation between individual *concentration* and *enlightenment* following the sequence of "concentration - calm down/meditation - open up wisdom/reinstate enlightenment." Hua required students to repeat the question to be solved and the procedures of solving that question in teaching, since while *concentrating* on something people's mind become *clear*, and this is *part of human instinc*t. She asked students to be calm and so that then they would know how to solve the mathematical questions. She taught students how to concentrate by reading the Chinese classics and spent 3 to 5 minutes reading the Chinese classics at most of mathematics lessons. Hua believed that by getting access to Buddhism, the students might learn how to *concentrate*, which would allow them to attain *precepts, meditation,* and *wisdom*. By concentrating on reading, the students would not be able to think of other things; and by meditating themselves, they would start to understand the true meaning of knowledge, which *inspires people's wisdo*m.

Why did Hua assume that concentration could get people to know the true meaning of knowledge? Because once being calm, people learn things efficiently, and she realized this through Buddhism. Although students might not understand fully, according to Buddhism, this shows a *karmic obstruction*. For example, listening, some kids look at the bright side but others see the dark side. Buddhism might be interpreted as one kind of education that *can enlighten people's inborn wisdom* and makes people understand the truths of the Universe and life. The basic purpose of Buddhism is to recover people's innate enlightenment, so Buddha means enlightened being. Therefore, learning "how to concentrate and enlighten?" would enable students to learn mathematical knowledge.

Moreover, the ideas of *self-awareness* also played a critical role in her pedagogical thinking. She suggested that the process should be followed by "student awareness of mistakes — student thinking/reflection — student awareness of enlightenment." For example, when a student got a mathematical question wrong, she would tell the student, "You are wrong!" instead of "showing them where it went wrong." She would ask students to find their mistakes themselves. She thought, "then students can have the opportunity to think and to see where the problem is. It can therefore awaken students' enlightenment." She recognizes this procedure as *improving student's nature of enlightenment*. Thus, enlightenment has to do with the varied degrees of self-awareness for the children.

The role of *life experiences* in re-instating enlightenment was also crucial in the logic of her teaching practice. She sequenced the steps as "sharing life experiences— re-thinking ideas and behaviors of life—reinstating enlightenment." For instance, she asked her students to write down the experiences that they learned everyday, and then shared these experiences each other in the morning before the first period of the day. The reason for doing so was "People's enlightenment is usually de-enlightened by greed, anger, ignorance, doubt, and pride, so that we need to practice Buddhism;" "to enact Buddhism is to adjust your improper behaviors;" and "experiencing and sharing helps students to realize the most precious parts of our real life."

To re-instate Buddhist views of enlightenment was of paramount importance in her mathematics teaching, as she cherished most the concept of enlightenment in her mathematics teaching since it is what her life is all about. She then used a metaphor concerning shadows and the brightness of the Sun to explain her ideas of enlightenment. She said that "self-awareness is usually concealed by oneself and the world, just like the sun is covered by cloud, and if those obstacles are removed then such self-awareness recovers."

On the other hand, she used conversations in classroom teaching in which the teacher asks questions, and students solve the questions and explain the procedures of solving them. She also used in-class tests to check and understand students learning. The purpose of checking assignments was to know the extent of the mistakes that students made. Therefore, the role of assessment in practice for the teacher is to *make sense of the students' learning situation*. The aim of assessment for Hua was diagnosing students' misconceptions rather than grading.

The teacher did not insist on her own teaching approaches; rather, she would try to modify teaching strategies to coordinate with the present state of students' learning. When students made mistakes in the mathematics exercises, Hua would ask student to correct and revise the mistakes. She professed,

> If the mistakes weren't corrected, students still cannot do those questions they did wrong. This habit could be analogized to living habits. People do make mistakes sometimes or have some bad habits in daily life. As long as you don't do it on purpose, you make mistakes and you correct them. It would be all right as long as you don't repeat these mistakes any more.

It is more important for her to guide students *not to repeat similar mistakes* than to know students' learning, because students might learn from mistakes. Therefore, helping students to avoid making similar mistakes is what concerns her most in teaching.

The more precious the values are, the more crucial they will be for the teacher. Hua professed that as far as she is concerned, to achieve *Buddhahood* and *life cultivation* is more important than general education for human beings. Therefore, the central value derived from Buddhism for her is to re-instate *enlightenment* and *concentration* in education. The values carried by the value statements related to the pedagogical component such as, "the aim of teaching is to help students understand mathematical content," "the purpose of mathematical assessment is to know student learning," and "mathematics learning depends on personal efforts and understanding," all seem peripheral for her.

This teacher would not have shared her meditations about Buddha with those who were not interested in Buddhism. In this case, it might not have been possible to find out her ideas of concentration and re-instatement of enlightenment about mathematics learning. Therefore, the common religious ground between researcher and teacher seemed to act as a catalyst that made the study plausible.

2.3   Revisiting the Two Approaches Used in Studying Teachers' Values

Social identity approach. Teachers' values were interpreted as "dually individual-social phenomena, the social identities concerning mathematics and pedagogy," as "the principles or standards of teacher choices and judgements on the importance or worth of using certain pedagogical identifications in his or her classroom teaching of mathematics" (Chin & Lin, 2000). The value system was then construed as "the internal-external dialectic of identification," as "the dialectical relationship between the varieties and complexities of individual pedagogical values," as the process whereby all values are constituted (Jenkins, 1996, p. 20).

Pedagogical values, therefore, are seen as personal principles of thinking and enacting of certain pedagogical identifications with which the teachers agree. Here we conceive the values that mathematics teachers have as their *Pedagogical identities* concerning mathematics and pedagogy, developing through a dialectical relationship between the varieties and complexities of individual pedagogical identifications. They are the results of a process of an internal-external dialectic of identification. We consider Ming as a member of the teacher group to which he belongs. The pedagogical values then reflect his principles of selection and judgement of certain identifications concerning mathematics and pedagogy, which are shared among group members. These identities describe not only the teacher's personal characteristics and preferences in mathematics teaching, but also the shared characters of his teachers' group. These shared identities reflect much of the specific features that mathematics teachers have in teaching within their context of schooling. The identities thus act as a set of consistent and coherent schemas showing both the conceptual and behavioral aspects of the teacher's principles of teaching and learning.

The teachers' pedagogical values were explored in the case of Ming through a *four-step dialectical procedure*, in which each step covered different features of teacher's pedagogical characteristics. In the first step of *observation* and *sensation*, we focused on some of Ming's observable teaching patterns or teaching styles. For example, we discussed the metaphorical story "King's Birthday Party," which started the mathematical induction lesson, and the follow-up game of "Hanoi Tower" (see Chin & Lin, 2000). Some personal characteristics of the teacher, such as the ideas of *sharing* and *discussing* with school colleagues, and the role of *metaphors* in teaching, became overt in the interviews. The teacher's styles and characteristics of teaching might in this case point to the phenomena that values uphold.

In the second step, the processes of *reflection* and *introspection* were used. It was crucial to initiate the teacher into reflecting on his own teaching activities. We used pedagogical reflections and introspection, focussing on "critical incidents" (Bishop, 1999, p. 4) selected from the teacher's classroom teaching, as the sources of interview to uncover his knowledge, thoughts, or identifications of mathematics and pedagogy. When a teacher thinks about his own teaching and the ways of teaching mathematics, then it is time to pose questions such as "Why did you teach that way? Were there any other alternatives? And for what reasons did you choose them?" or "Why is it so important for you to teach mathematics that way?"

Dialogue and *discussion* were then used to verify those principles that emerge in choosing and enacting certain pedagogical identifications. Value dialogue was crucial in the interviews, since this could bring out teachers' rationales or principles of thinking and action about values. It is an open and informal discussion in which some issues are clarified as similar to the approaches of "value clarification discussion" (Volkmor, Pasanella, & Raths, 1977) and "thinking aloud" (Clark & Peterson, 1986). In such dialogues, the researcher acts as a listener and inquirer in examining whatever he recognizes as relevant; the teacher on the other hand plays the role of a speaker in recollecting his thoughts and principles of judgement through introspection and retrospection on his teaching activities. It is a dialectical and discursive process in which the teacher tries to defend his or her value position in exchanges.

In the final step, the *recursive probing* approach, in combination with the previous three steps, was used to identify Ming's pedagogical identities. The empirical data referred to in this study were examined and verified in varied aspects and contexts. Different observers were involved in examining the empirical data, for instance, one colleague (Fan) and two student teachers (Wen & Yu). The reliability of the data was examined in terms of different data sources such as Ming's regular interviews, in-school colloquia, and out-of-school discourse. The focus of the data collection was therefore on the teacher's daily school activities.

Raths, Harmin, and Simon's valuing approach. From the perspective of the process of valuing, values were seen as teachers' pedagogical beliefs, attitudes, or feelings meeting the requirements of the "choosing," "prizing," and "acting" procedures suggested by Raths et al. (1987). There are three indicators, referring to one's free will to choose, choosing from alternatives, and choosing by thoughtful consideration of the consequences of each alternative, for examining the procedure of "choosing." The two standards for examining "prizing" concern either being happy with the choice, or enough to be willing to affirm the choice to others. Acting and repeated practice in some pattern of teaching are the two standards for testing the procedure of "acting." Teachers who meet each of the three grouped criteria were considered as satisfying the standards of value examination provided that action is repeated. In this case, pedagogical values were conceived of as *teachers' beliefs, attitudes, feelings which satisfy the examination of all the three main criteria: choosing, prizing, and acting.*

The Raths' dichotomous options given above were modified to either dichotomies or the preferences between the options. To verify the prizing procedure one should either be happy with the choice, or be willing to affirm the choice to others. Moreover, individuals have to either show or enact their preference, or cherish the options or execute the options. The criterion for checking the acting procedure is repeated action in some pattern of life.

A crucial question here is "How and why could the teacher express (or not) to outsiders his/her values?" This is the question of "How could teachers' pedagogical values become explicit or self-evident?" and "Why could teachers' pedagogical values not become acknowledged?" and "What characteristics and factors might enable teachers to clarify such values on their own?" In the light of this, Raths' valuing approach was applied to study Hua's pedagogical values.

3. DEGREES OF VALUE CLARIFICATION

In the discussion of the role and function that social speech, communicative speech, and inner speech play in an individual's thought and language, Vygotsky (1978, 1986) proposed that one can internalize social speech, and socialize inner speech, through intra-personal communication in terms of interpersonal dialogues. He suggested that thoughts could be expressed by words to initiate social speech while, at the same time, those words become part of the inner speech of the individuals. In this study, we conceive of mathematics teachers' pedagogical values as their implicit social characteristics concerning mathematics and pedagogy. It seems that these values might become explicit through a dialectical process of interaction between thoughts and words. This explicit process of values clarification might relate to the effects of individuals' mental development and socialization (Vygotsky, 1978). Therefore, making explicit teachers' pedagogical values probably has to do with the process of their professional development.

In the light of Vygotsky, a critical question for value clarification is "How can we help teachers express their pedagogical values explicitly and to be aware of such values?" Mathematics teachers, as value carriers, have certain forms of naïve pedagogical values as their "spontaneous concepts" (Vygotsky, 1986). Thus, the issue is how or in what ways can we as researchers assist teachers to explicate explicitly their naïve pedagogical values to outsiders; in other words, how can we help the teachers develop "the spontaneous concepts" (implicit values) into "the scientific concepts" (explicit values)?

In this section, we will describe the characteristics and factors relating to the processes of teachers' pedagogical value clarification as exemplified by Ming and Hua. While Ming was at a stage of high value clarification, Hua seemed to be still in the process of clarifying her own values.

3.1 Higher Value clarification: The Case of Ming

The process of value clarification. It was in going through a *suspicion-awareness-trial-understanding-clarification* process of transformation that Ming's pedagogical values became clarified. He asked on different interview occasions, firstly, "What do you mean by value?" then inquired, "Are the values we study to do with mathematics, mathematics teaching, or personal characteristics?" and in the end he recognized that "Values might be *something important* to me, the thing that makes me feel *happy* and gives me *pleasure*." Then, he tried to use the word *value* to describe an incident that happened in his school concerning the role and function of student test scores. Ming said that "some teachers would pay great attention to the scores that their students got in the tests, because they might *value* the idea that the higher the score their students have got, the better the status that they would have in the school." This value statement indicates exactly the value of tests in education for which such teachers are looking. But, for him, "education is to improve people's *abilities* and *the quality of life* rather than getting better scores on tests." This statement, however, shows the value of student ability that he values most.

He then understood the meanings of value through dialogue and discussion as the study proceeded. Ming said that,

> I think they (his values) were there for quite a long time; perhaps I didn't realize them before. People may have values that are very different in forms, content, or degree of awareness. But, it is not appropriate to say what kinds of value are better.

For Ming, values seem to be implicit in nature; not everyone can realize his or her own values of mathematics and pedagogy. These values would have *deep influence* on the teacher's *thinking* and *action*. However, people use different words with the same meanings, or different meanings with the same words. The values that Ming had were there for a very long time; and yet, he didn't find suitable words to speak them out, or perhaps he hadn't had an occasion to discuss his values with others. Finally, he understood and used the word *value* very often in the interviews, although the values that he has are difficult to express at the very beginning.

Vygotsky's (1978, p. 86) "zone of proximal development" describes the extent to which individuals' concepts might develop under external encouragement. Lave and Wenger (1991, p.48-49), use "individually active knowledge" and "socially understood knowledge" to describe the extent of different knowledge that we might learn between the daily-experiential and social-historical contexts. Ming's active knowledge reflects in the stages of suspicion and awareness; and the understanding and clarification stages show clearly his recognition of the word *value*. This five-stage pedagogical value clarification process describes a teacher's self-reconstruction of the recognition of educational values moving from individually active knowledge to socially understood knowledge. It reveals also the probable way of connecting spontaneous and scientific concepts about values, and the possibility of transforming mathematics teacher's personal inner speech into socially outer speech. This is also relevant to what Moscovici (1981, pp. 188-191) says in his theories of social cognition concerning the process of pedagogical value clarification as a teacher's social re-establishing and re-constituting processes, in which the unfamiliar become familiar through the disequilibrium-equilibrium procedure.

This five-stage model suggests a way for the transformation of mathematics teachers' values, from a *pedagogical value carrier* whose values play out as implicitly spontaneous concepts, to a *pedagogical value communicator* whose values act as explicitly self-evident scientific concepts that can be used to communicate with outsiders.

Characteristics of a value communicator. When Ming's values were being clarified, he became a preacher-like person. His values turned into a set of ideas used to persuade and share the underlining faiths with others. The value carrier cherished very much such faiths and values, but the preacher sees his faithful thoughts as personal pedagogical repertoires accompanying certain specifically personal characteristics. This is not to force somebody to listen to him; however, if he knows who are interested in what he is talking about, then he will be very happy to *share his ideas*. Ming said, "To speak out my own ideas is itself a kind of enjoyment, which one does not expect to have paid back." These characteristics his personality showing a teacher's values of mathematics and pedagogy being enacted daily in school, and can be recognized by anyone.

We consider these observable and sensible phenomena of such personalities to be the realization of teachers' pedagogical identities. They are the teachers' personalities about mathematics and pedagogy that are sensible for outsiders. This view of identities extends the concepts of beliefs or values as teacher's implicit characteristics (for example, Krathwohl, Bloom, & Masia, 1964; McLeod, 1992) to the explicit personality that can be felt and even observed by outsiders. The pedagogical values are therefore construed as the explicit identities of mathematics teachers.

In general, having understood a mathematical concept, one would be able to give relevant examples and analogues. In other words, one can use examples and analogues to explain the mathematical concepts. In the process of pedagogical value clarification, Ming was able to project his understanding of mathematics and pedagogy into some teaching incidents shown as *narratives* and *metaphors*. These situated examples of teaching incidents then operate as the catalysts for outsiders to make sense of his pedagogical identities. In other words, researchers can use these *narratives* and *metaphors* as the sources for discussion and sharing different ideas of mathematics teaching with teachers. For example, Ming sees mathematics teaching as drama, writing, composing, or painting in which the teacher plays the role of director, writer, composer, or painter. Mathematics teaching is just like the arts, reflecting details and delicacies showing a teacher's personal preferences of identifications concerning mathematics and pedagogy. Ming described his mathematics teaching as "Arts reflecting a teacher's *preferences* of teaching."

Using *narration* and *metaphoring*, mathematics teachers might explain and share their pedagogical identities with outsiders. These situated narratives and contextualized metaphors, on the one hand, reflect the state of cognitive balance after the teacher's values are clarified, showing the features of a value communicator's intellectual and ability. On the other hand, they can be used as indicators of examining whether the pedagogical values are clarified or not.

Factors relevant to value clarification. Two major factors initiating the clarification of Ming's pedagogical values were reflective dialogue and writing a textbook. The *experiences of writing a textbook* seem helpful, during which the writers have to think through how and in what forms they can best present the mathematical concepts to the students? On the other hand, *reflection in discussion* was an effective way of *stimulating* and *re-structuring* teachers' thoughts through which teachers might *re-organise* their own ideas and word descriptions of values.

Three critical activities relevant to the process of value clarification for the teacher are *dialogue, communication,* and *pedagogical reflection.* Mathematics teachers have to *reflect* on their teaching from time to time; otherwise, they would be like a recorder replaying the content of their teaching once every year. A *reflective teacher* would look for improvements in teaching and extend his or her sources of knowledge in mathematics teaching. Learning to *exchange* with colleagues, parents, and students may force teachers to reflect on what they have taught. As a result, we suggest that the activities of dialogue, communication, and pedagogical reflection are three useful catalysts for clarifying teachers' pedagogical values. This process also suggests a way of turning the inner aspect of value speech that mathematics teachers have to its social aspect.

Two keys that Vygotsky (1986) proposed, of moving people from individual inner speech to interpersonal social speech, are dialogue and communication. These two social activities of connecting individuals' thoughts with their words set up the bases of transforming inner speech, such as the word value, to communicative social speech as a commonly used and recognized language. As far as Ming is concerned, dialogue and communication are two useful activities in connecting teachers' inner thoughts and words of pedagogical value, and in transforming such inner speech to communicative social speech of pedagogical values through interpersonal pedagogical reflections. During such a process, a communicative language of pedagogical values emerges. It is in this case that mathematics teachers are capable of explaining their ideas of pedagogical value to outsiders by using narratives and metaphors derived from certain classroom teaching incidents.

3.2 Lower Value Clarification: The Case of Hua

The first time Hua was asked to be in our research sample, she thought she wasn't familiar enough with the new curriculum and the relevant materials; therefore at first she turned us down politely. After the researchers explained that this research was to study her values in mathematics teaching, but not her understanding of new curriculum, she promised to reconsider it. Later on, Hua told the researcher, "After your phone call, I considered and decided not to be in your research sample. The day when I went to your office to reject you, I saw the holy image of KWAN-YIN Buddha and the Heart Sutra posted in your office. I then changed my mind and was happy to be in the research." Hua agreed to be in our research sample only because she and the researcher were Buddhists, but not because of her interest in the research theme.

During the process of research, she never spontaneously asked what value was. She was at the state of unawareness of the concept of value when she initially participated in the research. During the research, the first time Hua saw her own teaching in the videos, she was surprised. She said, "How astonishing! Why did I talk in such a harsh tone? Perhaps I am not democratic enough when teaching students. I feel I am still authoritative." These words of Hua implied her idea and practice of obeying the authority were inconsistent. It seemed to her that her values at that moment were in the state of conflict. In terms of our data, Hua was a teacher who was concerned most with the discipline in the classroom, obeyed the school regulations, and asked students to respect teachers and rules, to be pious, and have a sense of shame. She also respected the experts regarding their opinions about mathematics curriculum and professional issues in mathematics teaching. Hua not only agreed with our descriptions but also thought that these were basic requirements to be an upright person. This indicated that Hua started to become aware of her values. Therefore, this seemed to suggest that Hua's process of understanding values was from unawareness, to conflict, and then to awareness, but lacking of the trial, understanding, and clarification stages in comparison with that of Ming's.

When she was asked if she would talk about original enlightenment with others ordinarily, she said,

> It depends on the opportunity. If the people I talked to would like to listen, I would talk about it. In fact, when there are people who really want to hear about it, I am very willing to share such nice teachings of Buddha. If the listeners don't accept it and you force them to do it, that will be what we said, the so-called unfavorable moment. Since the karma hasn't come yet, we wouldn't compel people to listen to the teachings of Buddha.

Under the influence of karma of Buddhism, Hua thought it was not necessary to discuss her values with other people openly. Hua always required students to concentrate in mathematics lessons. She told her students, "I don't like you to be absent-minded. Leo has been concentrating recently!" Hua would tell the intern teacher to remind students of being attentive in teaching and to say something like, "Listen carefully, class! Everyone should pay careful attention!" Her students and even the parents of her students all knew she demanded students to concentrate. For example, one student wrote, "We moved on quietly and then heard the tweet and moo. I then realized I could get everything done well as long as I quiet down in the composition about treasure hunting in fieldtrips." He also wrote, "As long as you pay attention to seek, to listen and to see, you would find lots of treasures and learn plenty of knowledge." In a parent-teacher meeting, the parents agreed "to encourage students to concentrate in doing things in cooperation with the teacher." All the information suggested Hua was very willing to share and discuss in public these values related to her teaching. Although Hua was a teacher willing to talk about her values with others, what she would like to make public was not the pedagogical aspect of the value but religious.

Once Hua asked several students to try, but yet no one could solve, a mathematics question; she then pointed to a student and said, "Good Horse, you have known. Go ahead and explain it." Through interviews, later we learned that Hua told students a story beforehand, in which a Good Horse was compared to a person with foresight. In addition to this story, Hua had told us many different stories in the Sutras. She said she usually told students those stories to cultivate the philosophy of self-improvement. Hua used metaphors in her teaching and these metaphors were related to self-improvement and Buddhism. Unlike Ming's case, we hardly heard her talk about any metaphors related to mathematics teaching, neither did we see Hua communicate her teaching values to others by using teaching incidents.

It is possible that this was because Hua was a Buddhist but not an efficient value communicator for public, or, she was not inclined to communicate her teaching values to others with mathematics teaching events.

Considering Hau's willingness to know the research theme, her current state of recognition about values, and that she was not a pedagogical value communicator, it seems that the teacher does not quite realize her own values of mathematics and pedagogy. She might be not quite sure of the values that she had before the interviews, but becoming more aware of them after such interviews. In this case, in comparison with the case of Ming, Hau might be still in the process of value clarification.

4. THE RELEVANCE OF VALUE CLARIFICATION AND MATHEMATICS TEACHING

Two corresponding forms of changes in classroom teaching were salient. A higher degree of pedagogical change is observed in Ming's case and a lower degree of change in teaching practices is shown by Hua. In this section, the relationship between the extent of value clarification and its effects on classroom teaching will be discussed. Moreover, the conjecture, *the more mathematics teachers understand about their own pedagogical value positions, the more flexible they will be in their thinking about, and practice in, their classroom teaching of mathematics*, will also be examined.

4.1 Higher Degree of Change in Classroom Teaching: The Case of Ming

Incidents referring to the movement of Ming's pedagogical thinking and action after his values having been clarified will be used to examine the conjecture above. In the discussion of teaching mathematical induction lessons focussing on how to assist the low achievement students, we found a pedagogical shift in Ming's classroom teaching, moving from the way of mathematics teaching that he valued previously to adjust for the students' needs of learning. He professed that,

> Having been involved in this research project for two years, I have also realized that I might have to modify the teaching strategies that I used, to a more *flexible* way in order to fulfil need of students who are in a lower achievement group. I would say that although it is not possible for me at this stage to value other values with which I do not agree, however, I would *try to refine my strategies and sequences of teaching to adjust to the students' background.* I used activities that I have used in the section of mathematical induction. In other words, I would say that it is *only strategy changes rather than value changes.*

Is the protocol above suggesting that the teacher becomes more flexible after pedagogical values have been clarified? Values are one of the most stable characteristics that mathematics teachers have (for example, Bishop, 1991; Raths et al., 1987; Swadener & Soedjadi, 1988); however, does this mean that the social context of learning and teaching could not play a role in re-shaping teachers' values?

Several substantial pedagogical refinements have been found recently in Ming's classroom teaching. One shift concerned his attitudes toward the educational responsibility for student learning. He argued that teachers should be fully responsible for the process and outcomes of student learning, as he said,

> I think that I have to take *more responsibility for student learning.* I think teachers should be *fully responsible* for students' educational outcomes. I once had a thought that teachers should only take *half of the responsibility,* till very recently when I found some of my students were interested in the invited speaker's talk on some occasions, while on other occasions they were bored. I started to think if this was the speaker's responsibility to make the audience feel interested? Therefore, I think the *responsibilities for students' learning outcomes are all mine.*

To take this idea into account in teaching, he then modified the strategy and sequence of teaching the mathematical induction section this year, although it was similar to what he used before, but he developed a more flexible and refined way of presenting the concept. Four aspects of refinement were observed in his teaching this year. Firstly, he tried to interview several students after the five lessons have been taught for re-confirming students' perception of his teaching. In other words, Ming wanted to know "What have the students learned and perceived in his lessons?"— a question that he has asked himself occasionally but never put into action to collect students' actual reactions to check his rationales of teaching and education— in terms of re-examining student learning outcomes. The four interview questions were:

1. Did you learn anything during the lessons of mathematical induction?
2. Did you feel anything pleasant in learning the concept?
3. Did you find any difficulties about learning the concept through these lessons?
4. Could you tell me what is mathematical induction for you?

Having got a highly positive response from the five sample students, he then said, "I am now very sure that I have passed and taught to my students what I wanted them to learn, although this idea was not considered seriously before." We then asked if this movement changed any value in him. He replied that,

> in order to involve the low achievement students in a *feeling* that the process of learning mathematical knowledge (in this case it means the concept of mathematical induction) may be *of interest* and they can easily *get access to* the knowledge without difficulties. I can't say it is nothing to do with the values that I have, however, I did try to give my students access to *the profits* (this means values in terms of the researcher's terminology) that I had expected through these lessons.

The second alternation was to use more familiar language for the students, such as, initial incentive and chain reaction to explain two steps of the concept "N=1" and "If N=k is ok, then N=k+1 is also sustained." He said, "The closer we use the language that our students' have to explain the ideas the better the concept might be understood by the students." Thirdly, as he recognizes the many difficulties with which his students might be confronted in learning the concept such as "How can the assumption N=k be sustained?' Ming then separated the natural numbers into two groups, in which set A consists of the numbers that meet the assumption, and the other set B includes those numbers that don't meet the assumption. There is at least one number (N=1) in set A, and he then explains how A is equal to N. This setting then helps him to guide his students to recognize that the assumption is plausible and should be true in the end by infinite iteration. Finally, before he taught the students the forms of mathematical induction, Ming asked them to write down their naïve ideas in proving the statement, using their own way of explanation or proof which is not necessarily formal. Then, he re-phrased those students' explanations, followed by introducing the forms of mathematical induction according to such student explanations. It was in this sense that the teacher learned to adapt his approach of teaching to student needs by refining his former teaching sequence and strategy.

The underlying rationales of doing this, for Ming, are closely related to the program of implementing the pedagogical values that he professed previously about those low achievement students. He wants to give his students access to, and enjoyment of, the activity of learning mathematics that is easy to know. He said in the interview "these are "*the hot points*" that I was intending to pass to my students through those teaching activities." In this sense, he seems to prize very much what he values in his classroom teaching and he wants to carry out this program even for low achievement students. He said,

> It is extremely important to modify my way of teaching in order to fulfil the students' needs, such as the approaches that I used this year in teaching mathematical induction. Since I have to *take full responsibility* for the learning outcomes of my students, including the low achievers. *There is no excuse for me for not doing so*, as I am the only person on whom they can count. If I hesitated to change my approach to teaching there would be no chance for them to *like mathematics and to learn mathematics confidently*.

He then followed by saying,

> I can't say it is nothing to do with the values that I have, however, it is *worth* to do so. Moreover, it is *the most important thing* for me in the teaching to get my students into the world of mathematics with *enjoyment, expectation*, and *pleasure*. I think this is exactly the point of which I want them to make sense.

In short, what Ming has done above in his later teaching of mathematical induction shows us the possibilities of pedagogical transition or teaching refinement for the teachers who are in a higher value clarification stage. To implement thoroughly those core pedagogical values and to take full responsibility for student learning, the teacher then modifies and also refines several strategies in teaching, for example, checking student perception of the mathematical concept taught; using familiar words that students might acknowledge better; revising and refining teaching steps to meet student needs; and connecting student's inner speech (thoughts and words) to their social speech with others. As a pedagogical value communicator, Ming becomes fully aware of his responsibility for learning and teaching, modifying his teaching activity to improve student ability and knowledge. This view of teacher accountability reflects also a movement in the professional growth in mathematics teaching of an expert teacher after pedagogical value clarification.

4.2 Lower Degree of Change in Classroom Teaching: The Case of Hua

To know the present status of student learning was the major purpose of assessment for Hua. On the one hand, she asked her students to solve the problems on their own and to share their strategies with peers, while on the other hand, she checked the assignments to figure out students' strategies. This helped the teacher to understand more about her students' mathematical thinking, and to modify her teaching strategies. For example, in the year of 1997 and 1999 Hua taught differently the following question: There are 10 peaches in one bag, and 10 persons share three bags of peaches, then how many bags of peaches for one person?

In 1997, Hua read the question three times. The third time she strongly emphasized the meaning of the word *bag*. She then wrote the whole question down on a small blackboard attached to the main chalkboard to remind the students. And then she spent about 15 minutes in solving this question. As a result, ten different mistakes were found. In 1999, Hua described and structured the question on the blackboard like this:

1 bag   10 peaches
3 bags   10 persons, no peach left
How many bags of peaches are there?

Then, by contrast, she required the students to write down their solution procedures and to explain the strategies of solving the problem to other students. A total of 9 minutes and 20 seconds was used in this activity. As a result, only two mistakes were found.

The above difference in teaching strategies seemed to be related to the teacher's knowledge about her students having trouble with the key idea of unit derived from the teaching activity in 1997. She wrote down the key concepts of the question on blackboard instead of the whole question, in order to make clear the main idea of the question. Having known the student difficulties with distinguishing unit, she figured out a different teaching approach this year. To discuss the relationship of packs and towels with students and to reinforce their concepts of unit, she used the following example as the pre-lesson exercise: "Five persons share one towel pack of 5 towels inside, then how many packs of towel will one person get?"

In 1997, she did not realize the question would help students to distinguish the relationship between units; therefore, more students made mistakes. Two value statements concerning the role of assessment in teaching that Hua described were "assessment is part of teaching process" and "the aim of assessment is to know the status of student learning." Thus, her knowledge of students' conceptions of unit might enable her to clarify the relationships between different units and then re-organize the question in 1999.

In 1999, she still taught her lessons in a question-and-answer way, and raised questions and asked   target students to answer. She seldom let the whole class answer or allowed group discussion. If students replied to or talked to the target student, or the target student peeped at another's answer, they would all be stopped by Hua. Though Hua arranged classroom seats by groups, she asked students to concentrate on their learning in mathematics individually. When we gave Hua our report on classroom observation, she disagreed with the descriptions of stressing individual learning over group discussions. Hua said that before she becomes more familiar with the new curriculum, she would not try to use group discussions. This, however, was contradicted by what we observed in her classes later. We wondered why she grouped students that way, and yet still asked students to solve the problems individually. She replied, "It is part of our school culture; if we do not arrange students' seats in groups, the principal will force us to do so."

Although Hua asked her students to concentrate, her demand originated from Buddhism. She hoped to reach the reinstatement of enlightenment through the process of concentration and then meditation. Thus, to her, concentration was a means of reinstating enlightenment. She didn't see concentration from the aspect of mathematics teaching. The concentration she required was individual concentration. The pedagogical aspect of concentration had not been clearly clarified for the teacher. And yet, the pedagogical concentration could expand to become a concentration of group discussion and the sharing of intelligence activities.

Therefore, the idea for her to require students to concentrate individually, and her way to practice this idea, didn't change in her teaching.

In summary, these differences in teachers' pedagogical value clarification seems to be related to the different degrees of change in classroom teaching, and clarifying teachers' pedagogical values might in this sense enhance the quality of mathematics teaching. As a result, the conjecture that "the more teachers understand about their own value positions the better teachers they will be" (Bishop, 1999, p. 5), would in this sense be partially sustained. However, for the teachers who are at the stage of higher value clarification but lower teaching change, the assumption might be rejected. In other words, the assumption will not be sustained for the teacher in a high value clarification position who refuses to modify his or her teaching strategy and sequence to adapt student needs. Hence, the conjecture, *the more mathematics teachers understand about their own pedagogical value positions the more flexible they will be in their thinking about, and practice in the classroom teaching of mathematics*, seems to be partially justified in terms of our two teacher cases.

5. PEDAGOGICAL VALUES IN MATHEMATICS TEACHER EDUCATION

What implications for teacher education do we learn from the understanding of teachers' value clarification processes? In what ways might we assist mathematics teachers to clarify their own value positions? How could we educate teachers about certain educational values? These are the questions that we will elaborate here. Some useful ideas for the development of teacher education programs through values will be brought out, and the difficulties of doing so will also be discussed.

5.1 On Value Clarification

The case of high pedagogical value clarification, described earlier, includes a *five stages of cognitive movement* relating to suspicion, awareness, trial, understanding, and clarification; a *three interactive activity of value transformation* consisting of dialogue, communication, and pedagogical reflection; and a *two mental characteristics of value communicator* concerning narration and metaphoring.

The three social interactive activities, enabling a teacher's identities from an implicit pedagogical value carrier to an explicit pedagogical value communicator, play the central role in teachers' value clarification. Moreover, the effectiveness of such a value transformation process is subject to teachers' ability in using narration and metaphoring. These two mental characteristics of a value communicator are very similar to those of the teachers who use exemplars and analogues to explain mathematical ideas. In other words, when values are explicit, mathematics teachers are capable of explaining their ideas of mathematics and pedagogy by using narratives and metaphors derived from critical teaching incidents.

On the other hand, the five stages of value clarification suggest a probable way of educating student teachers through different developmental stages. The two mental characteristics of value clarification might act as catalysts enabling teachers' values to become explicit. The cases of high and low value clarification describe a spectrum of mathematics teachers' value transform.

Moreover, adapting one's teaching strategy to meet students' needs, refining the classroom activity to assist student learning, and taking full responsibility for their educational outcomes show the extent of teachers' decisive intentions in implementing certain pedagogical values. In a way this also shows, to the outsiders, how much the teacher cherishes his or her own values in mathematics and pedagogy. To reflect this cognitive aspect of prizing values, the teacher modifies the forms and sequence of teaching activity in order to involve more students in understanding the concepts of mathematical induction.

5.2 On Teacher Education

Some researchers have argued for the need to promote high quality mathematics teachers and mathematics teaching through the awareness of the significant role that values play in teaching (for example, Bishop, 1999). However, several issues concerning the possibility of educating mathematics teachers about pedagogical values should be considered cautiously.

First of all, one effect derived from the process of pedagogical value clarification is to enhance teachers' abilities to reflect and to communicate personal views or thoughts about mathematics teaching and learning with others such as colleagues and students. This, then, might improve teachers' professional growth. Therefore, we suggest that the process of pedagogical value clarification is one mechanism for improving the professional development of mathematics teachers. Another effect is that this process might increase teachers' willingness to discuss their concepts of mathematical knowledge and ideas about mathematics teaching with others. Then, an expert mathematics teacher with these abilities and willingness is expected to be a better mentor. Moreover, the more we know about the characteristics and mechanism of teachers' value clarification process the better we could get access to the process of internalization of teachers' values.

The above understandings might be useful in designing the relevant program of teacher education through cognitive change and value clarification. The three catalyst activities that play the crucial roles in transforming a *pedagogical value carrier* to a *pedagogical value communicator* can be re-designed into relevant learning activities for mathematics teachers, mentors, and teacher educators in order to clarify their own values and to become value communicators. In this case, two mental features of pedagogical value clarification may operate as criteria to examine how much better communicators they would be. The cases of high and low value clarification and their relation to classroom instructional practices seem to indicate a plausible path of value transformation in teacher's professional growth.

Moreover, descriptions of teachers' sayings and doings, teachers' own teaching videos, and the dialogue interview process are three sources that might act as materials for identifying teachers' pedagogical values, since these value descriptions may encourage teachers to inform their teaching behaviors and lead to a higher value clarification status. To reflect on one's own teaching might help teachers to re-examine their value-related activities and to revise the content and approaches of conducting such activities. Finally, mathematics teacher educators may use the approach of value interview to clarify their student teachers' pedagogical values. In this case, the former two materials may act as the bases for developing and refining value-related activities, and the third as an approach for clarifying those values.

Therefore, the assumption, *the more we understand about the processes, features, and mechanism of teachers' pedagogical value clarification the better position we will take to develop relevant programs of educating mathematics teachers through pedagogical values*, seems to be apparent.

The second issue has to do with the characteristics of pedagogical values. Values have been argued as entailing an experiential, situated, and rationalized nature (Lave & Wenger, 1991; Raths et al., 1987; Stewart, 1987). The pedagogical values that teachers have are derived from and situated in the specific classroom teaching incidents. These incidents reveal the very nature of the teacher's daily teaching activity which is experientially based and knowledge situated. Having been derived from a long-term process of selection and evaluation, these incidents have become rationalized. In the case of Ming, these incidents became his personal resource for talking and sharing ideas about mathematics and teaching with people through narration and metaphoring. The teacher who is like a preacher, persuading people according to those ideas of mathematics teaching which are value-laden, is very difficult to be counter-persuaded.

The case of Hua, however, suggests that the professional development of teachers might be facilitated by the meditation in certain religions such as Buddhism, and the change in teachers' attitudes toward mathematics might also be anticipated through such meditation. Her pedagogical values were closely related to the religious faiths connected to two of the traditional and contemporary Taiwanese ethical values that Yang (1994) suggests. For instance, obeying authority stresses the personal roles of obedience and the social conditions that should be in an ordered, esteemed, and counted-on authority, and self-reliance impacts on one's independence of behavior and life management. In this case, teachers' pedagogical values may in a sense relate to religious faiths and social-ethical values. Therefore, should teacher education program take the basic tenets of Buddhism into account? And would that be plausible or effective in conducting such a program for mathematics teachers?

Further, values, as teachers' pedagogical identities of mathematics and pedagogy and as the products of valuing which represent their personal characteristics of the profession and status of teachers, are thought to be purposeful and evaluative in nature. The nature of pedagogical values discussed above raises the concerns of value change and value education of mathematics teachers, since, to educate or change certain values of teachers means to challenge the nature and mechanism of valuing. This idea does not seem plausible in the case of Ming, who is an expert teacher and whose values have been evaluated through a long-term process of pedagogical reflection. Hua, who is at the stage of low value clarification and teaching changes, has a higher possibility of success in professional development, perhaps through religious aspects.

The third issue concerns the plausible approaches of educating mathematics teachers about values. The crucial role that the degrees of awareness and willingness play in educating teachers' affective and evaluative mental quantities such as beliefs, has been suggested in the relevant researches (for example, Cobb, Wood, Yackel, & McNeal, 1992). Yet, on the contrary, it seems difficult to educate values through lecturing and demonstration, emphasizing a passively accepting point of view which is in contrast to the experiential, situational, and rational nature of values. Instead, values might be replaced or transformed through the self-developing or self-identifying processes associated with specific value-related teaching activities such as "The Hanoi Tower" (Chin & Lin, 2000). In this case, varied forms of pedagogical value might co-exist in the same value system. In the light of value clarification, the activities and criteria suggested in the previous section might be helpful for developing such approaches. Moreover, teachers' pedagogical values might be informed through experiencing the faiths of "social" religions such as Buddhism.

The above arguments are not saying that the pedagogical values of mathematics teachers are impossible to be changed or educated. However, it does mean that researchers should be more cautious in trying to apply the values that they think mathematics teachers should have. We, as researchers, might better conceive values as one part of a teacher's professional identity and personality.

ACKNOWLEDGEMENTS

Particular thanks are given to the two participant teachers (Ming and Hua), who have been kind and open to share their experiences and views with us. We also owe our colleagues Dr. Yuh-Yin Wu Wang and Dr. Chao-Jung Wu for their comments on the early drafts of this chapter and for their being involved in the two research studies for years. Also to our assistants Miss Huang and Miss Yang, who have done a great job with the audio-video tape translations. Finally, our thanks go to the National Science Council (NSC) for funding the research. The arguments in this chapter are the authors' own responsibility and do not necessary reflect the views of NSC.

REFERENCES

Bishop, A. J. (1991). Mathematical Values in the Teaching Process. In Bishop, et al.(Eds.), *Mathematical knowledge: Its growth through teaching*, Dordrecht: Kluwer.

Bishop, A. J. (1999). Educating student teachers about values in mathematics education. In F. L. Lin (Ed.), *Proceedings of the 1999 International Conference on Mathematics Teacher Education*. Taipei, Taiwan.

Brown, C.A. & Borko, H. (1992). Becoming a mathematics teacher. In D. A. Grouws (Ed.), *Handbook of research on mathematics teaching and learning*. New York: Macmillan.

Chin, C., & Lin, F. L. (1999). *A value-oriented mathematics teaching*. Paper presented at the Annual Meeting of Mathematics Education Research Projects Funded by NSC, Center for Teacher Education, National Tsing Hua University. (In Chinese)

Chin, C. & Lin, F. L. (2000). A case study of a mathematics teacher's pedagogical values: Using a methodological framework of interpretation and reflection. *Proceedings of the National Science Council Part D: Mathematics, Science, and Technology Education, 10*(2), 90-101.

Clark, C. M., & Peterson, P. L. (1986). Teachers' thought processes. In M. C. Wittrock (Ed.), *Handbook of research on teaching (3rd ed.)*. New York: Macmillan.

Cobb, P., Wood, T., Yackel, E., & McNeal, B. (1992). Characteristics of classroom traditions: An interactional analysis. *American Educational Research Journal, 29*(3), 576-604.

Committee of High School Entrance Examination – Taipei (CHSEE). (1999). Annual research report. Taipei.

Committee of University Entrance Examination (CUEE). (1999). Annual work report. Taipei.Jenkins, R. (1996). *Social identity*. London: Routledge.

Jenkins, R. (1996). *Social identity*. London: Routledge.

Krathwohl, D. R., Bloom, B. S., & Masia, B. B. (1964). *Taxonomy of educational objectives, the classification of educational goals: Handbook 2: Affective domain*. New York: Longmans.

Lave, J., & Wenger, E. (1991). *Situated learning: Legitimate peripheral participation*. Cambridge: Cambridge University Press.

Leu, Y. C. (2000). An elementary school teacher presents values in mathematics teaching. *Chinese Journal of Science Education, 8*(1), 57-76. (In Chinese)

Liou, Z. (1997). *Religion and education*. Taipei: Zan-Chung Publisher.

Mcleod, D. B.(1992). Research on affect in mathematics education: A reconceptualization. In C. A. Grouws (Ed.), *Handbook of research on mathematics teaching and learning*. New York: Macmillan.

Moscovici, S. (1981). On social representation. In J. P. Forgas (Ed.), *Social cognition: Perspectives on everyday understanding*. London: Academic Press.

Raths, L. E., Harmin, M., & Simon, S. B.(1987). Selections from values and teaching. In P. F. Carbone (Ed.), *Value theory and education*. Malabar: Krieger.

Stewart, J. S.(1987). Clarifying values clarificaton: A critique. In P. F. Carbone, (Ed.), *Value theory and education*. Malabar: Krieger.

Swadener, M. & Soedjadi, R. (1988). Values, mathematics education, and the task of developing pupils' personalities: An indonesian perspective. *Educational Studies in Mathematics, 19*, 193-208.

Tajfel, H. (1978). Social categorisation, social identity and social comparison. In H. Tajfel (Ed.), *Differentiation between social groups: Studies in the social psychology of intergroup relations*. London: Academic Press.

Tajfel, H. (1981). Social stereotypes and social groups. In H. Tajfel (Ed.), *Human groups and social categories*. Cambridge: Cambridge University Press.

Tomlinson, P. & Quinton, M. (Eds.). (1986). *Values across the curriculum*. Lewes: The Falmer Press.

Vygotsky, L. S. (1978). *Mind in society*. Cambridge: Harvard University Press.

Vygotsky, L. S. (1986). *Thought and language*. Cambridge: The MIT Press.

Volkmor, B. C., Pasanella, A. L., & Raths, L. E. (1977). *Values in the classroom*. Columbus: Merrill. (Quoted from the Chinese Edition Translated by O and Lin (1986), *Values in the classroom*, Kaohsiung: Fu-Wen Publisher.)

Yang, K.S. (1994). Could tradition values and modern values be co-existed? In K.S.Yang(Ed.). *Chinese views of values: From a social science aspect*. Taipei: Kwei-Kuang Publisher. (In Chinese)

Chien Chin
Center for Teacher Education
National Tsing Hua University
Taiwan

Yuh-Chyn Leu
National Taipei Teachers' College
Taiwan

Fou-Lai Lin
National Taiwan Normal University
Taiwan

KONRAD KRAINER

TEACHERS' GROWTH IS MORE THAN THE GROWTH OF INDIVIDUAL TEACHERS: THE CASE OF GISELA

ABSTRACT. This paper tells the story of Gisela, a mathematics teacher and vice-principal at an Austrian urban secondary school. Reflections on her pre-service teacher education and her struggle for professional growth in her teaching career will be combined with more general reflections on the interconnection between the further development of individual teachers in their own classes and the situation and the further development of their school. We see that in the case of Gisela, and more generally too, the systematic enhancement of the quality of teaching in a country (in our case taking mathematics as the example) cannot build only on the professional development of selected individual teachers (although this is very important), but must seriously take into account the involvement of as many (mathematics) teachers as possible in their schools, their regions, and so forth, as well as other relevant stakeholders such as department heads, principals, superintendents, teacher educators, parents, and students. Moreover, teacher education cannot be confined to an approach that regards only the individual as the learner, but must as well include groups of teachers, whole schools, and even the whole educational system. To touch the full complexity of teacher education, we need to build a bridge between classroom development, school development, and the development of the whole educational system. Overall, Gisela's story is a plea for broadening our scope from an individualistic to a systemic one.

Stories play a decisive role in our understanding of the educational processes in the field of teacher education (see, for example, Cooney, 1999, pp. 1-2; Krainer & Goffree, 1999, pp. 229-230). One important reason is that stories build a bridge between *three learning levels* that are often unconnected with one another. Firstly, stories provide us with authentic evidence and holistic pictures of exemplary developments in the practice of teacher education. Secondly, through stories we can extend our theoretical knowledge about the complex processes of teacher education. Thirdly, and possibly most important of all, stories are starting points for our own reflection and promote insights into ourselves and our challenges, hopefully with consequences for our actions and beliefs in teacher education.

The following story reflects on a *mathematics teacher's career*, aiming not only at describing her *individual development* but also at sketching how it is interconnected with the *development of her school* and the whole *educational system in Austria*.

Gisela—the name I have given her in this story—is in her mid-fifties and has more than 20 years of teaching practice. She is married and has three daughters who have now all left home. During her nearly 30 years of employment in the Austrian school-system she stopped teaching only for several years of leave in order to take care of her three children. My reflections on her professional growth – with the

F.-L. Lin & T. J. Cooney (Eds.) Making Sense of Mathematics Teacher Education, 271—293.

major emphasis on the last 15 years – will be combined with more general reflections on the interconnection between the further development of individual teachers in their own classes and the situation and the further development of their school. This will be accompanied by some considerations on efforts by educational systems to improve the quality of teaching.

Gisela has read the whole text of this paper and accepts that it is a viable description of her development. I dedicate this text to her and to all other teachers all over the world that do their best in continuously questioning and improving their quality of teaching and try to spread this attitude and competence to other colleagues and even to their whole school, while recognising that everyone has to find his or her own professional way, but that it is helpful to do it co-operatively as "critical friends" (see, for example, Altrichter, Posch, & Somekh, 1993, pp. 58-61).

1. MEETING GISELA

I first met Gisela in April 1985 when she came to the first seminar of the two-year *professional development program PFL-Mathematics* (see, for example, Fischer, Krainer, Malle, Posch, & Zenkl, 1985; Krainer & Posch, 1996; Krainer, 1999). She was one of the about 30 mathematics teachers from all over Austria that participated in that university program. I was one of the program leaders, and in addition, I was one of the staff members who was responsible for supervising the regional group in which Gisela was one of the about ten members. In sum, Gisela and I met eight times during the PFL-program 1985-1987. Her initiative for a further development of the quality of her school brought us together again in 1995, and led among other things to a two-and-a-half-day *seminar with the group of mathematics teachers* in 1996. Three *additional seminars* for this group and one for the whole school were held in the years 1997-1999; a further seminar for the group of mathematics teachers is planned for the year 2000. In addition to the data we gathered in the years 1985-1987 and 1995-1999 (protocols, field notes, evaluation), and some reports by Gisela and her colleagues in the annual school reports, I conducted in early 1999 a telephone interview with her. The focus of that interview was on Gisela's curriculum vitae, in particular putting an emphasis on her pre-service teacher education, her first experiences as a teacher, her participation in the PFL-program, and her career as a mathematics teacher and vice-principal. Since 1999 I have contacted her on several occasions for further feedback on current developments in her teaching and her school.

Why did Gisela take part in that professional development program and where did she come from?

1.1 Gisela's Pre-service Education at the University: A Pervading Influence

Gisela was born in 1946, one year after the end of the Second World War, in a rural region in Austria and grew up in a large and rather poor family. She intended to become a primary teacher but when she finished her studies she changed her mind and wanted to become a *mathematics and geography teacher in a secondary school.*

She therefore went to university, where she financed her studies by giving private lessons.

Her *teacher education at the university* was nearly completely dedicated to the study of the subject matter (mathematics and geography), as was the case no matter whether someone studied for a diploma or wanted to become a teacher. The only exception concerning her mathematics study was a seminar where the student teachers observed some mathematics classes and were introduced to the technique of calculating with the slide rule. The study of pedagogical issues was confined to elements of the history and theory of pedagogy. This was a big contrast to Gisela's *primary teacher education*, where she had learned to work with groups and had become familiar, for example, with the Montessori method. The mathematics teaching she experienced at the university was a pure mono-culture: one frontal teaching unit followed the next, and there were only some lessons where the students had to show their individual attempts to solve mathematical tasks. The student teachers were conveyed the knowledge in a broadcast-metaphor with nearly no content-related interaction among the students.

In 1971, Gisela finished her studies in geography, married, and began to teach mathematics at an urban *higher secondary school* in Austria. Although she had not yet finished her mathematical studies at that time (which she did in 1974), Gisela – like many other teachers – were offered a job as a teacher due to the immense shortage of mathematics teachers.

At her first school, Gisela primarily taught mathematics from grades 9 to 12. Although she felt *mathematically well equipped*, she *lacked pedagogical and didactic background knowledge* for teaching students of that age. As she had learned at the university, she used to teach the subject frontally, sometimes asking single students to work at the blackboard, neither of which allowed much communication among the class. This was partially also caused by the fact that Gisela had to work with about 36 students in small classrooms. Many of Gisela's students had poor marks and results in mathematics. Her *learning experience at the university* had a *great impact on her teaching* at school, and the learning and teaching culture at the university had a *deep socialising effect* on her. It was as if initiating learning higher mathematics in any other way was unimaginable.

There was practically *no professional communication among the teachers*, most of whom remained as *lone fighters* in their classes keeping their problems as well as their strengths to themselves. The longer Gisela taught, the more frustrated she became. She wanted to find opportunities to reflect on her teaching and to change it but she did not find adequate opportunities to do so. The in-service courses were rather traditional and did not meet this challenge. She attended courses for "communication for adults" in order to have a second choice for a career outside the school. Gisela seriously considered leaving the teaching profession.

So far, the story shows the *pervading influence* of Gisela's pre-service education at the university on her teaching, and the *interconnectedness* of the systems "university" and "school." The cycle "student teacher -> teacher -> (some of teacher's students later become a) student teacher -> ..." produces and reproduces patterns of attitudes and beliefs. It is essential to investigate this cycle more carefully for implications on both systems and to launch projects where this cycle can be designed constructively. An important feature seems to be the culture of the organisation (university, school, ...) in which individuals work and live. For example, Gisela's university was an organisation with a lone-fighter culture that in turn contributed to the situation that most teachers – like Gisela – left this organisation socialised as a lone fighter. At her school, Gisela experienced the same culture, each teacher focused on his or her own teaching. There was no sufficient professional communication among colleagues and no adequate internal support system for young teachers like Gisela. Although she had not yet finished her mathematical studies at that time, she taught mathematics due to the immense shortage of mathematics teachers. This general condition of the educational system intensified the lone fighter situation: There was no chance for her to move gradually into her new role as a teacher, as she immediately had to take responsibility and had to concentrate on her individual situation in order to master it as good as possible.

1.2 Gisela's Participation in a Professional Development Program

Gisela looked for opportunities to change her situation. She became curious when a mathematics teacher at a neighbouring school told her that she was participating in a *professional development program* for mathematics teachers based on a "teacher as researcher" philosophy (PFL-Mathematics 1982-84). Her colleague also stressed that she was learning a great deal there and she strongly recommended Gisela to attend the next run. Fortunately, the Austrian ministries responsible for education and research prolonged this pilot-project. Therefore, Gisela and Werner – a new young colleague at her school – were able to attend the two year university program 1985-87 together with about 30 other mathematics teachers from secondary schools in Austria.

In April 1985, Gisela came to the first of the three one-week *PFL-seminars* (in addition, over the two years, the participants attended five one-and-a-half-day regional meetings and carried out teaching experiments at their schools which were discussed at the seminars and at the regional meetings). As preparatory work for this first seminar Gisela brought with her a documentation of group work in one of her classes. The seven-page long report shows Gisela's wish to carefully observe and understand students' actions and to promote students' self-assessment of their work (e.g., they were asked to write down their views in protocols). Her report – like the reports by the other participants – was shared at this seminar in a regional group of about ten people, supported by two staff members. She felt that professional communication among colleagues is a central feature of her efforts to bring about change. These *regional groups* became for Gisela and many others a continuous, homelike, protected, and powerful learning environment within the program.

Gisela liked her regional group and voluntarily she became the host of the first (of the five) group meetings. She reported on her attempts to put more emphasis on the visualisation and interpretation of graphs, looking for interconnections to geography (her second subject). Gisela stressed that the interview activities at the first seminar enhanced her patience to wait for students' responses and to reflect on her teaching. Among others, she also motivated the students to work autonomously with the school book in order to investigate things on their own.

The fourth regional meeting of Gisela's group was extended to a four-day work and family meeting in June 1986, starting with a barbecue on a participant's patio. Gisela came with her husband and her three daughters. Besides the professional program, the meeting also included other events such as long walks together, swimming in a nearby lake, or self-organised circus attractions by the children of the participants and the staff members. One important issue of this meeting was the reflection on the catastrophe of Tschernobyl, on radioactivity and on dealing with this issue in mathematics teaching. The participants also reported about their activities at school. Gisela, for example, gave further insight into her teaching experiments with the extensive use of group work. For the next seminar her wish was for a working group on the issue "project work."

The biggest part of the third (and last) one-week PFL-seminar was dedicated to talks by participants on their studies, to working groups and to follow-up activities after the program. Gisela was not among the 17 participants who presented results of their systematic reflections on their practice. She did consider it, but finally she hesitated and did not. However, she really liked the reports by her colleagues and sometimes wished that she too had taken the plunge into the cold water.

Many personal benefits, but hardly any impact on other teachers: Professional development processes need time and support. During our recent interview, twelve years after having attended the professional development program, Gisela came to regard it as the *"rescue for her teaching career."* During the program, she never articulated that she really considered to leave the teaching profession. Of course, we had asked the participants for their reasons to join the program, but there have not been such dramatic explanations. This shows that we should be reluctant in interpreting statements of participants in evaluations referring to running programs. Gisela needed a lot of time in order to be able to have enough distance to see the situation from a more neutral point of view. In the interview, Gisela indicated that she had learned enough methods and ways of reflecting on and changing her teaching in the program. She also stressed that she had become more self-confident in respect to her didactic thinking and acting, a consequence which she had not expected before. Furthermore, she also learned to *"present my views and arguments* with *greater self-confidence."* Finally, Gisela became aware that she can *"learn a great deal from collaborating with colleagues,"* but nevertheless, she has to go her *"own way"* since specific competence cannot be transferred from other people's minds to her mind. As a consequence, Gisela increasingly also regarded her students as producers of *their* own knowledge, and not only as consumers of *her* knowledge. She introduced new modes of instruction where her students worked together and jointly reflected on their activities. However, sometimes general conditions, such as classes with more than 30 students, hindered her efforts and she was not successful in achieving her pedagogical ideals in practice.

However deep the influence of the professional development program was on Gisela's actions and beliefs, it had hardly any impact on other colleagues' teaching. On the contrary, certain other teachers at her school were irritated by her teaching experiments and showed some *resistance* to talk about teaching issues. Nevertheless,

Gisela had a good contact with her young colleague Werner who participated in the same program. They supported each other as "critical friends" but were relatively isolated among the other mathematics teachers.

In the interview, Gisela, looking back, stated that changing one's own teaching demands *"a lot of energy for several years"* and that this is also a reason why innovations concerning one's own teaching can only slowly have an impact on other colleagues. *Professional development processes need time and support.* The challenge for teachers is thus to be *lifelong learners* (see, for example, Fullan & Stiegelbauer, 1991, p. 289; Day, 1999).

The story of Gisela so far demonstrates that professional development programs might cause *considerable progress for individual teachers* (and even rescue them from burnout or from leaving the teaching profession) but *do not necessarily have any impact on other teachers* in their school. If professional communication among teachers is not an important feature of the culture of a school (see, for example, Hord & Boyd, 1995, p. 10, cited in Loucks-Horsley, 1998, p. 182), innovations by individual teachers remain limited to their heads and classrooms. Even *a pair of colleagues* – like Gisela and Werner in our case – co-operating successfully might not be enough as a *critical mass*. Similar experiences were reported in Borasi, Fonzi, Smith, & Rose (1999, p. 75) pointing out that their professional development program had additional benefits when not just pairs but a critical mass of teachers from the same school participated in the program. Gisela and Werner, at that time, were not able to take a *leadership role* among the group of mathematics teachers, due above all to the fact that they were too much involved in their own learning process. Nevertheless, their ability to act as critical friends for each other was sufficient to promote their own professional growth, as we will later see in Gisela's story (and in the story of Werner, who later became a regional co-ordinator of mathematics teachers).

Teachers' growth is a complex process. The story also shows that *teachers' growth* is not a linear progression. On the contrary, it is a *complex and continuous learning process* with a variety of local and individual phases of progress, stagnation, and regression. We should be cautious in regarding teachers' professional development as an individual's change from "bad" to "good" teaching, for example, believing that there is some kind of static perfection (therefore terms like "further development of teachers" or "teachers in transition" —see, for example, Fennema & Nelson, 1997— seem to be more viable than "teacher change"). This is in line with the research of Wilson & Goldenberg (1998, p. 274) which followed a teacher's intellectual development using Perry's scheme, and which reported that the result cannot be seen as *"an individual's dramatic transformation from rigid, dualistic practice to flexible, experimentalist practice,"* but instead as *"a less operatic, but admirable, human story of a successful teacher's struggle to become more effective because of his belief that his students are worth the effort."* Further, it should also be mentioned, that *professional growth* always goes hand in hand with *personal growth* and *social growth*, and that these are interactive and interdependent (see, for example, Bell & Gilbert, 1994, cited and discussed in Even, 1999, p. 16; Halai, 1998, p. 312).

It is not easy for individual teachers who have participated in professional development programs to find colleagues who really want to join in their efforts to improve, or for they themselves to have enough motivation and perseverance to realise changes in the short or long run. Furthermore, innovative action at schools is often regarded rather critically and causes open or hidden resistance or opposition. Nevertheless, engaging in *long-term in-service education programs* (see, for example, Grouws & Schultz, 1996; Borasi et al., 1999), or research projects (see, for example, Crawford & Adler, 1996; Jaworski, 1998) which place an emphasis on professional communication and co-operation of teachers through promoting the discussion of their *investigations into their own teaching*, more efficiently supports teachers' efforts to bring about change. That such a program gives birth to self-organised groups which remain together for a longer period (see, for example, Krainer, 1994) is more an exception of the rule. However, a lot of participants – like Gisela and Werner – act as *"agents of change"* in their region. But it has to be added that professional development seminars and programs never can reach all teachers. It is also often argued that participants on such seminars are "always the same" and those who really would need some improvement do not come.

Looking at alternative strategies to foster teachers' growth. All these arguments show that curriculum reforms, pre-service teacher education, and individual-oriented professional development programs – though very important – cannot be the only strategic intervention to improve the teaching of a subject in a national educational system. Alternative approaches which recently have become more popular are *school-based in-service courses* (for groups of teachers of a specific subject or combination of subjects, for example mathematics and science), *professional networks* of teachers and researchers, and *whole school development programs*. Concerning efforts of whole schools to grow professionally it is essential that the further development of the school as an organisation be interconnected to the further development of the teaching of subjects. It will be interesting to see how the story of Gisela relates to that challenge.

2. GISELA'S NEW SCHOOL AND HER NEW ROLES AS DEPARTMENT HEAD AND VICE-PRINCIPAL

When Gisela heard that a *new secondary school* in the city was to be opened in 1988, she immediately felt that this could be a new chance for her. She applied for a position as mathematics and geography teacher at this school and was lucky to get it in 1989. Gisela was *open for a change*, aimed at working with children at the age of 10 to 14 and was interested in helping to *build up a new school*. However, she was also sad because she lost Werner as a partner next door, and she was unsure whether she could establish an equally good relationship with other colleagues at the new school.

2.1 The Culture of the New School

In 1989, when Gisela joined the new secondary school (grades 5 to 12) in its second year of existence, the teaching staff was relatively small. Due to the challenges of a new school and the smallness of the staff there was a relatively *large amount of communication and collaboration* among the colleagues. Looking back, many colleagues saw this time as a kind of period with a relatively strong and jointly lived *"foundation spirit."* This brought some advantages for the early teachers and promoted the development of the school. This, however, partially also turned into a disadvantage when more and more new teachers came to the school and had to cope with the socially constructed and relatively fixed "foundation spirit" of the first teachers.

Gisela was among this first generation. In contrary to her old school, she was an "unknown quantity" and she liked not being "burdened with a specific image." At the very beginning, there were only three other mathematics teachers at this school. At her school, Gisela became the "custodian for mathematics," which is an Austrian lightweight form of a *head of department* of mathematics. She liked to have the opportunity now also to teach students in the lower secondary grades 5 to 8. Although the group of mathematics teachers was very small, there was hardly any professional communication about teaching among them at the very beginning; most communication was dedicated to school-organisational issues.

In 1991, two years after her start at this new school, Gisela was appointed as the "administrator" of the school by the regional school board. This position at secondary schools in Austria can be compared with that of a *vice-principal* of a school, being responsible primarily for administrative agenda, but also with the duty to teach some classes (dependent on the size of the school). Due to her new function and role, Gisela had to learn a lot of new things (regulations, computer software for developing time tables, etc.). Above all, her interest from now on was not only directed to improving her own teaching but increasingly also to contributing to the *further development of the whole school.*

Looking back, it is interesting that she initiated relatively few activities among the group of mathematics teachers, although she was their custodian. But there was no real tradition in Austria to do that. The custodians mostly dealt with administrative issues, whereas the teachers regarded themselves as *experts in their subjects* and worked as autonomous but lone fighters in their classrooms. The situation at Gisela's school was a typical example of that tradition.

In the organisational and school development literature terms like "professional bureaucracies," "expert organisations," or "fragmentary schools" are used to describe organisations where *experts* are more *committed to their expertise in a specific field* (for example, subjects in the case of secondary schools and universities, or domains like surgery in a hospital) than to the whole organisation (see, for example, Grossmann 1997). Austrian schools, universities, and hospitals, due to their *low degree of autonomy and decentralisation* until recent years, show a low but increasing level of individuals' corporate identity with the organisation in which they work. *Systematic reflection* and *networking*, if it existed, was traditionally more directed to colleagues *outside* the organisation than towards professional communication among the members *within* the organisation. Recently, this has been changing tremendously, in particular with regard to the school system. The increased autonomy and decentralisation gave rise to issues like the *quality of schools* and its comparability across their country. Studies like TIMSS accelerate this discussion, partially due to media reports which in many cases sketch only a superficial view of the situation. Nevertheless, TIMSS is a challenge and a chance to start a more open discussion about the quality of mathematics and science teaching in particular, but also more generally to reflect on the way in which a national educational system aims at establishing and promoting quality assurance and quality development.

2.2 A School Development Initiative Gives Birth to a Seminar for Mathematics Teachers

Gisela's school grew bigger and bigger and the vivid communication and co-operation decreased only slightly, but continuously. In addition, more and more things became routine and when the first students who had started in the lowest class (grade 5) came nearer to the highest class (grade 12) in order to pass the final examination, some parts of the teaching staff, the principal, and Gisela felt that the school would need a *refreshment*. Initiatives taken to start a school development process in the years around 1994 had no real success, however.

In 1995, Gisela was asked to find a way for a new attempt to revitalise the school development process. She remembered her good experiences with the PFL-program and contacted our department. We were interested because we saw the need not only to build on in-service teacher education when striving for the promotion of quality teaching in Austrian schools, but also to support whole school initiatives. It was arranged that a university team would support a team at the school to prepare a *professional development day* in October 1995 and that the presence of a well-known mathematics educator from the United States would be used to organise a two-and-a-half-day *seminar* in March 1996 for the group of mathematics teachers at this school. Gisela was happy that her relations with the PFL-people were being refreshed and promised a chance to initiate some change at her school, similar to her own experience.

The professional development day in October 1995 did not bring the expected success, namely a joint step of the whole teaching staff towards a renewal process. Some latent problems of the school which had been swept under the carpet came to light, but there was no chance of handling them in a really constructive way. Although working groups were initiated, Gisela, genuinely, was not really happy about the situation, as she had expected more concrete steps.

At that time, enhanced by this increased autonomy, more and more Austrian schools embarked upon similar attempts. Often it was a story of *enthusiastic individuals and groups* who experienced different kinds of *resistance from a considerable number of teachers*, and of a slow but continuous progress of schools in establishing realistic and joint steps towards improvement. The more schools were able to link the school development process with concrete improvements in teachers' classrooms and in the professional communication among the teachers, the more successful such attempts were. This assessment is supported by Fullan and Stiegelbauer (1991, p. 289) who argue that *"teacher development and school development must go hand in hand."*

2.3 The Preliminary Meeting and the First Seminar for the Mathematics Teachers

As fixed in the collaboration between the school and the university, six weeks before the seminar a *preliminary meeting* was held at the school. In an effort to encourage communication among the teachers in a reflective environment and to make their *different approaches to teaching* visible, the seven teachers were asked to think of a typical mathematics lesson they had taught over the last two weeks and describe the first five minutes of the lesson to the other teachers, then to identify those principles that guide their teaching, and finally to reflect on status quo and further developments of mathematics teaching at their school. The teachers' reflections gave a feeling for the heterogeneity of approaches among the participants. Planning the seminar was a challenging *negotiation process.*

The *two-and-a-half-day seminar* in March 1996 for the group of mathematics teachers at Gisela's school was led by two mathematics educators, one from Austria and one from the United States. As agreed at a preliminary meeting, the seminar for the eight participants was based, like the PFL-program, on a *"teacher as researcher" philosophy* and covered three major issues: 1) joint planning, carrying out, observing, and analysing *interviews with students* in order to understand better how they see mathematics, mathematics teaching, and so forth; 2) joint planning, carrying out, observing, and analysing a *little experiment towards more "open" mathematics teaching* in order to experience new approaches (e.g. , the use of open-ended tasks), methods (e.g., team-teaching), and so forth; 3) investigating *interconnections between mathematics and other subjects* in order to experience the potential of bringing the real world into mathematics teaching. Although the seminar language was English and some participants – like Gisela – sometimes had difficulties to follow the discussion, the evaluation showed that most teachers benefited from the seminar considerably. One of the four participants who gave their feedback on the seminar in English, for example, wrote in the questionnaire: *"Learning happened in different dimensions: concerning the subject mathematics, concerning methods of teaching (routines, patterns, ...), concerning communication behaviour (teacher – students, teacher – teacher), concerning interaction in the group (developing personal trust, team spirit)."* Gisela highlighted *"the creation of a very constructive working climate"* and the *"scope of freedom for necessary communication"* among the teachers. She also indicated that she became more aware that *"students can acquire much of their knowledge without the help of the teacher when they know the goal and the reason behind their activities."* A young teacher who participated in the seminar, positively surprised by the efforts of more experienced colleagues who also reflected critically on their teaching and strove for new ideas, commented: *"Even older colleagues try out new things."*

Gisela was very happy about the success of the seminar. Some participants declared at the end of the seminar that they came with some scepticism, but finally they found it helpful that the design forced them to communicate among each other in this intensive way. One colleague stressed very openly: *"I feared that the seminar would only be Gisela's pet idea, and the others had to join it because she was in a more powerful position. But I enjoyed the seminar, and like the attitude of the group members towards each others. I am now ready for further activities..* Obviously the seminar contributed – through joint actions and reflections, and through networking of the autonomous beliefs and actions of the individual teachers – to the development of *"shared meaning"* (see Fullan & Stiegelbauer, 1991, p. 5).

2.4 Two "Miniatures" Showing the Importance of Organisational Factors and Joint Activities

Of course, all *innovations at schools* (like the activities in this seminar) have their *general organisational conditions* that can promote or hinder them tremendously. In the following I refer to *two examples of "miniatures"* that had an impact on the seminar. The *first* one deals with the organisational background of the seminar. Gisela as the vice-principal of the school successfully managed the challenging task of arranging for the many classes of the participants to be taught by other teachers for three days. In addition, the school had a good connection to the regional in-service education institute, which had to be convinced it was worth contributing financial resources to the seminar. It must be said that at that time in Austria it was very unusual for a group of mathematics teachers to be aiming at initiating school-based professional development and wanting to have financial support for that. This is a good example of an *interplay* between a creative setting of *internal general conditions* and the *use of external resources* to make possible a self-organised activity which contributes to the professional growth of a school.

A *second "miniature"* example emerged from a specific activity within the seminar. The participants were invited to look in pairs for good examples of interconnections between mathematics and other subjects out of sets of journals, books, and other material the seminar leaders brought with them. A particular *mathematics education journal* from which different volumes were chosen and analysed by different teachers was found as very fitting for the use of these teachers. Gisela and some other members of the group immediately went to the *principal* and persuaded him that this journal would contribute to the further development of mathematics at this school. The next time I visited the school the journal had been subscribed to and was prominently displayed in the school library.

In particular, this second "miniature" tells a small story of its own. *Firstly*, it shows on a *micro level* the *importance of the principal* when, for example, financial resources come into play. As usual in Austria, the custodian or the group did not have the autonomy to decide to purchase the journal. They had to go to the principal and to convince him. Certainly, it was an advantage that Gisela was the vice-principal and so could help the group to get what it wanted. From this small example of "micro politics" at schools we can see that the leading staff has a great influence on innovations at schools and their willingness to support such initiatives depends tremendously on a variety of factors. For example, a principal's decision might depend on whether his or her view of mathematics or his subjective assessment of the professionalism of mathematics teachers is more or less positive. For this and other reasons many mathematics teacher educators (see, for example, Peter, 1996) highlight the importance of principals and other important stakeholders, and the necessity of multiple perspectives concerning the professional development of teachers. Besides examples where principals play a more indirect role, there are also opportunities where they can actively and directly influence mathematics teachers' work. Halai (1998, p. 298), for example, describes how a principal in Pakistan in tandem with a teacher educator worked out the strategy of implementing professional development for mathematics teachers at a school. Principals and *other important stakeholders* such as regional subject co-ordinators or superintendents with different roles and functions in the school system, have their own ideas and beliefs about the nature of learning, teaching, mathematical knowledge, and reform (see, for example, Nelson, 1998). They can influence greatly decisions concerning general conditions of the quality of teaching; therefore it is essential to pay more attention to their role in the professional development of teachers, both practically and theoretically.

Secondly, Gisela's group had the advantage that the *whole group* participated in the seminar, so that the idea for subscribing to the journal emerged as a *joint wish*, and thus the representatives of the group were able to speak for the whole group. It would have been much more difficult for a single teacher coming back from an in-service course to convince his or her colleagues as well as the principal that the journal was necessary for the whole school. The "miniature" underlines the benefit of joint activities by groups of teachers of one school.

Looking back three years to that seminar, Gisela stressed in the interview that *"the seminar was an important step for the group"* of mathematics teachers at her school. Above all, it *"created trust among the colleagues and the feeling that it is worth investing time to work together."* Gisela reports that *"other groups began to envy the good climate and communication among the mathematics teachers,"* which in turn motivated the group to proceed further.

2.5 The Importance of Making Good Work Visible

The *newly established reputation of mathematics* at the school was partially caused by an activity that I have only recently learnt about. After the seminar, Gisela, supported by others, wrote a short report about it. She published it in their *annual school report* and thus made the professional efforts of the group of mathematics teachers *visible* to all teachers, students, and parents of the school. The report mainly builds on results of interviews with students and other investigations expressing on the one hand students' views on mathematics and mathematics teaching, as well as on the mathematics teachers' attempts to improve their knowledge about students through a small research project within the seminar.

One *outstanding result* printed in the school report is a *picture* drawn by a female student of Gisela's grade 11 class. The students had been invited to draw a coloured picture that they felt characterised their notion of mathematics. Then they had been asked to create a subtitle for their picture and to write a short description of the picture. The girl whose picture is presented in the school report shows a thick book entitled "The Great Book of Mathematics" which is locked by a clasp and a seal. The girl gave it the subtitle "Where is the key?" and described it as follows:

> The sealed, closed book is not accessible to all. It is only possible to open the book with the key. But, even when the book is open one need not necessarily understand the content. Either you have the understanding or not! In order to understand the book it has to be read from the beginning to the end!

For Gisela these results were two sides of a coin. On the one hand, she liked the creative work of this girl and her other students, their openness to speak about their view of mathematics and the benefit she and the other teachers took in discussing these results in the group. On the other hand, this pupil's view of mathematics and how she might have contributed to it irritated her. Nevertheless, Gisela saw it as a learning chance for her students, their parents, herself, and other teachers, and therefore chose this very picture for the report.

2.6 The Second and the Third Seminar for the Mathematics Teachers

In February and April 1997, *two further seminars* (each of one and a half days) with this group of mathematics teachers were held, both again at the school. The *first* of these two seminars placed the *emphasis on content-related aspects* (for example, project-oriented teaching in descriptive statistics, and teaching that builds on the many-sidedness of geometry) and aimed at helping the eight participants to find starting points for jointly planning teaching units after the seminar. Some colleagues did indeed take some steps towards this direction but the time was too short to present concrete results at the next seminar.

The *second* of these seminars was the first where all ten mathematics teachers participated. There was one teacher who hesitated to join the seminars for the group so far. Due to the increasingly positive climate among the mathematics teachers she decided to take part, stressing that she found it helpful that nobody pressed her to join the seminars. This again shows that professional development needs time and patience, and is a complex process influenced by a variety of factors from which a lot are not always to grasp easily. The seminar had two major topics, the *mediation of a conflict* between two group members and an introduction to a particular approach to *alternative assessment*. The topics served as a starting point for interesting developments, both at the group level but also on the personal level and concerning the whole school. This *close interplay of professional, personal, social, and organisational learning* might explain why participants' feedback to this seminar was the best one of all meetings with that group.

2.7 Conflict Resolution Through Gathering and Analysing Data

The *first major topic* of this third seminar was not planned but arose in the first minutes of the seminar when the participants articulated their expectations towards the one-and-a-half-day program. A *hidden conflict* between two mathematics teachers surfaced. The group decided to change the program and to deal with that problem. The conflict basically was that one of the teachers had become the successor of the other one's mathematics class and argued that this class was the worst he ever had. This is in no way an isolated case at schools and often causes deep conflicts between teachers and hinders communication enormously. At this seminar, in a joint effort, an attempt was made to create a plan for coping with the challenge in a constructive way. Firstly the group aimed at a deeper understanding of the situation, in particular through listening to the different views of the two teachers (on the importance of listening see, for example, Cooney & Krainer, 1996), being allowed only to ask questions, but not to make suggestions or to criticise. The subsequent activity included planning, carrying out, and interpreting interviews with students of this class. The answers of the students were surprising and helpful at the same time (and showed their excellent expertise in evaluating teaching and their own work). Parallel to this work with the students one seminar leader interviewed the two teachers. The analyses of all data brought new views into play, enabled alternative ways of coping with the given situation to be found acceptable for all sides. Altogether, the group recognised their ability to succeed in dealing with bigger challenges. This "miniature" also shows that teachers' growth cannot be confined simply to the improvement of teaching skills or mathematical competence. Professional development has to invest in the *"whole teacher,"* one of Day's (1999, p. 206) three important *investment strategies*.

2.8 A Group Activity as a Contribution to School Development

The *second big topic* was a reaction to the group's interest in reflecting on alternative assessment. One seminar leader reported on her teaching experience with a specific method, the so-called *"learning goal oriented assessment"* (with the German abbreviation "LOB" which means "praise"). The teachers were really impressed by the method, which motivates students to take responsibility for their learning progress. Gisela and some other teachers took some concrete steps in this direction in their subsequent teaching. Again, the group reported on the seminar and their follow-up activities. This apparently created a deep impression on other teachers and led to the invitation of one seminar-leader to work half a day with the *whole school staff* on the topic "learning goal oriented assessment." The meeting was a big success. Some teachers were inspired to try this method in their teaching, and in particular Gisela was very happy. Although she had handed over her function as the school's mathematics custodian to another teacher of the group two years earlier, Gisela continued to feel co-responsible for the mathematics group's development and felt really proud that it was the activities of her group that had contributed to *an impulse at the school* to think about a new culture of teaching and assessing.

A fourth seminar with the mathematics teachers at that school in 1999 proved the continuous growth of this group, with the next seminar taking place in the year 2000.

2.9   Interpreting the Growth of Gisela and Her Group

How can we interpret the professional development of Gisela and the group of mathematics teachers since the school-year 1995/96? At least *three different phases* may be perceived.

The *first phase* started with Gisela's initiative to make use of the offer of the university institute to organise a two-and-a-half-day-seminar for the mathematics teachers of a secondary school. In this phase the mathematics teachers were more or less a loosely associated assembly of lone fighters that had been talked into the seminar by Gisela.

The *second phase* began with the preliminary meeting and had its most important milestone in the two-and-a-half-day-seminar which was then followed by the report on it in the school's annual report. The most prominent outcome of this phase was the *transition process* from the *loose association* to a *well-formed group*. At the organisational level, Gisela, as the custodian of the group, continued to play a leadership-role, whereas concerning the learning process she felt and behaved as a normal member of the group, just as one part of the newly established learning community of critical friends. This helped the others and her to maintain their progress as a group, and was supported through the report about their joint activity in the annual report. It was this phase where the story of Gisela basically became *a story of the group*.

The *third phase*, which started with two shorter seminars, was an additional step forward by the group. In particular, the joint work on the conflict was a crucial test. Strengthened by this experience of success as well as by the activities on alternative assessment which seemed to fit perfectly to their current needs for professional development, the group was encouraged again to report on their activities. Increasing *questions and feedback by other teachers* were the external appreciation of their process. The fact that Gisela had handed over the function of the custodian to Veronika, another member of the group, and that the report was a critical reflection on the activities of the whole group, made it easier for the other teachers and groups to regard the alternative assessment topic as a *possible starting point* for their own professional development. Like Gisela, who never claimed the ownership for the group's growth for herself, the group did not fall into the trap of playing missionaries for other teachers (an approach that hinders many innovations at schools) and were mainly interested in improving their teaching and their communication among the group. Gisela herself continued to work at and improve her teaching. For example, in the last school year she introduced "learning goal oriented assessment" in her new grade 5 class and was overwhelmed by her students' self-reliant work, their short oral presentations and written stories, and by the positive feedback of their parents. Even a previously sceptical colleague, an English teacher who for a long time had shown little interest in Gisela's activities, indicated that *"for the first time she could understand her"* and paid attention to her approach to assessment.

2.10 A Bridge Between the Group's Growth and the Whole School's Further Development

It was apparent to the other teachers of the school that the mathematics group seemed to have found *a joint basis* for their growth. Therefore, the initiation of the half-day seminar on alternative assessment for the whole staff was a natural step and built *a bridge* from the professional development of a group to an initiative in school development. Although the work on alternative assessment was by no means the only school development activity, it was a remarkable event as the majority of teachers participated in the seminar, and it gave them an insight into the mathematics group's *culture of organising professional development for themselves.* It must be stressed that this development was in no way only a one-way street from the group to the school. For example, without the school's long tradition in making good examples of students' and teachers' work visible (in the annual school report, through project presentations, ...) it would not have been automatically accepted for the group to write a report about their activities. Without a school culture that appreciates innovations (or even regards these as natural and daily actions), and without the support by the management of the school, the group's growth would not have had such an influence on the whole school.

It is interesting to see that the original impulse for the seminars for the group of mathematics teachers arose from an initiative to revitalise the school development process. Now the professional development of this group in turn contributed to the further development of the whole school. This shows again the interplay between the learning of individuals, groups, and the whole organisation. *Teachers' growth is more than the growth of individual teachers.* It is a crucial part of school development and, as we will see later, a contribution to the further development of the whole (regional) educational system.

2.11 Advantages of Continuous Professional Development

The group's growth since the preliminary meeting in February 1996 also showed that *working continuously* with such a group might yield some *advantages* which should not be underestimated when discussing professional development programs for mathematics teachers:

- It is possible to take the "culture" of the school (the context in which the teachers live and work and which is a decisive general condition of what is possible or not) into consideration.
- The collaboration among individuals might develop towards the establishment of a group.

- The teachers could have the encouragement of others (who work next door to them) or even colleagues who were ready to join their efforts to improve their mathematics teaching.
- Innovations would be more likely to become a relevant component of mathematics teaching (or even of the whole school).
- Mathematics teaching could be more visible and could play a greater role at this school.

3. GISELA'S CASE AS A STARTING POINT FOR MORE GENERAL REFLECTIONS

The story of Gisela and the group of mathematics teachers at her school tells us that professional development activities can promote an individual teacher's growth considerably. Nevertheless, different kinds of *internal and external impulses and support*, enough *time*, and *general conditions* on the *individual* and the *organisational level* (e.g., importance of principals and school culture) as well as on the *educational system level* (e.g., general conditions and support for school development processes, role of mathematics in society) that foster development are essential. The story shows that these three levels are *closely interconnected*.

3.1 Action, Reflection, Autonomy, and Networking: Dimensions of Teachers' Professional Practice

A very prominent feature of teachers' professional development in the story is the mathematics group's transition from an *assembly of lone fighters* to a *network of critical friends* (see also, for example, the term "critical colleagueship" in Lord, 1994, cited in Nelson, 1998, p. 210, or "professional culture" in Loucks-Horsley, 1998, p. 194). Let us briefly review the story and interpret it using the *four dimensions of teachers' professional practice* as described, for example, in Krainer (1998):

Action: The attitude towards, and competence in, experimental, constructive, and goal-directed work;

Reflection: The attitude towards, and competence in, (self-)critical and one's own actions systematically reflecting work;

Autonomy: The attitude towards, and competence in, self-initiative, self-organised and self-determined work;

Networking: The attitude towards, and competence in, communicative and co-operative work with increasing public relevance.

Each of the pairs, *"action and reflection"* and *"autonomy and networking,"* expresses both *contrast and unity*, and can be seen as complementary dimensions which have to be kept in a certain balance, depending on the context. Figure 1 shows a qualitative diagram in which the point in the middle means a balance with regard to each of the two pairs, whereas deviations from the middle can be interpreted as preferences for one or two dimensions (for example, marking the point further right and higher means more emphasis on action and autonomy).

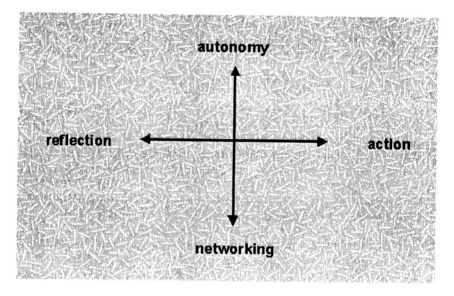

Figure 1. Four dimensions of teachers' professional practice

Based on various experiences, the place of most teachers (and also schools) in this diagram is, in general, in the first quadrant. One could say: *there is a lot of action and autonomy but less reflection and networking,* in the sense of critical dialogue about one's teaching with colleagues, mathematics educators, the school authority, the public, and so forth. Therefore promoting reflection and networking seems to be a powerful *intervention strategy* in the professional development of teachers. This is in line with the assumption of Fullan & Stiegelbauer (1991, p. 5) who regard the development of *"shared meaning"* as the central feature of educational change. Let us now come back to the story of Gisela.

Growth of individuals. Gisela, being accustomed to *acting autonomously* as a lone fighter in her classrooms, was challenged to *reflect* on her actions and to *share* her individual experiences and beliefs with other colleagues when she entered the PFL-program. Since *reflecting* and *networking* was a fundamental principle in the learning community of this professional development program, Gisela had to practice exactly those things which had been a blind spot in her career previously. She became aware that she can also regard her students as producers of *their own* knowledge, and not only as consumers of *her* knowledge. Therefore she increasingly introduced new modes of instruction where *students' reflection and networking* played an important role. This marks the personal growth of Gisela and her students, being the individual aspect of her story.

Growth of the group. It was very helpful for Gisela to have Werner as a critical friend at her old school, and when she came to the new school she aimed at promoting professional communication among the teaching staff. The seminars with the group of mathematics teachers also place the emphasis on reflecting and networking. Through joint efforts the mathematics teachers, slowly but continuously, turned into a *network of critical friends*.

Growth of the school. It was essential that the group *wrote down their experiences* and *made their reflections visible* to all teachers, students, and parents of the school. This form of *networking of innovations* finally led to a seminar for the whole staff of the school, which means that, at least concerning a specific topic, the group's innovations spread to a bigger circle. On a more general level, promoting school development processes means initiating learning environments where teachers, and in many cases also students and parents, jointly reflect on recent and future activities of the school, thus increasing the network of critical friends of that school and building a *corporate identity* that sees *innovations as natural and daily actions*.

On all these levels the *promotion of reflection and networking* plays a decisive role. Concerning the further development of the teaching profession, the educational system and its interaction with the society as a whole, one might ask, for example, the following *critical questions*: Is there efficient communication among mathematics co-ordinators (in regions, countries, or internationally)? Is there a fruitful collaboration between mathematics teachers (researchers, ...) and teachers (researchers, ...) of other subjects? Is mathematics seen as an important learning field at schools and in society? Do the general conditions at schools (e.g., working climate, curriculum, availability of new media) promote innovations in classrooms? What kinds of influence do teachers have on regulations (curriculum, assessment, etc.), on standards, or on the status of their profession? Is teachers' reflection on their profession seen as a relevant contribution to the educational system? Does it promote professional communication and collaboration among teachers? Is it promoted by mathematics educators and researchers?

Growth of the educational system. The story of Gisela, her group, and her school might find a *natural continuation*, for example, as follows: Another principal, mathematics custodian or superintendent hears or reads about the developments at Gisela's school and begins to initiate a similar process at his or her own school, or tries to find other schools to join in a series of "reflection workshops" or other kinds of networking between mathematics groups or schools. As a matter of fact, I was contacted by the school board of this region to hold a half-day workshop for principals dealing with mathematics teaching, in particular putting an emphasis on alternative modes of assessment. In addition, my colleague who had led a professional development day at Gisela's school, has been invited to hold a seminar for teachers of all subjects that focused specifically on that topic. This seminar will be continued because the regional in-service education institute found it a useful way of promoting professional development. It seems realistic that some initiatives will take place at different schools in the future, as it is a reality in Gisela's school now. This means that the development at Gisela's school would have had some impact on development in the regional educational system. However, a lot of factors have contributed to that situation, for example: the culture at Gisela's school, the principal, the group of mathematics teachers, the regional school board and in-service education institute, and, above all, Gisela, who initiated big parts of the process. But what factors influenced Gisela's actions and reflections? Surely her whole curriculum vitae, her experiences as a child and student, her pre-service education, her first teaching, and also – as she stresses several times – the PFL-program. But what would have happened if the Austrian ministries hadn't prolonged this professional development project in 1984? In the meantime, the PFL-program has had the participation of about 500 teachers all over Austria (and also some from neighbouring countries), many of whom are now acting as "agents of change" in their region, and in some cases nationwide. They may be engaged in teacher pre-service and in-service education, as textbook authors, as (vice-) principals and superintendents, or they may actively participate in conferences in which they present the innovative work they are doing in their classrooms (see, for example, Krainer & Posch, 1996, chapters 5 – 8).

3.2   The Need for a Systemic View on Teacher Education and on Reform

These considerations and the questions above again show that the *professional development of individuals, organisations, and the educational system are closely linked with one another*. Here is an example (which intentionally assumes rather unfavourable general conditions in order to highlight its implications more clearly): teachers, who work in an educational system with narrow regulations on curriculum and assessment, who have no influence on those regulations in the past, and who will not be having any in the future, who were educated at universities where lecturing was the dominant teaching method (which leaves the audience to reflect the learned content), currently teaching at a school with a low level of communication among the teachers, and who are now confronted with in-service courses oriented only towards their weaknesses, need a very strong motivation not to regard students as "received knowers," in the way they themselves have been socialised. On the other hand, too often teachers complain about restrictive regulations that tend to hinder their innovations in classrooms, underestimating thereby the freedom of action they have or could establish. However, in just the same way as research on students' mathematical understanding shows that we systematically underestimate students' creative ways of thinking (when our focus is not restricted to hearing only things we want to hear), *we seem to systematically underestimate teachers' creative attempts to improve their teaching*. Many experiences of our work with teachers prove that fact. Gisela is one example for many. However, we should not confine ourselves to see only the individual aspect of Gisela's story. To some extent, it is a story that shows the *development of an educational system*. Her story raises the question of how national efforts and reforms should be arranged in order to stimulate growth at all levels of the educational system, including students, teachers and schools, and taking into account the learning of the educational system itself.

3.3 Some Consequences for National Efforts and Reforms

How does our story of teachers' efforts to grow professionally relate to national efforts to improve the quality of teaching? The story of Gisela and her group raises two issues, at least, that should be taken into consideration.

A good balance between supporting "bottom-up" and establishing intelligent "top-down" initiatives. A first issue refers the question of the *ownership of reform*. On the one hand, the story of Gisela and her group tells us that teachers have the attitude towards, and the necessary competence for carrying out, self-initiated innovations and for reflecting on them self-critically once they have the feeling that it contributes to their students' and their own growth. On the other hand, the story shows that internal and external impulses and support were essential for the process. This implies a *balanced policy*, on the one hand relying on teachers' efforts to take care of the quality of teaching themselves and *supporting* such *"bottom-up" activities*, and on the other hand *establishing an intelligent "top-down" approach* that does not undermine the "bottom-up" one but, nevertheless, secures a kind of guarantee that quality assurance and quality development are taken seriously. In Austria, for example, it is planned to introduce an obligation for teachers and schools for self-evaluation. The quality of this self-evaluation will be assessed in a kind of meta-evaluation, occasionally accompanied by initiating nationally focussed evaluations on specific issues (e.g., integration) and by participating in international comparative studies. Since schools received extended autonomy concerning the curriculum, colleagues teaching the same subject are increasingly challenged of developing steps towards a joint position, thus making professional communication within (and partly among) subject groups necessary.

A good balance between initiatives focusing on individual aspects, on organisational ones, and on those related to the whole educational system. A second issue that has to be considered seriously is the *role of individuals* in transition processes. On the one hand, the story tells us that innovations in schools are deeply influenced by individuals and might have implications for many other teachers and even for a whole school. On the other hand, it shows the interconnectedness of individuals' actions and beliefs with the culture of organisations (schools, universities, teacher in-service institutes, ...) and with the whole (educational, political, societal, cultural, ...) system in which they work and live. This implies a *systemic view on reform* and has consequences for all who are concerned with the initiation, financing, implementation, promotion, evaluation, or investigation of reform initiatives. The consequence is that reform should be promoted on all levels, for the individual, for the organisation, and for the overall educational system. Not only individuals (students, teachers, principals, superintendents, teacher educators, ...) have to learn, but also organisations (schools, universities, in-service education institutes, ministries, ...), and, as I want to add, we all as a society have to learn continuously.

Professional development programs and related investigations should more clearly be seen as *interventions on all three levels*: the individual, the organisational, and the educational system level. Maybe not enough has been done in the past concerning the last two levels. We need not only stories about students, teachers, teacher education programs, but increasingly also *stories about the further development of mathematics teaching at whole schools, in school networks, in regions, in nations, on continents*, and so forth, which take into account organisational and societal issues. Otherwise we run the danger of creating knowledge which has only little impact on practice and educational policy. If we, as mathematics educators, are not ready to raise these issues we will be confined to work only in general conditions that are constructed by politicians, researchers from other fields, test developers, and so forth. It is essential to demonstrate the value of innovations in teacher education and its results to teachers, parents, departments, schools, principals, superintendents, and so forth. In the same way we should support mathematics teachers to make visible their efforts to further develop their teaching. In *professional development*, in particular, the challenge for us is to regard it as a contribution to the whole educational system. In broadening our (mostly individualistic) approach, we need to find a *more systemic approach*, both practically and theoretically, for dealing with the quality of teaching. This means *"to understand both the small and big pictures"* of educational change and to place the emphasis on *"active initiation and participation, pressure and support, changes in behavior and beliefs, and the overriding problem of ownership"* (Fullan & Stiegelbauer, 1991, pp. 4, 91).

It might be seen as a paradox that a story of an individual teacher might also tell a story of the complexity of teacher education or of an educational system. But maybe – as in the case of chaos theory – the whole pattern can also be seen in the details. From a methodological point of view, we need a sound *balance* between the *search for the general*, and the *search for the particular*. Stories provide a good chance to meet this challenge.

REFERENCES

Altrichter, H., Posch P. & Somekh, B. (1993). Teachers investigate their work. An introduction to the methods of action research. London: Routledge.

Bell, B. & Gilbert, J. (1994). Teacher development as professional, personal, and social development. *Teaching and Teacher Education, 5*, 483-497.

Borasi, R., Fonzi, J., Smith, C.F., & Rose, B. (1999). Beginning the process of rethinking mathematics instruction: A professional development program. *Journal of Mathematics Teacher Education, 2*, 49-78.

Cooney, T.J. (1999). Stories and the challenge for JMTE. *Journal of Mathematics Teacher Education, 2*, 1-2.

Cooney, T. J. & Krainer, K. (1996). Inservice mathematics teacher education: The importance of listening. In A. Bishop, K. Clements, C. Keitel, J. Kilpatrick, & C. Laborde. *International handbook of mathematics education, Part 2* (pp. 1155-1185). Dordrecht, The Netherlands: Kluwer.

Crawford, K. & Adler, J. (1996). Teachers as researchers in mathematics education. In A. Bishop, K. Clements, C. Keitel, J. Kilpatrick, & C. Laborde (Eds.), *International handbook of mathematics education, Part 2* (pp. 1187-1205). Dordrecht, The Netherlands: Kluwer.

Day, C. (1999). Developing teachers: The challenges of lifelong learning. London: Falmer Press.

Even, R. (1999). The development of teacher leaders and inservice teacher educators. *Journal of Mathematics Teacher Education, 2*, 3-24.

Fennema, E. & Nelson, B. S. (Eds.). (1997). *Mathematics teachers in transition.* Mahwah, NJ: Erlbaum.

Fischer, R., Krainer, K., Malle, G., Posch, P., & Zenkl, M. (Eds.). (1985). *Pädagogik und Fachdidaktik für Mathematiklehrer.* Vienna: Hölder-Pichler-Tempsky.

Fullan, M. & Stiegelbauer, S. (1991). *The new meaning of educational change* (2nd ed.). New York: Teachers College Press.

Grossmann, R. (Ed.). (1997). *Besser billiger mehr – Zur Reform der Experten Organisationen Krankenhaus, Schule,* Universität. iff-Texte, Band 2. Wien: Springer.

Grouws, D. & Schultz, K. (1996). Mathematics teacher education. In J. Sikula, (Ed.), *Handbook of research on teacher education* (pp. 442-458). New York: Macmillan.

Halai, A. (1998). Mentor, mentee, and mathematics: A story of professional development. *Journal of Mathematics Teacher Education, 1,* 295-315.

Hord, S. M. & Boyd, V. (1995). Professional development fuels a culture of continuous improvement. *Journal of Staff Development, 16*(1), 10-15.

Jaworski, B. (1998). Mathematics teacher research: Process, practice, and the development of teaching. *Journal of Mathematics Teacher Education, 1,* 3-31.

Krainer, K. (1994). PFL-mathematics: A teacher in-service education course as a contribution to the improvement of professional practice in mathematics instruction. In P. Ponte & F. Matos (Eds.), *Proceedings 18th International Conference for the Psychology of Mathematics Education* (PME 18) Vol. III (pp.104-111). Lisbon, Spain:University of Lisbon.

Krainer, K. (1998). Some considerations on problems and perspectives of inservice mathematics teacher education. In C. Alsina, et al. (Eds.), *8th International Congress on Mathematical Education. Selected lectures.* S.A.E.M. (pp. 303-321). Sevilla, Spain: Thales.

Krainer, K. (1999). PFL-Mathematics: Improving professional practice in mathematics teaching. In B. Jaworski, T. Wood, & S. Dawson (Eds.), *Studies in mathematics education series. Mathematics teacher education: Critical international perspectives* (pp. 102-111). London: Falmer Press.

Krainer, K & Goffree, F. (1999). Investigations into teacher education: Trends, future research, and collaboration. In K. Krainer & F. Goffree (Eds.), *On research in Mathematics teacher education. From a study of teaching practices to issues in teacher dducation* (pp. 223-242). Osnabrück: Forschungsinstitut für Mathematikdidaktik. Internet: http://www.fmd.uni-osnabrueck.de/ebooks/erme/cerme1-proceedings/cerme1-group3.pdf

Krainer, K. & Posch, P. (Eds.). (1996). *Lehrerfortbildung zwischen Prozessen und Produkten.* Klinkhardt: Germany: Bad Heilbrunn. [See review in: *Journal of Mathematics Teacher Education, 1,* 1998, 113-116.]

Lord, B. T. (1994). Teachers' professional development: Critical colleagueship and the role of professional communities. In N. Cobb (Ed.), *The future of education: Perspectives on national standards in America* (pp. 175-204). San Diego: California Academic Press.

Loucks-Horsley, S., Hewson, P. W., Love, N., & Stiles, K.E. (1998). *Designing professional development for teachers of science and mathematics.* Thousand Oaks, CA: Corwin Press.

Nelson, B.S. (1998). Lenses on learning: Administrators' views on reform and the professional development of teachers. *Journal of Mathematics Teacher Education, 1* (2), 191-215.

Peter, A. (1996). Aktion und Reflexion. Lehrerfortbildung aus international vergleichender Perspektive. Weinheim, Germany: Deutscher Studien Verlag.

Wilson, M., & Goldenberg, M. P. (1998). Some conceptions are difficult to change: One middle school mathematics teacher's struggle. *Journal of Mathematics Teacher Education, 1,* 269-293.

Prof.Dr. Konrad Krainer
University of Klagenfurt / IFF
Sterneckstrasse 15, A-9020 Klagenfurt
Tel.: ++43 463 2700 738 (Fax: 759)
konrad.krainer@uni-klu.ac.at
http://www.uni-klu.ac.at/iff/schule

BARBARA JAWORSKI

DEVELOPING MATHEMATICS TEACHING: TEACHERS, TEACHER EDUCATORS, AND RESEARCHERS AS CO-LEARNERS

ABSTRACT: This chapter addresses mathematics teaching and teacher development from the perspective of teachers and educators working together in co-learning partnerships to improve the learning of mathematics in school classrooms. From a recognition of the complexities involved, in theory and in practice, the need for and nature of a co-learning partnership is discussed. Reference is made to a particular example in which mathematics teachers and educators have worked together, sometimes as researchers, for the development of teachers and educators, jointly and in parallel. Significance here lies in the complementary roles, relationships, and learning outcomes of the various participants. From these illustrative examples, some general principles for co-learning partnerships are suggested and issues raised, followed by questions and areas for further research.

This chapter addresses the relationship between mathematics teachers and mathematics educators, both of whom are practitioners in an enterprise which is about developing and improving mathematics teaching for the more effective learning of mathematics in classrooms. It recognises the value of teachers, as well as educators, engaging in research as part of the process of developing their teaching. It goes further to suggest that "co-learning partnerships" between teachers and educators, enabling teachers to share responsibility in the development process, lead to more effective development.

The idea of co-learning comes from an article by Wagner (1997), who analyses relationships between researchers and practitioners in educational settings. One style of such relationship is called a "co-learning agreement." According to Wagner,

> In a co-learning agreement, researchers and practitioners are both participants in processes of education and systems of schooling. Both are engaged in action and reflection. By working together, each might learn something about the world of the other. Of equal importance, however, each may learn something more about his or her own world and its connections to institutions and schooling. (Wagner, 1997, p. 16)

In this chapter, I extend this notion of co-learning agreement to relationships between educators and teachers, recognising at the same time that the vision I have of such relationships includes all of the participants being also researchers in their own educational settings. Thus "researchers and practitioners," from Wagner's definition, become researchers *and* educators *and* teachers where the relationship might be three-way but is often just two-way where participants are playing a dual role – that is the teacher and/or educator is also a researcher.

F.-L. Lin & T. J. Cooney (Eds.) Making Sense of Mathematics Teacher Education, 295—320.
© 2001 *Kluwer Academic Publishers. Printed in the Netherlands.*

I start by taking a look at the complex scene of mathematics teaching and its development as seen by educators who take some responsibility in promoting more effective teaching of mathematics. I recognise at the same time that it is only teachers who can make a difference in classrooms.

1. RECOGNITION OF COMPLEXITY

It needs little justification that the issues in developing teaching are weighty and complex. I have detailed some of this complexity in Jaworski (1999) where I mentioned the following as some of the elements to consider (p. 184):

1. Educators' theories which relate to mathematics teaching, to the development of teaching and to knowledge which underpins this development.
2. Mathematics itself and the potentially special nature of mathematics. How do effective teaching approaches – those which lead to effective learning – relate to the special nature of mathematics?
3. The recognition of "good" or "expert" teachers, and questions about how such expertise might be communicated to others. What is the knowledge on which this expertise rests? How does the recognised expertise reflect the theories referred to in (1) and (2)?
4. The recognition that much mathematics teaching is not effective – it does not seem to promote effective mathematical learning. We need to consider carefully what might improve it, and how this relates to the three points above.

I shall address each of these elements briefly before going further.

1.1 Educator's Theories

The development of teaching, and of knowledge within teaching, can be addressed at a number of theoretical levels including theories of pedagogic practice which are specifically directed at the development of mathematical understandings in classrooms. For example, theory which rests on the importance of teachers' own mathematical learning and understandings of mathematics to their teaching of mathematics (e.g. Schifter, 1997); theory which rests on teachers' knowledge of students' mathematical understandings, and the preconceptions they bring to learning mathematical topics (e.g. Fennema, et al, 1996); and theory which is related to classroom interactions and modes of mathematical argumentation (e.g. Cobb, Wood & Yackel, 1990). Such theories, often developed in close relation to practice, are not in competition but rather together enrich our understandings of issues in teaching. Most offer research evidence from real classroom teaching and learning situations which can serve as a basis for development programmes and further research.

At the root of such theoretical perspectives are considerations of knowledge growth, and in particular how *teachers'* knowledge grows. Two influential areas of theory, drawn on by educators to explain knowledge growth in teaching, and to situate the more localised theories, are *Social Practice Theory*, and *Constructivism*.

Social Practice Theory is concerned with the socially-embedded growth of knowledge within communities of practice. Where teachers are concerned, the relevant practice is *teaching*; a relevant *community* of practice embraces schools and other institutions concerned with teaching and developing teaching. Provision for teaching development often takes the form of courses for teachers, from which teachers' practices are expected to develop. Adler (1996), speaking explicitly of mathematics teacher education, has written

> Knowing about teaching and becoming a teacher evolve, and are deeply interwoven in ongoing activity in the practice of teaching. Knowledge about teaching is not acquired in courses about teaching, but in ongoing participation in the teaching community in which such courses may be a part. (p. 3)

Adler follows sociocultural theorists Lave and Wenger (1991) in conceptualizing teaching as a process of apprenticeship into a community of practice with its novices and old-stagers, with newcomers growing into the community through their participation in its practices. She does not deny the value of courses, but rather emphasizes the importance of the *community* through which teaching evolves. We might ask, nevertheless, what role courses play within this community. Lave and Wenger speak of the development of communities of practice within which novices develop as full members of the community through apprentice-type relationships. Learning is seen to be a process of enculturation where learners as "peripheral participants" in the community grow into "old stagers," those who represent the community of practice. They write, "... newcomers legitimate peripherality ... involves participation as a way of learning – of both absorbing and being absorbed in – the "culture of practice" ... mastery resides not in the master, but in the organization of the community of practice" (Lave and Wenger, 1991, p 95). Thus, knowing, or cognition, is *situated* in the practice. Teachers might be seen as growing into the practices of the community where their teaching is situated – those of schools and classrooms. These classrooms are situated within a wider socio-political community with a variety of cultural influences. The development of knowledge of teaching is seen as a fundamental part of *participating* in teaching within this social setting. Seeing growth of teaching knowledge in terms of participation has implications for educators working with teachers to develop teaching; and this raises questions about certain approaches to teaching development, courses for teachers being one such approach. To what extent, for example, are teaching development programmes a part of the community of practice of teaching? Also, where and how do teacher educators fit into this community?

Constructivism deals with the construction of knowledge, individually or socially, through interactions between humans and their physical and social worlds. It has been drawn on extensively by mathematics educators as a basis for programmes of teaching development (e.g. Murray et al., 1999; Markovitz & Even, 1999). At its most basic level, constructivism suggests that learners construct knowledge relative to the experiences they encounter in the world around them. Where teachers are concerned this might be seen as teachers' personal construction of the processes of teaching relative to their ongoing experiences in schools and classrooms – an individual process involving reflection and adaptation (the Piagetian view, e.g., von Glasersfeld, 1987). Alternatively, individual knowledge might be seen to develop from intersubjectivity between teachers working together: knowledge is constructed first within the teaching community; interactions within the community lead to a growth of intersubjectivity, or *common* knowledge, from which individual perceptions of teaching derive (the Vygotskian view, e.g. Bruner, 1996). Certain incompatibilities have been observed between these two positions (e.g. Confrey, 1995). For the former, there is no possibility of recognising the existence of knowledge external to individual experience. However, this is incompatible with seeing knowledge *within* the social dimension, only later to be synthesised by the individual. In terms of teacher education, do we see a teacher's growth of knowledge as a personal synthesis from experience, or as deriving from interactions within social settings in which teachers work?

As is the nature of theory and its links with practice, certain aspects of these theories seem to fit with the development of teaching but are contradicted by others. Theory is no more than an attempt to organise knowledge and offer ways of seeing situations whose complexity always defies theory. Yet it is easy to be seduced into a belief that some theory might be found to express and explain the complexity. Jere Confrey (1995), for example, explores the possibility of some encompassing theory that will unify diverse perspectives and overcome dichotomies such as that apparent between Piagetian and Vygotskian constructivism. In seeking for effective teaching, a less ambitious position seems tenable: that is to draw on what seems relevant or valuable in competing theories as lenses through which to *view* practice. This allows the viewer to explain or predict , while recognising differences and limitations as a *productive tension* (the grit in the oyster) in addressing teaching practice for both teachers and educators. So, for example, a critique of courses as a vehicle for teaching development might involve viewing them through various theoretical lenses and looking critically and comparatively at resulting implications for learning.

This discussion has to be seen relative to relationships between teachers and teacher-educators, with recognition that it is typically the educators and not the teachers who know of and have access to external theory and research, while it is the teachers who have to develop practice or implement change. Teachers' own theories are often neither recognised nor acknowledged by teachers themselves (e.g. Othman, 1996), so that they are not available for scrutiny which would aid development (Jaworski, 1994). In order for theories to be of use to teachers, teachers have to gain access to theories (including their own) and develop a vision of ways of interpreting them in practice. Gaining access is not straightforward, and cannot realistically be the responsibility of teachers. It is then a serious question for educators as to how such access might become a reality in the pressured world of the classroom teacher of mathematics.

1.2 The Potentially Special Nature of Mathematics

How we see *mathematics* has been recognised as central to the way we conceptualise its teaching and learning, both as teachers and educators (e.g. Thompson, 1984; Lerman, 1990; Schifter, 1997). Cooney and Shealey (1997) have expressed relationships between Khunian paradigms of knowledge growth, Lakatosian models of mathematical growth, and our desires as educators to develop conceptual understandings of mathematics. For many mathematicians the beauty of mathematics lies in pure abstract forms, but formalisation and abstraction are notably contributory to the problems mathematics creates for many students (Sierpinska, 1994; Nardi, 1996). Mathematical utility has been viewed as essential to creating realistic situations in classrooms from which conceptualisations can arise. However, classroom interpretations of utility often run counter to everyday experiences where realistic situations make little use of mathematics. Also utilitarian approaches to mathematics can reduce mathematics to particularised forms rather than leading to generalised relationships. It is a serious issue for teachers how to approach abstract ways of expression which are not a natural part of everyday life. For teachers individually, tackling such mathematical issues as part of the wider demands and pressures of school life is seriously challenging. Inability to deal adequately with such challenges, among the many other demands on a teacher, might be seen as contributory to teaching which, viewed from the outside, is deemed ineffective and in need of change.

Of course, before we can tackle what is perceived as ineffective, we have to identify what we mean by 'effective' learning of mathematics. If effective learning means "conceptual" learning, then involving learners in developing a relational and conceptual understanding of mathematics (e.g. following Skemp, 1976), which goes beyond instrumental rule following and stereotypical problem-solving, can be seen as a major aim of effective mathematics teaching. This is not to suggest that memory, recall, use of algorithms, and the practice of standard types of problems are not valuable aspects of learning, but that by themselves they do not constitute mathematical understanding. At any phase of education, it seems desirable that students have opportunity to do and conceptualise mathematics in a generalised way which includes appropriate levels of abstraction.

A problem with such mathematical theorising is that it often ignores the complexity of knowledge teachers bring to designing mathematical activities in classrooms. Such knowledge weighs up the socio-political pressures of institution, curriculum, assessment and society, which militate against conceptual learning, and makes decisions about teaching mathematics relative to these pressures. The purity of theories of conceptualising mathematics often excludes this social knowledge. Social practice theory would account for practices as seen and established, by recognising teachers' knowledge as central to the practices which pertain. Constructivist theory would see pertaining practices being a result of teachers' constructions of teaching relative to the pressures within which they work. Either theory allows us to make some sense of classroom situations, but it is less clear how to address issues such as those of enabling students to deal with mathematical formalization and abstraction.

Here again we find ourselves in the realms of theory – theories relating to the nature of mathematics itself and to its effective learning, theories charting the growth of knowledge in and beyond mathematics, and theories recognising the effects of social forces on teaching mathematics. Educators' knowledge of theories in mathematical domains is a guiding force in conceptualising effective mathematics teaching. Teachers bring very specialised social knowledge to their conceptualisations. Teaching approaches need to take account of both mathematical and social knowledge, or fail to be effective, as do also approaches to teaching development.

1.3 The Recognition of "Good" or "Expert" Teachers

Despite concerns about the complexity of teaching, and weighty questions of theory and epistemology, we can still recognise teaching in classrooms which goes some way to achieving conceptual understanding of mathematics. In the mathematics education community, we are all aware that there are many people we regard as "good" teachers because of the ways in which they work effectively for students' mathematical learning. This is achieved despite all the constraints posed by socio-political pressures mentioned above. It would be useful to know something about the knowledge and personal theories, explicit or tacit, that underpin such teaching.

In the UK, Brown and McIntyre (1993), have studied teaching with precisely this aim, to identify general teaching characteristics which relate to "good" teaching. In my own work I have characterised "investigative" mathematics teaching, which has had the explicit aim of fostering conceptual understandings of mathematics (Jaworski, 1994). In these and other of the studies mentioned above (e.g., Schifter, 1997; Fennema, et al., 1996; Cobb, Wood, & Yackel, 1990) characteristics of "good teaching" are *identified*. It is more difficult, however, to *communicate* the elements of such teaching in a way that they might become accessible to other teachers. Can the theories outlined above offer models – social practice models, or constructivist models for example – through which teachers might develop knowledge and expertise related to identified characteristics of "good practice"?

1.4 The Recognition That Much Mathematics Teaching Is Not Effective

We are also aware that much mathematics teaching does not achieve effective learning of mathematics. The salutary nature of the recent TIMSS results emphasised this for many countries. Here is where the issues start to bite! When we see ineffective teaching, and recognise its implications for learners in classrooms, we cannot avoid responsibility that something needs to be done, and the question of *what* becomes impelling.

In terms of social practice theory, if the old-stagers of a community are ineffective, then it appears that there will be a perpetuation of practices which continue to promote ineffective teaching. If we believe in teachers' construction of teaching practices relative to their experiences, we have to recognise that such construction has resulted in practices we find inappropriate. Changes are needed, but it is far from clear how such changes can occur.

From such considerations, it is but a small step into what Brown and McIntyre (ibid) have called a "deficit" model of teaching. As Dawson (1999) indicates, it is easy to point to teachers who are not achieving goals we have identified and consider how we might change such teaching. He suggests that one (international) "manifestation of inservice culture" has the following basic principle:

> [that] there is something wrong with mathematics teaching worldwide, and that we as mathematics educators must fix it. (p. 148)

But deficit attitudes do not start to address effective ways in which such change can take place or, indeed, what are the fundamentals of such change. What are the ways in which ineffective practices can become effective? Such questions are indicative that educators, despite sophisticated theories and theorising, do not have answers to some very basic questions.

2. THE TEACHER-EDUCATOR AS LEARNER

The questions and issues identified above are but a few of the many which can be asked and raised. The complexity sketched provides the back-drop for conceptualisation of the role of the teacher-educator. Unlike most teachers, under too much pressure to have time to identify and work on issues at theoretical levels, the teacher-educator is expected to be both a theorist and a practitioner. There are expectations that the teacher-educator will make overt attempts to link theory and practice in promoting effective teaching. However, despite, often, many years of relevant experience at a variety of levels, and considerable associated knowledge, teacher-educators are themselves learners (and I acknowledge myself firmly in this position). Moreover, it is *only* as a learner that I can justify the position I take in my discussion and argument in this chapter. The very nature of the complexity is that issues are not clear cut, or answers easy to find. The interpretation of ideas and theories into modes of teaching for effective mathematics learning is as difficult for teacher-educators as it is for teachers. The main difference between the two, in most circumstances currently, is that teacher-educators, being more knowledgeable about theory, have more responsibility for finding solutions to this problem.

It seems important to recognize three levels of consideration for teachers and educators, as they tend to become intertwined[ii]. In in-service provision for the development of mathematics teaching, it is impossible to avoid questions of what makes good teaching. Such questions have to take into account mathematical learners in classrooms. Hence the learning of mathematics has to be a key consideration for in-service provision. Thus there are three levels at which teachers and teacher-educators need to operate and reflect:

Level 1. Mathematics and provision of classroom mathematical activities for students' effective learning of mathematics;

Level 2. Mathematics teaching and ways in which teachers think about developing their approaches to teaching;

Level 3. The roles and activities of teacher-educators in contributing to developments in (1) and (2).

Presented in this way it might seem a linear process, but in fact each higher level encompasses those below it. The teacher-educator as learner is operating at

Level 3, which involves dealing directly with issues at Level 2, which requires attention at Level 1. Teachers work mainly at Level 1, with some engaging in thinking at Level 2.

As an example of what is involved I draw on Tom Cooney's (1994) concepts of *Mathematical* and *Pedagogical Power*. *Mathematical power*, for the learner of mathematics, is "the ability to draw on whatever (mathematical) knowledge is needed to solve problems" (Cooney 1994, p.15). Cooney & Shealy (1997, p.105 citing Cooney, 1994) point to mathematical power as "the essence of intelligent problem solving within the context of teaching mathematics." *Pedagogical power*, can be defined similarly – the ability to draw on whatever *pedagogical* knowledge is needed to solve problems. Cooney writes "pedagogical problem solving has to do with recognizing the conditions and constraints of the pedagogical problems being faced" (1994, p.15). I would add to this the aims, possibilities and opportunities provided by such problem solving. Pedagogical power is seen to be vested in such pedagogical problem solving through processes of reflection[iii] and analysis. In this context, Cooney and Shealy ask, "But how can we *engender* such an orientation among teachers with whom we work?" (p. 105, my emphasis). This is a Level 3 question. The constructs of mathematical power and pedagogical power can be seen to apply respectively at Level 1 and Level 2 above. At Level 3 are questions about the roles teacher-educators can play in the development of pedagogical power by teachers, and the word "engender" is a key term here. We might coin the term "educative-power" to capture this engendering.

Here we have an example of a theory espoused by educators: that is, the importance of the link between pedagogical power and intelligent problem solving in mathematics teaching. As educators, we want teachers to be aware of this link, to have access to both mathematical power and pedagogical power; we want to engender these qualities. The word "engender" carries a wealth of meaning with it and encapsulates the problem for educators. *What is it that educators can do that will result in teaching which manifests in practice such theoretical concepts?* Moreover, and this is not always asked, what exactly might such theoretical concepts – in this case, "intelligent problem solving" – look like in the community of practice of teachers and teaching? How would we recognize it, and would we like what we see? These questions lead to a scrutiny of links between theory and practice, and ways in which practice fits with or mirrors theory. Through such questions we search for insights into the development of practice in terms of its desired theoretical outcomes.

In all of this complexity, what is it that mathematics educators do, or can do, to promote, enable, facilitate, support, or engender (or even *recognize*) effective mathematics teaching in classrooms? This question is fundamental to the learning of a teacher-educator. However, seeing the position in these terms leaves educators still in the deficit mode of trying to "fix" teachers. Teachers are seen as having a responsive role but not a generative role in the process.

3. MOVING FROM EDUCATORS TO CO-LEARNERS WITHIN A RESEARCH CULTURE

Our learning as teacher-educators often takes the form of research. Through research into our own or others' practices, and the sharing through dissemination of outcomes, we learn about practices and issues. Such learning comes from a deep engagement with the fundamental notions we are seeking to know. From research programmes we see the value of, for example, the importance of students' preconceptions to their mathematical development, or the value of teachers reflecting on their own mathematical learning, and other theoretical syntheses from research, as mentioned above. Often, we go from here into the devising of programmes for teachers through which they too can appreciate these realisations and interpret them into effective classroom practices.

The process hypothesised is one of

research by educators --> programmes for teachers --> effective practices.

Through this process it is expected that educator-researchers will "engender"effective practices in teachers; in Dawson's words (1999) "fixing" the teachers. Dawson writes:

> Many mathematics teachers seem to be seeking new ways to fix their practice. But this places mathematics teachers in a relationship of co-dependence with mathematics teacher-educators. Mathematics teachers need someone to fix them and mathematics teacher-educators need someone to fix. The two groups seem made for each other. (Dawson, 1999, p.148)

Dawson's heavy irony points toward one explanation for the perpetuation of ineffective practices, despite multitudes of well-meaning programmes devised by educators. The imbalance of power in the teacher/educator relationship places educators in a superior position to teachers, despite the fact that all are learners. Both groups have both theoretical and professional knowledge, but it is as if only the knowledge of the educators is valued. Despite their position as learners (which is mainly under-acknowledged) educators are seen as the ones who know what it is that teachers ought to know and need to learn. However, educators do not know how teachers will learn; they can only conjecture approaches which might be effective and put these to the test in research programmes. The status of this conjecturing is not always clear to teachers who see the enterprise ultimately either in terms of their failure to learn, or of the worthlessness of the programme in which they have participated. (See, for example, Emily in Irwin & Britt, 1999)

From both psychological and sociological perspectives, educators, with theories and research tools at their disposal, and the respect of teachers and colleagues, are in an ideal position to learn. Educators are in a position described by Belenky et al. (1986 – speaking of *women's* ways of knowing) as having *constructed knowledge*, "a position in which women view all knowledge as contextual, experience themselves as creators of knowledge, and value both subjective and objective strategies for knowing." This position might be explained from either a social-constructivist or a social-practice theory of coming to know, from either of which we might suggest implications for practices through which this position might be achieved by other practitioners.

Isolating contributory elements to our "constructed knowledge" we might point to autonomy in making decisions about styles of teaching and focuses for research; to opportunities for sharing and negotiating theoretical ideas with colleagues in the wider research community; to reflective critique in observing and questioning our practices; and to responsibility for the outcomes of our teaching and research. These elements are powerful in our growth and conceptualisation in teaching and learning – how might we use them, and our awareness of them, in conceptualising our work with teachers? How might we, *jointly* with teachers, experience the *pedagogical power* of which Cooney speaks? How might we draw teachers into negotiation of these issues, for example to debating the pros and cons of various theoretical positions?

One obvious response to this question is to seek to engage teachers themselves in the research activities through which we acknowledge our own learning. Research has shown that teachers' thinking develops when mathematics teachers enquire into aspects of their teaching (Jaworski, 1994; 1998). In fact many programmes, both outside and within mathematics education have seen teachers' engagement in research as one means of teaching development. In mathematics education this is demonstrated by substantial projects, for example, in Austria (Krainer, 1993), New Zealand (Britt et al., 1993) and in the UK (Jaworski, 1998). All these programmes testify to the depth of issues, the quality of thinking, and the influences on teaching which are associated with teachers engaging in research into their own teaching. A working group which met at the PME conference[iv] over the course of about 6 years was devoted to considerations of mathematics teacher research; from this effort a book elaborating theories and practices emerged (Zack, Mousley, & Breen, 1997). These studies show that engaging in research is a strong force for teaching development with positive indications for effective mathematics learning in the associated classrooms.

It is evident from many of these programmes that teacher-research is particularly successful when associated with academic opportunities for teachers to access the theories and research this chapter has been addressing. This can be possible through having teachers read appropriate literature or through providing them opportunities for sharing experiences, synthesising from and explaining outcomes of research, and developing critical frameworks related to practice. In such programmes, teachers and educators work side by side to conceptualise and resource appropriate directions for teachers' personal study. Groups of teachers and educators, forming communities of practice, provide for knowledge growth in social settings. When teachers develop overt awareness of theoretical principles guiding such practices, these practices are more effective as they are examined critically by all participants in the learning enterprise.

To illustrate and support these ideas, I now refer to an example of the development of three teachers within a teacher-development programme which espoused collaboration between teachers and educators at a variety of levels in the development of both teachers and educators. The programme, an M.Ed. in Teacher Education, educated teachers to become teacher-educators, ultimately working alongside those teaching the M.Ed. programme. Research into the learning of participants in the programme demonstrates the co-learning of teachers, novice educators, and experienced educators.

4.   ONE MATHEMATICS TEACHING DEVELOPMENT PROGRAMME

The programme on which I shall draw, to provide examples of co-learning in action, has taken place in Pakistan over the last 6 years[v]. At the beginning of this programme, twenty-three experienced teachers, from various subject disciplines, went through an 18 months MEd degree course, followed by a three-year internship as teacher-educators in which they worked each year for half a year in school (teaching and helping other teachers develop) and half a year in the university (running Visiting Teacher (VT) courses for their teacher colleagues). Thus, alongside the teacher-educator internship programme, ran a teacher-development programme in which teachers and teacher-educators developed side by side. I shall focus on three of the teachers who were mathematics specialists in the teacher-educator programme.

From a starting position as a tutor in the M.Ed. programme (working with the whole cohort), my own role in this process developed through mentor, co-researcher and ultimately close colleague to the three mathematicians during their three years of internship. My own learning is evidenced through syntheses such as those expressed in this chapter, and derives from research and personal reflection during this time. The learning of the teachers, evident to me through close observation, and access to the teachers' personal writing, will be evidenced here with reference to their own words as quoted from their journals or from written responses to questions I asked them directly.

A study of the outcomes of this programme adds an extra dimension to the three levels of operation of teacher-educators. It might be seen as a split at Level (3):

3a   Mathematics teacher education and ways in which educators think about developing their approaches to teacher education;

3b   (The old 3) The roles and activities of teacher-educators in contributing to developments at (1), (2) and (3a) above.

This new level involves the ongoing development of experienced teacher-educators. It also involves the development of teachers to become teacher-educators working in ways similar to those who are instrumental in their education, and in a reflexive relationship with them. Models of apprenticeship might be seen to describe this situation, with novice teacher-educators apprenticed to the old-stagers, those who are "teaching" them (Lave & Wenger, 1991). However, the reflexive nature of the enterprise led to my re-conceptualisation of it as a "co-learning partnership" building on the terminology from Wagner (1997)[vi] quoted at the beginning of this chapter. I point here to an important step in my own thinking and development to which I will return later in the chapter.

4.1 A small study of three programme participants[vii]

I asked the three teachers[viii] a number of questions about their thinking/teaching before the degree course, their learning in the degree course, and their teaching as a result of the degree course. All spoke initially of their developing knowledge of mathematics and mathematical learning, and ways in which their thinking had developed.

One teacher wrote,

> A significant aspect of my learning during the MEd programme was a deeper understanding of how learning takes place. In pre-MEd days, I had an idea that pupils had different needs regarding the kind of support they needed in learning mathematics. However, I looked at these needs being different because I thought one was bright, the other dull, and so on. In the MEd ... I was exposed to a variety of learning strategies which allowed me to learn by interacting with people and materials. I also had an opportunity to find out by reading and in sessions what others had found out about how learning takes place. I now realize the significance of allowing pupils to make meaning in mathematics. An important aspect is acknowledging that different people will make meaning and hence represent their ideas and understanding through different ways.

The teacher also made reference to various forms of input which had contributed to her growth of knowledge in the formal programme (such as modelling of learning strategies, interactions with people and materials, opportunities to read what others had written) and their significance for her own learning, for example, in emphasizing meaning making in mathematics. Thus the programme offered opportunities to reflect on multiple sources of interaction and their contribution to her learning process. In becoming aware of their effects on her own learning, she was able to form principles about working with students in classrooms. Co-learning is evident here, in terms of the teachers' interactions in a course designed by educators, and one educator's synthesis of the resulting learning.

Another teacher offered me excerpts from her journal (from the early days of her M.Ed. course) which exemplify aspects of her learning and her ways of expressing her learning, speaking of "thinking questions," and to new ways of seeing "sharing" and "talk." She indicated a developing awareness of qualities of the classroom environment which contributed to the children's mathematical learning. Opportunities, during the programme, to work with students and reflect on interactions, contributed to her developing thinking. For example, she had written,

> Mathematics is fun. The children were so happy while doing activities; how they were convincing each other: "no, this is half, give me two thirds, 1/6 is less than 1/3,". When they were talking they were very relaxed and comfortable. Why? Did they feel they were in a safe environment? Is it because they were allowed to talk and do themselves? I was surprised to see their level of confidence, and making decisions.

She emphasised her enhanced perceptions of the nature of mathematics and of mathematical activity, in comparison with her own previous practice in teaching. Her remarks reflect both her awareness of the mathematics per se and some analysis of qualities of the classroom environment which contributed to the children's mathematical development. Through applying her learning in the programme to small-scale activities with students, she became aware of approaches to classroom activity of which she had been previously unaware. The research showed many other remarks of this kind which provide evidence of these teachers' development of thinking and practice at Level 1 deriving from the M.Ed. programme and its activities.

In working with these teachers over a four-year period, I observed closely growth and change in their thinking and ways of working, both personally in their classroom teaching and in their work with other teachers. I thus felt able to ask them if they recognised shifts in their knowledge and awareness during their M.Ed. studies and subsequent work. As I had asked about *knowledge*, it was unsurprising that the teachers addressed the concept of knowledge directly. Nevertheless, their responses indicated a deeply thoughtful consideration of what knowledge meant for them, and of their shifts in knowledge. For example, one teacher wrote,

> Reading books and listening to teachers lecture was the important tool of receiving knowledge. I never thought that knowledge always has context and meaning. But as I am getting experience to work with other teachers my own knowledge or understanding about knowledge is being changed. Knowledge is not only to learn new subject or content, but understand and get meaning. Knowledge should include: what is being taught, to whom it is being taught, e.g. students' background, learning style, level ... why it is being taught.
>
> Knowledge is power.

The words "knowledge is power" emphasised the importance for both teachers and teacher-educators of our knowing, our ways of knowing and our ways of relating this knowing to constructions of the practices of teaching and teacher education. Co-learning is again evident here. Theoretical conceptualisations of changes in practice were highlighted by one teacher who listed decisions which "reflect my changed thinking as a result of this wider understanding about learning." Her list included new uses for textbooks, a variety of teaching strategies ("to allow pupils room for active participation and social interaction in class") and the representation of mathematical ideas in pictures, words, concrete models, or symbols

These are concrete manifestations of the general principles highlighted by the teacher who spoke of knowledge, above. Although my questions might be seen to pre-empt the teachers' responses, presupposing shifts of thinking and changes in practice, the teachers' words provided ample justification for my assumptions. All the teachers sent me either quotations from, or portions of, their journals to read. These were not constructed for my benefit, to answer my questions, but were deep and searching reflections into knowledge and practice, documented over considerable time periods. This use of personal journals was a significant part of the co-learning process. Important was that the journals were private to their authors, but sharing of chosen sections was encouraged between all participants within the co-learning partnership.

I felt that the responses I received provided many examples of the different levels of knowing quoted from Belenky et al. (1986) earlier, particularly of personal, procedural and constructed knowledge. Such growth and development was not always comfortable as reflected in this quotation from one journal:

> In one task of the module I took the initiative to be the group presenter, and describing the task I wrote 'roll model' instead of 'role model'. The facilitator of the group laughed at my English, and I was so hurt that immediately I lost all my confidence. Read my

> reflection of the day: "Today is the worst day of my life. I am very stupid. Why did I have a desire of learning? High qualification is only for the people who have the power of English language."

Reading this passage was salutary for me. I do not know who this facilitator was, but I recognise the sensitivities involved and the care with which we need to act in order to nurture the delicate relationships on which co-learning is based.

After M.Ed. graduation, the three teachers, now PDTs, worked over a three year period of 6 months in their schools teaching and working with other teachers to enhance teaching, and six months in the Institute running courses for teachers from their schools. Putting their own enhanced knowledge of mathematics teaching into practice was not always straightforward. For example, one PDT, in response to my questions, wrote about her own struggles with teaching,

> Teaching Class VI through the use of multiple strategies was not a smooth affair. The issues and concerns can be seen in my journal entries.

The following quotation from her journal is indicative of her development at Level 2:

> I must do something about the issues which are coming out of my teaching. First, pupils are not used to working with each other – it is obvious from the way they work, the individualistic approach to group tasks, the squabbles and so on. This means that, for meaningful learning to take place, I have to focus more on using strategies specific to co-operative learning. I also feel that in a whole school day, just 35 minutes of working with each other, and the remaining time working individually, competing against each other, is not going to help. I will have to convince other teachers also to use cooperative learning in their class.

References to the use of co-operative learning could be seen as an extension of co-learning into the classroom in work between teacher and students in learning mathematics. Here we see the teacher's struggles, at Level 2, to implement her enhanced knowledge at Level 1 into effective classroom approaches. Her remark at the end heralded a shift into developing knowledge at Level 3. As a result of working with other teachers in her school, and observing the problems they had in conceptualizing changed practices, she wrote,

> Now I understand why teachers just resort to plain telling. It is so easy compared to pupils' reasoning out the whole problem themselves with appropriate support and guidance from the teacher.

In Jaworski and Watson (1993), in a discussion of processes in *mentoring*, we talk of the shift from co-mentoring to the *inner* mentor. Recast in terms of co-learning, I believe we see here a significant part of the learning process in a co-learning situation. During the M.Ed. course, the teacher learned from reflections on interactions to develop her personal theories of working with students in classrooms. Her developed ability to observe and reflect in the application of her theoretical knowledge led to her enhanced ability to analyse new situations and to struggle with the issues they raised for her – the development of an inner mentor. It is possible to cast this growth of knowledge theoretically in both individual and social terms, and through such theoretical analysis to start to address the learning paradox (Bereiter, 1985) concerning how we are able to develop more sophisticated concepts than those we already know, without having already constructed the mechanisms by which this is possible.

The three PDTs worked with other teachers in three separate environments, firstly providing guidance and support in their schools, secondly in running courses for teachers (from their own and other schools) at the Institute, and thirdly through a small-scale research project in which they worked with teachers engaging in classroom action research. One PDT sent me 100 pages from her journal, written during research with her two teachers. My analysis of this writing resulted in a categorization of the substance of remarks in the journal which are significantly indicative of knowledge and growth, both personal and social. Out of 125 items recorded, the largest categories were:

1. *Personal learning/evaluation of the PDT*. (21 items). For example, "I have learned that you can't do something to teachers, you need to do it <u>with</u> them - or even better they must feel the need to do it themselves."

2. *Issues related to reading of the literature by the PDT and her associated teachers* (19 items). For example, "The meeting with Habiba was very interesting. Her reading of Hargreaves has led her to reflect on the issue of empowerment".

3. *The learning/growth of her associated teachers* (13 items). For example, "Through the action research Farah has started examining her role as a teacher, not only in a particular classroom but in a school and in society. ... When did this interest in self emerge? Was it the reading? Was it her ability to apply that reading to her experiences? Was it that while working on a project she saw a difference in approach between [another teacher] and herself?"

Here is evidence, at Level 3, not only of the development of the PDT, but also of the two teachers with whom she was conducting research. Their growth of knowledge was significantly enhanced by their co-working. The PDT's report of her research project, written for publication, provides ample further evidence as well as insights and issues into teaching development through classroom research. The joint research of these two teachers and the educator points powerfully to a research environment as an effective co-learning situation.

My observations of these programmes provided overwhelming evidence of PDTs' knowledge, understanding, and expertise, consolidated during their degree programme and in their subsequent work in school. Their comments on work with other teachers indicated a deep understanding of issues in teaching and learning (at Levels 3a and b), and they struggled with ways of communicating their knowledge to others and enabling others to develop and grow. Unsurprisingly, their own knowledge and understanding were both questioned and strengthened during this time. One of them wrote, "I have not found all this easy. Teachers depend on me and sometimes I have no solutions. At times I have felt quite alone." More recently, this PDT, working full time in her school as a teacher-educator, has emphasised the difficulty of this alone-ness. Although engaging with teachers in projects where teaching knowledge and understanding can be seen to develop, both for herself and the teachers with whom she works, she now indicates her need for further stimulus to continue her own learning, perhaps in a Ph.D. programme.

4.2 Significance and Implications of the Programme

The PDTs' growth of knowledge in both theoretical and practical domains is evident from their own words quoted above. This knowledge encompasses mathematical knowledge, knowledge of mathematical learning, pedagogical knowledge related to mathematical learning, knowledge of theories in mathematics education, and knowledge of wider theories and issues in schooling.

The PDTs' teaching in school and in the Visiting Teacher programmes at the university, and reflection on this teaching, is evidence of their development of highly successful approaches to teaching mathematics. This evidence is seen in the mathematical activities of students in classrooms and the development of teacher colleagues with whom they have worked. Such evidence is currently largely idiosyncratic. It was not possible to study and document children's learning or fellow-teachers' development in a systematic way. Further research would be needed to provide more objective evidence. However, where fellow teachers are concerned, there is evidence from those who worked directly with the PDTs in the classroom research project that this work was highly important to their development of both thinking and teaching. This was hinted at indirectly in the quotations above.

Towards the end of their three-year internship, PDTs worked with faculty at the Institute in teaching current cohorts in the master's degree programme, which is ongoing in developing future PDTs. At the end of their internship, two of the three PDTs embarked on doctoral programmes in anticipation of joining ultimately the central faculty of the Institute.

Within the programme described, co-learning has been emphasised between faculty members (acting as tutor, mentor, co-researcher and colleague) and developing teacher-educators (the PDTs). Of course, co-learning was also taking place between PDTs and teachers: teachers in the PDTs' schools, teacher-participants in the VT programmes, and teacher-researchers in the action research programme. A very significant culture of practice is still is in the process of development. The wider educational and cultural issues surrounding such an ambitious programme cannot be addressed in the space of this chapter (see Jaworski, 1997, for further insights and issues). It needs to be recognised that there are many problems and ramifications which the programme is gradually addressing as practices become adapted and established. It is not my intention to suggest this is a miracle in teaching development.

4.3 The Learning of an Experienced Teacher-Educator

I have hinted throughout this chapter at my own learning as a teacher educator during my involvement in this programme. I shall now attempt to use some of my own experiences to further exemplify, and to raise issues for, the concept of co-learning partnership.

As an educator and researcher I am strongly aware of the reflexive nature of theory and practice in contributing to my developing thinking, teaching, and research (see for example, Jaworski, 1994). The knowledge on which I drew in designing and teaching the modules of the M.Ed. programme for which I was responsible had both theoretical and practical roots. These are not always separable. As educators, I believe we integrate theory and practice to such an extent that it is not always easy to trace contributory factors. Nevertheless, we become used to articulating practice in theoretical terms, and I know I do this regularly in most of my teaching. As I speak theoretically, I have in mind images of practice that are part of the culture in which I operate. However, these images are not always available to the teachers with whom I work, and I have to recognise the different cultures from which they draw their images. This is more complex than merely *national* differences, although these can be very significant. Thus there is real value in trying to explore together the various images we have in our divergent cultures. Sometimes, as the partner with greater knowledge and experience of teacher education, I have the responsibility to initiate sharing. As I undertake this responsibility I learn through reflection on experience which ways are fruitful and which are not. So, in the MEd programme, over the years I have had to learn what seems fruitful in particular cases and to generalise from these as appropriate. Thus I learn about the contexts of the teachers with whom I am working, and I learn about ways of working in these contexts. As I work in alternative contexts I also learn about approaches which are effective in a localised way, and those which are more universally applicable. This is ongoing learning which feeds back into future work in all the programmes in which I operate. I have seen this largely as a constructive process within the social domains in which co-learning occurs. However, these social domains constitute communities that are growing and changing as interactions occur, and so the learning processes involved can be cast as participation in social practices. A Vygotskian view might see learning in terms of our multiple zones of proximal development with respect to which we scaffold each other's learning.

Providing examples of this learning is not straightforward. There are certainly many examples, but none seem especially outstanding. It is together that they contribute to the overall learning experience. However, to illustrate the points I am making I will offer some examples.

4.4 Learning About Pedagogy

Three examples show different dimensions of this learning.

1.   In the first M.Ed. programme, I had been offering a number of problems to the teachers to engage them in mathematics and encourage feelings of success and pleasure in doing mathematics successfully (for example, handshakes, paper folding, pentominos). I congratulated one of the teachers on her successful completion of a problem. She had claimed earlier that she could never do mathematics, and would never be able to do mathematics. So I said something like, "Look, this shows you *can* do mathematics." Her response was, "Oh, this isn't mathematics, it's just common sense!" Since this event, I have been challenged to identify what aspects of the problems I offer are indeed mathematical, and what it means for them to be mathematical problems. A further challenge is to enable students to

recognise mathematics in their approaches to problem solving, and to extend their own perceptions of mathematics. Neither of these have been trivial tasks. In a spirit of co-learning, I now discuss with students what exactly they and I mean by mathematics and how we each distinguish between mathematics and common sense. I am now clearer about what *I* mean when I talk about a mathematical problem, but this deserves a paper all to itself!

2. The paper folding problem involves folding a piece of paper a number of times and predicting the number of regions to be found when it is unfolded. When a group of teachers engaged in this problem, those who were non-mathematicians could generalise using words, but found it difficult to express their generality in mathematical symbols. When shown by their more mathematical colleagues, they were delighted with the resulting notation. Later in the course, the teachers were invited to write a short piece on their learning of algebra to share with other teachers. It was amazing to me the number of them who chose to write about their work on the paper-folding problem. Their perception of generalisation and its mathematical expression had clearly been significant. However, the various writings had a stereotypical similarity, which led me to question what had been achieved in the activity, and what this had contributed to the teachers' wider perceptions of algebra. I am still working on these questions as I devise activities (such as paper-folding) related to algebraic learning for future groups.

3. Asking questions has been an important part of learning and teaching for me as both teacher and learner. I therefore encourage all those I work with to ask, and address, questions – about mathematics, about pedagogy, about classroom practices widely. For her assignment, one of the M.Ed. teachers chose to address *questioning* as a pedagogic approach. In her essay, she drew attention to the fact that in Pakistani society, questioning is largely discouraged; certainly it shows a lack of respect to question parents, teachers, or indeed anyone senior in the community. Her pointing this out to me provided a new dimension to my future use of questioning. In the M.Ed. modules, it is now an issue we address overtly – to consider its value, but also to address its implications for teachers in Pakistani schools.

4.5 Learning About Mathematics

The examples above point to the importance of the *mathematical* nature of the learning discussed in this chapter. Much of what I have written is about learning to be a teacher of mathematics and learning to be a mathematics teacher educator in which the mathematical basis of the learning has not been made explicit. To what extent are all the co-learning participants also learning mathematics, as this is certainly the focus of our enterprise in terms of students' learning in classrooms. In the examples above, both my mathematical knowledge and my knowledge of mathematical pedagogy was extended through the experiences I described. One module of the M.Ed. programme has focussed explicitly on subject learning, or on the learning of Pedagogic Content Knowledge (Schulman, 1987). In our case the content is mathematics. In this module teachers work overtly on mathematical concepts to enhance their own mathematical understanding. In addition, they reflect on the way we as tutors teach the mathematical content of the module and consider their own subsequent teaching in classrooms and ways in which they might work with other teachers to enhance mathematical learning.

A discussion of the multiple learning opportunities and issues arising from them which this teaching afforded is beyond the scope of this chapter (but see Jaworski and Nardi, 1998) However, I must make clear here that my own learning of mathematics was significantly enhanced through this teaching, as was my awareness of classroom approaches for effective learning of students of mathematics. One small example involved a teacher's recognition of the effect of multiplying by (-1) firstly a quadratic equation,

$$\text{for example, } x^2 - 3x - 4 = 0 => -x^2 + 3x + 4 = 0$$

and subsequently the corresponding quadratic function,

$$\text{for example, } f(x) = x^2 - 3x - 4 => -f(x) = -x^2 + 3x + 4$$

as made evident in a graphical representation (the reflection of the curve in the x-axis). The invariance of the solution of the equation relative to the changing function was shown as a graphic image, which I had not perceived before. Of course, I had a knowledge of quadratic functions and equations before the classroom event, but this event allowed me to gain new perspectives of relationships and hence to enhance my own knowledge. Sharing this with the teachers was a powerful tool for enhancing the co-learning environment in this mathematics class, as it inspired them to know that their tutor's learning could be enhanced through their own mathematical insights.

Although much of the discussion in this chapter does not address mathematical learning so explicitly, it is nevertheless true that all the reported learning is firmly rooted in a growth of knowledge and awareness of how mathematics can be learned and taught.

4.6 Learning About Co-Learning

I acknowledge the importance of sharing and interaction in this learning, both with teachers, my educator colleagues, other researchers, and the wider research literature. Without these resources my thinking becomes unrooted and fanciful, and I lose sight of the evidential base necessary for real growth of knowledge. Although I have a well-developed inner mentor, I need the co-mentoring of my students and colleagues for continued growth. All of this points towards the essential nature of social interactions at a variety of levels for my students, the teachers with whom I work. Relationships between participants in any programme are crucial to such interactions, and time given to establishing good relationships is well spent.

A problem I and my colleagues are still addressing concerns relationships between teachers in the M.Ed. course and teachers we work with in schools. The M.Ed. programme is extremely selective of its participants, and most are proud to have been selected. Very quickly, these participants meet new concepts, new ways of working and become excited by the ideas and possiblities with which they are bombarded as part of their course. When they go into schools, they see teachers struggling with impoverished situations both in terms of resource and in terms of ideas and concepts. Albeit unconsciously, some respond with an elitist attitude which is unhelpful both in relationships and in potential for learning. As course leaders we have to find sensitive ways of overcoming such reactions.

The above paragraphs highlight practical concerns that can lead to important theoretical principles for ways of working for fruitful learning. Although these principles derive from practice, practice, nevertheless, reminds us that applying such principles is far from simple. For example, the time given to establishing relationships might be spent several times over. In an M.Ed. module this year, practices of journal exchange, writing comments on journals, and one-one meetings between students and tutors were all seen as immensely valuable in developing relationships and understandings between tutors and students. However, the time needed for tutors to undertake required assessment of students interfered with that needed for journals and meetings. Compromises by tutors had to be made, and corresponding issues addressed. Students were not always happy with these compromises. Tutors felt, in evaluating the programme, that not enough care had been taken to share with students the dilemmas that were faced, and that closer understandings could have resulted from a tutor-student discussion of the time problems. As the M.Ed. has developed over the years, closer understandings of the roles and relationships of tutors and students have developed, but there are always issues such as those related to *time* and *assessment* which continue to challenge us.

The time when a more helpful understanding has developed has been during the three years when graduates of the M.Ed. programme have worked alongside us as PDTs, delivering courses for teachers and engaging together in research projects. These relationships might be seen to involve an apprenticeship model, with the newcomers learning from the old stagers. However, overt discussion with PDTs of how, as educators, we achieve objectives and deal with the issues which arise leads to our learning, too. As an experienced educator I learned a lot from my PDT colleagues. I shall never forget when a number of teachers were dominating a conversation in a session, and one of the PDTs raised her arm and said simply "social skills." These brief words were sufficient to alert teachers to issues of effective social interaction within a group, and it was simply done. The issue of how to intervene effectively might have resulted in more heavy handed intervention (from me!) and I gratefully learned a strategy that I could now use. The issues raised in discussion with PDTs inevitably took me beyond my current understandings, and contributed to my knowledge as teacher and educator.

Two of the PDTs have continued with me as doctoral students, time-sharing between Oxford and Karachi. They have joined a doctoral group (in Oxford) where research into the teaching and learning of mathematics usually involves working in classrooms or tutorials studying students' learning or teachers' teaching or both.

This group meets periodically to share ideas and issues related to their research. Such meetings are always thought provoking. Alongside my own research, working with research students is one of my most rewarding learning experiences. We are all participants in a research endeavour of differing degrees of peripherality where our learning is concerned (Lave & Wenger, 1991). There are no ultimate "old stagers," i.e., those who have reached some kind of knowledge nirvana. The quality of the learning relationship is that we recognise the co-learning nature of our enterprise. It was through sharing with this group the Wagner article quoted earlier that I came to appreciate the essential nature of co-learning, despite writing about co-mentoring so many years earlier (Jaworski & Watson, 1993)

Extending co-learning beyond the research environment to that of teacher education came as a result of an international collaboration with teacher educators (Jaworski, Wood & Dawson, 1999) and contributions to PME conferences in 1998 and 1999 where I had again opportunities to share experiences with educators internationally. The learning which resulted from these interactions has been fed into my teaching this year, both in the M.Ed. programme described above and in other courses that I teach. I am currently working overtly on ideas of co-learning with student-teachers in Oxford, and am conducting a small-scale research project with them to explore their notions of co-learning as they develop as beginning teachers.

The above paragraphs testify to the powerful nature of the co-learning concept for myself as teacher, educator, and researcher, so that it is inevitable that I seek to understand better how co-learning partnerships can be developed and grow between participants in educational settings at all levels. I am aware of many of the issues to be faced, and the research that needs to be done to take these ideas further.

5. A CO-LEARNING PARTNERSHIP MODEL OF MATHEMATICS TEACHING DEVELOPMENT

The nature of a co-learning partnership is that teachers and educators work and learn together in a reciprocal relationship of a reflexive nature. This might involve co-operation, working communicatively and supportively, or collaboration, working jointly. Roles, relationships, and responsibilities within the partnership develop throughout its life. In the programme described above, original roles were more traditionally those of teacher and student, while later roles developed through mentoring relationships to collegial ones. Thus roles do not have to be equal, and will rarely be equal. The nature of the partnership involves recognition of, respect for, and responsibility in interpreting and developing roles so that each partner maximises learning opportunities. The balance of power will shift as roles develop. Initially it is likely that educators hold most of the power. However, the early responsibilities associated with this power are to enable teachers as rapidly as possible to take on their own mantle of responsibility within the relationship. This includes teachers' development as critical thinkers, alongside their educator partners, through reflection at all levels of learning and practice. Programmes which are devised to be co-learning partnerships would typically be explicit about the reflexive nature of roles and ways in which the programme would facilitate their development.

The term "engender" was highlighted and questioned earlier in the chapter. Within a co-learning partnership, it would be the responsibility of those devising the programme to engender reflexivity through specifically designed activities and ways of acting and inter-relating. Part of this engendering would involve educators in gradual withdrawal from the engendering role as teachers take on responsibility as co-learning partners. A principle motivation for this process would be avoidance of the deficit model through which development is weak and unsustainable due to too much dependence being placed on programme leaders and inability to continue development once support is withdrawn.

The co-learning model needs still a great deal more thought in its conceptualization, through suitable research in devised programmes. However, initial discussions with partners in a variety of educational settings suggest it is a fruitful basis for conceptualising effective teaching development. Examples of failure in the programme discussed – such as teachers who have been unable to sustain new practices in their classrooms beyond their initial return from VT programmes – can be attributed to some failure in the co-learning agreement, either in initiating it or sustaining it[ix]. Further research will seek particularities of such initiation and sustaining, in order to work towards general principles which can be applied more widely. There will be many other such issues to address.

Indications from the discussed programme suggest the following areas for (ongoing) exploration in effective teaching development:

- Consistency of approaches throughout stages and programmes. (e.g., in the programme discussed this might involve PDTs using materials and approaches from their degree programme suitably modified for Visiting Teacher programmes).
- Extending short teacher education programmes through continued co-learning partnerships to provide a professional route for teachers into academic qualifications.
- Co-learning partnership programmes for Head Teachers which extend the co-learning culture into in-school relationships.
- Co-learning partnerships between universities and schools to allow mutuality of research and development.
- Development of co-learning partnerships in classrooms between students and teachers.

Although these suggestions are deeply ambitious, the overriding aim of the proposed "co-learning partnership model of teaching development" is to remove the "deficit" stigma and change a culture of dependency at so many levels of teaching and learning into one of mutual respect and responsibility. Thus, learners at all levels would have confidence in their own determination of their learning process with support from the co-learning partnerships in which they are engaged.

ACKNOWLEDGEMENTS

I should like to thank Razia Fakir Mohammed, Anjum Halai and Yasmin Mehta for their collaboration in the research documented above, and for making these conceptualisations possible.
My thanks too to Tim Rowland for helpful critical comments on an earlier draft of this manuscript.

REFERENCES

Adler, J. (1996). Lave and Wenger's social practice theory and teaching and learning school mathematics. In L. Puig & A. Gutierrez (Eds.), *Proceedings of the Twentieth Conference of the International Group for the Psychology of Mathematics Education, 2*, 3-10. University of Valencia, Spain: Psychology of Mathematics Education.

Belenky, M. F., Clinchy, B. M., Goldberger, N. R. & Tarule, J. M. (1986). *Women's ways of knowing: The development of self, voice and mind.* New York: Basic Books.

Bereiter, C. (1985). Towards a solution of the learning paradox. *Review of Educational Research, 55*(2), 201-226.

Britt, M.S., Irwin, K.C., Ellis,J., & Ritchie, G. (1993). *Teachers raising achievement in mathematics: Final report to the Ministry of Education.* Auckland, NZ: Centre for Mathematics Education, Auckland College of Education.

Brown, S. & McIntyre, D. (1993). *Making sense of teaching.* Buckingham: Open University Press.

Bruner, J. (1996). Celebrating divergence: Piaget and Vygotsky. Keynote address delivered in Geneva on 15th September, 1996 at a joint meeting of the Growing Mind Conference in honour of the centennial of Jean Piaget's birth, and the Vygotsky-Piaget Conference of the 2nd Congress of Socio-Cultural Research.

Cobb, P., Wood, T., & Yackel, E. (1990). Classrooms as learning environments for teachers and researchers. In R.B. Davis , C. Maher, & N. Noddings, (Eds.), Constructivist views on the learning and teaching of mathematics. (pp. 125-146). *Journal of Research in Mathematics Education Monograph Series, No 4.* Reston, VA: National Council of Teachers of Mathematics.

Confrey, J. (1995). How compatible are radical constructivism, sociocultural approaches and social constructivism? In L. P. Steffe & J. Gale (Eds.), *Constructivism in education.* Hillsdale, NJ: Erlbaum.

Cooney, T. (1994). Teacher education as an exercise in adaptation. In D. B. Aichele & A. F. Coxford (Eds.), *Professional development for teachers of mathematics: 1994 yearbook.* Reston, VA: National Council of Teachers of Mathematics.

Cooney, T. J. & Shealy, B. (1997). On understanding the structure of teachers' beliefs and their relationship to change. In E. Fennema & B. Scott-Nelson (Eds.), *Mathematics teachers in transition.* Mahwah, NJ: Erlbaum.

Dawson, A.J. (Sandy) (1999). The enactive perspective on teacher development: A path laid while walking. In B. Jaworski, T. Wood, & A. J. Dawson (Eds.), *Mathematics teacher education: Critical international perspectives.* London: Falmer Press.

Dewey, J. (1933). *How we think.* London: D.C. Heath & Co.

Fennema, E., Carpenter, T., Franke, M., Levi, L., Jacobs, V., & Empson, S. (1996). A longitudinal study of learning to use children's thinking in mathematics instruction, *Journal of Research in Mathematics Education, 27*, 403-434.

Halai, A. (1997). Secondary mathematics teaching: Should it be all chalk and talk? *Mathematics Teaching, 161,* 18-19.

Halai, A. (1998). Mentor, mentee and mathematics. *Journal of Mathematics Teacher Education, 1* (3).

Irwin, K., & Britt, M. (1999). Teachers' knowledge of mathematics and reflective professional development. In B. Jaworski, T. Wood, & A. J. Dawson (Eds.), *Mathematics teacher education: Critical international perspectives.* London: Falmer Press.

Jaworski, B. (1994). *Investigating mathematics teaching: A constructivist enquiry.* London: Falmer Press.

Jaworski, B. (1997). The implications of theory for a new masters programme for teacher educators in Pakistan. *Oxford Studies in Comparative Education, 6, 2.*

Jaworski, B. (1998). Mathematics teacher research: Process practice and the development of teaching. *Journal of Mathematics Teacher Education, 1* (1), 3-31.

Jaworski, B. (1999). The plurality of knowledge growth in mathematics teaching. In B. Jaworski, T. Wood, & A. J. Dawson (Eds.), *Mathematics teacher education: Critical international perspectives.* London: Falmer Press.

Jaworski, B. & Nardi, E. (1998). The teaching-research dialectic in a mathematics course in Pakistan. In A. Olivier & K. Newstead (Eds.), *Proceedings of the 22ndConference of the International Group for the Psychology of Mathematics Education, 3,* 80-87.

Jaworski, B. & Watson, A. (1993). *Mentoring in mathematics teaching.* London: Falmer Press.

Jaworski, B., Wood, T., & Dawson, S. (1999). *Mathematics teacher education: Critical international perspectives.* London: Falmer Press.

Kemmis, S. (1985). Action research and the politics of reflection. In D. Boud, R. Keogh, & D. Walker (Eds.), *Reflection: turning experience into learning.* London: Kogan Page.

Krainer, K. (1993). Understanding students' understanding: On the importance of co-operation between teachers and researchers. In P. Boero (Ed.), *Proceedings of the 3rd Bratislava International Symposium on Mathematical Teacher Education.* Comenius Univ.: Bratislava.

Lave, J. & Wenger, E. (1991). *Situated learning: Legitimate peripheral participation.* New York: Cambridge University Press.

Lerman, S. (1990). Alternative perspectives of the nature of mathermatics and their influneces on the teaching of mathematics. *British Educational Research Journal, 16* (1), 53-61.

Markovitz, Z., & Even, R. (1999). Mathematics classroom situations: An inservice course for elementary teachers. In B. Jaworski, T. Wood, & A. J. Dawson (Eds.), *Mathematics teacher education: Critical international perspectives.* London: Falmer Press.

Murray , H., Olivier, A., & Human, P. (1999). Teachers' mathematical experiences as links to children's needs. In B. Jaworski, T. Wood, & A. J. Dawson (Eds.), *Mathematics teacher education: Critical international perspectives.* London: Falmer Press.

Nardi, E. (1996). *The novice mathematician's encounter with mathematical abstraction: Tensions in concept-image construction and formalisation.* Unpublished doctoral dissertation, University of Oxford, Oxford.

Othman, M. Y. (1996). *A pilot study into the teacher craft of three mathematics teachers and its relation to learning in the classroom: Methodological issues and indications for future research.* Unpublished master's thesis, University of Oxford, Oxford.

Schifter, D. (1997). *Learning mathematics for teaching.* Newton, MA: Centre for the Development of Teaching.

Schön D.A. (1987). *Educating the reflective practitioner.* Oxford: Jossey-Bass.

Shulman, L.S. (1987). Knowledge and teaching: Foundations of the new reform. *Harvard Educational Review, 57* (1), 1-22.

Sierpinska, A. (1994). *Understanding in mathematics.* London: Falmer Press.

Skemp, R. R. (1976). Relational understanding and instrumental understanding. *Mathematics Teaching, 77.*

The Aga Khan University Institute for Educational Development (1990). *A proposal to the AKU Board of Trustees.* Karachi, Pakistan: Author.

Thompson, A. (1984). The relationship of teachers' conceptions of mathematics teaching to instructional practice. *Educational Studies in Mathematics, 15,* 105-127.

von Glasersfeld, E. (1987). Learning as a constructive activity. In C. Janvier (Ed.), *Problems of representation in the teaching and learning of mathematics,* Hillslade, NJ: Erlbaum.

Wagner, J. (1997). The unavoidable intervention of educational research: A framework for reconsidering researcher-practitioner cooperation. *Educational Researcher, 26*(7), 13-21.

Zack, V., Mousely, J. & Breen, C. (Eds.). (1997). *Developing practice: Teachers' inquiry and educational change in classrooms.* Geelong, Australia: Centre for Studies in Mathematics, Science and Environmental Education, Deakin University.

University of Oxford
United Kingdom

NOTES

[i] I recognise use of the pronoun "we" as problematic in parts of this text. In parts it is an appeal to the reader to join with me, the author, in observations about the issues under discussion. In other places it reflects the community of mathematics teacher educators of which I am a member. The reader, of course, is not necessarily a member of the community. I hope context will make usage clear.

ii These were presented first in Jaworski (1999). Here they are elaborated particularly with regard to the concept of co-learning.

[iii] Reflection in this chapter is interpreted in the spirit of Dewey (1933), Kemmis (1985) and Schön (1987) as involving critical thinking which demands action. I have written extensively of this elsewhere, see for example Jaworski, 1998.

[iv] An International Group for the Psychology of Mathematics Education (PME) meets every year in a different country to discuss research in mathematics education.

[v] In 1994, the Aga Khan University in Pakistan inaugurated an Institute for Educational Development (IED) with a mission to enhance teaching and hence schooling in Pakistan and beyond. A team of educators from Oxford joined local faculty in the IED's teacher/teaching development programme.

The IED's initial framework had twin goals of enhancing teachers' skills by enabling teachers to reflect on their practice, their classroom situation, and the ways in which children learn; and rewarding teachers' progress by the granting of internationally recognized qualifications, the first of which was a masters' degree programme (M.Ed.) in teacher education for selected experienced teachers.

At the end of the M.Ed. course (18 months, then; now 2 years full time), graduates returned to their own schools as Professional Development Teachers (PDTs) with responsibilities to develop their own teaching relative to their learning in the M.Ed. course and to work with other teachers in their school to facilitate development and contribute to school improvement. They were also contracted to devote 6 months of each year, for three years, to delivering two-month education programmes at the IED for *Visiting Teachers* (VTs) from schools. Thus an aim of the programme was that these people would not only develop as teachers, they would take on the mantle of teacher-educators.

The initial framework for the IED included the following statement on complementarity between research, reflective practice and teaching programmes:

... inquiry is at the heart of both teaching and learning. Teachers who view learning as inquiring into the natural and social world relate to subject matter in characteristic ways. These ways differ markedly from those that characterize teachers who view themselves as conduits for received knowledge and their students as empty vessels. Teachers who view themselves and their students as inquirers rather than receptors are more inclined to encourage students to challenge their own thinking and that of others, to foster the kind of open debate and discussion critical to sharpening and refining ideas and concepts. (1991 proposal, p 24)

Thus, the IED set out to encourage enquiry, mutual challenge, and critical reflection. Consistent with the above aims, M.Ed. participants wrote reflective journals which were shared with tutors and peers for communication and feedback. Theories of cooperative learning were pursued in the practice of the course, leading to the development of a community of learners for support and challenge. During taught modules, participants worked with students and/or teachers in schools on the same campus as the IED. Gaining practical experience alongside theoretical input, with encouragement to reflect and critically review their learning was central to the philosophy of the programme (see for example Halai, 1997; 1998).

In the taught programme, all participants took part in modules in English, Mathematics, Social Studies and Science. In mathematics, participants engaged in mathematical tasks themselves and reflected on their own learning within these tasks. They were introduced to the mathematics education literature which addressed issues in the learning and teaching of mathematics. They conducted small-scale research with students to devise activities and study students' thinking and interactions in those activities. They spent time with mathematics teachers both in classrooms and in workshops outside classrooms, working together on issues in mathematics teaching. Participants specialising in mathematics also spent time working in areas of mathematics to update their own mathematical knowledge and consider further mathematical pedagogy. All participants engaged in modules addressing mentoring, teacher change, and school improvement.

[vi] Wagner 's typology of research partnerships with practitioners speaks of Co-learning Agreements as one of the extremes of relationships between researchers and practitioners, the other extreme being "Data Extraction Agreements," in which researchers conceptualise and conduct the research with minimal inclusion of practitioners. These research relationships seem to have much in common with the teacher and educator partnership in teaching development.

[vii] More detail from this research is presented in Jaworski (1999). Extracts here are chosen to illustrate educator development in co-learning situations.

[viii] In the early days of the programme participants were teachers. After their degree course ended they became Professional Development Teachers (PDTs). See Note 5 above.

[ix] One PDT is now studying this phenomenon in her research at doctoral level.

Index

Printed in the United States
33669LVS00001B/2

9 780792 369868